The Mad Sculptor

Also by Harold Schechter

The Mad Sculptor

The MANIAC, *the* MODEL,
and the MURDER THAT
SHOOK THE NATION

Harold Schechter

New Harvest
Houghton Mifflin Harcourt
BOSTON   NEW YORK
2014

For information about permission to reproduce selections from this book,
write to Permissions, Houghton Mifflin Harcourt Publishing Company,
215 Park Avenue South, New York, New York 10003.

www.hmhco.com

Library of Congress Cataloging-in-Publication Data
Schechter, Harold.
The mad sculptor : the maniac, the model, and the murder that shook the nation /
Harold Schechter.
pages cm
ISBN 978-0-544-11431-9 (hardback)
1. Irwin, Robert, 1907–1975. 2. Serial murderers—New York (State)—New York.
I. Title.
HV6534.N5S343 2014
364.152'32092—dc23
2013032240

Book design by Brian Moore

Printed in the United States of America
DOC 10 9 8 7 6 5 4 3 2 1

In Memory of Harvey Shapiro

Contents

Cast of Characters

The Beekman Place Murders

VERA STRETZ, the "Skyscraper Slayer," mistress and murderer of Fritz Gebhardt.

FRITZ GEBHARDT, prominent German industrialist with high political ambitions, Vera's "Nazi Loverboy."

NANCY TITTERTON, the "Bathtub Beauty," editor, writer, murder victim.

LEWIS TITTERTON, Nancy's husband, head of the script department of NBC radio.

JOHN FIORENZA, upholsterer's assistant, Nancy's killer.

The Artist and His Mentors

ROBERT IRWIN, the "Mad Sculptor," artist, divinity student, mass killer.

CARLO ROMANELLI, renowned Hollywood sculptor, Robert Irwin's first mentor.

LORADO TAFT, famed Chicago sculptor who took Irwin under his wing.

ANGUS MACLEAN, professor of religious history and future dean at the St. Lawrence University Theological School.

The Irwins

BENJAMIN HARDIN IRWIN, evangelist, founder of the Fire-Baptized Holiness Church, philanderer, father of the Mad Sculptor.

MARY IRWIN, Benjamin's wife, religious fanatic, member of Florence Crawford's Apostolic Faith Mission, mother of the Mad Sculptor.

VIDALIN IRWIN, older brother of Robert Irwin, juvenile delinquent, future inmate of Oregon State Penitentiary.

PEMBER IRWIN, younger brother of Robert Irwin, juvenile delinquent, also a future inmate of Oregon State Penitentiary.

The Gedeons

ETHEL GEDEON, older daughter of the Gedeon family, object of Bob's amorous obsession.

VERONICA "RONNIE" GEDEON, party girl, artist's model, murder victim.

JOSEPH GEDEON, Hungarian-born upholsterer, head of the Gedeon family, suspect in the "Easter Sunday Massacre."

MARY GEDEON, Joe's wife, speakeasy operator, landlady, murder victim.

JOE KUDNER, Ethel Gedeon's second husband.

FRANK BYRNES, waiter at Manhattan's Racquet and Tennis Club, boarded with the Gedeons, murder victim.

BOBBY FLOWER, briefly married to teenage Ronnie.

The Shrinks

FREDRIC WERTHAM, prominent New York psychiatrist who would treat and befriend Irwin.

CLARENCE LOW, president of the board of Rockland State Hospital and Bob's patron.

DR. RUSSELL E. BLAISDELL, superintendent of the Rockwell State Hospital.

The Cops

FRANCIS KEAR, Deputy Chief Inspector, NYPD.

JOHN A. LYONS, Assistant Chief Inspector, NYPD.

ALEXANDER O. GETTLER, renowned "test tube sleuth" of the NYPD crime lab.

LEWIS VALENTINE, Commissioner, NYPD.

The Newsmen

WEST PETERSON, editor of *Inside Detective* magazine, offered one-thousand-dollar reward for help in Irwin's arrest.

HARRY ROMANOFF, city editor of the *Chicago Herald-Examiner*.

JOHN DIENHART, managing editor of the *Herald and Examiner*.

The Good Samaritan

HENRIETTA KOSCIANSKI, Cleveland hotel pantry girl who recognized Bob from *Inside Detective* article.

The Suits

SAMUEL LEIBOWITZ, the "Great Defender," lawyer for clients ranging from Al Capone to the Scottsboro Boys.

THOMAS DEWEY, Manhattan District Attorney, future governor of New York and Republican presidential candidate.

JACOB J. ROSENBLUM, Assistant District Attorney, Dewey's right-hand man, assigned to try Robert Irwin.

PETER SABBATINO, lawyer hired by Ethel to represent Joseph Gedeon.

Prologue

From the window of his rented attic room, he can look across the low rooftop of the adjoining building and watch the hectic scene in front of the police station on 51st Street: the grim-faced detectives shoving their way through the clamorous mob of reporters, the squad cars delivering a steady stream of witnesses and suspects, the neighborhood gawkers jamming the sidewalks. On a couple of occasions, he spots the old man being hustled in and out of the precinct house, doing his best to ignore the shouted questions of the newshounds.

By midweek, his meager provisions, the stuff he removed from their icebox, have run out. He will have to risk a trip outside for some food. Luckily, the scratches on his face have begun to fade. She had mauled him like nobody's business. Put up a hell of a fight. Must have taken her twenty minutes to die.

He waits until nightfall, then slips downstairs and out the front door. After a hasty bite at an all-night cafeteria, he returns to his room with a sackful of groceries and the final editions of the Mirror, *the* Journal, *and the* News.

The papers are full of the story: "The Mystery of the Slain Artist's

Model," "The Easter Sunday Murders," "The Beekman Place Massacre." Not one fails to mention its "curious parallels" to the Titterton killing during Holy Week a year before. Or to the Stretz case of 1935, also in the ritzy neighborhood of Beekman Place.[1]

He counts more than twenty photographs of Ronnie in the tabloids, most in cheesecake poses, her nakedness barely concealed by a gauzy, airbrushed veil. By contrast, he finds only a couple of Ethel, bundled in a fur coat, her face drawn, her frowning husband beside her. The grainy pictures do nothing to capture her perfection.

He is sorry to have caused Ethel grief. If she had been home that night, none of this would have happened. Otherwise, he feels not a twinge of remorse. Why should he? They aren't really dead. Sure, they might be gone from this plane. But their lives aren't lost. You can't destroy one atom of matter. How are you going to destroy spirit?[2]

He reads about the growing list of suspects—Ronnie's countless boyfriends, Mary's former boarders, the Englishman's shady acquaintances. Every cop in the city is on the lookout for the "mad slayer." And all the while, he is right under their noses, holed up just a block away. He has made absolutely no effort to cover his tracks. Must have left dozens of fingerprints all over the apartment. Didn't even bother to go back for the glove when he realized he'd left it behind. The incompetence of the police and their supposed scientific experts amuses him.

Still, he knows it is only a matter of time before his name comes up. By the end of the week, he decides to skip town. Someday, when he has made his great contribution to the human race, he will be able to travel just by visualization. Time and space will mean nothing. For now, he will have to rely on more prosaic means.

On Sunday, April 4, exactly one week after the Easter morning slaughter, Robert Irwin boards a train to Philadelphia.

Part I

Beekman Place

Dead End

B EEKMAN PLACE — A TRANQUIL East Side enclave just north of the United Nations and one of Manhattan's most exclusive addresses—hasn't always been home to the rich. Its name derives from the Beekman family, whose American branch dates back to 1647, when the wealthy Dutch merchant Wilhelmus Beekman arrived in the New World on the same ship carrying Peter Stuyvesant. In 1763, his descendant James Beekman built a stately country home on the high bank of the East River at what is now 51st Street. Furnished with costly imports and the handiwork of the finest colonial craftsmen, Mount Pleasant (as the picturesque white mansion was named) was commandeered by the British during the Revolutionary War and used as their military headquarters. The patriot-spy Nathan Hale was tried there for treason in September 1776 and held overnight in the greenhouse before being hanged the next morning in a nearby orchard. Following the war, George and Martha Washington are said to have paid frequent visits to Mount Pleasant, where "Mrs. Beekman would refresh them with lemonade made from fruit which she gathered from her famous lemon trees."[1]

Abandoned by the Beekman family in 1854 when a cholera epidemic drove them from the city, the venerable mansion stood for another twenty years. By the time of its demolition in 1874, the once-bucolic area had been transformed into a stretch of stolid middle-class row houses, bordered by a shorefront wasteland of coal yards, breweries, and so many cattle pens, tanneries, and meatpacking plants that the neighborhood just to the south was known as Blood Alley.[2] Following an evening stroll around Beekman Place in 1871, the diarist George Templeton Strong wryly noted its "nice outlook over the East River," which included "a clear view of the penitentiary, the smallpox hospital, and the other palaces of Blackwell's Island."[3]

Over the following decades, the neighborhood continued to decline. As waves of European immigrants poured into the city and surged northward from the teeming ghettos of the Lower East Side, Beekman Place became engulfed by slums, its aging brownstones reduced to cheap boardinghouses for the foreign-born workers eking out a living at the waterside factories and abattoirs.

Its rehabilitation began in the 1920s when the East Side riverfront was colonized by Vanderbilts, Rockefellers, and other adventurous blue bloods. The old brownstones were renovated into stylish town houses, while several elegant apartment buildings, designed by some of the era's leading architects, arose on the site. One of the most impressive structures was the twenty-six-story Art Deco skyscraper at the corner of East 49th Street and First Avenue. Intended as a club and dormitory for college sorority women, it was originally known as the Panhellenic House but was renamed the Beekman Tower when it became a residential hotel for both sexes in 1934.[4] By then, the now-fashionable neighborhood was home to a particularly rich concentration of artists, writers, and theatrical celebrities, among them Katharine Cornell, Ethel Barrymore, and Alfred Lunt and Lynn Fontanne. In later years, the neighborhood would boast such residents as Irving Berlin, Greta Garbo, and Noël Coward.

While Beekman Place and its even swankier neighbor, Sutton Place, were undergoing their revival, however, the surrounding streets remained untouched by gentrification. In the early 1930s, the area was a glaring study in contrasts, a neighborhood where luxury towers soared amid grimy tenements, where frayed laundry hung on lines within sight of private gardens, and where young toughs frolicked in the river beside the yachts and motor launches of the super-rich.

In October 1935, New York theatergoers got a vivid look at this "strange otherworld" when the socially conscious crime drama *Dead End* opened on Broadway. Written by Pulitzer Prize–winner Sidney Kingsley (and later adapted for the screen by Lillian Hellman), the play concerns a poor aspiring young architect named Gimpty, hopelessly in love with a beautiful society girl; a vicious gangster named Baby-face Martin, drawn back to the old neighborhood by vestigial stirrings of human sentiment; and a gang of adolescent wharf rats seemingly doomed to criminal lives of their own. Its setting, inspired by the dock off 53rd Street just north of Beekman Place, is described in stage directions that perfectly capture the jarring contrasts that characterized the area in the mid-1930s:

DEAD END of a New York street, ending in a wharf over the East River. To the left is a high terrace and a white iron gate leading to the back of the exclusive East River Terrace Apartments. Hugging the terrace and filing up the street are a series of squalid tenement houses. And here on the shore, along the Fifties is a strange sight. Set plumb down in the midst of slums, antique warehouses, discarded breweries, slaughter houses, electrical works, gas tanks, loading cranes, coal-chutes, the very wealthy have begun to establish their city residence in huge, new, palatial apartments.

The East River Terrace is one of these. Looking up this street from the vantage of the River, we see only a small portion of the back terrace and a gate; but they are enough to suggest the towering magnificence of the whole structure. . . . Contrasting sharply with all this richness is the diseased street below, filthy, strewn with torn newspapers and garbage from the tenements. The tenement houses are close, dark and crumbling.

They crowd each other. Where there are curtains in the windows, they are streaked and faded; where there are none, we see through to hideous, water stained, peeling wallpaper, and old broken-down furniture. The fire escapes are cluttered with gutted mattresses and quilts, old clothes, bread-boxes, milk bottles, a canary cage, an occasional potted plant struggling for life.[5]

Exactly two weeks after *Dead End* premiered, Beekman Place was suddenly in the news—not as the inspiration for Broadway's latest hit but as the site of a shocking murder, a crime that swiftly turned into New York's biggest tabloid sensation in years. Two other, even more gruesome killings would occur there within an eighteen-month span. One helped ignite a nationwide panic over a supposed epidemic of psychopathic sex crimes. The other came to be viewed as among the most spectacular American murder cases of the century.

If *Dead End* was meant to convey a message about the roots of criminality—"that mean streets breed gangsters"[6]—these grisly real-life crimes carried a moral of their own, one that had less to do with Kingsley's brand of 1930s social realism than with the Gothic nightmares of Edgar Allan Poe. Beekman Place—a supposed bastion of safety for the privileged few—turned out to be much like Prince Prospero's castellated fortress in "The Masque of the Red Death." For all its wealth and glamour, it could not keep horror at bay.

Vera and Fritz

T O BECOME A TRUE TABLOID sensation, a murder has to offer more than morbid titillation. It needs a pair of outsized
characters—diabolical villain and defenseless, preferably female,
victim—a dramatic storyline, and the kind of lurid goings-on that
speak to the secret dreams and dangerous desires of the public. In
short, the same juicy ingredients we look for in any good potboiler.

Certainly there was no shortage of shocking homicides during the latter half of November 1935. In upstate New York, sixteen-
year-old Sylvester Lancaric—resentful of the attentions his mother
lavished on his baby brother, John—stomped his little sibling to
death. Not many miles away, twenty-three-year-old LeRoy Smith
of Ladentown was kidnapped, held captive for three days, then shot
through the heart by the jealous ex-boyfriend of his teenage sweetheart, Mary Swope Philpot. A twenty-one-year-old Virginia woman,
Edith Maxwell, killed her father by "beating him over the head with
her high-heeled shoe when he attempted to whip her for staying out
until nearly midnight" with her date. In Columbus, Texas, Benny
Mitchell and Ernest Collins, both seventeen, brutally murdered

nineteen-year-old Geraldine Kollman when she caught them stealing pecans on her father's ranch. And in Washington, D.C., the body of twenty-six-year-old stenographer and choir singer Corinna Loring was found dumped in a park, her neck bound with wrapping cord and "wounds on her temple looking as though her head had been clamped in a pair of ice tongs."[1]

Gruesome as they were, however, none of these murders earned more than a few fleeting columns in the tabloids. The case of Vera Stretz, by contrast, dominated the front pages for weeks.

At around 2:30 a.m. on Tuesday, November 12, 1935, Miss Mary Hazelton, a guest on the twentieth floor of the Beekman Tower, was startled awake by a noise never heard before inside the exclusive residential hotel: a series of rapid cracks, unmistakably the sound of gunfire, coming from somewhere overhead. She immediately telephoned the assistant night manager, Mr. Leslie Taite, at his post at the front desk.

Taking the elevator to the top story, Taite began a fruitless check for signs of disturbance, working his way down floor by floor. When he emerged onto the nineteenth floor, he spotted a woman perched on the little sofa beside the elevator, wearing a gray cloth coat with a chinchilla collar and a close-fitting gray felt hat. Clutched in her hands was a large black handbag of crushable pin seal leather. She appeared, Taite later testified, "a little dazed."

"Have you found him?" asked the woman.

Taite replied that he hadn't found anyone and didn't know what the woman was talking about.

"He's on the twenty-first floor," said the woman. "Room 2114. Rap on the door. If no one answers, go in. There's a man there who may need some help."

Leaving the woman, Taite immediately rode back up to the twenty-first floor, hurried to the designated room, and knocked on the door. When no one responded, he entered with his passkey.

Lying motionless on his side in the bedroom was a middle-aged man in a blood-soaked nightshirt. Taite knew who he was: Dr. Fritz

Gebhardt, a prominent German financier and regular tenant of the hotel. Taite saw at a glance that Gebhardt was dead. Snatching up the phone from the bed table, he called the police.

By then, the woman who had directed him to the room was making her way down the staircase. At the third-floor landing, however, her progress was barred by a padlocked accordion gate. Abandoning the stairwell, she rang for the service elevator. A few moments later, the elevator arrived and the door slid open. Inside was a pair of police officers, John Holden and Walter A. Mitchell, who had just arrived in response to Taite's call.

"Where are you going?" asked Holden.

"I want to go down," said the woman, though she made no move to get into the elevator.

As Holden stepped out and approached her, she suddenly said: "How is he?"

"Who do you mean?" said Holden.

"The man upstairs," said the woman. "Is he all right?"

"I don't know," said Holden. "Why?"

"I shot him," the woman said calmly.

"Let me see that handbag," said Holden.

Shaking her head, the woman clutched the purse more tightly to her body.

Holden reached out and tore it from her grasp. Undoing the chromium clasp, which bore the monogram "VS," he pulled the bag open, peered inside, then reached in and removed a .32-caliber double-action revolver, still warm to his palm.

"All right, you have the gun," said the woman. "Now give me back my bag."

"I think I'll hold onto it," said Holden. Later, in the station house, detectives emptied the bag and—along with a compact, lipstick, and embroidered handkerchief—found a box containing forty-six .32-caliber cartridges, four discharged shells, the key to the dead man's room, a platinum ring set with a square-cut aquamarine, and a crumpled silk woman's nightgown, badly stained with blood.

Escorted to the twenty-first floor by the two patrolmen, the woman—who had given her name as Vera Stretz—was led into Gebhardt's room, shown the bullet-riddled body, and asked "why she did it."

"Please don't ask me that," she said. "I'll only talk to a lawyer."[2]

At the East 51st Street precinct house, she was questioned by Deputy Chief Inspector Francis J. Kear, in command of Manhattan detectives. Beyond admitting to the murder, Stretz—so cool and composed that the tabloids quickly branded her the "Icy Blonde"—stubbornly refused to discuss it. By then, reporters had gotten wind of the murder and dozens of newspapermen had gathered at the station house, among them the celebrity columnist Walter Winchell, who, on the following morning, would describe Stretz as "an attractive blonde woman—nothing sassy or brassy about her—but wholesome, sweet, her clothes were plain and in good taste." As she was being led off to Homicide Court for her arraignment, several newsmen called out, "Why did you do it, Vera?" All she would say was: "It's a long story—a very long story."[3]

Investigators, however, already believed that they had pieced most of that story together. Searching Vera's apartment on the nineteenth floor of the Beekman Tower Hotel, they had discovered a cache of correspondence between the couple, along with a suicide note and a will written out by Vera two days before the slaying. The thirty-one-year-old Stretz—the cultured, NYU-educated daughter of a well-known musician and bandleader—had met the dashing Gebhardt the previous December on a holiday cruise to the Caribbean. During a romantic New Year's Eve stop at Havana, they had danced through the night and exchanged a romantic kiss at the stroke of twelve. Their shipboard flirtation had swiftly blossomed into a full-blown affair.

By June 1935, Vera had gone to work at his Fifth Avenue import firm, Frank von Knoop & Co., where she served as both his personal secretary and, as the tabloids put it, his "office wife" (a phrase only recently popularized by Faith Baldwin's best-selling novel of that name). That same month, the two had taken a vacation to Lake George, New York, registering in a hotel as Mr. and Mrs. Gebhardt.

Not long after their return, Vera had moved into an apartment in the Beekman Tower, two floors beneath her lover's. Sometime in late July, before leaving on a business trip to Europe, Gebhardt had presented her with the aquamarine ring.[4]

Throughout their lengthy separation, they had exchanged scores of impassioned letters. He was her "Darling Fritzie" who made her feel "feverish" with desire. She was his "Veralein," his "dear girlie," who filled him with such longing that "the fastest steamer" was "not fast enough to take me home to you."[5] She was understandably stunned, therefore, when, upon his long-awaited return on November 8, he revealed the existence of a wife and children in Baden-Baden — a family he had no intention of abandoning.

"The belated discovery that Dr. Gebhardt, whom she had told girl friends was her 'fiancé,' already had a wife in Germany sent her on her errand of death," the *Daily News* reported on the morning after the murder:

> As detectives reconstructed the tragedy, Miss Stretz went to the fashionable apartment of the German industrialist intending to slay both him and herself after learning that he had a wife living abroad. As a prelude to her adventure with death, she participated in a highly romantic interlude — as the negligee bore witness. Sometime during — or after — this impassioned scene, the role of the blonde secretary changed. From her handbag she obtained the revolver she had brought to the tryst and sent four shots into Dr. Gebhardt's body through his old-fashioned nightgown. . . . The finding of the will, made out by the girl two days earlier, led to the deduction that she had planned not only the murder of her lover but her own suicide as well. If such was the case, she lost her nerve after firing the four shots into Dr. Gebhardt.[6]

As a category of crime, such "love killings" weren't particularly uncommon. At virtually the same time as the Gebhardt murder, a platinum-blond showgirl named Bunny Williams shot her two-timing husband dead in an Atlantic City hotel room, and the crime was barely noted in the papers.[7] Though the Stretz case had more than its share of prurient ingredients—one tabloid writer described it as "a scorching story with all the elements of a banned-in-Boston novel"[8]—what made it so irresistible was, as much as anything else, the social standing of its principals, not only the classy, college-bred killer but also her prominent lover and victim.

A handsome, cosmopolitan forty-three-year-old, Gebhardt had been a decorated World War I flying ace, serving in the squadron of Manfred von Richthofen, the legendary "Red Baron." Following the war, he had earned his doctorate degree in political economy from Frankfurt University with a dissertation on "The International Trade in Machinery." After a brief teaching stint, he had gone into business, earning a fortune in the automobile and locomotive industries before establishing a highly successful import-export firm that specialized in "exchanging German raw material for American commodities." Charming, cultured, fluent in several languages, he also harbored political ambitions and had hopes of being named German ambassador to the United States—a fair expectation, given his close friendship with high Nazi officials, particularly Hermann Göring, a fellow Richthofen pilot during the Great War.[9]

The tabloids had a field day with the story of the demure "Skyscraper Slayer" and her philandering "Nazi Loverboy."[10] Since it quickly emerged that Vera had known about Gebhardt's wife all along, new theories about her motives abounded. He had been cheating on her with another woman. He had reneged on a promise to ask his wife for a divorce during his recent trip to Germany. He had attempted to end their affair after learning of his imminent appointment as the German ambassador to the United States, brusquely informing her that "no breath of scandal must attach to me."[11]

Vera herself wasn't talking, not to the press, not to her father, Frank, not even to family lawyer Arthur Moritz. Emerging from an interview with Vera the day after the shooting, a grim-faced Moritz advised Frank Stretz that, though Vera had offered few specifics, it was clear that she was "in a bad spot." He himself could do nothing for her. His specialty was civil law, and what Vera needed was "the best criminal lawyer in the country."

That same afternoon, a telegram went out in Vera's name: "I desire to confer with you. Come immediately." It was addressed to Samuel S. Leibowitz.[12]

Brought to this country as a four-year-old boy by parents fleeing the rampant anti-Semitism of their native Romania, Samuel Simon Leibowitz had the kind of life that typifies the immigrant dream.[13] Arriving in Manhattan on St. Patrick's Day 1897, his family took up residence in a two-room tenement flat on the Lower East Side, where they shared a water tap, bathtub, and toilet with the neighbors. Within a few years, his hard-working father, Isaac—who had sold dry goods in the Old Country—went from pushcart peddler to owner of his own store on Second Avenue and 107th Street, housing his family in the rear of the shop. Six years later, when Sam was thirteen, Isaac was able to open an even bigger store in Brooklyn and purchase a tidy home in the borough's then-peaceful neighborhood of Cypress Hills.

By all accounts, Sam, though an undistinguished student in other respects, displayed a precocious flair for elocution. No schoolroom activity gave him greater pleasure than standing in front of his classmates and declaiming "The Charge of the Light Brigade" or the Gettysburg Address. It was an early outlet for the strong theatrical streak he would later bring to bear in the courtroom, and his first taste of "the excitement and satisfaction of performing before an audience."[14]

Though Sam himself leaned toward a career in civil engineering, his father—typical of first-generation Jewish immigrants—wanted his son to be a lawyer. In the fall of 1911, Sam entered Cornell University Law School, where he shone not only academically but also as a star of the intercollegiate debating team and the first Jewish member of the Dramatic Club. In his senior year, he was elected president of the Cornell Student Congress. An ambitious young man with such a record of distinction, graduating from a top law school, would have been snapped up by one of Manhattan's elite white-collar firms—assuming he was a WASP. Realistically assessing his prospects—and eager to exercise his particular combination of forensic and histrionic skills—he opted for criminal law.[15]

His earliest clients were a colorful assortment of petty crooks and lowlifes. Typical of the breed was one "Izzy the Goniff," allegedly caught while lifting the wallet of an unwary stroller on the Coney Island boardwalk. Less concerned with the legal outcome of his case than with his professional reputation—"I've been a pickpocket for twenty-five years," he told Leibowitz, "and no sucker ever felt my mitt in his pocket"—he proceeded to demonstrate his prowess by stealing back the hundred-dollar retainer he had just paid the lawyer. At his trial, Leibowitz won over the jury by arguing that, though "his client was indeed a professional pickpocket and, if acquitted, would probably remain one, he was too good at it to be caught in the act by an ordinary citizen."[16]

By 1923, Leibowitz had racked up such an impressive record of acquittals for his small-time clientele that he began attracting a new and far higher-paying class of criminals, among them some of the country's most notorious gangsters: Benjamin "Bugsy" Siegel, Abe "Kid Twist" Reles (feared hit man for Murder, Inc.), mob boss Albert Anastasia, and Al Capone.

One of his most celebrated cases was his defense of Vincent "Mad Dog" Coll, charged with the murder of five-year-old Michael Vengalli, one of five children hit with machine-gun fire when Coll sprayed bullets into a crowded summertime street during the attempted drive-by assassination of a gangland rival. The main witness against Coll was a professional stooge named George Brecht who claimed he had been on the block selling Eskimo Pies and had recognized Coll as the death car sped by.

Ordering his assistant to go out and buy fourteen Eskimo Pies, Leibowitz handed out the ice cream bars to the jury members, judge, and prosecutor. "While they ate, he proceeded to question the witness," one journalist reported. "The man couldn't describe the label, had no idea how the pies were made, and had never heard of dry ice.

He said he carried the pies around in a cardboard box in the July sun and their own coldness kept them from melting."

His credibility completely undermined, Brecht quickly lost his composure and was caught in lie after lie by Leibowitz. Coll ended up walking free, the beneficiary of what the tabloids quickly branded the "Eskimo Pie Defense."[17]

The so-called "Christian Fish Defense" became another enduring part of the Leibowitz legend. His client in this case was one Viscenzo Santangelo, charged with shooting a police officer responding to a domestic disturbance call at the Santangelo home. Despite the testimony of five eyewitnesses who swore they had seen him at the crime scene, the defendant claimed that he had been working all day at a fish store in Harlem. Employing a Leibowitz-like tactic of his own, the prosecutor had a basket of fish brought into the courtroom, then held them up one by one—a flounder, a mackerel, a porgy, twenty-one in all—and asked Santangelo to identify them. Displaying a degree of ignorance unusual for a fish-store employee, Santangelo guessed wrong every time. Leibowitz, however, had a riposte at the ready. Recognizing by their names that four of the jurymen were his coreligionists, he declared, in a voice ringing with indignation, that the prosecutor had perpetrated an unconscionable fraud:

> Was there in all that array of fish a single pike, or pickerel, or whitefish, or any other fish that can be made into gefilte fish? There was not! My client told you that he worked in a store at 114th Street and Park Avenue. The prosecutor knows that is a Jewish neighborhood and he did not show a single fish that makes gefilte fish. What a travesty of justice! My client is an Italian who works in a Jewish fish market and they try him on Christian fish!

The jury took just ninety minutes to acquit.[18]

Though a consummate performer who could, as the occasion demanded, elicit laughter, tears, or heart-swelling sympathy from a jury, Leibowitz was far more than a showman. He himself claimed that success "was due to preparation rather than to courtroom legerdemain":

> He investigated the facts and the evidence—including the scene where the relevant events had taken place—for himself. He constructed the case as if he were the prosecutor, identifying the elements of the case and the strengths and weakness of each. Only then did he begin working on a defense. He learned everything available of the life history, personality, habits, and character of his client, potential witnesses, prosecuting attorney, presiding jurist, and potential jurors. He would also do careful research into specialized fields of knowledge related to his case, whether ballistics, medicine, psychology or chemistry.[19]

Always good for colorful copy, the stocky, balding, immaculately groomed attorney—a master of press manipulation—was a media darling, the starring attraction of such tabloid sensations as the Gigolo Murder Widow Trial, the Gravesend Bay Rowboat Murder Trial, the Honor Slayer Murder Trial, the Dream Slayer Murder Trial, the Phantom Slayer Murder Trial, the Four-Gun Sweeney Murder Trial, and the Insurance Death Plotter Murder Trial. By 1932, he had defended seventy-eight people accused of first-degree murder. His record stood at seventy-seven acquittals, one hung jury, no convictions.[20]

In January 1933, Leibowitz was retained as the lawyer for the Scottsboro Boys, the nine African-American teenagers falsely accused of gang-raping two white women aboard a freight train headed from Chattanooga, Tennessee, to Huntsville, Alabama. In the face of constant death threats from Southern racists—who openly declared their desire to lynch the "Jew lawyer from New York"—he devoted the next five years to the cause célèbre. Working without pay or reimbursement for his expenses, he eventually brought the case all the way to the U.S. Supreme Court, where he earned a place in civil rights history by convincing the justices that the Alabama trial system—which excluded African-Americans from serving on juries—was unconstitutional and had deprived his clients "of the equal protection of the laws as provided for the Fourteenth Amendment."[21]

By then, the "Great Defender" (as his admirers now called him) had resumed his criminal law practice in New York, though with one crucial difference. He was far less inclined to represent high-profile gangsters, turning down both Lucky Luciano and Louis "Lepke" Buchalter, despite the latter's offer of a $250,000 fee.[22] In early 1936, he became involved in the single most spectacular case of the century, that of Bruno Richard Hauptmann, convicted kidnapper-killer of the Lindbergh baby. Retained by a wealthy socialite convinced that Hauptmann had been railroaded, Leibowitz conducted a series of jailhouse interviews with the prisoner, trying to convince him that his only hope of avoiding the chair was to admit his guilt. Even Leibowitz's famously persuasive powers, however, could not wrest a confession from Hauptmann. In a rare admission of defeat, Leibowitz quit the case on February 19.

One month later, he would dazzle observers with "his most brilliant performance yet" in the trial of Vera Stretz.[23]

No sooner had he taken over the Stretz case than Leibowitz began to work the press. To counter the public perception of her as a coldblooded femme fatale, he arranged a jailhouse interview for his client, attended by a dozen reporters from the city's major papers.

Dressed in a polka-dotted, Alice-blue frock and devoid of makeup (in accordance with prison rules), Vera met with the newsmen in the reception room of the Women's House of Detention on the day after Thanksgiving, Friday, November 29. With Leibowitz at her side, she fielded their questions with a fervor that, as one attendee wrote, successfully "demolished her image as an emotionless 'icy blonde.'"[24] She grew particularly impassioned when one reporter asked, "Do you regret the circumstances which brought you here?"

"Any decent woman would have done the same thing," she replied with a quavering voice.

His own voice ringing with indignation, Leibowitz interjected:

"Legally, ethically, and from every human standpoint, Gebhardt got what was coming to him. He was the kind of creature that any red-blooded man here present would just love to take out to the nearest back yard for the purpose of knocking his head loose from his torso."

From this and similar statements, the newsmen concluded that Leibowitz planned a self-defense plea based on "some vile insult directed by Dr. Gebhardt against Vera's womanhood," on a "gross violation of his secretary-sweetheart's fundamental faith in the purity and cleanliness of his affection," as the tabloids put it. Though tantalizingly vague as to the nature of Gebhardt's "vile," "gross" behavior, these reports left little doubt that Leibowitz meant to dish up some particularly steamy revelations when the trial got underway.[25]

When it finally opened on Friday, March 20, 1936, it was the hottest show in town, drawing a huge crowd of spectators, among them such luminaries as Walter Winchell, actress Tallulah Bankhead, and Dudley Field Malone, Clarence Darrow's co-counsel in the famous Scopes Monkey Trial.[26] Even before the first witness was called to the stand, the outlines of Leibowitz's "decency defense" began to emerge. Questioning prospective jurors, he startled observers—and drew heated objections from his opponent, Assistant District Attorney Miles O'Brien—by grilling them on their knowledge of "the philosophical superman theories of Friedrich Wilhelm Nietzsche." Given Gebhardt's nationality—and his close ties to Nazi bigwigs (at his funeral service several months earlier, a swastika flag had been draped over his coffin)—reporters inferred that Leibowitz intended to draw a link between Gebhardt and the author of *Thus Spake Zarathustra*, whose attitude toward the opposite sex was summed up in such maxims as "Man shall be trained for war and women for the recreation of the warrior," "A man who has the depth of spirit . . . must conceive of woman as a possession, as confinable property, as being predestined for service," and "Thou goest to woman? Do not forget thy whip!"

Leibowitz also made it clear that he was looking for jurors with a highly developed sense of old-fashioned chivalry. Knowing "what a high value Southerners place on a woman's virtue," he seemed especially eager to empanel William A. French Jr., a radio engineer and native of North Carolina. First, however, there was a potentially disqualifying matter to resolve. "Would you be prejudiced against me," asked Leibowitz, "because I was counsel for the Scottsboro Boys?" When French replied with an emphatic "no," the lawyer then asked the same question he would pose, in one form or another, to every talesman: "If a woman killed to protect her body and no matter what form that protection took—would you find her not guilty because of the law of self-defense?" Satisfied with French's response, Leibowitz quickly accepted him.[27]

At the end of the first day's proceedings, Leibowitz met with reporters, who peppered him with questions about his focus on Nietzschean philosophy. "Nietzsche was Gebhardt's god," he informed them. The remark confirmed what they had already deduced about Leibowitz's strategy. "It seems obvious that he will argue that the defendant killed Gebhardt to prevent an unnatural assault," the papers reported—"that Vera squeezed the trigger to protect herself from the degrading advances of a brute who had sopped up a superman complex from Nietzsche's writings."[28]

In contrast to his flamboyant opponent, Prosecutor O'Brien proceeded in a dry, matter-of-fact way that bordered on the bland. His opening statement, lasting a mere twenty minutes, was a straightforward recounting of the events of November 12, 1935, when Dr. Gebhardt's 168-pound, five-foot-eight, nightshirt-clad body was found on the floor of his Beekman Tower Hotel room, perforated by four bullets from Vera Stretz's pistol. The deadpan manner in which he delivered his statement made it clear that he felt he had an open-and-shut case—that the facts spoke so loudly for themselves that they required no undue emphasis on his part to impress themselves on the jury. As one chronicler puts it:

> O'Brien, in effect, was saying to the jury, "This woman and Gebhardt were having an affair. Something went wrong with it

and she killed him. It's that simple. Why cloud the issue with irrelevant nonsense about Nietzsche or about possible unnatural acts? She was in her right mind and deliberately killed him. That's all that counts and that constitutes first-degree murder."[29]

A parade of prosecution witnesses offered devastating testimony, including future chief medical examiner Dr. Milton Helpern and ballistics expert Sergeant Harry Butts, who established that Gebhardt had been shot at point-blank range, twice in the back. Listening at the defense table, Vera repeatedly broke into convulsive sobs and, on several occasions, fell into a swoon and had to be revived with smelling salts. By the time the prosecution rested, O'Brien, in his dry, methodical way, had done a seemingly unassailable job of depicting the death of Dr. Gebhardt as "a cold-blooded premeditated execution."[30]

When the courtroom opened on the following morning, Friday, March 27, the eager, largely female crowd surged through the doorway, filling up the spectator section within minutes. Out in the corridor, a hundred or more disappointed sensation-seekers clamored vainly for admission. They had come for the trial's long-awaited climax, the testimony of Vera Stretz, Leibowitz's sole witness. For weeks, the tabloids had offered lurid hints about the motives that drove Vera to kill—the "abnormal," "weird and repulsive," "dangerously sadistic" practices that Gebhardt had tried to force upon her.[31] Now, with Vera finally slated to take the stand, the public would learn if the prurient rumors were true. They would not be disappointed.

Under Leibowitz's questioning, Vera—looking "pathetically pale" and twisting a handkerchief nervously in her hands[32]—related the familiar story of her passionate love affair with the dashing German financier. She told of their initial meeting aboard the Caribbean cruiser *Vulcania*, of their shipboard flirtation, of their first New Year's Eve kiss in Havana. By the time they returned to New York City, their friendship, she said, was already "very deep."

Soon he was phoning her regularly, squiring her to expensive restaurants, sending her flowers, candy, books. She was swept off her feet by the "fascinating," "gallant," "brilliant" man of the world, so "ardent" in his attentions.[33]

Shortly afterward, upon returning from one of his frequent business trips to Europe, he took her to a supper club, where he declared his love for her. Vera—who, it emerged, had been briefly married in her midtwenties to a man twice her age and now affected a world-weary cynicism—told him that she "didn't believe in love."[34]

"What did he say to that?" asked Leibowitz.

"He said, 'All right, I'll teach you.'"

And how, inquired Leibowitz, did she respond?

"I told him I would be charmed to have him teach me."

"Despite his being to your knowledge a married man?" asked Leibowitz.

"He said he and his wife had not lived together for years," said Vera. "That was all dead. He said that ordinary laws were made for ordinary men, but he was not an ordinary man."

"A superman perhaps?" said Leibowitz, provoking a swift—and sustained—objection.[35]

With "the humility of a slave," Vera surrendered herself utterly to his tutelage—to his "love school," as the tabloids called it.[36] She first gave herself to him sexually during a trip to Lake George the preceding May. "He wanted to pretend it was our wedding trip," said Vera. "We registered as Mr. and Mrs. Gebhardt."

"Why," asked Leibowitz, "did you have intimate relations with him?"

"Because I loved him intensely," said Vera. "I could not help yielding to him."

At the time, Vera was living on 57th Street in a one-room apartment with a window that opened on a fire escape. Visiting one night, Gebhardt expressed his concern that "someone could come up that fire escape and into this room and run away with the little girl I love." Vera reassured him that she could scare off any intruder with a licensed pistol she owned, purchased for protection several years earlier when she resided in East Harlem. Gebhardt, according to Vera's testimony, "asked me to show it to him and I did. He didn't want me to have it—thought it was dangerous for me. He took it and the cartridges and put them in his coat pocket. He kept the gun from then on."[37] Shortly afterward, Vera moved into the Beekman Tower Hotel to facilitate their affair.

She was unashamed of her behavior, as one of her many love letters—read aloud by Leibowitz—made clear. "The basis of my self-content," she wrote, "is the good old-fashioned theorem that sexual intercourse is sacred and lovely, a unity of everything fine."[38] Gebhardt's own letters to her smoldered with passion. "I look around and I feel your eye and I feel your kiss on my lips," he wrote during one of their separations. "I long to caress you with my hands. A thousand dear kisses."

Their correspondence grew increasingly torrid. He mailed her picture postcards from European art museums of the most risqué paintings he could find—nymphs and satyrs disporting themselves in scandalous ways, languid odalisques reclining on rumpled beds, naked female slaves lounging in Oriental seraglios.

In return she copied out an entire passage from D. H. Lawrence's *Lady Chatterley's Lover.* Preparing to read this excerpt aloud in court, Leibowitz asked that the spectator section be cleared. "If there are any women who will be shocked," the judge announced, "they may leave the courtroom now."

No one budged from her seat.

As the spectators cupped their ears and strained forward, Leibowitz—speaking so softly that his voice barely carried to the jury box—read the controversial passage in which the gamekeeper Mellors rhapsodizes about his enforced celibacy while separated from his married lover:

> If you're in Scotland and I'm in the Midlands, and I can't put my arms around you, and wrap my legs round you, yet I've got something of you. My soul softly flaps in the little Pentecost flame with you, like the peace of fucking. We fucked a flame

into being. Even the flowers are fucked into being between the sun and earth. But it's a delicate thing, and takes patience and the long pause. So I love chastity now, because it is the peace that comes of fucking. I love being chaste now. I love it as snow-drops love the snow. I love this chastity, which is the peace of our fucking, between us now like a snowdrop of forked white fire. And when the real spring comes, when the drawing to-gether comes, then we can fuck the little flame brilliant and yellow, brilliant.[39]

That the demur, respectable, college-educated woman had penned such pornography (as most of the public still viewed it) was proof of how thoroughly subjugated she had become to her Teutonic "super lover," of how masterfully he had turned her into his sexual plaything.[40] Or so Leibowitz wished the jurors to think.

For all of her slavish devotion to Fritz, however, Vera still retained sufficient self-respect to crave a conventional relationship. When, fol-lowing a business trip to Boston in June 1935, he presented her with the aquamarine ring, she assumed that they were now formally en-gaged.[41] Not long afterward, he left again, this time for Germany. It was Vera's understanding that he intended to ask his wife for a divorce to clear the way for their own marriage. She was stunned, therefore, when, immediately upon his return on November 8, he in-formed her that "he had discovered in his travels that he was not the marrying kind." He wanted their relationship to remain as it was, with Vera as his mistress.

Vera would have none of it. "I told him I couldn't have that kind of life anymore," she testified. "I couldn't bear it. I wanted a home and husband." If Gebhardt wouldn't wed her, she announced, "it was all over" between them.

Her declaration evoked a side of her "Darling Fritzie" she had never witnessed before. "No one has ever left me before," he sneered. "And you are not going to leave me."

The climactic act of the drama occurred the following night. Be-sides ministering to his sexual needs, Vera had frequently been called upon to play nurse to Gebhardt, who suffered from chronic abdominal pains. She was asleep in her room on Monday, November 11, when, at around 11:00 p.m., she was awakened by the telephone. The call was from Fritz, who claimed to be stricken with a severe gastric attack and unable to find his heating pad. Could she please come help him?

Throwing her coat over her nightgown and slipping on her shoes, she hurried to his room. When he opened the door to admit her, she saw that he looked flushed, feverish. Ordering him back to bed, she followed him into his bedroom, then stepped over to the bureau to look for the pad. In the top drawer, among various "odds and ends"—a collar box, some neckties, cuff links—she saw the pistol he had confiscated from her several weeks earlier. She was still searching for the heating pad when Gebhardt snuck up from behind and grabbed her.

"If you don't need me," she said, struggling vainly to break free, "I'm going."

"You're not going anywhere," he said. "You're staying here as long as I want you."

"You beast," she cried. "Let me go!"

Throwing her onto the bed, he "flung himself on" her, pinned her arms over her head, and raped her.

"It was excruciatingly painful," said Vera in a quavering voice. "I lay there moaning. Then he reached for me again and I sprang out of bed. I looked for my shoes. I saw one of them on the bureau. I found one mixed in the bedclothes. I put them on and said, 'I hate you. I never want to see you again.'"

As she stood by the bureau, getting into her shoes, Gebhardt rose from the bed and came at her. "You damned whore," he snarled. "You are not like my others—but you *will* be before you leave this room. I will make you."

At this point in her narration, Vera faltered, as though reluctant to relive in her mind the sheer horror of that moment.

"Then what happened?" asked Leibowitz.

"I said, 'Let me go, let me go,' and he lifted"—here, tears began to flow from Vera's eyes—"he lifted up his nightgown—he took— he lifted up his nightgown and he took his penis—"

"Go on," said Leibowitz, his voiced resounding in the hushed courtroom.

"And he said—"

Raising her balled-up handkerchief to her eyes, Vera broke into sobs.

"You'll have to control yourself, young lady," said the judge. "Tell your story to the jury."

It took a few moments for Vera to pull herself together and re- sume her story. Standing before her, exposed in that obscene fash- ion, Gebhardt had said: "You will do everything I want."

What Gebhardt wanted was so repulsive—such a "crime against nature," in the view of Vera's contemporaries—that, though her very life hinged on convincing the jury that the murder was jus- tified, she could barely bring herself to repeat his monstrous de- mand. Finally, "choked with sobs," she spoke "the ugly words he had used." The newspapers of the time could only hint at the nature of this grotesque "indignity." Years would pass before chroniclers of the case revealed that Gebhardt had attempted to force her to per- form fellatio.[42]

"No, no, never!" Vera cried as Gebhardt stood leering at her.

Suddenly she "remembered the gun" and snatched it from the drawer. "Let me out," she warned, "or I'll do something desperate."

"You damned bitch," said Gebhardt. "I'll kill you."

With that, Vera testified, "he grabbed my hand and he pulled me toward him and I pulled away from him and that is when the gun went off. He fell on the bed and he staggered up. And I shot him again."

Leibowitz—who had opted not to make an opening statement at the start of the trial—delivered a five-hour summation on Friday, April 3. He began at 10:00 a.m. in "a mild, chatty voice but turned up the heat quickly. He shouted, pounded the table, tore off his coat and put it on again," treating the courtroom to "one of the choice performances of his long life at the bar."[43]

In his version of events, Vera—despite her mature years, college degree, and taste for Lawrentian "obscenities"—was a starry-eyed innocent who, like so many American women, was a "sucker" for a smooth-talking foreigner like Gebhardt.

"You know these men," said Leibowitz in a mocking, mincing voice. "The gallant, Continental manners—he can hold a coat just so. You know we Americans can't hold a candle to them. The girls love these pseudo attentions. Women cry for it." Speaking as one regular "red-blooded" guy to twelve others, Leibowitz could only wonder at the mysteries of the opposite sex. "What do we men know about love? What do we know about those complex wheels that turn in the skulls of those creatures we call women? He whispers sweet nothing in her ears and her heart says, 'Why, this is love.'"

Far from being "an enchantress or an adventuress," all Vera wanted was a "home, respectability. She wanted to be able to say to her neighbors, 'Meet my husband, Dr. Gebhardt.'" When he gave her a "cheap little ring," she eagerly seized on it as a "promise of marriage." To her, it "epitomized a home and children, her very life itself."

Gebhardt, however, was interested in only one thing. A "professional heartbreaker," a "gigolo," a "roamer" who "didn't care a hoot about his wife," he regarded Vera as nothing more than "his toy, his human plaything." "The man was an egomaniac," Leibowitz declared. "He determined to conquer her, like a superman." When Vera finally attempted to break free of his nefarious clutches, he resolved to make her submit one last time to his perverse desires. "That's why he lured her to his room with that last foul pretense that he had been taken ill in the night. And she trustfully answered his call."

When Gebhardt attacked her, she had every right to use violence to protect herself. The fact that she had previously "submitted to his importunities does not mean that she was bound to submit always.

If to prevent the commission of a crime upon herself she resorted to whatever form was necessary, she did not commit murder or manslaughter or any other crime," said Leibowitz.

"She warned him she'd do something desperate. The warning didn't stop him. The bullets did." Indeed, it was "an act of God" that her pistol was in Gebhardt's bureau drawer that night. "God knows what might have happened to this girl if the gun weren't there."

"She had a right to kill to get out of that room," said Leibowitz, after reminding the jurors of the sexual abomination she had been threatened with. She was "a poor girl trying to get away from a lecherous beast."

"Give this little girl a fair shake," begged Leibowitz. "She suffered her Calvary that day. She walked with a cross on her back and a crown of thorns on her head.

"Let her go free. She's entitled to it. Even though it is raining outdoors, let her go free clad in her thin coat—let her stumble out into the world, let her breathe God's free air, as she has a right to do!"[44]

The jury received the case at 3:34 p.m. and—not having eaten since breakfast—immediately broke for lunch. Their deliberations began in earnest at 5:15. Less than three hours later, at 8:10 p.m., they announced that they had reached a verdict.

When, a few minutes later, jury foreman Curtis L. Lee declared the defendant not guilty, the largely female audience broke into a wild applause, while Vera herself—"the Weeping Willow love slayer," as the tabloids now called her—collapsed in a faint and had to be revived with spirits of ammonia. As the congratulatory crowd swarmed around her, several guards "formed a flying wedge and whisked her to an anteroom," while Samuel Leibowitz, making "no attempt to conceal his elation," offered exuberant thanks to the jurors.[45]

Less than a half hour earlier, the Lindbergh baby kidnapper, Bruno Richard Hauptmann, following several stays of execution, was finally led to the chair in the New Jersey State Prison, still protesting his innocence. Given his infamy as perpetrator of the single greatest American crime of the twentieth century, the front page of the next morning's *New York Daily News* served as striking testimony to the notoriety the Stretz case had achieved. In equally bold letters it read: "BRUNO DEAD. VERA FREE."[46]

Meeting with reporters that same morning in Leibowitz's office, Vera—looking refreshed and wearing "a smart new green ensemble and black pancake hat"—struck a solemn note when asked about her future. She was "through with men," she announced. "Marriage, a home, babies—those are for normal people, not me." When one female reporter called out, "Don't let this ruin your life," Vera sadly replied: "My life has been ruined already. I can never be the same woman again."[47]

By the following day, Vera had apparently settled on a plan. Accompanied by a photograph captioned, "PRESENTING THE STRETZ GIRL . . . AUTHOR!," the *Mirror* reported that she intended to write a "prison novel" based on her experiences in the Women's House of Detention while awaiting her trial. She had already come up with a title: *The House of Innocence.*[48]

The article on Vera's authorial aspirations, appearing on Monday, April 6, was the *Mirror*'s last piece on the Stretz affair. For devoted tabloid readers, the months-long circus surrounding the Beekman Place murder had come to an end.

They wouldn't have to wait long for a new one.

"Beauty Slain in Bathtub"

W HETHER VERA STRETZ COMPLETED any part of her projected prison novel is unknown. Certainly no such book
ever appeared in print. As with so many others who dream of literary glory, her plans of becoming a published author remained in the
realm of the hypothetical.

Nancy Evans Titterton, on the other hand, was the real thing.

A native of Dayton, Ohio, Nancy had been involved with literature from her earliest years. A graduate of Antioch College, where
she won honors in English, she had briefly operated a small book-
shop in her hometown before moving to New York City in 1924 to
pursue a literary career. Renting an apartment in Greenwich Village,
she went to work in the book department of Lord & Taylor while
writing newspaper book reviews in her spare time. After a few years
as a bookseller, she was hired by the publishing house of Doubleday,
Doran, where (in a grimly ironic coincidence that the tabloids never
tired of noting) she helped develop the company's popular Crime
Club series.[1]

She met her future husband, Lewis H. Titterton, in 1927. A slight, sandy-haired Englishman who sported a neatly trimmed moustache and round, horn-rimmed eyeglasses, Titterton had studied ancient Middle Eastern languages at Cambridge University and Harvard. In 1925, still in his twenties, he was offered the prestigious post of assistant editor of the *Atlantic Monthly*. From there he moved into the book business as assistant sales manager and later associate editor of the Macmillan Company. During his spare time, he translated French novels and turned out several hundred book reviews, mostly for the *New York Times*.

In 1929, after a two-year courtship, he and Nancy were wed in the picturesque Little Church Around the Corner on East 29th Street. They lived briefly on West 47th Street—the heart of Manhattan's notorious Hell's Kitchen—before moving to the far more congenial milieu of Beekman Place, renting an apartment in a handsome five-story walk-up overlooking the East River. "I'm so glad to get out of Hell's Kitchen," she wrote to one friend shortly after the move. "Even though we had bars on the window, I never felt safe there. Nothing could happen to anyone on Beekman Place."[2]

By then, Titterton had gone to work at NBC, where he quickly found himself promoted to chief of the script division, a somewhat incongruous position for so bookish a man. Intent on elevating the cultural quality of radio programming, he commissioned scripts from serious dramatists and hosted a weekly interview program featuring eminent men of letters. Even among his competitors at rival stations he was regarded as a force for good, a champion of literacy in a world of *Amos 'n' Andy*, *Gang Busters*, and *Chandu the Magician*.[3]

Nancy, in the meantime, had left her job and was devoting herself full time to fiction writing. After publishing several pieces in *Scribner's*, she achieved a breakthrough in August 1935 when her poignant tale "I Shall Decline My Head" appeared in *Story* magazine, the prestigious journal that would introduce the work of J. D. Salinger, John Cheever, Joseph Heller, and Tennessee Williams, among others.[4] On the strength of that story—about an old man adrift in dreams of the past—she was given a contract for a first novel and immediately set to work on it.

Compared to the literary luminaries she counted as her Beekman Place neighbors, Nancy Evans Titterton was still a relative unknown. For a few weeks in the spring of 1936, however, she became the biggest name in town.

Good Friday fell on April 10 that year. After breakfast that morning, Lewis Titterton left his fourth-floor apartment in the five-story walk-up building at 22 Beekman Place and strolled the few blocks to his office at Radio City. In his mailbox he found "an amusing letter from a friend" and telephoned his wife to read it to her. They shared a laugh over the letter before hanging up. The time was approximately 9:00 a.m. They would never speak again.[5]

Nancy had another telephone conversation that morning, this one with Mrs. Georgia Mansbridge of 12 St. Luke's Place in Greenwich Village. They chatted for a few minutes at around 10:15 a.m. about a dinner party scheduled for the following night. "I feel sure no one was in her apartment when we spoke," a distraught Mrs. Mansbridge would tell reporters the following day. "Poor little Nancy— she couldn't fight. She had no strength, and she wouldn't know what to do. All she could do was scream."

The only person to hear Nancy scream—other than the man who raped and killed her—was Oneda Smithmead, a "colored maid" in an apartment one floor below. At around 11:30, Smithmead heard a woman call out "Dudley, Dudley, Dudley!"—the name of the building handyman, Dudley Mings. There was an urgency to the cry, but since the tenants routinely shouted for Mings whenever a toilet overflowed, a ceiling light blew, or a sash window wouldn't open, Smith attached little significance to it. Only in retrospect (as the *New York Post* reported) was "the cry interpreted as a desperate plea for the help of the only man who might be about the premises" at that hour of the workday.

Not long afterward, Wiley Straughn, a fourteen-year-old delivery boy for a local dry cleaners, the London Valet Service, arrived at 22 Beekman Place with a dress for Mrs. Titterton. He pressed the downstairs bell repeatedly but got no response. Assuming that no one was home, he returned to the shop with the dress.[6]

Later that day, another delivery arrived for the Tittertons. At approximately 4:15 p.m., a small truck pulled up in front of 22 Beekman Place and two men emerged from the cab. The driver was Theodore Kruger, the stocky, middle-aged owner of a local upholstery shop. With him was his assistant, John Fiorenza.

A grade school dropout with a "dull normal" IQ, a stunted personality, and a face that seemed fixed in a perpetual smirk, Fiorenza, twenty-four, shared a Brooklyn apartment with his mother, Theresa, and her second husband, Ignazi Cupani, a WPA carpenter. Withdrawn to the point of extreme social isolation, he barely communicated at home—his stepfather claimed that Johnny had spoken to him no more than seven times in the past eleven years—and didn't have a girlfriend until the age of twenty-one, when he began seeing a quiet, strictly raised young woman from the Bronx, Pauline D'Antonio. After two years of "keeping company" under the chaperoning eye of Pauline's Old Country grandmother, the couple had gotten engaged. Hoping to wed in the fall, Pauline had recently taken a job in an underwear factory to earn money for her dowry.[7]

John himself had been working at Kruger's shop for the past three years, sweeping out the place, cleaning the display windows, and helping with the upholstery, a skill he had picked up during one of his stints in the Elmira Reformatory in upstate New York. From the age of twelve—when he was arrested for stealing a bicycle—Fiorenza had been in and out of trouble with the law. In the scheme of things, his offenses were trivial. His most serious conviction to date, on a charge of grand larceny, had resulted from the theft of two snare drums and a trombone from the basement of a neighborhood music shop. A psychiatrist who examined him at the time diagnosed Fiorenza as a "neurotic type of personality deviate" with poor impulse control: "with him, the wish is father to the thought and leads quickly to action without consideration or foresight." On two occasions, he had given in to an "uncontrollable urge to take 'joy rides,'" making off with stolen cars in broad daylight, once with the owner clinging precariously to the running board and shouting for him to stop. "Perhaps," a prominent New York City psychoanalyst named Walter Bromberg ventured, "this urge to drive cars could be interpreted as a symbolic expression of the pressure of unrecognized, powerful sexual drives." Bromberg, of course, had the benefit of hindsight. Until Good Friday 1936, no one—John Fiorenza included—realized just how dangerously explosive his sexual drives were.

Kruger—who regarded his assistant as a "good-natured" if "not very quick-witted" young man whose troubles had been "over little things"—knew all about John's police record. Indeed, that very morning, Fiorenza had shown up late for work in order to keep an appointment with his probation officer, Peter Gambaro. Or so Theodore Kruger had been led to believe.[8]

From the rear of the truck, Kruger and his assistant removed a loveseat, newly upholstered in green fabric. They had picked up the little sofa the previous day from the Tittertons' apartment and were now returning it as per prearrangement. Their load wasn't heavy and the two men had no trouble carrying it up to the fourth floor, where they found the Tittertons' door ajar. After rapping on the door and getting no response, they carried the loveseat inside and set it down in its original location in the living room. Kruger called out for Mrs. Titterton. Receiving no answer, he left the bill on the seat cushion, then motioned for his helper to follow him from the apartment. They had just started down the stairway when Kruger—thinking he would telephone Mrs. Titterton once he returned to his shop and make sure she was satisfied with the job—decided to go back and get her phone number.

"I found the phone in the bedroom and took the number," Kruger told reporters later that day. "Suddenly I noticed the bathroom light was on and the door was open a few inches. I walked over and knocked. Finally I pushed the door wide open."

A woman's foot hung over the edge of the bathtub. Kruger called out Mrs. Titterton's name, but the figure in the bathtub did not stir. He went closer and peered into the tub. "My knees began shaking and I felt sick," he related. "I shouted to Johnny, 'My God, something's happened to the missus! Call the police!'"

Fiorenza did as he was told. Kruger was so rattled that only much later would he recall something strange. Though Fiorenza had not yet even glanced into the bathroom, he told the sergeant who answered: "There's a woman tied up in the bathtub."[9]

In less than five minutes, a half dozen homicide detectives were crowded inside the Tittertons' bathroom. Inside the tub, Nancy lay on her stomach, naked except for a torn white slip bunched around her waist and the sheer magenta-colored hose hanging down her legs. Twisted around her neck was a makeshift noose, fashioned from a pink pajama top and a matching silk dressing jacket, tightly knotted together. Water dripping from the showerhead had pooled around her dark, swollen face.

From the state of the apartment, the detectives were able to reconstruct the general circumstances of the crime. There was no sign of forced entry; evidently, Nancy had freely admitted her killer. The kitchen, living room, and library were undisturbed. The assault had taken place in the bedroom, where one of the twin beds was in disarray and the victim's garter belt, brassiere, blue tweed skirt, and pink blouse were strewn around the floor, violently ripped from her body by her attacker. Ligature marks on her wrists showed that he had bound her hands together before raping her. Afterward, she had been garroted and dragged into the bathroom. An autopsy revealed that she was still alive when she was dumped in the tub and had died of slow asphyxiation.[10]

At approximately 5:45 p.m., Assistant Medical Examiner Thomas A. Gonzales arrived on the scene. Moments later, Lewis Titterton returned from work. He had not been notified of the tragedy and was startled by the milling crowd outside his building and the fleet of police cars at the curb. He collapsed in horror at the news that greeted him upstairs.

After finishing his preliminary examination, Dr. Gonzales ordered the body removed. Lying beneath it on the bottom of the tub was a strand of cord about thirteen inches long, cleanly cut at both ends. Though it matched the marks on Nancy's wrists, it was too short to have kept her hands tightly bound. Detectives immediately deduced that it came from a longer piece of rope. Evidently, the killer, intent on removing all physical evidence, had sliced off the rope and carried it away with him. In his haste, however, this segment, concealed beneath Nancy's body, had escaped his notice.

To the naked eye, there was nothing at all distinctive about the piece of cord. In the end, however, it would prove to be the key element in a landmark feat of forensic detection: "the string," as the *Daily News* declared, "that tied the slayer to the chair."[11]

From the moment the story broke, the Beekman Place "Bathtub Murder" became the talk of the town, thanks to the gleefully exploitive coverage by the tabloids. That the killing occurred exactly one week to the day after Vera Stretz's acquittal and just a block north of the building where Fritz Gebhardt was shot to death only added to its lurid appeal.[12]

Hearst's *Mirror* did its usual shameless job of turning the tragedy into prurient entertainment. On Saturday, April 11, under the headline "HOW WOMAN WAS FOUND STRANGLED TO DEATH IN MURDER MYSTERY," it presented the gruesome sex-killing as a five-panel comic strip, complete with graphic drawings of the corpse and a fedora-wearing detective bearing a marked resemblance to Dick Tracy. The following day, its entire back page—normally reserved for the latest sports headlines—was devoted to a voyeuristic photo of Mrs. Titterton's body being removed from the apartment on its way to the morgue.[13]

In the relentlessly titillating coverage of the case, the victim—by all accounts a demure, "owlishly solemn" woman who favored modest tweeds and sports clothes and wore her hair in a mannish cut—was portrayed as a slinky redhead who liked to parade around her apartment in a negligee, even when "delivery boys and workmen" were present. As if the particulars of the murder weren't sensational enough, the tabloids spiced up their stories with hints of sexual perversion. According to the *Mirror,* Dr. Gonzales's initial examination of the violated corpse revealed "evidence of abnormality that convinced him that only a degenerate could have committed the crime." Citing experts like Arthur Carey, former head of the NYPD's homicide bureau, the *News* informed readers that "crimes of this shocking type" are "relatively frequent," as should be expected "with so many perverted, twisted, and mentally unbalanced persons on the loose."[14]

The *Mirror,* true to its three-ring-circus sensibility, cited experts of its own, like "Mrs. Myra Kingsley, prominent astrologist of 225 East 54th Street," who determined from the victim's horoscope "that the crime was due to the conjunction of the planet Mars—the War God—with the Sun in the Eighth house, which signifies DEATH." Mrs. Kingsley also deduced from Nancy's "chart that the murderer was an older man, and that he either came from or has gone to a distance since the crime was committed." Not to be outdone, the *Post* hired its own astrologist, Mrs. Belle Bart, who insisted that "the murderer is German or English, has a light complexion, takes drugs or drinks, met Mrs. Titterton in the fall of 1935, escaped from Beekman Place in a southwesterly direction and would probably be arrested in Washington Square or thereabouts."[15]

Within a week of the murder, the unknown, aspiring author had become such a tabloid sensation that the headlines simply called her by first name: "NANCY KNEW KILLER," "MAN OF MYSTERY BOUGHT NANCY FLOWERS," "NANCY'S HUSBAND NAMES MURDER SUSPECT."[16] Visiting from England at the time was a writer of authentic renown: Marie Belloc Lowndes, best known for her novel *The Lodger,* a thriller about Jack the Ripper made into an early Alfred Hitchcock film. On the evening of Friday, April 18, she dined with Edmund Pearson, dean of American true crime historians. Her diary entry about the occasion records only a single topic of conversation: "All New York is horrified over the murder of a woman writer, Mrs. Titterton, strangled on Good Friday. She was about thirty and happily married." Speculating on the identity of the killer, Mrs. Belloc Lowndes could reach only one conclusion: "It was a lunatic's murder."[17]

There was no shortage of suspects, beginning with Lewis Titterton. He was not only the victim's husband—always the likeliest perpetrator when a married woman meets a violent death—but also a bookwormish Brit "whose accent and manner were alone enough to put the average detective's back up," as one commentator noted.[18] Titterton, however, had no trouble proving he was at work all day. And even the cops most inclined to sneer at his egghead demeanor were moved by the depth of his grief.

For a few days, investigators focused on a "sandy-haired young man with needlepoint eyes and a manner that verged on the feminine" who, according to the Countess Alice Hoyos—a beautiful divorcée occupying the apartment directly below the Tittertons'— had been skulking around the neighborhood for the previous week. W. A. DeWitt, a writer for *Reader's Digest* who lived in the neighboring building, claimed that, on the morning of the murder, he had glanced through his window and seen a "Negro in dungarees walking across the roof of No. 22 Beekman Place from which access to the fire escape leading to the Titterton apartment was readily accessible." Other supposed witnesses pointed their fingers at "a shifty-eyed youth loitering in front of the building," "a reputedly demented man who had been annoying maids and matrons in the neighborhood," and a pair of mysterious "prowlers, one in his early twenties with several missing teeth, the other a forty-year-old man with a florid face."[19]

From Police Chief George Fallon of Quincy, Massachusetts, came a tip about a fugitive wanted for a similar bathtub strangling in that city. Another official, Dr. Carleton Simon, "former Special Deputy Commissioner of the NYPD and present criminologist of the International Association of the Chiefs of Police," opined that Mrs. Titterton died "as the innocent victim of a sexual adventurer who, obeying an uncontrollable emotional urge, set out to talk his way into apartments in the Beekman Place district. He planned to force his attentions upon any women he met who challenged his bestial desire. Mrs. Titterton chanced to be that woman."[20]

That Nancy had admitted her killer into the apartment and even, as the evidence suggested, allowed him into her bedroom fueled a host of scandalous rumors that the tabloids were only too happy to promote. Every day brought unsubstantiated stories of another secret paramour. There was the "rejected suitor of her bachelor girlhood who had been in touch with her since her marriage." The "brilliant literary figure widely known to millions" who urged Nancy to "divorce her husband and marry him." The mysterious gentleman who, according to a neighborhood florist, "frequently bought gardenias there for Mrs. Titterton." At one point, the *Mirror* even had her consorting with "a youngish male adventurer of the type known as a 'gigolo.'"[21]

Her family and friends reacted with outraged denials. From Dayton, her grieving mother, Mrs. Frank Evans, issued a statement affirming the warmth of Nancy's marriage: "She never mentioned the name of any other man but Lewis to me in her letters. They were completely devoted to each other." A close friend of the Tittertons, Caroline Singer—well-known writer of travel books and wife of famed illustrator Cyrus LeRoy Baldridge—concurred. "I never saw more devoted persons than Nancy and her husband," she told reporters. "There was no possibility of an outside love interest in her life. She was too fastidious for anything so sordid as a semi-Bohemian relationship with some other man. She had an integrity of character which would have prevented any second-rate love affair." Besides, added Singer, even if Nancy *had* been unfaithful, she would certainly have chosen a tender and sensitive lover, not "the brute type of man" who might resort to physical violence.[22]

The police, too, swiftly dismissed the love-affair angle. On the day of Nancy's funeral—a simple Episcopalian service attended by more than two hundred people, most from the publishing world— Assistant Chief Inspector John A. Lyons cautioned reporters not to leap to salacious conclusions. "We are satisfied now that Mrs. Titterton voluntarily admitted the man. This does not mean, however, that he was a lover or even a close friend. It may have been a salesman or repair man of some sort, someone who made a casual call."[23]

By then, the hunt for Nancy Titterton's killer had become the biggest homicide investigation in the city's history, with sixty-five detectives on the case. On Thursday, April 16, forty of those detectives gathered for a two-hour conference at police headquarters to compare notes. Afterward, their commander, Deputy Chief Inspector Francis J. Kear, appeared before reporters to offer a bleak assessment. After running down scores of tips and following every possible lead, his men were no closer to making an arrest than they were at the beginning. "POLICE AT A LOSS IN THE TITTERTON CASE," read a headline in the next morning's *Times*, while the *Mirror* declared that the murder was shaping up to be "the perfect crime."[24] Even as New Yorkers were reading these gloomy reports, however, developments were taking place behind the scenes that would break the case wide open.

When Dr. Charles Norris became New York's first chief medical examiner in 1918, he immediately recruited Bellevue biochemist Alexander O. Gettler as his toxicologist. Setting up a laboratory on the fourth floor of the city mortuary at Bellevue, Gettler quickly earned a reputation as a "modern Merlin," a master of "criminological chemistry." Newspaper photos accompanying the stories about his forensic feats invariably showed the white-coated Gettler posed with some impressive piece of lab apparatus—a kind of 1930s CSI whiz capable of cracking seemingly unsolvable crimes with one of his "well-nigh magical scientific techniques." By the time of his retirement in 1959, he was internationally renowned as the "father of forensic chemistry," the "world's greatest test-tube sleuth." By his own estimate, he and his assistants worked on approximately two thousand cases a year. Of those, one of his greatest triumphs would be the solution of the Titterton mystery.[25]

Studying it under his microscope, Gettler discovered that the piece of twine found in the tub beneath the dead woman's body contained a strand of istle, a stiff fiber obtained from several species of Mexican plants and used in the manufacture of cheap scrubbing brushes, burlap, and cordage. Inspector Lyons immediately had a circular sent to more than two dozen rope-makers in the region: "ADVISE IMMEDIATELY WHETHER YOU MANUFACTURE QUARTER INCH HEMP FIBER TWISTED TWINE WITH SINGLE STRAND ISTLE. TWINE THIS DESCRIPTION IMPORTANT IN HOMICIDE INVESTIGATION."

Twenty-three telegrams with negative replies came back before an executive with the Hanover Cordage Company of York, Pennsylvania, telephoned to say that his firm made a similar product. Carrying the telltale piece of twine, a detective set out for York at once, where Hanover officials confirmed that it came from their factory. They also explained that the cord was commonly used as upholstery binding.

A check of company's sales records showed that several rolls of the rope had recently been purchased by a New York City wholesaler. When police paid a visit to the wholesaler, they learned that on Thursday, April 9 — the day before Nancy Titterton's murder — one of these rolls had been delivered to the East Side shop of Theodore Kruger.[26]

Kruger himself had long been dismissed as a suspect, having been in his shop all Good Friday morning, as several witnesses testified.[27] His twenty-four-year-old assistant, however, was a person of interest to the police. Not only had they learned of his lengthy arrest record, they had also turned up the psychiatric report that described him as a "personality deviate" and predicted that, without ongoing treatment, the young compulsive car thief would "have difficulty in learning to refrain from illegal acts from time to time."[28]

Fiorenza was placed under twenty-four-hour surveillance. In the meantime, Dr. Gettler continued his hunt for forensic evidence that would tie the killer directly to the crime. He found it on Monday, April 20. Going over Nancy Titterton's rumpled bedspread inch by inch with a high-powered magnifying glass, Gettler discovered a single odd-looking hair, less than half an inch long. It was white and "strangely stiff"—certainly not human. Placing it under his microscope, he determined that it was horsehair of the type used as furniture stuffing. Obtaining a sample from the Tittertons' newly reupholstered loveseat, Gettler confirmed that the two hairs matched. There was only one plausible way that the horsehair could have ended up on Nancy's bed: the killer must have had it on his clothing when he attacked her. And he had gotten it on his clothing while working in Kruger's shop.[29]

Questioned about his employee, Kruger insisted that, despite his various run-ins with the law, Fiorenza was "a perfect gentleman." "There was never anything about him that was bad," said Kruger. "Why, I've seen him take meat out of his sandwich for lunch and give it to our dog." He was a good worker, too, very reliable, always on time. True, he'd shown up a few hours late on the day of the murder, but he had a solid excuse: his weekly appointment with his probation officer, Peter Gambaro.[30]

When detectives visited the probation office in the Criminal Court building, however, they discovered that Gambaro, a practicing Catholic, had taken Good Friday off. And no one else in the office had any memory of seeing Fiorenza that morning.[31]

With his alibi blown, Fiorenza was immediately taken into custody and whisked to an undisclosed location in the Bronx, where he underwent sixteen hours of relentless grilling. He didn't break down until 10:30 the next morning, when he turned to Police Commissioner Lewis Valentine and, in a voice hoarse with exhaustion, said: "Give me a cigarette and I'll tell you all I know."[32]

According to his confession—transcribed by Detective George Swander and signed by Fiorenza—he had gone to the Tittertons' apartment on Thursday afternoon, April 9, to pick up the loveseat with Kruger. As soon as he set eyes on Nancy, the "idea came to me of doing what I did to her afterward." He could see that she was too slight to put up much resistance and so soft-spoken that she would be unable to make much of an outcry. All the rest of that day and night, he brooded on his plan.

The next morning, after telephoning Kruger to say that he would be late because of an appointment with his parole officer, he proceeded to 22 Beekman Place. In his pocket was a fifty-two-inch length of cord he had taken from the shop the previous day.

"I rang the downstairs bell. The latch sounded. I went upstairs. Mrs. Titterton answered the door. She was all dressed and had a garment—a dress or a pair of pajamas, something like that—in her hand. I told her I came about the loveseat. Just to get her in there I asked her, didn't she want to have the loveseat in the bedroom? She didn't know. But that made her go into the bedroom to see in her mind how the loveseat would look there. I went in there with her."

No sooner were they inside the bedroom than Fiorenza lunged at Mrs. Titterton. She just had time to let out a scream before he "grabbed whatever it was she had in her hand and stuffed it into her mouth, so she couldn't yell any more." Throwing her facedown on the bed, he pulled the cord from his pocket and tightly bound her wrists. He then turned her over on her back and, in a blind frenzy, tore off her clothes and raped her. "From time to time, when she started to scream as the gag worked loose, I throttled her with my hands. She raised an awful fuss."

Afterward, as she lay whimpering on the bed, he snatched up the pajama top and a thin dressing jacket, knotted them together, and strangled her. She was still breathing when he carried her into the bathroom. He thought about filling the tub to make it look as if she had drowned but couldn't find the plug. Grabbing a knife from the kitchen, he sliced the rope in several pieces from her wrists. He thought he "put it all in my pocket and took it away."

He got out of the building without being seen and hurried around the corner. A block away, he tossed the cord into an ash can, never guessing that he had left a piece behind. He then ducked into a drugstore on First Avenue and called Kruger to say that he had been delayed longer than expected but was on his way.

He reached the shop at around 11:50. "I helped fix the loveseat. I didn't say anything about killing the woman." At 4:00 p.m., he "went back with my boss to the Tittertons," taking care to let Kruger enter the apartment first and discover the body.

When Fiorenza's interrogators asked him why he had targeted Nancy Titterton, even he seemed baffled. "She wasn't my type," he said. "If I saw her on the street, I would not give her a second look."[33]

The woman who presumably was his type, his fiancée Pauline D'Antonio, initially refused to believe any of it. "He did not do it," she told the reporters who swarmed to her apartment at 2385 Lorillard Place in the Bronx (just a short block away, as the tabloids delighted in noting, from the home of Anna Hauptmann, widow of the convicted killer of the Lindbergh baby). "They are telling lies about him. He did not confess. He could not have confessed to such a thing. He will be back and we will be married in September."

By the following morning, however, she had undergone a change of heart. "It's all over," she said. "I can have nothing to do with him. Thank God I found out before we were married. I'd have died if he'd been the father of my child, my husband."

Informed of her comments in his cell at police headquarters, Fiorenza looked glum: "I guess she'll never come to see me now. Well, what can I do? I made a serious mistake."[34]

Not content to titillate its readers with the lurid details of Fiorenza's actual confession, Hearst's *Daily Mirror* resorted to a stunt so brazen that it made the city's other tabloids seem like models of journalistic sobriety. Beginning on Saturday, April 25, it ran a sensational six-part series headlined "Fiorenza's Own Amazing Story," trumpeted as the exclusive firsthand account of "the events leading up to the fateful Good Friday when the body of Mrs. Nancy Titterton was found in the bathtub at 22 Beekman Place." A prefatory note claimed that Fiorenza had dictated the story from his cell in the Tombs to a staff reporter from the *Mirror* named David Charney.

According to this startling tale, Fiorenza had first encountered his future victim six months earlier when "she called up Kruger's where I worked and I went up to see her about fixing some furniture and upholstery work. She was a fine-looking woman. She had a lot of class." Much to his surprise, she "started to ask me questions about myself. Gee, I couldn't get over her being so nice to me, just a plain working fellow." Noticing the dirt under his fingernails, he felt embarrassed in her presence, but "she told me not to worry about my hands" and invited him to sit down in the living room. "She seemed anxious to talk more about me. Among other things, she asked about my fiancée. She also asked if I was interested in the arts. I didn't get that. It was very highfalutin talk." Initially flattered by her attention, he began to feel "dopey" when he realized that "she was a writer" and "was studying me like them doctors study guinea pigs to see what they got behind their minds. I was a type to her. When I left she asked me to come back again. I was thinking of her. She was thinking of a guinea pig."

The remaining five installments of this sleazy potboiler describe Fiorenza's burgeoning obsession with the beguiling Mrs. Titterton, who comes across as a careless, high-society tease, inviting him back repeatedly to pump him for material she can use in her fiction while ignoring the erotic effect she is having on him. Before long, Fiorenza is in the grip of a "wild, uncontrollable passion" for her. "Every other woman I saw looked to me like Mrs. Titterton. I'd pick up a magazine and all the faces of the good-looking women in it were like her. Daydreaming about her, I pictured myself dressed up in a swell tuxedo, married to her. We just finished up a cocktail and the butler comes up, bows, and says the car's waiting." By its final chapter, "Fiorenza's Own Amazing Story" has turned into a cut-rate version of Theodore Dreiser's *An American Tragedy*: the story of a poor working boy engaged to a doting girl of his own class who becomes infatuated with an upper-crust beauty and dreams of possessing her. In this account, however, it is the beautiful socialite who ends up dead.[35]

Even by tabloid standards, "Fiorenza's Own Amazing Story" was outrageous, provoking a furious response from one of Hearst's main competitors, Julius David Stern, publisher of the *New York Post*. After contacting the district attorney and confirming that "no reporter from any newspaper had ever talked to Fiorenza in jail," Stern published a scathing front-page editorial denouncing the purported autobiography as "the baldest fake in years"—a semipornographic thriller, "so written as to blacken a dead woman's character and build up sympathy for a confessed murderer." Besides its defamation of the victim—"a woman who, during her lifetime, was respected by all who knew her"—what made "the Hearst hoax" particularly disgraceful was its potential to influence Fiorenza's future trial.

"How many prospective jurors have read the *Mirror*'s vile insinuations that Mrs. Titterton led Fiorenza on," thundered Stern, "that she encouraged him to spend time with her while she probed him for literary material? Hearst's fake is so abhorrent that it shames the whole newspaper business. It is so dangerous that it can lead to a miscarriage of justice."[36]

In desperation, several friends of Fiorenza reached out to the courtroom miracle worker who had just performed the seemingly impossible in the case of Vera Stretz. Samuel Leibowitz, however, flatly refused. "I wouldn't touch it with a ten-foot pole," he told reporters. "That guy is sitting in the electric chair right now."

"Are you afraid you might spoil your record if you took the case?" one of the newsmen suggested.

Leibowitz bristled. "It isn't that," he snapped. "It's a dirty, nasty affair and I don't want anything to do with it."[37]

On May 19, just a month after his arrest, Fiorenza went to trial, represented by Manhattan defense lawyer Henry Klauber. Dressed in an ill-fitting blue-serge suit, with his slick-backed black hair "accenting the whiteness of his sharp features," he sat through the weeklong proceedings with an air of bland indifference. Only once—when his stricken mother took the stand to testify (falsely) that he had been at home on the morning of the murder—did he display any trace of emotion, wiping his eyes, burying his face in his hands, and shaking his head.

After a fruitless attempt to show that Mrs. Titterton had actually been killed by a shadowy "fiend" who had been on the loose in the neighborhood at the time of the murder, Klauber switched to an insanity defense. His main witness was Dr. James Lincoln McCartney, former psychiatrist at Elmira Reformatory, who (using the now-outmoded terminology for schizophrenia) characterized Fiorenza as "a dementia praecox case." In rebuttal, the prosecution called a quartet of experts, including Dr. Perry Lichtenstein—author of a magazine article, among other professional publications, titled "Who's Looney Now?"—and Dr. Thomas Cusack, who insisted that Fiorenza was not nearly "wacky" enough to be diagnosed with dementia praecox. All four prosecution experts agreed that the defendant was "keenly aware of the nature and quality of his behavior at the time of the crime."

The conflicting psychiatric testimony left the jurors deeply divided. Retiring to the jury room at 3:00 p.m. on May 27, they deliberated for more than eleven hours without reaching a verdict. When Judge Charles C. Nott Jr. received word shortly after 2:00 a.m. that they were deadlocked, he refused to let them go to their hotels, ordering them locked up in the jury room until they came to a decision. Finally, at precisely 10:07 a.m., they emerged with a verdict. Fiorenza was found guilty of first-degree murder.

The following week, on Friday, June 6, he was sentenced to die in the electric chair. Standing before the bench in his blue suit, blue shirt, and white tie, he displayed not a flicker of emotion. He was equally impassive when he went to his death on January 22, 1937, one of four prisoners executed within a twenty-minute span that night. Accompanied by the Catholic chaplain the Reverend John P. McCaffrey, Fiorenza walked calmly into the execution chamber and said nothing as he sat on the chair. The switch was thrown at 11:09 p.m. Three minutes later, he was pronounced dead.[38]

4

Sex Fiends

FROM THE SALEM WITCHCRAFT trials of the 1690s to the so-
called "day care hysteria" of the 1980s—when ritual sex abuse
was reputedly epidemic in our nation's preschools—Americans have
regularly been seized with panic over one supposedly rampant evil
or another. Every era seems to produce its own defining monster,
from the arsenic-dispensing "domestic poisoner" of the 1890s to the
switchblade-wielding juvenile delinquent of the 1950s, the suburban
Satan worshipper of the 1970s to the suicidal mass-murderer of our
own terrorism-obsessed age. Beginning in 1937, the boogeyman that
haunted the American psyche was the "sex fiend."

Appalling sex crimes, of course, were nothing new. In 1934, for
example, the maniac Albert Fish was arrested for the dismemberment-murder, committed six years earlier, of schoolgirl Grace Budd,
a portion of whose flesh he took away with him and made into a cannibal stew. The following year, Francis Flynn—a divorced, thirty-
nine-year-old taxicab dispatcher and father of a seventeen-year-old
daughter—made tabloid headlines after luring six-year-old Mar-
garet Parlato into his Queens apartment, molesting her, drowning

her, then disposing of her body down the dumbwaiter shaft of his building.[1]

It wasn't until 1937, however, that—if the media were to be believed—a so-called "sex crime wave" engulfed the nation. Under titles like "Sex Crime Wave Alarms the U.S.," "Can We End Sex Crimes?," and "Is the Sex Criminal Insane?," popular newsstand magazines—among them *Time*, the *Saturday Evening Post*, the *Nation*, the *Literary Digest*, and *Cosmopolitan*—ran panic-inducing articles about the purported plague of psychopathic sex-murders. In a widely syndicated piece called "War on the Sex Criminal!," FBI chief J. Edgar Hoover declared that "the sex fiend, most loathsome of all the vast army of crime, has become a threat to safety of American childhood and womanhood." Even the staid *New York Times*, famed for its high-minded avoidance of anything that smacked of sensationalism, found itself running so many articles on the subject—one hundred and forty-three in 1937 alone—that it had to create a new "Sex Crimes" subject heading in its annual index.[2] Book publishers, quick to capitalize on the scare, rushed out works like *The Sex Criminal* by Dr. Bertram Pollens, senior psychologist of the New York City penitentiary on Rikers Island and head of its clinic for sex offenders.[3]

Historians of the phenomenon point to a string of sensational New York City sex-murders that sparked the hysteria. In March 1937, Simon Elmore, a fifty-seven-year-old housepainter, encountered four-year-old Joan Kuleba on a Staten Island beach. Promising to show her "a place where grasshoppers did all sorts of wonderful things," he led her to a tumbledown house in a nearby marsh, where —after sexually assaulting her—he strangled her with the shoulder straps of her bathing suit, dropped "a fifty-pound clump of bricks on her back," then strolled home for lunch. That August, Lawrence Marks, a forty-nine-year-old unemployed hospital worker, strangled eight-year-old Paula Magagna in her Brooklyn home, raped her after death, and left her nude body lying in the cellar. Not long afterward, twenty-six-year-old Salvatore Ossido, a Brooklyn barber and father of two small children, lured a nine-year-old parochial schoolgirl, Einer Sporrer, into the back room of his shop, crushed her skull with a hammer, raped her corpse, then stuffed it into a burlap sack and dumped it on the stoop of a house a block and a half away.[4] And of course there was the rape-murder of Nancy Titterton, a crime that "sent a wave of horror and fear across the whole United States" and that rarely went unmentioned in the many newspaper and magazine articles on the "rising tide of perversion" supposedly sweeping the nation.[5]

Fiorenza was prominently cited in a feature that appeared in the *New York Daily News* on March 28, 1937—Easter Sunday. Written by journalist Arthur Watson and titled "Sex Criminals Nearly Always Repeaters," the article detailed the futile efforts of both the legal system and the psychiatric establishment to "cure and control the abnormalities of these perverts." Concluding with the sobering assessment that, apart from either permanent institutionalization or castration, there was no way to protect society from the depredations of these creatures, the story was illustrated with portraits of three of the most notorious "sex fiends" of recent years: Fiorenza, Albert Fish, and Salvatore Ossido, whose brutal murder and postmortem rape of little Einer Sporrer had occurred only a week earlier.[6]

Even as New Yorkers were digesting Watson's disheartening report, a new atrocity was taking place in their midst—a crime that would stun the nation, set off one of the largest manhunts in U.S. history, and confirm the growing belief that the psychopathic "sex fiend" had become "the most terrible menace now confronting American people."[7] For New Yorkers, the shock of the Easter Sunday horror was amplified by its timing and locale. Not only did it occur exactly one year after the Good Friday rape-murder of Nancy Titterton but it also happened just a block and a half away from that earlier outrage, in a neighborhood that suddenly seemed to have fallen under an inexplicable curse: Beekman Place.

Part II

Fenelon

The Firebrand

I N LATER YEARS, after he had perpetrated one of the most sensationally savage murders of his age, psychiatrists would find much in his background to account for his fanatical temperament.

His father, Benjamin Hardin Irwin, was born in 1854 and grew up in Missouri until the age of nine, when the family traveled by covered wagon to the Nebraska Territory, settling near the town of Tecumseh. Benjamin was still an adolescent when, tired of tending his father's cattle, he fled the farm and found work in a stone quarry. There, he saw firsthand "the power of dynamite to blow things up"—an experience that would leave a lasting imprint on his imagination. A brilliant, if largely self-educated, young man, he taught school for a while, dabbled in local politics, and—after immersing himself in Blackstone's *Commentaries*—moved into town and set himself up as a lawyer, continuing to practice for about eight years. It was during this period that he married and had a son.[1]

A turning point in his life occurred in 1879. By then, Irwin had sunk into a deep well of self-loathing. In his own estimation, he was "the most wicked man" in the community—a black-hearted sinner who lied to friends, cheated clients, quarreled constantly with neighbors, and beat his wife and child when drunk. Overwhelmed with disgust at his wickedness, he was saved when, during a meeting at the local Mount Zion Baptist Church, his soul was converted to Christ.

His awakening took place at a time of intense religious ferment, when a great wave of revivalism swept over the land. Inspired by the teachings of John Wesley, the founder of Methodism, ministers of the burgeoning holiness movement preached that salvation entailed "two separate phases of experience for the believer." In the first— conversion or justification—"the penitent was forgiven for actual sins of commission, becoming a Christian but retaining 'a residue of sin within.'" The second, more controversial, experience was known as "entire sanctification," a work of divine grace that "purified believers of this remaining 'inbred sin' and gave a person 'perfect love' of God and humanity."[2]

Through his contact with itinerant holiness preachers, Benjamin Hardin Irwin learned of the doctrine of sanctification and received the experience himself at eleven o'clock, Saturday night, May 16, 1891. In the grip of an agonized realization of the "turpitude and vileness" of his "inherent depravity," he began to pray so loudly that he woke up his neighbors. All at once—as he later testified—"the flood gates of Heaven were opened wide, and there came into my soul successive waves and mighty inundation of light, and love and joy and faith, and power and glory and loyalty to God." He "melted into a flood of tears" at the realization that "the Holy Ghost in his fullness had come into my soul. *I was sanctified.*"[3]

Embarking on the life of a revivalist preacher, he conducted hundreds of camp meetings over the next few years in small towns throughout Nebraska, Iowa, Illinois, Kansas, Oklahoma, and Colorado. He was, by all accounts, a riveting, larger-than-life figure —"magnetic in personality, charismatic in delivery, able in mind, handsome in build, and articulate of tongue."[4] His own son would compare him to Elmer Gantry, the barnstorming preacher of Sinclair Lewis's scathing attack on American evangelism. Gantry, of course, is the very embodiment of religious hypocrisy, a compulsive womanizer who rails against sexual immorality even while ogling the nubile girls in the choir. In this regard, too, the analogy with Irwin would prove to be apt.[5]

As Irwin pursued his ministry, he found himself yearning for an even more "intimate acquaintance with the living God." Possessed of "an unspeakable soul-hunger," he turned for solace to the writings of the Methodist theologian John Fletcher, who spoke of a spiritual experience beyond conversion and sanctification — a third work of grace he described as "the baptism of burning love."

Seeking such experience for himself, Irwin received it near midnight on October 23, 1895. As he lay in bed, he

> saw in the room above me a cross of pure, transparent fire. It was all fire. I have been able to see that cross in the same place above me every moment from that time to this. No fire that was ever kindled in earth was half as pure, so beautiful, so divinely transparent as that. In a few moments the whole room where we were lying seemed to be all luminous with a seven-fold light, and a little later still the very heavens were all aglow with transparent flame. The very walls of the room seemed to be on fire.

Two days later, following a trip to Enid, Oklahoma, he was returning home by train when a "second wave struck":

> All at once I became conscious that I was literally on fire. This expression may seem a strange one, but I cannot express it any other way. Everything about me seemed to be on fire — actually burning, blazing, glowing. I felt that I was in the midst of a fiery presence. At no time in my life have I known or felt such unutterable bliss. For five hours I felt that I should certainly be consumed — and there I entered into an infinitely deeper and more wonderful rest than I have ever known before.[6]

Aflame with the spirit of the living God, the newly "fire-baptized" Irwin began to preach his message of a "third experience" in holiness periodicals, self-published pamphlets, and raucous tent meetings that were soon attracting huge throngs of believers, hungry to receive the "blessed fire" themselves. Under the ministry of the firebrand preacher, thousands of believers were soon testifying to the powerful new baptism. "Some said they felt fire burning in their souls, but others claimed it as a burning in their bodies also. It was felt in the tongue, in the fingers, in the palm of the hand, in the feet, in the side, in the arms. . . . The church would seem to be lighted with fire, the trees of the wood would appear as flames of fire, the landscape would seem to be baptized in the glory of the fire." Whipped into a frenzy of "godly hysteria" by Irwin's exhortations, those who received the fire would shout, scream, laugh, bark like dogs, speak in tongues, fall into trances, or shake with the "jerks."[7]

As Irwin's message spread throughout the South and Midwest, he met with bitter, sometimes violent, opposition. More moderate holiness leaders denounced him as a "mystical renegade" promoting a heretical doctrine. At one camp meeting, a mob of rowdies broke up his wildly convulsive services, tearing down and burning his tents, pistol-whipping some congregants and hurling chairs at others. At another, one of his closest associates was plunged into a horse trough and nearly drowned.[8]

Such hostility did nothing to daunt "the apostle of fire." "People may oppose us," he declared, "preachers may preach against the experience, and devils may howl, but we have come to preach blood and fire till Jesus comes." In a pamphlet titled "Pyrophobia (A Morbid Fear of Fire)," he lashed out at his critics, deriding them as mealymouthed defenders of a "fossilized" faith and assuring his followers that "God would soon strike dead those who opposed his ministry."[9]

For two years, beginning in 1896, Irwin brought his fiery crusade to two dozen states, proclaiming the glory of the "blissful, burning, leaping, love-waves of God's living fire" and thundering against the vices of the age, from "the handling of tobacco in every form" to the "use of slang language" to the wearing of such "prideful" adornments as male neckties ("I would rather have a rattlesnake around my neck than a tie," he declared).[10]

Even while decrying every stimulant from cigars to coffee to Coca-Cola, however, Irwin himself seemed addicted to ever-increasing doses of ecstatic experience. By 1899, he was trumpeting a series of new, even more explosive works of grace: the baptisms of dynamite, lyddite, selenite, and oxydite, guaranteed to "utterly demolish" the "strongholds of Satan," blast "into atoms his deepest laid and most systematic plots and plans," and "blow sin back to hell." Critics, convinced of his growing fanaticism, suggested that the only blessing Irwin lacked was "the baptism of common sense."[11]

Irwin was at the height of his power and influence when, in 1900, his world combusted. In the spring of that year, his followers were stunned by reports that he had been spotted in Omaha, drunk and smoking a big cigar. Enemies within the holiness movement began mocking him in print as the "Whiskey Baptized" preacher. Rumors of financial chicanery also circulated, one critic claiming that "at times, the collections entrusted to him could not be accounted for." Later, an even more shocking revelation came to light: that Irwin's "life for many years alternated between the pulpit and the harlot house. He would go from the pulpit to wallow with harlots the rest of the night."[12]

Publicly confessing to a life of "open and gross sin," Irwin resigned from his church in disgrace and dropped from sight. Several years would pass before he resurfaced.

The modern Pentecostal movement was born on January 1, 1901, in a small midwestern Bible school run by evangelist Charles Fox Parham. A preacher since his early adolescence, Parham had crossed paths with revivalists, faith healers, and holiness ministers of various stripes, including Benjamin Hardin Irwin. Impressed with the wild emotionalism of Irwin's followers, Parham came to share the belief in a work of grace beyond conversion and sanctification. Unlike Irwin, however, he concluded that the one true sign of this "third baptism" was not an overwhelming experience of holy fire but the miraculous onset of glossolalia—the gift of tongues, the power bestowed upon Jesus's disciples on the feast day of Pentecost, as recorded in the Book of Acts: "And suddenly there came a sound from heaven as of a rushing mighty wind, and it filled all the house where they were sitting. . . . And they were all filled with the Holy Ghost, and began to speak with other tongues, as the Spirit gave them utterance."[13]

Establishing his headquarters in Topeka, Kansas, Parham started an educational institute, the Bethel Bible College. In late December 1900, his students undertook a concerted effort to receive the gift of tongues. At around 7:00 p.m. on New Year's Day, one of them, thirty-year-old Agnes Ozman, asked her teacher to lay his hands upon her. He did so and began to pray. "I had scarcely repeated three dozen sentences," Parham later recounted, "when a glory fell upon her, a halo seemed to surround her head and face, and she began speaking in the Chinese language and was unable to speak English for three days." In short order, the entire student body, along with Parham himself, was speaking in tongues.[14]

Over the next few years, Parham and a band of young acolytes spread the Pentecostal message into Missouri, Oklahoma, and Texas. In January 1906, he opened a Bible training school in Houston. Among the twenty-five students who signed up to hear Parham lecture on "the Holy Spirit in His different operations" was William J. Seymour.[15]

The Louisiana-born son of former slaves, the thirty-six-year-old Seymour had taken up preaching several years earlier after surviving a near-fatal bout of smallpox. Eager to learn from Parham, he was allowed to listen in on a few weeks' worth of lectures from the hallway outside the classroom, safely segregated from his white brethren. In February 1906—having imbibed Parham's belief in glossolalia as the true "Bible evidence" of third baptism—Seymour accepted an invitation to preach in Los Angeles. By the beginning of April, he had moved his services into a boxy, ramshackle building on Azusa Street.

Within a matter of weeks, Parham's preaching had sparked an explosion of religious hysteria that "beggared description. Men and women would shout, weep, dance, fall into trances, speak and sing in tongues, and interpret their messages into English."[16] In the third week of April, the *Los Angeles Times* ran a page-one story, describing the "riot of religious fervor" at the Azusa Street Mission, where the wildly gesticulating congregants "work themselves up into a state of mad excitement," which "ends in a gurgle of wordless prayer. . . . They claim to have 'the gift of tongues' and to be able to comprehend the babel."[17]

As news of the revival spread across the nation, mobs of people flocked to Azusa Street, some merely to gawk at the delirious antics of the "holy rollers" (as critics branded the worshippers) but most to experience the Pentecostal baptism for themselves. By late 1906, the movement claimed at least thirteen thousand adherents who had spoken in tongues.[18] Among them was Benjamin Hardin Irwin.

As he reported in an issue of the holiness magazine *Triumphs of Faith*, Irwin's embrace of Pentecostalism took place on Christmas Day 1906, when he renounced his former belief in spiritual pyrotechnics and began speaking in tongues.

> I felt my lips and tongue and jaw being used as they had never been used before. My vocal organs were in the hands and control of another, and the Other was the Divine Paraclete within me. He was beginning to speak through me in other tongues. . . . He caused me to use words which I had never heard or conceived of before. I was enabled to speak with greater fluency than I had ever spoken in my native English. . . . Since that time, I have been used of God in speaking many times in Chinese, Hindoostani, Bengali, Arabic, and other languages unknown to me.

Following this transformative experience, Irwin became an Azusa Street missionary, "leading Pentecostal services from California to Oakland."[19]

Exactly what had transpired in the time between Irwin's scandalous resignation from the Fire-Baptized Holiness Church he had founded and his reemergence on Azusa Street is, for the most part, a mystery. From the few surviving records of that period, however, we do know one crucial fact. During that six-year stretch, he took a second wife and sired three sons with her.[20]

Her maiden name was Mary Lee Jordan. Born in Carthage, Texas, in 1870, she came from an old Southern family that, while boasting a number of prominent "businessmen, judges, and men of wealth," was known for "a certain degree of mental instability." One of her brothers "was a known sex pervert who had been sterilized after it was found that he had been committing sodomy upon his young nephew." Another suffered from "mental amnesia." Her sister was "described as excitable and emotional," her mother "was adjudged by authorities as insane," and her father was "said to have been impetuous, highly nervous, and to have been shot by an enemy while on horseback."[21]

Surviving descriptions of Mary are full of contradictions. Some say that she was "college trained," others that she had a "secondary school education." At times, she is characterized as "easy-going," at others as possessing a "nervous, high-strung temperament." She is sometimes portrayed as a semi-invalid who, by her own admission, "was not brought up to work," though documents indicate that she "worked as a washerwoman and cleaning lady to make a home for her sons." All accounts agree on one point, however: that her most salient trait was her "extreme religious fanaticism."[22]

She dated her spiritual awakening to an experience that occurred in her early girlhood. As she later testified, she "was walking at night" when, all at once, she "saw a ball of light, fell down on her knees, prayed all night and was converted."[23] Soon she was swept up in the fast-rising tide of the holiness movement. She appears to have met her charismatic husband-to-be around the time of his sudden plunge from grace. They were married in Canada in 1902.

Their first son was born the following year. As with all their children, his name would reflect the extravagant zeal of his parents: Vidalin Bathurst Irwin, after the famed Icelandic bishop Jon Vidalin and the Reverend Jess Bathurst, one of Benjamin's closest associates in the holiness movement. Their youngest son, born six years later, would be christened Pember in honor of G. H. Pember, English evangelist and author of such works as *The Antichrist Babylon and the Coming of the Kingdom*, *The Great Prophecies of the Centuries Concerning Israel and the Gentiles*, and *Mystery Babylon the Great*. Both Vidalin and Pember would grow up to be hardened criminals and do long stretches in prison for assorted felonies.

Their middle brother would outdo them both in iniquity. He was born in a gospel tent during a massive camp meeting held in Arroyo Seco Park, just outside Pasadena, on August 5, 1907. No doctor was there to assist with the delivery. His first name was a tribute to one of his father's spiritual heroes, the seventeenth-century French theologian François Fénelon, while his middle name commemorated the place of his own birth: Fenelon Arroyo Seco Irwin. The world would come to known him by other names: Robert Irwin. The Beekman Hill Maniac. The Easter Sunday Slayer. The Mad Sculptor.

6

The Brothers

BENJAMIN IRWIN'S PENTECOSTAL baptism did nothing to reform his character. Even after receiving the blessing of tongues—the supposed sign of his spiritual cleansing—he continued to consort with other women. His long-suffering wife was well aware of his infidelities. "He was definitely immoral," Mary would later report, "and a slave to his passions."[1] Even worse than his womanizing, however, was a secret she learned after nearly nine years of marriage: Benjamin had never bothered to divorce his first wife. He was not only a philanderer but a bigamist, too. In early 1910, not long after Mary made this shocking discovery, Benjamin Irwin deserted his family, running off with a younger woman.

Burdened with the sole support of three young sons, Mary took on a number of menial jobs. Her chronically poor health, however—which proved resistant to the divine healing promised by her faith—made it impossible for her to work on a regular basis. Often she was bedridden. With the pittance she earned as a part-time house cleaner and laundress—never more than a few dollars a day—she kept her children fed on whatever meager provisions she could afford. Their diet was heavy on potatoes, turnips, and cabbage. Often, they were reduced to begging day-old bread from neighborhood bakers.

They moved repeatedly from one run-down section of Los Angeles to another, finally settling in a ramshackle cottage on Omaha Street. The place had no indoor plumbing or electricity and was so cramped that the boys took turns sleeping on the porch. Its interior decor featured stretched flour sacking on the walls and a few old sticks of furniture. The sole item of value was Mary's prized pump organ. A talented musician, she would gather her sons in the evening and lead them in singing "He Calleth Thee," "I've Been Washed in the Blood," "Resting Safe with Jesus," and other favorite Pentecostal hymns.[2]

Religion remained the center of her life. She awoke at five each morning to pray for an hour and spent every available minute at the Azusa Street Mission, seeking respite from her troubles in the ecstatic transports of Pastor Seymour's revival. Her middle son—"intensely devoted to his mother" in his early childhood—often accompanied her to the meetings. Throughout his life he would carry "memories of religious fervor, fanaticism and terror"—of men and women babbling in unknown tongues and offering witness to the miraculous cures effected by "hysterical prayer." After one frenzied service, he ran home through a storm, shouting, "I'll be good! God save me! I'll be good!"[3]

His father exposed him to a very different side of existence. Once, when Fenelon was five, Ben paid him an unexpected visit and ended up taking him "downtown to a house where two women lived" (as Irwin later recalled). "These women were very nice to me and they put me in a room and my father went away with these women for an hour or two. The women were about thirty years old." It wasn't until many years later, of course, that he understood the purpose of his father's visit to the house where the two nice women lived.[4]

Typical of some early Pentecostals—who, placing the love of Christ above all else, "virtually abandoned regular family life to follow the Lord"[5]—Mary was increasingly neglectful of her children. "Her religion was the consolation from all the woes that flesh is heir to," Irwin would recall. "Though affectionate in her way, she was wedded to God's mission and with this absorbing interest she became . . . oblivious of our growing needs. So we were reared in squalor, under-nourished, poorly clothed and our housing was merely a shelter. Our life was drab, insecure, deprived of the natural life of the normal child. Mother had her religious emotions to sustain her, while we had but empty stomachs to go to bed on."[6] With their mother otherwise occupied, her sons found themselves free to run wild.

Wildest of all was Vidalin, a textbook delinquent clearly marked for a criminal future. A real-life version of the stereotypical street toughs Sidney Kingsley would depict in *Dead End*, he began smoking at the age of eight and was soon up to forty cigarettes a day. At nine, he was hanging around neighborhood pool halls. By ten, he was engaged in petty theft, stealing pigeons from their sidewalk coops outside of local butcher shops and selling them for twenty-five cents a pair.

His serious troubles began at the age of eleven when he entered sixth grade and befriended a young hoodlum named Gale Wing. Two years his senior, Wing had already been arrested once for stealing copper wire from the city's Bureau of Power and Light, burning off the insulation, and selling it to an unlicensed junk dealer for ten cents a pound. He was also the leader of the self-styled "Pasadena Avenue Gang," a bunch of juvenile miscreants described by one social worker as "a menace to the neighborhood." Inducted into the gang, Vidalin was soon skipping school to join them in their criminal escapades—mostly housebreaking, petty larceny, and the occasional theft of an automobile, which was either abandoned after a wild joyride or dismantled and sold to shady dealers in used car parts.[7]

On the evening of August 24, 1917—two months past his fourteenth birthday—Vidalin was arrested for the first time. Loitering outside the Sunbeam Theater on Pasadena Avenue with a couple of pals, he began pelting moviegoers with handfuls of gravel as they emerged from a showing of the William S. Hart horse opera, *The*

Gun Fighter. Unfortunately for Vidalin, the police station was directly across the street. Charged with truancy and public nuisance, he was given probation, which he promptly violated by playing hooky during the day and "loafing on the streets late at night." In the first week of October, upon the petition of his mother, he was declared a ward of the court and sentenced to the Whittier State School until the age of twenty-one.[8]

While awaiting transfer to the reform school, he was confined to Juvenile Hall, the short-term detention center for delinquents (equivalent to county jail for adults). Within days, he and a trio of fellow inmates had engineered an escape, using a chisel stolen from the woodworking shop. Caught in San Bernardino and returned to his cell, he escaped again less than two weeks later, this time making his way to Tijuana, where—according to a doubtful yarn he told to one social worker—he "won fifty dollars gambling with two Mexicans." He was picked up in Oceanside a week later and brought back to Juvenile Hall, where he promptly found himself in trouble for stealing a sweater from another boy.[9]

He was finally admitted to Whittier in September 1918. In a published report on the remedial goals of the reform school, Superintendent Fred C. Nelles explained that its inmates "could be divided into three groups": "those who are feeble-minded," those "of sound mind whose delinquency is associated with some form of misunderstanding or neglect," and "those who wrong-doing has become habitual and who are intentionally, deliberately, and willfully guilty of misconduct."[10] From the start, it was clear that Vidalin Irwin fell into the last category.

Interviewed upon admission by the resident psychologist, a Dr. Hoag, the fifteen-year-old delinquent crowed about his criminal exploits, boasting that he had committed as many as twenty "housebreaking jobs" on his own and another ten with fellow members of the Pasadena Avenue Gang and had once netted $150—roughly $2,500 in today's money—from robbing a grocery store in Alhambra. To gauge his ethical development, Hoag posed a hypothetical question: "If you were walking along the street and there was no one

in sight except a man in front of you who, in pulling out his handkerchief, dropped a ten-dollar bill, what would you do?" Without hesitation, Vidalin replied: "I would be inclined to put the money to my
own use."

Hoag was impressed with Vidalin's intelligence, describing him
as "one of the brightest boys he had ever examined." At the same
time, the psychologist found him "unmanageable," "quarrelsome,"
"deceitful," and "possibly psychopathic," with "blunted moral reac-
tions."[11] His diagnosis was quickly confirmed by Vidalin's behavior.
Within weeks of his arrival, he was sent to Whittier's penal farm for
"disobedience, refusal to work, refusal to answer when spoken to,
and a determination not to succeed." After thirty-one days, he was
returned to the general population, only to be banished again a mere
five days later for an attempted escape. On January 29, 1919, just nine
days after his release, he hurled a stone at a boy named Charles Smith
and was returned to the penal farm, where he remained until February 17. After a few months of relative calm, he was charged with
participating in a plot to attack the watchman with a baseball bat.
This time, he earned a stint in a lightless solitary confinement cell,
euphemistically known as "the rest room." By the time he was freed
from the penal farm on July 22, he had secured his reputation as one
of the reform school's most incorrigible cases.[12]

Taking his big brother as role model, Pember—the youngest of the
three Irwin boys—began running afoul of the law at the age of
nine. Possessed of both a superior IQ and a variety of nervous disorders—one social worker described him as a nail biter and bed wet-
ter, with "spasmodic twitching of the eyelids" and other tics—he
was first arrested in July 1918 after snatching a change purse from
a playmate and running off to Eastlake Park, where he spent the
money riding the miniature railroad and visiting the nearby alliga-
tor farm. Owing to his "persistent thefts and disobedience of his
mother," he was committed to Juvenile Hall, where he remained
until the following April, when he was placed in the foster home of
a family named Canty. Two months later, he ran away. Turned in by

his mother, he was sent to the Strickland Home for Boys, a five-acre farm on the northern fringe of Los Angeles, converted into a refuge for wayward youths. Its stated aim was to promote character development in its troubled young charges—a worthy endeavor that, in the case of Pember Irwin, would prove entirely futile.[13]

Though his criminal notoriety would, in the end, far exceed that of his brothers, Fenelon was the least ungovernable of the three as a young child. Often, while the other two were out looking for trouble, he "stayed at home . . . to help his mother with the housework."[14] Studious and exceptionally bright, he did so well upon entering school that he skipped second grade. He was, from his earliest years, a voracious reader. Eventually, he would devour every book on the family shelves, beginning with Plutarch's *Lives*, Bunyan's *Pilgrim's Progress*, and—his favorite—François Guizot's *A Popular History of France from the Earliest Times*.[15]

Before he reached ten, however, he was beginning to show signs of disturbance. At school, he grew "more unruly, less attentive, and developed a tendency to truancy." Later, he would blame his problems on his "growing class consciousness"—his shameful realization that he "was more poorly clothed than his fellow students, had worse shoes and sometimes no shoes at all, and had no lunch while they were all furnished with lunch by their families." He was also prone to violent outbursts of temper and—though not particularly big for his age—gained a reputation as a fearsome fighter, ready to "beat the tar" out of anyone who "got fresh" with him.[16]

He began fighting with his mother, too, mostly over religion. He resented her demand that he study at least three chapters of scripture every night when he preferred reading dime novel Westerns, Hugo's *Les Misérables*, and the stories of Mark Twain. She also insisted that he memorize a new psalm every Sunday—a chore he found increasingly onerous and eventually refused to perform. She called him a young infidel. He told her to stop "stuffing the Bible down his throat." Their quarrels grew increasingly bitter.[17]

In July 1919, less than a week before Fenelon's twelfth birthday, his mother filed a court petition, charging that she was unable to supervise or care for him. A few weeks later, he was committed to Juvenile Hall. "It relieved her of a heavy burden," Irwin would bitterly recollect, "and she had more time to serve the Lord."[18]

Like every new admittee to the detention center, Fenelon was given a medical exam—the first thorough checkup he had ever received. His blood sample tested positive for syphilis.

In later years, reports would circulate that the disease had been transmitted by his mother. According to these accounts, his maternal grandmother, who owned slaves in Louisiana, had mistreated one of them, a "black mammy" infected with syphilis. To get her revenge, the woman snuck into the nursery of Fenelon's mother— still, at that time, a suckling infant—and "fed her from her black breasts."[19]

This remarkably unpleasant tale has all the hallmarks of an urban legend—one of those widely credited scare stories that have more to do with lurid (and in this case racist) fantasy than historical fact. A more likely explanation, given the whoremongering hypocrite who sired him, is that Fenelon's father was the ultimate source of the disease.

Whatever the case, the results of Fenelon's blood test was consistent with those of his brothers. As authorities had already determined, both Vidalin and Pember Irwin, like twelve-year-old Fenelon, were afflicted with congenital syphilis.[20]

Epiphany

AFTER THREE MONTHS IN JUVENILE HALL, Fenelon was sent to join Pember in the Strickland Home for Boys. Not long after his arrival, he badly beat up another inmate who (so he claimed) had called him a sissy. A few days later, convinced that "the other boys there hated him," he ran away, taking his little brother with him. Within twenty-four hours, a railroad guard found the pair sleeping in a freight car. Fenelon—indulging his dime novel fantasies—explained that he had planned to go to Montana "to fight Indians." Returned to the Strickland Home with Pember, he continued to get embroiled in fistfights and, in March 1920, was committed to the Whittier reform school, where he was reunited with his older brother, Vidalin.

With her children now wards of the state, Mary was free to devote herself fully to her Pentecostal pursuits. By 1919, when Fenelon was sent to Juvenile Hall, she had become an acolyte of a former Azusa Street coworker, Florence L. Crawford.

A close associate of William Seymour, Mother Crawford (as she came to be known) conducted an evangelistic campaign that took her throughout the Midwest and as far north as Winnipeg. After receiving a direct communication from God that she "establish the headquarters of her ministry in Portland, Oregon," she repaired to the "Rose City" and began holding meetings in an old converted blacksmith shop. Her charismatic preaching quickly attracted followers from throughout the Pacific Northwest. Within a year, she had established her own church, the Apostolic Faith Mission.[1]

Her annual camp meetings, held in the summer and lasting as long as two months, became more elaborate by the year. A great open-walled tabernacle, surrounded by a city of tents, stood in a clearing in the woods. Adherents from as far away as Pennsylvania and New York filled every one of its 1,200 seats, wailing, weeping, and raising their hands high in prayer, while hundreds of redeemed souls hurried up to the altar to kneel in the sawdust and testify to "the great things God had done for them." Ministers preached fiery sermons, and rousing hymns were chanted to the accompaniment of a sixty-piece orchestra—coronets, slide trombones, clarinets, saxophones, mellophones, and stringed instruments of every variety. A chartered barge, the *Bluebird*, ferried hundreds of worshippers to a nearby island for the water baptismal service.[2]

In the summer of 1920, Mary Irwin journeyed northward to take part in Mother Crawford's camp meeting, held in Rose City Park in northeast Portland. By the time the meeting ended seven weeks later, she had decided to make Portland her permanent home. With no place to live or means of support, she turned to her coreligionists for assistance. One, a widow, Mrs. L. M. Bispham, offered to take Mary in "until she found work and established herself." Mrs. Bispham also urged Mary to send for her two youngest sons. There was plenty of room in the house, and they would make good companions for her own son, a ten-year-old named Royal.[3]

In later years, Fenelon would remember his brief time at Whittier as one of happiest periods of his boyhood. Supplied with a clean suit of work clothes and three substantial meals a day, he was better dressed and fed than at any other time in his life. Unlike his incorrigible older brother, he maintained a spotless record of behavior, did well in his vocational training classes, and was awarded first prize in a school-wide essay-writing contest. His stay there lasted less than seven months. In October 1920, by order of the juvenile court, he was discharged from Whittier and restored to his mother's custody. Bidding farewell to Vidalin—who, having recently turned seventeen, still had four years to serve on his sentence—Fenelon reluctantly took his leave of the reformatory and, with Pember in tow, boarded a train to Portland.[4]

A strong creative streak ran in the Irwin family. Mary was a talented pianist who, during her time in Los Angeles, had met the celebrated composer (and future Polish prime minister) Ignacy Jan Paderewski and impressed him with her playing. Pember had inherited some of her talent and, in his later years, earned a living as a teacher of classical guitar.[5]

Fenelon's forte wasn't music but the visual arts. Throughout his life, he loved looking at paintings and statues and, from his early boyhood, showed a particular aptitude for sculpting. His earliest creation, molded out of strained mud when he was twelve years old and inspired by a picture of Michelangelo's *Moses*, was a bust of Abraham.[6] It was while boarding at the Bispham home in Portland, however, that his hobby blossomed into a passion. Deprived of conventional art supplies, he worked with whatever materials came to hand. Initially, his preferred medium was oleomargarine, taken from the Bisphams' icebox and fashioned into busts of his two main historical heroes, Attila the Hun and Napoleon. He also sculpted little figures out of pilfered laundry soap.

On one occasion, he and Pember went to visit the grave of a local celebrity, Sam Simpson, Oregon's unofficial poet laureate and author of the beloved lyric "Beautiful Willamette." Coming upon a shattered tombstone, Fenelon took a small piece home with him "and carved a hand on the back of it in relief." Eventually he managed to scrounge up enough money to acquire a small quantity of modeling

clay and used it to produce "his first permanent piece of sculpture."
Titled "The Horrible Greek," it was "a nine-inch bust molded on
classical lines but with wildly bulging eyes and a fantastically leering
mouth," toothless except for a single tusk-like canine.[7]

Enrolled in the local public school, Fenelon distinguished himself scholastically, though he ran afoul of officials after removing
several art history books from the library and returning them with
torn-out illustrations—a practice that would eventually land him
in far more serious trouble. When he completed seventh grade with
honors in June 1921, his formal education was over.[8]

By then, Mary had scraped together enough money from her
work as a cleaning lady to move herself and her sons into a little corner shack at 170 NE 3rd Avenue. That summer, she spent every spare
moment at Mother Crawford's camp meeting, where she served as
an exhorter, helping to guide the assembled sinners on the road to
salvation. What little income she earned as a menial was further reduced by her regular donations to the church. Left largely unat-
tended, her sons were "forced to subsist for weeks at a time on bread
and buttermilk begged from bakeries and dairies."[9]

Their situation improved somewhat when fourteen-year-old
Fenelon got a job as a stock clerk at the Meier & Frank department store in downtown Portland. He lasted there for less than six
months. Sometime in early 1922—in a pattern that would repeat itself throughout his working life—he was fired after savagely assaulting a coworker over some trivial slight. It took two burly men to
subdue the frenzied Irwin. "He was crazy mad," the store manager
recalled.[10]

This shocking outburst of rage was not the only early sign of his
growing instability. During that same brief period of employment,
he conceived an idea that, elaborated into a full-blown delusional
system, would come to dominate his later life.

It first occurred to him while he was folding up a bolt of polka-
dotted silk fabric in the department store stock room. All at once, as
he described it, "the material seemed to leave my hands and without

any human effort move straight up to my face." He felt his legs go weak and had to lean against a doorway for support. His boss, who was standing nearby, saw him falter and asked what was the matter.

"That's when the whole thing came to me in full force," Irwin later explained. "The reason people have so much difficulty in doing things is that they have such a hard time getting things in their head. You have to visualize first. Before a sculptor can make a statue he has to make a mental statue, and the reason that even the greatest sculptor has such a difficult time making a statue is because he doesn't get it clearly in his mind first."[11]

This realization—that an artist has to create a "mental prototype" of his subject before giving it material form—seems not merely self-evident but blindingly obvious. After all, what novelist, in describing a scene, doesn't first imagine it in all its physical and sensory richness? What painter doesn't first see with his mind's eye the design he then renders on canvas? Moreover, the practice of "visualization"—as Irwin would call his supposedly revolutionary theory—was already a well-established aspect of the late-nineteenth movement known as New Thought. Springing, among other sources, from the Transcendental philosophy of Ralph Waldo Emerson, who spoke of an all-pervasive "Over-Soul" accessible to individuals through the faculty of intuition, the various organizations and sects of this widespread metaphysical movement shared a belief in the miraculous healing and creative power of human thought—that disease could be cured, riches acquired, and happiness attained through the power of positive thinking.

As someone who gobbled up all manner of writings on religious and philosophical subjects, Irwin was likely familiar with some of the popular New Thought literature of the day, such as the best-selling self-help books of Wallace D. Wattles, who preached that "creative visualization" was a key to success. "Man," wrote Wattles, "can form things in his thought and, by impressing his thought upon formless substance, can cause the things he thinks about to be created."[12]

Immediately following his epiphany with the polka-dotted cloth, Irwin became convinced that, with enough concentration, he could create a mental picture so utterly real that he merely had to copy it in clay to produce an artistic masterpiece. "I expect some day to be able to form an absolutely clear and perfect image in my mind; to be able to actually *project* it into the air before me so that I can actually *see* it there with my material eyes just as I see material objects. I expect to be able to hold it and make other people see it." He would then "become the most famous and unique sculptor that ever lived."

To achieve this end, he threw himself into a series of daily exercises, designed to perfect his powers of visualization. The art illustrations he had torn from his school library books, originally intended as inspirations for his sculptures, were put in the service of this new obsession. He would study them for hours—François Joseph Sandmann's painting of Napoleon in exile on Saint Helena, Antonio Canova's statue of Theseus slaying a centaur, Arnold Böcklin's eerie *Isle of the Dead*. Then, seated on the edge of his bed in his darkened room, he would attempt to re-create them so completely in his mind that he "could project them in front of him at will and actually see them," like a moviegoer watching images onscreen.[13]

His initial results were not encouraging. Try as he might, he found it difficult to maintain the necessary focus to form a complete mental image of his subject. "Anybody can concentrate entirely on a thing for a moment or two," he later explained. "But after that, it gets to be a strain." Deciding that he needed assistance, he enlisted a young boy from the neighborhood, hiring him to sit in an adjoining room with a pocket watch and call out the time at regular intervals, while Irwin "concentrated on one mental picture after another," gradually increasing the clarity and duration of each visualized image. "This form of behavior led other people to consider him as being queer," one psychiatrist would subsequently note with classic clinical understatement. When the father of Irwin's young assistant got wind of "what was going on, the boy's services were summarily terminated."[14]

To augment the stolen pictures in his collection, Irwin began to borrow art books from various branches of the public library, often under a fictitious name, strip them of their illustrations, then toss the mutilated volumes into the Willamette River. Eventually, he would acquire an enormous number of these plundered images—at least a thousand, according to one official estimate—all carefully indexed and catalogued.[15]

In the meantime, Pember had reverted to his own delinquent ways. In early 1923, he stole several bicycles. Exactly what he did with them is unclear, though he evidently gave one to his older brother. Records show that, on February 16 of that year, Pember was sentenced to a term at the Oregon State Training School for Boys. Fenelon, charged with possession of stolen property, was given probation.[16]

By then, Mary had found work in a shirtwaist factory. Between her job and her evangelical activities, she was rarely at home. On those infrequent occasions when she and Fenelon were together, they were generally at each other's throats. He remained bitterly resentful of the tithe exacted by her church and continued to blame her for their indigent circumstances. For her part, Mary had come to see her middle son as the most irredeemable of her offspring. Though she supported his artistic ambitions and listened patiently to his rambling "discourses on the great powers that would come to him through visualization," she was horrified by another passion he had recently acquired: the writings of Robert Ingersoll.[17]

Known to his freethinking admirers as the "Great Agnostic," Ingersoll, born in upstate New York in 1833, was the son of an itinerant preacher. Seeking to account for his intense antireligious convictions, critics would later offer two contradictory theories: "On the one hand, they suggested that he was reacting to an upbringing filled with hellfire and damnation called down on him by his father; on the other, that young Robert had not been threatened with *enough* hellfire during his childhood."[18] Following a brief stint as a schoolteacher in southern Illinois, he apprenticed himself to a prominent attorney and, after assiduous self-study, was admitted to the bar. Though his uncompromising attacks on religious benightedness made him too controversial for political office (a term as attorney general of Illinois was the only post he ever held), he was a brilliant orator on behalf of other candidates and gained national renown after delivering an electrifying speech at the 1876 Republican National Convention, naming James G. Blaine as the party's presidential nominee.

For the next two decades—an era when public lectures were a major form of popular entertainment—he crisscrossed the country on more than a dozen tours, drawing sell-out crowds who often stood in line for hours and paid hefty ticket prices to hear him speak (one dollar or more at a time when the average American worker earned less than five hundred dollars a year). Luminaries from Mark Twain to Thomas Edison, Andrew Carnegie to Eugene Debs, Walt Whitman to Clarence Darrow regarded him as the greatest of all their country's orators. Speaking without notes for as long as three uninterrupted hours, he offered spellbinding talks on literary, scientific, political, and historical subjects: Shakespeare's plays, the poetry of Robert Burns, the life and work of Alexander von Humboldt, the Declaration of Independence, women's rights, and dozens more, all eventually published in a twelve-volume collection.

His greatest fame and notoriety, however, derived from his scathing attacks on religion. He proudly proclaimed his iconoclasm. "I care nothing for what the church says, except insofar as it accords with my reason," he declared, "and the Bible is nothing to me, only insofar as it agrees with what I think and know." One of his best-known talks, "Some Mistakes of Moses," was a ruthless dissection of "the errors, contradictions, and impossibilities contained in the Pentateuch"—a document he characterized "simply as a record of a barbarous people, in which are found a great number of ceremonies of savagery, many absurd and unjust laws, and thousands of ideas inconsistent with known and demonstrated facts."[19] Little wonder that this stalwart champion of science, rational thought, and humanism was reviled by fundamentalists, who regarded him as "one of the Devil's chief allies."[20]

Besides the art books he was vandalizing, Fenelon had been borrowing a wide range of reading material from the public library—everything from Bulfinch's *Mythology* to John Clark Ridpath's three-volume *History of the World*. Sometime around his fifteenth birthday, he discovered—and became enthralled by—Ingersoll's collected essays. His mother was predictably appalled at Fenelon's enthusiasm for the godless "Injuresoul" (as his religious critics called him). Worried that he might corrupt his impressionable younger brother, still confined to the Oregon State Training School, she dashed off a letter to Superintendent L. M. Gilbert, urging him to intercept any correspondence from Fenelon to Pember. "Fenelon is my child and has some good qualities, but he is brimful of poison," she wrote. "He is an atheist and well-versed in that pernicious literature. . . . Pember is just as easily influenced as can be toward the good or toward the evil. Just a little association with Fenelon will ruin him forever."[21]

In the fall of 1924, a public librarian named Anne Mulheron filed a complaint charging seventeen-year-old Fenelon with the destruction of dozens of books. Convicted as a delinquent minor on December 6, 1924, he was given a suspended sentence on condition that he pay restitution of $53.88 as his share of the cost of the mutilated books. To earn the money—roughly $800 in today's dollars—he found another job as a stock boy but was fired within weeks after flying into a rage at his supervisor and giving him a vicious beating. That June, his mother moved out of the house to reside for the summer at the Apostolic Faith Mission campgrounds. Penniless and alone, Fenelon went to the Domestic Relations Court and asked to be committed to reform school. His request was granted. On August 25, 1925, just past his eighteenth birthday, he joined Pember in the Oregon State Training School for Boys.[22]

Mary's fear that Fenelon would fill his younger brother's ear with atheistic "poison" was not unfounded. From the moment he arrived at the reformatory, Fenelon made no secret of his contempt for religion. "He was a fountain of abuse against God," Superintendent Gilbert later testified. "He was the most blasphemous infidel I ever beheld. So imbued was he with bitterness against Christianity that he could talk of nothing else for weeks after he arrived. He was possessed of an incredible fund of knowledge and seemed to take high pleasure in his incessant ranting against God."

Even more disconcerting to authorities than these antireligious tirades were his violent mood swings. "For no reason we could understand he would explosively transform from a smiling, pliable boy into a brutish, belligerent animal," recalled a school official named Lloyd E. Darling. During these spells—which sometimes lasted for days—he was a danger to the other boys. "Once roused to a fighting pitch," said Darling, "he had no other thought than to destroy his foe."[23]

Fenelon himself offered a reason for these murderous outbursts. As had happened at the Strickland Home, he was convinced that the other boys at the reformatory "looked upon me as a sissy." "That happens all the time," he told a psychiatrist some years afterward. "They all think I'm a sissy, so I smash them in the jaw and then I become their enemy."

He was particularly provoked by a boy named Danny, a swaggering bully who (in Irwin's telling) "used to hog all the bread at mealtimes, which meant that somebody had to go without bread." One morning at breakfast, as Danny and Fenelon were still seating themselves, "everybody else at the table grabbed the bread, so there was only one big slice left and one little heel." Before Danny could reach for the remaining slice, Irwin snatched it away. Danny spat out an insult that brought Fenelon out of his chair with a roar. Only the intervention of the dining hall supervisor kept the two teenage combatants apart.

Later that day however, Fenelon confronted Danny in the shoemaking shop, where both were employed as part of their industrial training. "You son of a bitch," said Fenelon, "if you're looking for a scrap just start something." When Danny responded with a curse,

Fenelon "smashed him in the jaw. For an hour about fifty people were trying to take me away from him. Finally when it ended, his finger was broken and I had given him a big cauliflower ear."

While Danny was led off to the infirmary, Fenelon was taken to the office of G. I. Stahl, the school's designated disciplinarian, and given what the inmates called a "dinging"—a severe lashing on his right hand with a heavy leather strap. "When he got through with me," Fenelon subsequently related, "my hand looked like a ham."[24]

He received another "dinging," this time on the buttocks, in late June 1926 after trying to escape from the reformatory. For the previous few months he had gone without lunch, turning over his food to a boy from the machine shop who, in exchange for the extra portions, had tinkered together a small apparatus constructed according to Fenelon's specifications. Built from the motor of an old Victrola phonograph, it functioned as a kind of metronome. As Irwin described it, the machine "ticked like a clock, only you could regulate it so that it ticked once every minute or whatever you wanted. By regulating the tick, I could find out how long I could concentrate." The device was designed to help him develop the power that would make him the world's greatest sculptor. He called it the "visualization machine." When school authorities prevented him from using it, however, he ran away in a fit of anger, only to be caught and returned to the reform school that same night.[25]

Paroled in November 1926, Fenelon returned to live with his mother, who had just received word that Benjamin Hardin Irwin, the man who had abandoned her sixteen years earlier, had died at the age of seventy-two in a boardinghouse in Brickstore, Georgia, where he was cohabiting with a forty-year-old widow named Fannie Norris.[26] For a few weeks, Fenelon labored in a cast-iron stove factory before taking a more congenial job with a firm specializing in ornamental modeling. His employment there ended in the usual way, when he assaulted a fellow worker who cast aspersions on his manhood. As he explained in a subsequent interview: "There was a fellow there who was a fairy and one of the other fellows said to me, 'That guy will give you five dollars if you suck him off. You have a nice ass—why don't you take a chance?' So I jumped up and beat him up and got fired."[27]

Still enthralled by the "Great Agnostic," Irwin not only used his earnings from his two short-lived jobs to purchase his own copies of Ingersoll's essays but also announced that he was adopting the first name of his intellectual hero. For his mother, it was the final proof that her middle son was beyond redemption. Sometime in the early weeks of 1927, he returned home from an outing to find that she had burned all of the offending books in the kitchen stove. They quarreled violently. The next morning, twenty-year-old Robert Irwin packed a bag and left Portland.

He never saw his mother again.[28]

Romanelli and Rady

W ORKING AT A VARIETY of manual jobs — dockhand, lumberjack, fruit picker, cannery worker — Irwin made his way to San Francisco. In a published reminiscence, he described the tawdry temptations of that "Sodom-by-the-Sea": its "liquor joints, dance halls with lurid dames . . . coke dens, and all the vices one could pay for." While others happily wallowed in such wickedness, Irwin (so he claims in his memoir) wanted no part of it. The fleshpots of the Barbary Coast might exert a forbidden allure, "but not enough for me to dwarf the soul I had been blessed with."[1]

Toting a battered suitcase stuffed with his precious collection of art illustrations, he hitchhiked down the coast, arriving in Los Angeles in late summer 1927, not long after his twentieth birthday. By then, he was in a desperately bedraggled state. "I had been on the road for a long time and presented a horrible picture — in dirt and rags." Wandering around a "tough section of town," he came upon a barbershop and stopped in for a haircut and shave.

"There were two barbers there," he told one of the many psy-

chiatrists who would examine him in later years. "One was small
and one was big, and the big one immediately took me for a fairy.
When he was shaving me, he got some hair in my mouth and he said
it looked like I had been sucking somebody." For reasons he could
never understand, Irwin was always being "mistaken for a queer,"
something that never failed to lash him into a rage. He managed to
suppress his fury until the haircut was done, then sprang to his feet
and "tore into the son-of-a-bitch." As he "beat the tar out of him
with my fist," the man's partner came up behind Irwin and "hit me
on the head with a bottle." Swiveling, Irwin delivered a punch to
the smaller man's jaw that knocked him senseless. With his two adversaries dispatched, Irwin, still in the grip of his frenzy, rampaged
through the shop, knocking every bottle of hair tonic, eau de cologne, and aftershave off their shelves and onto the linoleum floor.
He then strode out the door and hurried away, just as the neighborhood beat cop—alerted by a passerby who had witnessed the brawl
through the barbershop window—showed up.[2]

Shortly afterward—seeking work as a sculptor and trusting to
his "guiding star"—Irwin presented himself at the studio of Carlo
Romanelli. Member of an eminent family of Florentine artists, Romanelli had come to America at the age of thirty and, after settling
in Hollywood, quickly established himself as a highly successful
commercial sculptor. During the silent-movie era he produced props
for dozens of motion pictures—everything from a marble reproduction of ingenue Clara Kimball Young's hands for the 1922 melodrama *The Hands of Nara* to replicas of monumental Roman statuary for the 1925 version of *Ben-Hur*. His best-known works, however,
were the life-size lions and elephants commissioned by pioneering
movie producer William Selig for the entranceway to his personal
zoo—a menagerie of more than seven hundred animals assembled
for the studio's popular jungle pictures.[3]

In his periods of seeming normality—when he wasn't flying
into a murderous rage or spouting his wild-eyed theories about art
—Irwin could be a thoroughly engaging young man: polite, well-

spoken, brimming with energy and enthusiasm. He was attractive, too, with wavy brown hair, boyish good looks, and a compact build sculpted by his long months of physical labor. Freshly barbered and wearing a fresh suit of clothes he had purchased with his last twenty dollars, he made a favorable enough impression on Romanelli to be hired on the spot.

At twenty years old, Bob Irwin was still a virgin. He had been masturbating regularly since the age of ten, when his big brother, Vidalin, took him into the bathroom of their Los Angeles home and showed him how to do it. At eighteen, he had his first girlfriend — the sister of a fellow inmate at the Oregon State reformatory who took a shine to him on a visit to her brother. On subsequent visits, she had snuck into his room, where the two engaged in some furtive petting — "monkeying around," as Bob put it. Owing to his own bashfulness, however, they never had sex, though the girl was more than willing.[4]

Shortly after he went to work for Romanelli, he was finally relieved of his virginity. He was out with a buddy one night when they were approached by a pair of prostitutes who took them to a seedy hotel. Bob got the prettier of the two. "She was a very beautiful girl," he recalled. "I went upstairs with her and as soon as I got in there I began to stutter and she took in the whole situation at a glance. She said, 'I'm glad I got you. I'll take care of you.' I was deadly afraid of her and she took off her clothes and she washed off my penis with that warm stuff and saw if I had any clap. Then she lay me down on the bed and put her arms around me and made me forget about being afraid." To his astonished delight, she eagerly performed fellatio on him — "gave me a good French," in the words of Irwin, who would remember the moment as "the nearest I ever got to heaven in this world." As soon as he climaxed, "she immediately jumped up and went out and washed out her mouth and then she laid me down in the bed again and instead of being like a prostitute she was very nice and I played with her awhile and sucked her breasts. Then I had real intercourse with her." He "saw her quite a number of times after that" until she got arrested and vanished from the streets.[5]

Though he would continue to patronize prostitutes on a regular basis, sex was always secondary to Irwin's main preoccupation: his increasingly obsessive efforts to achieve artistic supremacy through the practice of visualization. During cigarette breaks at Romanelli's studio or over coffee at a local greasy spoon with the other assistants, he would hold forth on his favorite subject, waving his hands excitedly and speaking with an intensity that more than one of his listeners would describe as "fanatical."

"Sculptors today are like blind men feeling around in the dark," he proclaimed. "We keep on changing and changing our sculpture till we get it pretty near as we want it, but it's a long and laborious process, and we're never satisfied because we're copying something we can't clearly see."

Even Augustus Saint-Gaudens—the master sculptor best known for the Robert Gould Shaw Memorial on the Boston Common and his design for the 1905 "double eagle" gold piece, considered the most beautiful coin ever minted in the United States—went about his art in a misguided way. "He spent fourteen years on the Shaw Memorial, making it over and over again because he could never get it quite like he wanted it," said Irwin, "Fourteen years! And in the end he still wasn't satisfied. Yet he had all the academic training in the world."

Traditional academic training, Bob insisted, was precisely the problem. "The sculptors of today think the only way to develop artistic talent is to practice drawing and modeling from the nude. They don't realize that artistic genius resides not in the hand but in the brain, and by all this modeling and drawing, they're using material methods to remedy a mental fault. I say, why not get at the heart of the trouble from the start and develop your mental sight by practicing visualization? If Saint-Gaudens only could have gotten his mental picture clear, he could have finished his memorial in two or three days instead of fourteen years."

Bob had no intention of making the same mistake as Saint-Gaudens. "I mean to be able to get my mental picture clear. And then I'll be able to do things that no sculptor ever dreamed of. I'll be able to make a bust of somebody I haven't seen for years, just by copying my mental picture of that person. And I'll do it so fast that Michelangelo himself would say to me, 'How the hell did you do that?'"[6]

Bob remained at Romanelli's studio for nearly a year—the longest he would hold onto any single job in his life. Like other mentors he would find in the coming years, Romanelli took a shine to the earnest young sculptor, regarding him as "an excellent workman, clean in his habits and with talent and unusual ambition." Romanelli's wife, on the other hand, developed an active distaste for Bob's pontificating and saw him as "overbearing and a braggart." Several of the other assistants, too, grew fed up with his pompous pronouncements on art and told him so to his face. When Bob responded with his fists, Romanelli was compelled to let him go.[7]

He wasn't entirely unhappy to be relieved of the job since it had demanded so much of his time. Now that he was free, he could devote himself to the far more urgent matter of developing his visualization skills. To keep body and soul together, he took a string of part-time jobs. He did some life modeling for the Norwegian-born sculptor Finn Frolich, best remembered today for his bust of his good friend and sailing buddy Jack London. He spent a few months crafting celebrity likenesses in the waxworks studio of "encausticist" Katherine Stuberg, Hollywood's answer to Madame Tussaud. He did ornamental plasterwork for a concern called the A-1 Decorating Company.[8]

By the spring of 1929, however, he found himself longing for more fulfilling ways to exercise his artistic gifts. Like other young sculptors before him, he was an ardent fan of the eminent Chicagoan Lorado Taft, responsible for some of the city's most impressive monuments. He had read captivating accounts of Taft's famed atelier on the grounds of the 1893 World's Fair. In the first week of May 1929, Bob packed up his ever-growing picture collection, along with a sample of his work—a small plaster bust of Charles Lindbergh—and hopped a freight train bound for Chicago.

There were some odd affinities between Lorado Zadok Taft and the former Fenelon Arroyo Seco Irwin, beginning with their parents' habit of bestowing highly eccentric names on their offspring. Lorado and his siblings—his brother Florizel and sisters Zulime and Turbia Doctoria—were the children of Don Carlos Taft, a Congregational minister and teacher of geology at the University of Illinois (then known as Illinois Industrial University). Taft traced his fascination with sculpture to an incident that occurred in 1873, when a shipment of carelessly crated statues, destined for the university's new art museum, arrived from Europe in badly damaged condition and thirteen-year-old Lorado was called upon to help his father reassemble them.[9]

After graduating from the university in 1879, he spent four years in Paris, mastering the traditional techniques of clay modeling at the venerable École des Beaux-Arts. Back in America, he eked out a living with whatever odd sculpting jobs he could land: everything from death masks and parlor statuettes to bas-relief fireplace screens and butter sculptures for county fairs. Gradually, as his reputation grew, he won larger and more lucrative commissions—portrait busts of prominent citizens, Civil War monuments, and other public memorials. None of this work, however, was especially fulfilling to a man with Taft's exalted sense of calling, his determination to improve his fellow citizens by exposing them to the glories of classical art—statuary in particular.

His breakthrough came in 1893 when, at the invitation of Daniel Burnham, chief of construction for the Chicago's World Fair, he helped design the facade of the Horticultural Building, one of the architectural splendors of the great "White City." Other major commissions quickly followed: large-scale public monuments done in the classical Beaux Arts style and reflecting Taft's belief that the purpose of art "was to convey a noble message, to teach, to uplift."[10]

Typical of his lofty, allegorical approach was *The Solitude of the Soul*, a group of four idealized nudes—two male, two female—who, clutching at one another's hands as they weave their way around a central core of stone, symbolize the poignant "truth that each one of us, despite the best will on all sides, must pass through life more or less alone."[11]

As important to Taft as his sculpture was his role as cultural missionary—"an evangelist preaching the gospel of art," in the words of his brother-in-law, Pulitzer Prize–winning author Hamlin Garland.[12] When he wasn't in the studio, Taft was on the road, delivering lantern-slide lectures on art history and related subjects to rapt audiences throughout the Midwest and beyond. In his popular "clay talks"—performed, by his own estimate, more than 1,500 times in virtually every state of the union—he would set up a mock studio on stage and sculpt the portrait bust of a "Grecian beauty," explaining the process of clay modeling as he went along. For more than four decades, he also taught classes at the Art Institute, the University of Chicago, and the University of Illinois. His lectures were collected in various volumes, and in 1903 he published his authoritative *History of American Sculpture*, which remained the standard text on the subject for more than fifty years.[13]

In 1906, Taft, needing a larger workplace for his increasingly imposing commissions, took a lease on an abandoned brick stable on the Midway Plaisance. Almost at once, he began expanding the space by annexing a pair of frame barns. Eventually, the structure housed thirteen separate studios; a roofed courtyard with a fireplace, fountain, and sunken goldfish pond; and two dormitories for his growing corps of assistants.

For the next two decades, Taft's Midway Studio served as a mecca for aspiring sculptors throughout the country. Hardly a week went by without letters arriving from hopeful young artists, pleading for admission to his atelier. Others simply showed up at his door. No one with real talent was turned away by Taft, who cherished his role as mentor. Those accepted into Taft's "studio family," as he called it, could scarcely believe their good fortune. "If you can imagine yourself transformed into a place people call Heaven, that will give you some idea of how I felt," wrote the renowned sculptor and medalist Trygve A. Rovelstad, recalling his own induction into that privileged realm. "My dream had been realized."[14]

When Bob first stepped through the front entrance of the Midway Studio on a radiant morning in May 1929, he found himself in an enclosed, cement-floored courtyard flooded with sunshine from a large roof skylight and suffused with the odor of damp clay, plaster, and stone dust. At the far end of the space loomed a statue that he immediately recognized from various magazine illustrations as the full-scale plaster model of Taft's monumental *Fountain of the Great Lakes*—a dramatic grouping of five graceful maidens, allegorical symbols of the "inland seas," each bearing a large scalloped basin.

No one was in sight, though the studio was clearly not deserted. From behind closed doors came the sounds of a busy workplace: hammering, footsteps reverberating on the stone floor, the slapping of clay upon armature, somebody whistling one of the popular tunes of the day, "Painting the Clouds with Sunshine." All at once, the door to Bob's right flew open and out strode a strapping young man, floppy cap on his head, long workman's apron over his coveralls, his hands caked with clay—clearly one of Taft's assistants. Spotting Bob, he asked if he could be of help, then offered to escort him to Taft.

They found him in the main workroom, supervising a half dozen of his helpers who were working on the figure of a colossal armored knight, a few perched on ladders, others on a wooden scaffold surrounding the half-finished statue. Tall, straight-backed, and still strikingly handsome in his late sixties, the elderly sculptor cut an elegant figure even in his shapeless linen smock. By contrast, Bob—who had hoboed his way from California—looked so unkempt that Taft initially took him for a "tramp."[15]

"Honored to meet you, sir," said Bob, extending his right hand. "I've come two thousand miles to study with you."

After examining the sample that Bob had brought along and declaring it "the best head of Lindbergh he had ever seen," Taft invited him "to come and visit the Midway Studio for a week, and see how he should like the studio family, and how it would like him."[16]

Between his innate abilities and the skills he had acquired during his year-long apprenticeship with Romanelli, Bob had no trouble impressing the members of Taft's atelier and was quickly taken on at a pay of forty dollars a week. Besides his energy and raw talent, there was something else about the fresh-faced young sculptor that Taft warmed to. A product of the provincial West whose tastes ran to nineteenth-century neoclassicism, Bob cared nothing about avant-garde art—a sentiment he shared with the hidebound Taft, who viewed modernism with absolute disdain, deriding the work of Matisse, Braque, and their peers as "puerile effrontery," "willful bungling," and "sheer imbecility."[17] Within a short time, Bob had so worked his way into the older man's affections that Taft began to regard him as his protégé. While his other assistants bunked in the barnlike dormitories, Taft found lodging for Bob at the home of his widowed stepmother, Mary.[18]

With forty dollars a week in his pocket—roughly equivalent to four hundred today—Bob felt prosperous for the first time in his life. He treated himself to a snazzy new wardrobe and, during his free hours, took advantage of the many leisure-time opportunities Chicago offered a footloose young man. A lifelong boxing fan whose ever-growing picture collection included dozens of photos of professional prizefighters, he attended matches whenever he could. He was particularly enamored of German heavyweight and future world champion Max Schmeling—"the best-looking man in the world," in Bob's estimation. He also enjoyed the movies and would see anything starring his favorite actor, the matinee idol Ramon Novarro, known to his swooning admirers as "Ravishing Ramon." To Bob, Schmeling and Novarro (who would ultimately meet a grisly death at the hands of a pair of male hustlers he had brought home for sex) embodied opposite poles of his own character. "I have two sides to my nature," he would later explain. "One is that I like force, and that's why I like Schmeling. The other side of my nature is very spiritual—there's something very spiritual about Novarro. He is very much like Sir Galahad or Tristan."[19]

Bob's less spiritual inclinations found an outlet not only at the weekly fights but also in the city's many brothels and burlesque houses. He would always remember a stripper named Sally Swan, endowed with "the most beautiful breasts I ever saw in my whole life. Her breasts were so big that they touched in the middle and yet they didn't hang down one bit." A "beautiful tableau" of topless women costumed as Indian squaws, one of the highlights of a show at the Star and Garter burlesque house, also left a lasting impression.[20]

When the weather turned warmer, he liked to swim in the lake. There was one stretch of beach he particularly enjoyed, a secluded spot on the South Shore where people routinely went skinny-dipping. One sweltering afternoon in midsummer, as Bob later told the story, he was lounging there naked when another man—blue-eyed, blond-haired, and "sort of a fairy"—"swam towards me and came over to me and without warning said to me, 'Can I suck your cock?'"

"So I gave it to him," Bob related. "I just said, 'There you are, go to it,' and he did it. I just sat there and enjoyed it. I came once and he just swallowed it up."

Bob—who'd been "Frenched" by only one person before, the young prostitute in Los Angeles—decided that oral sex "was a million times nicer with a girl." Still, he had to admit that getting "sucked off by that fellow wasn't so bad." Of course, he would never do anything like that himself. It was one thing to be on the receiving end of the act. But performing fellatio on somebody else was "an abominable business," "the lowest and dirtiest thing a guy could do." Before he would "suck somebody else off," he would "kill himself." If there was one thing that made Bob Irwin "so goddamned mad" that he was ready to kill anybody who suggested it, it was being mistaken for that most loathsome of all creatures, a "queer."[21]

For a while, everything seemed to be going Bob's way. Though his landlady, Mrs. Taft, was "so old and utterly wrinkled" that Bob found her "sort of repelling," she treated him so kindly that he would forever feel a filial tenderness toward her.[22] Lorado him-self—"Rady" to his intimates—continued to take a fatherly interest in him. When the Steuben Club, a 2,500-member organization of prominent German-American citizens, was looking for a sculptor to make a bust of Max Schmeling, Taft recommended Bob. The club's vice president, Judge Walter W. L. Meyer—a power in the Chicago Democratic machine—was so pleased with the result that he offered Bob an even greater opportunity: the chance to do a portrait bust of New York State governor Franklin Delano Roosevelt, who was scheduled to speak at the Steuben Club in the fall. There was already talk of a Roosevelt run for the presidency in the 1932 elections, and Bob, as he wrote in a letter, could foresee a glorious future for him-self should FDR agree to pose for him: "If he did get elected, I could be personal friends with the President of the United States, with all kinds of political pull & right in line for a lot of commissions!"[23]

Bob had already done a bust of the man Roosevelt would ulti-mately defeat, Herbert Hoover. When a friend of Lorado Taft's, a fellow named Wardlaw, sent a photo of the bust to the White House, Bob received a personal reply from the president's wife, Lou Henry Hoover, commending him "for the high order" of his work. "You are indeed fortunate to have been recognized by such a man as Mr. Taft," Mrs. Hoover continued, "and I hope that you will work long and hard and some day be a great sculptor."[24]

For the first time in his life, Bob also had a large circle of friends. Taft's quiet Hyde Park neighborhood was full of young men Bob's age who shared his love of boxing. One of them owned some boxing gloves, and on warm summer days, they would gather in this fellow's backyard and, stripping to the waist, hold amateur matches. Bob, proud of his physique and fighting prowess, almost always emerged victorious.

Some evenings, Bob and his buddies went to the Trianon in the hope of meeting girls. A palatial ballroom with mock-Versailles de-cor and a white maple floor big enough to accommodate more than a thousand twirling couples, the Trianon, situated on the South Side at Cottage Grove and East 62nd, was Chicago's classiest dance hall.

It was there, sometime in late summer 1929, that Bob met Alice Ryan.

Apart from her age—twenty-two—and her love of the Charleston and fox-trot, virtually nothing is known about Alice. Bob himself assumed she was "fast," since she readily accompanied him back to his room on one of their first dates. When he began to "neck with her," however, he discovered that she was really "quite maidenly." As soon as he fondled her breasts, she burst into tears and exclaimed, "Oh, you men are all alike." Bob immediately desisted. Though his sex drive was as strong as any other young male's, he was happy to keep their relationship platonic since making love to Alice was far less important to him than enlightening her about the great truth he had discovered: the awesome potentialities of visualization.

Alone with her in his room, seated together on the edge of his bed, he would spend hours expounding on his theories, which had grown increasingly bizarre in the months since he left California.

"There's only one thing in the universe that counts," he explained. "Some call it the Universal Mind, some Spirit or Soul or the Life-Force. The Old Greeks called it the Logos. Today we call it God. It has a thousand different names but they all mean the same —that unseen *Something* that fills the whole wide universe with life and meaning, the way a broadcasting station fills the air with music.

"Now, in every human being evolution has given us a mechanism to make contact with that station—our brains. But since we are creatures of the material world, our brains can only catch a tiny portion of that heavenly music. We're like Hottentots. Give a Hottentot a radio and tell him to turn it on and he'll just turn the dial around and around and all he'll get is a bunch of squawks. But someone who knows how to run a radio can get beautiful music out of it from any station he wants.

"Do you get what I'm saying?" he continued, growing more excited by the moment. "This Universal Mind I'm talking about is, by its very nature, all-wise and all-powerful. It knows every damn thing there is to be known and can do any damn thing that can be done. So once we know how to work our mental radios correctly, we'll be

able to learn anything just by tuning in to the right station and pulling it out of the air—Greek or Latin or art or mathematics. And
not just any mathematics but such mathematics as would make Einstein's head swim. The Universal Mind would broadcast it directly
into our brains, just"—here he stuck out a hand and gave a sharp
snap—"like *that!*"

The question, of course, was "How do we learn to run this radio?
How can we enter this new and glorious world?" And the answer,
according to Bob, was obvious: through visualization.

"Let me ask you this," he said, leaping to his feet. "How do we
manage to move or lift a finger or do any god-darn thing? Through
our five senses, pretty miss, through our five senses. All our per-
ceptions of the *material* world are transmitted to us through sight,
touch, hearing, taste, and smell. So if you put two and two together,
you can see that the only way we can ever hope to explore the *higher*
world is to develop our *mental* senses. Now the sense we use most is
sight. So it naturally follows that if we can develop our inner, mental
sight—if we can see things absolutely clearly with our mind's eye—
we'll achieve such mastery over the world as no man ever dreamed
of. And here's the whole thing in a nutshell: to develop this sight,
you simply exercise it just as you would exercise a muscle. In other
words, you sit down every day and practice visualizing."

Exactly how developing a visual skill would allow someone to
hear heavenly music wasn't entirely clear. Alice, however—who, despite her exerted attempts to follow Bob's harangue, was finding it
harder and harder to keep up—said nothing.

"I wonder if you realize just what this whole thing means," said
Bob, staring down at her. "Everyone's read Shakespeare. How much
do you remember? Very little. And yet it's all there, right in your
head, every line, every word, every syllable. And let me tell you,
baby, once you learn to visualize, you'll be able to go to bed at night
and lie there in the dark and open *Hamlet* or *Macbeth* or *Othello* in
your mind and read the whole damn thing with your eyes closed.
And what's more you'll be able to *see* those plays enacted in your
mind. Those characters will step forth in living projected reality and

play their parts like actors on the stage—only with infinitely greater artistry and majesty and power. Have you ever seen a movie twice? We all have. Well, once you learn to visualize, you'll be able to stay home the second time and see that movie in your mind any time you please.

"Do you sense the magnitude of this thing?" he cried, waving his hands so wildly that Alice feared he would knock over the bedside table lamp. "Holy mackerel, there are no limits to it. It's beyond our dreams. After you became an expert at visualizing, you could amass more knowledge than the wisest man ever dreamed of possessing. How? Just go to the library every day and pick up book after book and turn the pages without reading them, and you'd have every word in every book in that library by heart and you could read it any time in your mind without any effort at all."

Stepping to his bureau, Bob rummaged in a drawer and came out with an art-book illustration that he handed to Alice. "Here, take a look at this picture of Napoleon for a minute. Now close your eyes and try to visualize it. Can you see him standing there on the rock of St. Helena, wearing that old hat of his and the great gray overcoat? Can you see the set look on his face? His great sad eyes, his Roman nose, his mouth, his binoculars hanging from his neck, his hands clasped tight behind his back, his white pants, his black boots on the rock? Can you see how he sticks out his jaw in that stubborn way of his? Can you see the majestic ocean rolling beneath the rays of the setting sun, can you hear the roar of the surf, can you feel the stiff ocean breezes on your cheeks, can you smell the salt tang of the sea? Can you see it clearly just as though you were there?

"Pretty tough, isn't it?" he said, removing the picture from her hand and returning it to the drawer.

"Here's the thing, though," he said, coming to stand before her again. "You'd be surprised how easy and interesting it becomes when two people work on it together. All the difficulties disappear and it becomes the most fascinating game you ever tried."

When Alice expressed some confusion about the exact nature

of the "game," Bob explained that, over the years, he had clipped nearly ten thousand pictures from books, newspapers, and magazines. Each had been glued to a sheet of paper and labeled with a title. He was looking for a partner who would play the role of "title caller." Seated across the room from him, the caller would select a picture at random and, holding it so that Bob couldn't see it, read its title aloud. Bob would "then proceed to describe the picture in minute detail from memory."[25]

Dropping to one knee in front of the startled young woman, he took her hands in both of his. "Alice," he said, staring into her eyes, "if only you and I could work together on this, there'd be no limit to the things we could do. You know what I'd like to do? Go off to some lonely lighthouse with you. It would be just the thing for us—nothing to take our attention away, no eight-hour workday, no dances, no shows, no friends to bother us. I want so much to get away from the trouble and turmoil of this material world into the solitude of some such place until I could master this. I don't know what you think, but I could be happy—supremely happy—out there with you."

It took a moment for Alice to find her voice. "Are you proposing to me, Bob?"

"God knows that if you want looks, connections, money, and all that sort of thing, you can make a hell of a lot better match than me," he said. "But if you and I could just work together, what progress we'd make. Why, the potentialities of the whole business are almost beyond our grasp. Of course, it will take some time until we get our ears fully attuned to the music of the Universal Mind—maybe twenty years. But in the meantime, you and I would be so in love with mastering this thing that material pleasures wouldn't really matter to you."[26]

Unless she dreamed of living in a lighthouse and practicing visualization for twenty years, Bob's idea of wedded bliss couldn't have seemed very alluring to Alice. Still, it's easy to see how an impressionable young woman might be taken by his good looks, talent, ambition, and seemingly brilliant mind. In the fall of 1929—the precise date is impossible to determine—Alice Ryan agreed to become Bob Irwin's wife.

A few weeks later, Bob received a letter from Joe Halliburton, a friend from his days in Los Angeles. Halliburton—who regarded Bob as "one of the most talented people he ever knew"—had a younger brother, Arthur, who had just moved to Chicago from Alabama to study at the Art Institute. Arthur had been staying at the local YMCA but was unhappy because the place (so he claimed) was full of sexual degenerates. Joe was wondering if Bob knew of any decent, affordable lodgings for his kid brother, someplace where he wouldn't be surrounded by "a bunch of perverts."

As it happened, there was another vacant bedroom on the second floor of Mrs. Taft's home that she was happy to rent for the same rate that Bob was paying—five dollars a week. In October 1929—at around the time of the great Wall Street crash—Arthur Halliburton became Bob Irwin's housemate.

Though he was an art student at the time he knew Irwin, Halliburton would end up as a journalist, with a long and varied career as a reporter for the King Features Syndicate, an editor and crime writer for the *New York Sunday Mirror*, a contributor to national magazines like *The New Yorker*, and, in later life, the owner of a small Florida weekly, the *Baker County Press*. Years after his former housemate gained nationwide infamy, Halliburton would recall his time living with Irwin, providing a firsthand account of that moment when Bob's life—and sanity—began to seriously unravel.

At first, Halliburton reported, Bob was "very friendly" to him, introducing him to the other young men on the block, who welcomed him into their little group and included him in their various recreational activities, including their regular backyard boxing matches. It wasn't long, however, before Bob began to get on his nerves.

"He always talked about himself to the exclusion of any other subject," wrote Halliburton. "He was a complete egomaniac." He seemed shockingly ungrateful to Lorado Taft, who had given him so much encouragement and support. The path to fame that Taft had followed—his slow, patient rise, through unrelenting effort, from obscurity to renown—filled Bob with nothing but scorn.

"I don't intend to gradually build up a reputation," he declared. "Sooner or later I'll hold in my hands and in my head an inconceivable power—and once I do I'll have this world by the tail. And then I won't need *anybody's* backing!"

When Halliburton expressed curiosity about this "inconceivable power," Bob took him into his room, showed him his "immense file of pictures," and gave him a lecture on visualization. Far from being impressed, Halliburton became convinced that "Irwin had no pre-imagination, none whatsoever. That was his whole problem. He could imitate things. He couldn't create things." Halliburton's failure to appreciate his housemate's genius did not sit well with Bob. Their relationship quickly deteriorated.

A few weeks later, while hanging around with their neighborhood pals, Bob challenged Halliburton to a friendly sparring match. They spent most of the first round circling each other and exchanging a few jabs. No sooner did the second round start, however, than —as Halliburton later recounted—"Irwin tore into me very furiously and surprised me by knocking me down." Bob, who loved to flaunt his physique and boast of his fighting prowess, raised his arms in triumph, as though declaring himself champ. It was a "great injury to his pride," therefore, when, during the following round, Halliburton unleashed a flurry of blows that sent Bob sprawling. His face flushed with anger and humiliation, he demanded another round, but Halliburton refused. For days afterward, Bob refused to speak a word to his housemate.

The climax of their relationship occurred about a week later. Halliburton, who never forgot the terror of the moment, vividly recalled it years later:

> One cold night I came into the kitchen. Mrs. Taft used to leave food for me to eat. I sat down in the corner of the kitchen at the

table. The stove with the oven door was open and the gas was turned on. Irwin was drying some socks in the stove. I said to him: "Bob, that doesn't seem like a very good place to put your laundry, in a place where someone is eating." Without any comment or word of warning, he suddenly attacked me, leaned over the table and hit me some hard, stunning blows. I was trapped and almost helpless. By the time I could wiggle my way out, I was badly hurt. He was off in a fury. To me the situation was very bad. . . . I was trying to push him off, but then I saw it was hopeless and tried to fight, but I was already beaten. I was bleeding so much from the nose and mouth that the floor became slick with blood. I wanted to end this, picked up a milk bottle and was going to hit him on the head. But I didn't have the strength do it. He just kept beating me on and on and on. By then a man from next door came running in and tried to stop him. But he was too little. Somebody called the police. Suddenly Irwin slipped on the blood. I seized the opportunity to run downstairs. I ran down and he ran after me. We struggled a while but then I got away. I went next door to a friend's and spent the night. The next day I moved to a hotel nearby.

When word of Bob's savage assault got around, he found himself an outcast. "None of the fellows in the neighborhood would speak to him after that," wrote Halliburton. "One fellow told me that Bob came up to him a few days later and tried to start a conversation," wrote Halliburton. "But he just turned away."[27]

Having alienated his entire circle of friends, Bob proceeded to cut himself off from the man who had shown him such kindness and done so much to advance his career. Leaving Taft's studio, he took a job at a company called United Pressed Products, designing plastic novelty items for sixty dollars a week—twenty more than Taft had been paying him. Money had become increasingly important to Bob since he hoped to quit work entirely and live off his savings while perfecting his powers of visualization. He had a fantasy of becoming rich by mass-producing little plaster busts of celebrities—Rudolph Valentino, Greta Garbo, Jack Dempsey—and selling them for one dollar apiece. Recognizing the star power of America's most infamous gangster, he even put in a phone call to Al Capone, who had just been paroled after serving ten months on a concealed weapon conviction and was holed up in the Lexington Hotel. Bob, who hoped to persuade "Scarface Al" to pose for him, managed to get through to Capone, who politely refused, explaining that he was about to leave for his Miami estate.[28]

Bob's job at United Pressed Products ended in the usual way, after he beat up the factory foreman because (as Bob explained) "he wanted to boss me around and butt into my business." He then found similar work at a place called Silvestri Art Manufacturing but lasted only three weeks before being fired for starting a fight with a coworker. By the summer of 1930, the only job he could find that related even remotely to sculpting was carving tombstones for a Jewish stonecutter. (Bob, who prided himself on his open-mindedness, believed that "the Jews have some objectionable traits but they have some good traits, too, and if I were a Jew I would hold my head up as high as anybody.")[29]

Desperate for a way to put his artistic talents to better and more lucrative use, he decided that his prospects were much brighter in New York City. Telling Alice that he would write to her as soon as he was settled, he headed east by train, arriving in Manhattan in August 1930, just as the economy was slipping into chaos.

Part III

The Shadow of Madness

9

Depression

C ONTRARY TO POPULAR MYTH, the sidewalks around Wall Street were not littered with the bodies of suicidal stockbrokers who had flung themselves from the rooftops following the catastrophic events of late October 1929. In truth, though the market continued to fall until the second week in November, concerted efforts by the titans of finance put a halt to the slide. In the early months of 1930, the stock market turned upward again. Optimism was in the air. President Hoover pronounced the economy "fundamentally sound," while John D. Rockefeller proclaimed that the crisis was a strictly temporary state of affairs. "In the ninety-three years of my life, depressions have come and gone. Prosperity has always returned and will again."

In the end, however, it was the recovery that proved fleeting. By April 1930, it had fizzled out. In June, the stock market plunged again. By the time Robert Irwin arrived in New York City on August 8, the country was headed inexorably toward a decade of hardship and suffering. Before the year was out, the unemployment rate —though still nowhere near the staggering 25 percent it would hit at the depth of the Depression—had nearly tripled from its 1929 low of roughly 3 percent. Breadlines were growing throughout the country.[1]

At first, however, Bob had little trouble finding well-paying work. Within a few weeks of his arrival, he had been hired as an assistant at the Ettl Studios on West 13th Street, a sculpture-casting firm that specialized in enlarging small-scale plaster models into full-size bronze statues. He managed to hold onto the job until mid-January 1931, when he was discharged after a string of fights with other employees.

That same month, he was arrested for disorderly conduct after assaulting a cabbie. As Bob later told the story:

> There was a taxi driver and he was bigger than me and he was just a big pile of crap. We had an argument about the fare and he said to me, "You goddamned little pansy, I'll smack your face if you don't come across with the money." So I said, "Why the hell don't you try to?" We got out the cab and he hit me in the face and I only hit him once in the face and I was never so astonished in my life because he was so big and he just turned around and ran like holy Moses, all the time yelling, "Help!" Finally I caught him by the coat tails and he started yelling like hell. A cop came and he had me arrested.

After a night in jail, Bob was taken to Magistrate's Court, where the charge was dismissed.[2]

Soon afterward, he got a job at the venerable taxidermy shop of Thomas Rowland, a world-renowned figure in his field who had mounted many of the specimens in the American Museum of Natural History. By the time Bob went to work there, the business— now run by the founder's son, Elmer—dealt mostly in hunters' and fishermen's trophies, though it also did a steady business in deceased domestic pets.[3] Bob remained there for eight months, stuffing everything from parrots and pug dogs to moose heads and marlins.

It was during this period, sometime in April 1931, that Bob came across a book that had a decisive—and deeply unfortunate—impact on his life: Will Durant's 1926 best seller *The Story of Philosophy*. A highly readable survey aimed at a lay audience, the book devotes each of its nine main chapters to one of the giants of Western philosophy beginning with Plato and ending with Nietzsche. It was the section on Arthur Schopenhauer, however, that proved disastrous for Bob.

As Durant explains in his direct, clear-spoken way, the famously pessimistic Schopenhauer saw the world and everything in it as the product of a ceaseless, striving force he called *will*, whose primary manifestation in human behavior is the sexual impulse. Though we think of ourselves as rational beings, we are dominated, like every other living thing, by the blind, unconscious drive to perpetuate the species, at the inevitable cost of our own individual existence. "Reproduction is the ultimate purpose of every organism, and its strongest instinct; for only so can the will conquer death," writes Durant. "From the spider who is eaten up by the female he has just fertilized, or the wasp that devotes itself to gathering food for offspring it will never see, to the man who wears himself to ruin in an effort to feed and clothe and educate his children, every organism hastens, at maturity, to sacrifice itself to the task of reproduction."[4]

Schopenhauer's bleak view of existence—his insistence that we are the slaves of desires that can never achieve more than fleeting satisfaction, that suffering is the essence of life, that we inhabit the worst of all possible worlds, and that death is the only cure for the sickness of being alive—had a profound effect on artists and thinkers from Tolstoy and Turgenev to Wagner and Wittgenstein to Nietzsche and Freud. For Bob Irwin, the whole of Schopenhauer's philosophy boiled down to a single revelation. Since the will, the all-powerful life force, "uses every living organism for its purpose of prolonging the race," we would have enormous reserves of energy at our disposal if we managed to free ourselves from the compulsion to reproduce. In short, if the sex drive could only be "bottled up," it could be "utilized for higher purposes"—namely, the attainment of the "inconceivable power" of visualization.[5]

His first step was to break up with Alice. Though their relationship had remained platonic, it would certainly turn sexual once they were wed. He felt bad about giving her up, but the sacrifice was small relative to the ultimate reward—like "foregoing five dollars to get a million," as he put it. With all the energy of his pent-up sex drive devoted to visualization, he would finally break through the barrier of material reality and merge with the Universal Mind. When that happened, he would achieve powers that were nothing less than godlike: communication through mental telepathy; senses so acute that he could "detect odors on Mars"; the ability to transform himself into "anything in the universe—a jackrabbit, a dragon, a thunderstorm."[6]

That June, less than two months after he devoured Durant's book, he sent Alice a brusque letter calling off their engagement. A few weeks later, in early August, he lost his job at the taxidermy shop. The problem, for once, wasn't his violent temper but the economy. In the short time since he had gone to work there, business had fallen off so dramatically that the owner had no choice but to let him go.[7]

At first, Bob wasn't entirely unhappy about losing his job. Though it paid a decent salary, he had always regarded the work—arranging dead creatures into lifelike poses—as a poor use of his sculptural talents. It quickly became clear, however, that—with the Depression in fill swing—even taxidermy was a more creative occupation than any job he was likely to find.

Since coming to New York City, he had lived in a succession of Manhattan boardinghouses. Now, to husband his meager savings, he moved out to Brooklyn and found a cheap room in a flat owned by an elderly woman.[8] Abandoning his hopeless search for fulfilling work, he spent days at a time in his darkened room, practicing visualization. With the shades drawn and his eyes shut tight, he strained to transform mental images into material objects. The abject failure of these attempts plunged him into a severe depression, made worse by some news that had recently reached him from the West. Both his brothers had been arrested and sentenced to long terms in the Oregon State Penitentiary, Vidalin for car theft, Pember for armed robbery and assault with a dangerous weapon.

His deteriorating mental state was manifested by a host of physical symptoms. On September 5, 1931, he was treated for chronic abdominal pains in the outpatient department of Kings County Hospital in the East Flatbush neighborhood of Brooklyn. Three days later, he was back at the hospital, complaining of "headaches, disturbed vision, and a queer taste in throat." The examining physician noted that Bob had Hutchinson's teeth—notched, narrow-edged incisors, a common sign of congenital syphilis. Bob acknowledged that he had been diagnosed with the condition as far back as 1919. A Wassermann test, administered on September 9, came back positive. Informed of the result the following week, he was urged to undergo a regimen of salvarsan injections, the preferred pre-penicillin treatment for the disease. He ignored the advice.[9]

Back in his room, he began contemplating suicide. "I was living with a nice old lady in Brooklyn and she was just like a mother to me," he later explained to a psychiatric interviewer, Dr. Samuel Feigin. "I was so miserable and so sick that I thought I would commit suicide. But I wasn't going to kill myself. I thought I would kill her and go to the electric chair."[10]

On October 5, alarmed by his increasingly violent fantasies, he presented himself at the psychiatric ward of Kings County Hospital. Complaining that "his nerves were shot, that he could not concentrate, and that he had 'figured on suicide' by killing someone so that he would be hung," he was admitted to the ward, where his condition was described as "psychoneurosis, psychasthenic type" (a now-obsolete diagnosis referring to a disorder "characterized by phobias, obsessions, compulsions, or excessive anxiety"). Exactly three weeks later, on Monday, October 26, 1931, he was discharged as "improved" and sent to the Burke Foundation in White Plains, New York.[11]

Named after the mother of its benefactor, the Winifred Masterson Burke Relief Foundation (as it was officially known) was created with a $4 million endowment by the New York City merchant John Masterson Burke, a lifelong bachelor who made his fortune in the South America trade and—except for some piddling bequests to long-serving domestics and a handful of cousins—left it all to charity. Situated on sixty acres of rolling lawns and wooded groves, it was established as a convalescent care facility, its stated purpose to provide for "the relief of worthy men and women who, notwithstanding their willingness to support themselves, have become wholly or partly unable to do so by reason of sickness and misfortune." Work on the complex—twelve neoclassical buildings designed by the renowned architectural firm of McKim, Mead and White—began in 1912. Three years later, the first patients were admitted. By the time of Bob's arrival, it had treated nearly 100,000 men and women recuperating from various disorders, primarily heart attacks, pneumonia, ulcers, thyroid disease, and "borderline nervous, mental and other psychoneurotic conditions." During their stays, patients were offered "fresh air, sunlight, good food, quietness, mild recreational opportunities, and occupational therapy." Those who remained for extended periods were generally put to work for three to six hours a day at modest wages.[12]

During his nearly nine-month residence at Burke's, Bob was assigned a part-time job as a dining hall waiter. Working alongside him was his best friend at the institution, a fellow convalescent named Charles Smith. In later interviews with investigators seeking insight into Irwin's psychology, Chuck (as everyone called him) would recall his former friend's more notable peculiarities. "It seemed like he had a lot of nervous energy," Smith reported. "He would overdo anything that he undertook. He would talk about the benefit of deep breathing and in cold weather would run around without a coat. On two or three mornings I heard him singing loudly at 5 o'clock in the morning. He explained that he did it to develop his lungs."

These eccentricities, however, paled in comparison to his friend's "fanatical" theorizing. "He has ideas that are more abstruse than Einstein's," said Smith, who was subjected to endless harangues on Bob's latest obsession, his determination to funnel every ounce of his libido into visualization. For all his talk about "bottling up" his sexual energy, however, Bob seemed incapable of chastity. "He was always admiring women's breasts" and carrying on various flirtations, Smith recalled. "He used to sneak out with the girl patients all the time. One night, I came in rather late and I happened to see him having intercourse with one of the girls."[13]

Bob himself would later describe this episode to a psychiatric interviewer:

> There was a woman at the Burke Foundation. She said she was 32 but she looked older because her hair was gray. She was a waitress. She got to monkeying around with me one night down in the basement. She just began to act kittenish and I grabbed a hold of her breast and she started giggling. I took her out one night and we saw Greta Garbo in *Mata Hari* and then we had a chicken sandwich and coffee and after we had a milkshake and she paid for everything. When we got back I had intercourse with her right in the dining room.[14]

Afterward, Bob felt deeply debased by the incident. "I was so damned ashamed of myself for taking such an old-looking bitch," he said. Even more mortifying to him, however, was his inability to control his sex drive. The entire unfortunate incident only confirmed in him a resolution he had recently formed.

As he explained to Chuck Smith—who initially dismissed the whole business as just another of his friend's oddball ideas—Bob had decided that the best way to conserve his sexual energy for the sake of visualization was to chop off his penis.

The Gedeons

A CCORDING TO BOB, he left the Burke Foundation to get away from a couple of female employees who began to make life miserable for him after he rebuffed their sexual demands. "There were two girls there," he told an interviewer. "One I had intercourse with and she asked me to do it again and I said 'No,' and from that time on she hated me like bloody murder. The other girl I didn't do anything with and she hated me like bloody murder, too. There was so damn much trouble that I decided to leave." A report by a social worker, however, tells a different story. By July 1932, Bob had gotten into so many "violent quarrels with other patients" that he fled the convalescent home before his "unmanageable temper" landed him in serious trouble.[1]

Back in Manhattan, the only work he could find was washing dishes in the cafeteria of the New York Supreme Court building, a job so low-paying that he could barely afford a bed in a Bowery flop-house. Within a few weeks of his arrival, he was spending his nights in a cardboard shack in the homeless community that had sprung up in Central Park—one of the makeshift shantytowns known as

"Hoovervilles" that proliferated across the United States during the Great Depression.

A chance encounter with his friend Chuck Smith changed the course of his life. Smith, who had left Burke's a few weeks before Bob, was working as a short-order cook and renting a room in a brownstone belonging to the family of an acquaintance, a young woman named Ethel. Hearing of his friend's desperate circumstances, he offered to let Bob share his bedroom, free of charge, until he was back on his feet. Of course, Chuck would have to get his landlords' permission. Why didn't Bob come to the house that evening and Chuck would introduce him to the family? The address was 240 East 53rd Street. The family's name was Gedeon.

A Hungarian émigré who had come to New York City twenty-five years earlier, Joseph Gedeon was a slight, skinny fellow whose hollow cheeks, long, pointed nose, scraggly moustache, and piercing eyes—magnified by pince-nez spectacles—gave him the look of an unusually cunning rodent. Though capable of a certain dapperness, his preferred outfit at home and at work—baggy trousers, frayed suspenders, and an old buttoned undershirt—endowed him with a vague air of seediness, made more pronounced by the hand-rolled cigarette perpetually dangling from his lips.

He met his wife, the former Mary Caratsoki—Hungarian-born like himself—at a dance. They married after a brief courtship and moved to Astoria, Queens. A "Magyar beauty in her youth," Mary allowed herself to slide into a plump and dowdy middle age, though, even in her forties, she retained enough traces of her former loveliness to strike most observers as "still a comely person."[2] A small dowry she brought to the marriage, supplemented by the savings they managed to scrape together from Joe's assorted odd jobs —janitor, bartender, industrial painter—allowed them to purchase a run-down brownstone on East 53rd Street in 1929. Moving into the ground floor, they rented the other bedrooms to boarders and briefly operated a basement speakeasy that was quickly shut down by police. In the meantime, Joe—who had apprenticed in his youth to an upholsterer—opened his own shop a few blocks away.

There were two daughters in the family. The elder, twenty-year-old Ethel, affected a severe look—horn-rimmed eyeglasses, brunette hair brushed back into a tight bun—that did little to disguise her beauty. Three years earlier she had been swept off her feet by a smooth-talking cabbie named Louis Gramatecki and eloped with him. The marriage was swiftly annulled, evidently because Gramatecki proved impotent on their wedding night—"ice cold," as Ethel put it. Within twenty-four hours, she had returned to her parents' brownstone, while Gramatecki moved into his widowed mother's apartment, where, the following year, he "locked himself inside the kitchen, closed the windows and turned on the gas."³

Even lovelier than Ethel was her kid sister, Veronica—Ronnie, as everyone called her. At fifteen, she already exuded a lush sexuality that, in coming years, she would cheerfully exploit and that would ultimately turn her into an icon of tabloid titillation.

Meeting no objections from the Gedeons, Bob moved into Chuck Smith's room in the third week of October 1932. His efforts to suppress his sexual urges on behalf of his visualization had been markedly unsuccessful. He was plagued by lewd fantasies of Alice and found it impossible to keep from masturbating. The proximity of the two nubile Gedeon sisters only made matters worse. On Wednesday, October 27, less than a week after he moved in with the Gedeons, he resolved to end his torment once and for all.

That evening, he went into the toilet and, as he afterward described it, "put a strong rubber band around my prick to make it numb so it wouldn't hurt." Leaving the house, he "walked the streets, then went all the way to Brooklyn by subway in order to kill time to leave it on till my penis got numb so that I wouldn't feel the pain." It was one in the morning by the time he returned to the brownstone. Inside the bathroom, he took "a brand new Gillette razor blade" he had bought for the purpose and placed the edge against the base of his penis. Then he started to cut.⁴

Wertham

DESCRIBING HIS FAILED ATTEMPT at "self-emasculation,"
Bob later explained that he'd been forced to stop when the
pain became too intense. "On the outside of my prick, I didn't feel it
at all. When I got to the inner cords—Jesus Christ, it hurt so damn
much, you have no idea. I kept on trying just a little bit at a time until I got to the place I couldn't stand it."

With the rubber band tourniquet still binding the base of his penis, Bob made his way to the Bellevue Hospital emergency room, arriving shortly before 2:30 in the morning. Giving his name as "James
Adamson," he calmly explained what he had tried to do and asked
the young night intern to finish the job. Utterly nonplussed, the intern bandaged the cut and advised Bob "to come back the next day."

Another slightly older physician was on duty when Bob returned
just after daybreak. Ignoring Bob's pleas that he complete the amputation, the doctor snipped off the rubber band with surgical scissors,
sutured the wound—an "ugly, deep laceration" requiring seven
stitches—applied antiseptic dressing, and had him admitted to the
psychiatric ward.[1] He would remain there until March 17, 1933.

During his five-month stay at Bellevue, Bob was examined by some of the city's most eminent psychiatrists, including Drs. Menas Gregory, head of the hospital's psychiatric division, and Walter Briehl, an acolyte of Wilhelm Reich's and, later in his career, a pioneering practitioner of group therapy. The physician who spent the most time with him, however—and with whom he formed the deepest and most enduring bond—was Fredric Wertham.[2]

At the time he first treated Bob Irwin, Wertham was still twenty years away from becoming the boogeyman that, in certain circles, he remains to this day. He attained his enduring notoriety in 1954 with the publication of his best seller *Seduction of the Innocent*, a luridly illustrated attack on comic books as the leading cause of criminal behavior in children. In a decade when, according to one national poll, juvenile delinquency ranked higher on the list of public concerns than open-air atom bomb testing, Wertham's screed helped incite a nationwide campaign against the comic book industry, culminating in a Congressional investigation that drove dozens of publishers out of business and forced the rest to adopt a strict (and, in the minds of most fans, ruinous) censorship code.[3] To comic book devotees then and now, "Dr. Werthless" (as he was caricatured in the pages of *Mad* magazine) was nothing but a witch-hunting zealot, stirring up a panic among the parents of America for his own self-promoting reasons.[4]

That Wertham has earned such a nefarious reputation in the cultural history books seems sadly unfair, since—far from being an unscrupulous fearmonger in the mold of Joe McCarthy—he was one of the city's most liberal and enlightened psychiatrists. However misguided his crusade against the comics, it was motivated by a passionate concern with the psychological and social roots of criminal violence.

Born and raised in Nuremberg, Bavaria, Friedrich Ignanz Wertheimer (as he was originally named) developed an early love for British culture during summertime visits to relatives in England. He was especially enamored of the novels of Charles Dickens and deeply impressed by their power to stir the conscience of the public and in-spire social reform. As he later told an interviewer, Dickens taught him a lesson he never forgot—"that by expressing oneself properly, one can affect lives."[5]

Following a year at the University of Munich, where he began his medical studies, Friedrich left Germany and enrolled in King's College London. His schooling was interrupted by the outbreak of the Great War. As a German national, he was sent to an internment camp, where he worked in the infirmary and spent his free hours reading texts on psychology. When the war ended, he returned to Germany to complete his medical studies, receiving his MD from the University of Würzburg in 1921. He interned briefly in Munich with Emil Kraepelin—the psychiatric pioneer who devised the stan-dard system for the classification of mental disorders—and, during postgraduate study in Vienna, paid a memorable visit to Sigmund Freud. Not long afterward, in August 1922, the twenty-seven-year-old Wertheimer left Europe for good, emigrating to America to work with Professor Adolf Meyer, director of the Phipps Psychiatric Clinic at Johns Hopkins University in Baltimore.

It was during Friedrich's years in Baltimore that he became a nat-uralized U.S. citizen and changed his name to the marginally more American-sounding Fredric Wertham. In other ways, too, this pe-riod proved the most transformative of his life. Under the influence of Meyer—who stressed the "importance of the home, the school, and the community in shaping the development of young minds"[6]—he began to look beyond traditional Freudian theory, with its em-phasis on infantile sexuality, and to focus on the larger social forces that help shape the personality (an approach that would ultimately lead to his concern with media violence). As one of the only psychi-atrists in the city willing to treat African-Americans, he formed a close association with the legendary attorney Clarence Darrow, who frequently called upon him to examine and testify on behalf of indi-gent black defendants. A highly cultured man with a lifelong passion for art and literature (his correspondents included George Bernard Shaw, Thomas Mann, and W. Somerset Maugham, and in later years, he counted Arthur Miller and Richard Wright among his friends), he became part of H. L. Mencken's Saturday Night Club, an informal gathering of two dozen members who met weekly to play music, dine on traditional German fare, and drink home-brewed beer. Among his patients at Phipps was Zelda Fitzgerald, several of whose watercolor paintings would eventually form part of his impressive art collection.[7]

Wertham remained at Phipps until December 1931, when he moved to New York to assume the position of senior psychiatrist at Bellevue Hospital. That same month—following years of concerted effort by a committee composed of jurists, criminologists, and mental health experts—New York City passed a law establishing a psychiatric clinic for the Court of General Sessions, at that time Manhattan's major criminal court. At a "moment when American courts, prisons, and asylums were beginning to look to psychiatry for scientific explanations of criminal activity,"[8] the clinic—staffed by members of Bellevue's psychiatric department—was responsible for evaluating the mental condition of all convicted felons and providing a report to the presiding judge that would assist him in determining an appropriate sentence. When the clinic went into operation on January 4, 1932, Fredric Wertham was one its three full-time members.[9]

Though he had been involved in various criminal cases in Baltimore, providing assistance to Clarence Darrow, it was his work for the new Court of General Sessions clinic that altered the course of Wertham's career and turned him into one of the nation's leading forensic psychiatrists. Within a few years, he had become a familiar name to readers of the tabloids as an expert witness in some of the most sensational trials of the day, including that of the cannibal pedophile Albert Fish.

To Wertham, the sixty-five-year-old Fish—who had spent his entire adult life preying on children and practicing "every known sexual perversion and some perversions never heard of before"—was manifestly insane, and he was stunned when the jury returned a guilty verdict and the old man was sentenced to death. In a subsequent meeting with Governor Herbert Lehman to plead for commutation, Wertham argued that, with Fish spared from death and committed to an institution, science would have a chance to study the man's twisted psychology and learn something that might help prevent future crimes against children. "Psychiatry is advanced enough," he insisted, "that with proper examination such a man as Fish can be detected and confined before the perpetration of these outrages."[10]

This argument (which failed to sway the governor) reflected not only a larger trend in 1930s America—the growing belief in the power of psychiatry to heal society's ills—but also Wertham's personal and unabashed idealism. Rejecting the view that humans are an innately savage species, he clung to the conviction that, by eliminating the social conditions that gave rise to criminal behavior, murder itself could be abolished—that "the ways of violence will eventually be replaced by reason."[11]

Despite a crushingly heavy case load—his work for the Court of General Sessions alone required him to evaluate roughly five hundred prisoners a year—Wertham made time to conduct "practically daily sessions" with Bob Irwin. For various reasons, Wertham found the younger man a fascinating figure. Besides his personable qualities—he initially impressed Wertham as "a nice, frank-looking young man who spoke with emphasis and conviction"—Bob presented the psychiatrist with a rare clinical opportunity. While the notion of a "castration complex" loomed large in Freudian theory, Wertham could think of no cases of "actual attempts at self-emasculation" in the annals of psychoanalysis.[12] That Bob was a sculptor made him even more intriguing to the psychiatrist. Not only was Wertham a connoisseur and collector of fine art but he also had recently married a sculptor himself—Florence Hesketh, a Maine-born, Wellesley-educated artist whose work would eventually be exhibited in some of the country's leading museums.[13]

For weeks after his admission to Bellevue's "psycho ward," Irwin persisted in his efforts to have his penis cut off. At one point, a young surgical intern informed Wertham that Irwin had called him aside and "asked me to do a great favor for him, namely, to remove his penis. He told me he knew a doctor who could do it properly. He said if I didn't, when he got out—even after a stay in a state institution —he'd find someone, even a man on the street, and pay him to amputate his penis."[14]

During their lengthy psychoanalytic sessions—held in a cubicle, with a female stenographer named Moore transcribing their exchanges—Wertham did his best to convince Bob of the impracticality of his plan. "When once the penis is removed that does not necessarily mean that the sexual libido disappears," said Wertham. "As a matter of fact, one cannot tell whether the sexual urge may not come back in the form of some undesirable perverse acts when the normal sex act cannot be executed any more." Prisoners in Sing Sing who "cannot have intercourse with women" don't lose their "sexual desire," he explained. On the contrary, "their brains are filled with sexual things. From what I've been told, a large percentage of them become homosexual or act homosexual in jail. Have you considered that?"

Bob conceded that, while he did in fact worry that "I will become a cocksucker," he was "willing to take the chance." The potential benefits of cutting off his penis far outweighed that risk.

Where had Bob gotten the idea in the first place? asked Wertham. Had he "ever heard or read about anybody doing what he had attempted to do?"

"No," Bob replied with a distinct note of pride. "It was completely my own grand invention."

Pressed about the supposed benefits he would derive from such an operation, Bob treated Wertham to one of his extended disquisitions on visualization and the half-baked Schopenhauerian ideas he had formed after reading Will Durant. Without his penis, he explained, he would be able to bottle up enough psychic energy "to solve the riddle of existence."

"I want to get my mental radio running in such a way that I can get in complete touch with the Universal Mind," he declared. "It sounds as fantastic as can be, but it isn't."

"It doesn't sound fantastic," Wertham replied. "It *is* fantastic."

"Okay," said Bob with a dismissive shrug.[15]

Seeing that there was no point in mounting a logical argument against these deeply bizarre beliefs, Wertham turned to the classic techniques of Freudian psychoanalysis, leading Bob "to talk about his dreams, his daydreams, his earliest memories."[16] From these lengthy sessions of free association, Wertham was able to get a general picture of Bob's family history. He learned about Pember and Vidalin, both now doing time in the Oregon State Penitentiary, and about Bob's lifelong sense of inferiority to his tough-guy siblings, his sense that he wasn't man enough to measure up to such "commanding" figures. He heard about the charismatic evangelist B. H. Irwin, "a plain lowdown hypocrite" (according to his son) who — in one typical episode — "was given nine hundred dollars to start a new church and went out and spent it all on women."

Unsurprisingly, given the preoccupations of Freudian theory, Wertham pushed Irwin to talk at length about his mother, particularly after Bob shared a tidbit about her child-rearing practices.

"My mother read books prior to my birth about how to raise children and to acquaint them with sex knowledge rather than let it get to us in a smutty way," Bob explained. "They were about how a mother should behave in front of her children so that it wouldn't be a mysterious thing, and she used to bathe in front of us and we could see from the waist up."

"Do you remember seeing your mother's breasts?" asked Wertham.

"Absolutely. Oh, she had nice breasts. They were neither too large nor too small. They didn't hang or anything and she was quite old at that time. She was about forty-five."

"And how old were you at the time you saw your mother's breasts?"

"Oh, about nine."

Perhaps, Wertham ventured, Bob's "later interest in breasts" could be traced to this childhood experience. "Tell me," said Wertham, "what do you like to do with breasts? Are you interested in the nipple itself? Do you have fantasies of doing what a baby does?"

"I know what you're aiming at," said Bob, who had picked up a smattering of Freud in the course of his omnivorous reading. "You're aiming at the Oedipus complex."

Though he staunchly denied that the sight of his naked mother had aroused conflicted sexual feelings in him, Bob admitted to a deep ambivalence toward her. "I can't understand it for the world, but even though I would do anything for my mother, I don't love her," he said in a voice thick with emotion. "I'm ashamed to say it, but it's so. The only explanation I have is this. When I was from this high up, I was stuffed so full of religion that for years I was an agnostic. I completely turned against it. I hated the religion."

Here, he burst into such violent sobs that he was unable to continue for several moments. "My mother is a wonderful woman," he said after regaining a measure of control. "I don't know how the devil I can feel that way about her but I realize that for the first time in my life not only that I don't love my mother but I hated her all my life."

Wertham had no doubt that Bob was in the grip of a severe mother complex. Equally striking to the psychiatrist was the young man's fear of being perceived as effeminate. "Whenever I went to a new school I was always considered to be a sissy," Bob related. "I don't know why they called me a sissy. The only way I could convince them out of it was to knock the tar out of them." As Wertham delved more deeply into Bob's past, it became clear that his patient had a long history of near-homicidal outbursts directed at men who had questioned his masculinity.

Given the act that had brought Bob to Bellevue—the attempted self-amputation of his male member—Wertham could not help but wonder if the young man's inordinate sensitivity to being branded a sissy was a classic case of "reaction formation": an exaggerated form of behavior concealing an unacceptable, diametrically opposite impulse (as when, to use the most obvious example, a man engages in violent acts of gay-bashing to protect himself against his own latent homosexuality). When Wertham explained this principle to Bob and suggested that his actions might mask "a deep, underlying desire to be a woman," the younger man conceded that the interpretation made sense from a psychoanalytic point of view but insisted that "in my case it is not true."

Gradually Bob began to show signs of improvement. In a session that took place on January 26, 1933—exactly three months after he was admitted to Bellevue—he recounted a joke he had first heard two years earlier.

"I thought of a dirty story that fits my case," he told Wertham. "There was a Scotchman, an Irishman, and a Jew and they didn't have anything to do, so they raped a woman. They got in court and the judge said, 'We will cut your prick off, but just to show I'm a regular fellow, I'll give you a break and let you choose the way.' The Scotchman says, 'Hell, get a hatchet and chop it off.' The Jew insisted upon the finest doctor and anesthesia. The Irishman says, 'Well, if you don't mind, you can just suck mine off.'"

By the time he reached the punch line, Irwin was already laughing so hard that he could barely finish the joke. Wertham waited until his cackling subsided, then asked, "Why does it fit your case?"

"Well," said Bob, "it doesn't really fit my case, only I wanted to cut my penis off, too."

Though Wertham was distinctly unamused, he thought it significant not only that Bob was able to joke about what he had done but also that, in speaking of his desire to cut off his penis, he used the past tense—a sign, as the psychiatrist saw it, that his patient's obsession with castrating himself was beginning to "loosen up."

That impression was confirmed in the following days. Discussing "the idea of self-emasculation" in the first week of February, Bob confessed that he was "really a little shaken in my belief in it. I don't have that inner determination to have it done at all costs." Now, he was willing to settle for a far less radical procedure: surgical sterilization by "ligation of the seminal cords, as is done to sex criminals in California."

Before long, he had given up even this fantasy. "During the last few weeks, he has never mentioned the idea of amputation or operating at all," Wertham recorded in his case notes in early March. By then, Bob had made such progress that Wertham—no longer afraid that his patient might attempt another act of self-mutilation—"permitted him, under the supervision of an attendant, to use sculpture tools."[17] Bob now spent much of his time on "serious efforts to improve his sculpturing and drawing." Eager to wean him from his bizarre obsession with visualization, Wertham encouraged him to abandon his preferred method—studying a book or magazine illustration, then replicating it from memory—and draw directly from life. When a few of the older, married nurses saw his work, they asked if he would be willing to make small portrait busts of their children. Bob agreed, charging them a modest fee and working from photographs supplied by the mothers.

Still, for all the strides he had made, Bob clearly had a long way to go on the road to recovery. On two occasions he threw the entire ward into an uproar when he flew into a rage over trivial provocations, beating up a medical student who "touched a clay model on which he'd been working" and attacking an orderly "over some question of whether or not he should be shaved."

And then there was the incident with the stenographer, Miss Moore. A pretty young woman, she had been impressed by Bob's sculptures and commissioned him to make a little bust of her. Wertham saw the piece when it was nearly completed and thought it "beautifully done." Not long afterward, when Wertham arrived for one of his sessions with Bob, he found the young sculptor in a savage mood. Miss Moore, Bob bitterly related, had "backed out of the deal on account of money." After agreeing to his original asking price, she had "tried to vamp me into doing it for nothing." When Bob offered to lower his fee, she had given him the go-ahead. Then, just as he was putting the finishing touches on the piece, she informed him that she couldn't afford it and was canceling their arrangement.

"And how does that make you feel?" Wertham inquired.

Bob considered the question for a moment, then answered with a vehemence that took Wertham aback.

"I'd like to cut the titties off the damned bitch," said Bob.

Bug in a Bottle

O N MARCH 17, 1933, after five months as an inmate of Bellevue's "psycho ward," Bob Irwin was transferred to Rockland
State Hospital in upstate New York.

Situated on a six-hundred-acre "rural campus" in the hamlet of
Orangeburg, twenty miles north of Manhattan, Rockland was regarded as "among the best-planned psychiatric hospitals in the
world" when it took in its first patients in February 1931. By the end
of the decade, however, this supposedly model institution had de-
generated into a grim, prison-like asylum, known to its inmates as
the "House of Despair."[1]

In early 1938, after posing as a mental patient and having himself
committed to Rockland for several weeks, Allen Bernard, a reporter
for the *New York Journal-American*, published a series of scathing,
page-one exposés on the nightmarish conditions at the hospital: The
endless hours locked in a dayroom with seventy-five other men and
no diversions besides a single checkerboard, a partial deck of cards,
and a broken player piano. The barely edible meals and forced feed-
ings with a nasogastric tube for recalcitrant eaters. The medieval

"treatments" with electroshock therapy, Metrazol injections (to in-
duce convulsions), and hours-long immersions in cold, constantly
running baths. The brutal beatings by sadistic orderlies. The acci-
dental lethal overdoses administered by careless nurses. The hopelessly inadequate psychiatric care meted out to the 4,700 inmates
who—in a hospital staffed with thirty full-time physicians—could
expect to see a doctor only once a month. A few years after Bernard's
series caused an uproar, the asylum gained even greater notoriety
with the publication of Mary Jane Ward's bestseller *The Snake Pit,* a
thinly disguised account of her hellish experiences at Rockland following a nervous breakdown.[2]

The records of Bob's life at Rockland have, by and large, been lost
to time. From the few surviving documents, we know that, owing
partly to his willingness to perform menial chores—making beds,
mopping floors, cleaning windows—he was afforded certain privileges. Unlike the typical male patient who (as Allen Bernard discovered) slept in communal wards with seventeen other men—"manic
depressives, dementia praecox patients, paranoiacs, sex maniacs, and
syphilitics in advanced stages of the disease"[3]—Bob was given a
room of his own. Thanks to Wertham's influence, he was also encouraged to pursue his sculpting as part of his occupational therapy and even permitted to use sharp-edged modeling tools. As in
Bellevue, he took commissions from staff members for small portrait
busts of themselves and their family members and managed to squir-
rel away more than fifty dollars for future use.[4]

Periodically, he exploded in one of his uncontrolled outbursts of
rage. One newspaper reported that Bob "was in no less than twenty-
five fights during his stay" at Rockland and that "even the attendants were afraid of him."[5] Following a particularly vicious assault
on a fellow patient in early June, he was briefly banished to the hospital's "Siberia"—Building 37, the violent ward, where, in violation
of a state law that required "that a patient be taken out of restraint
at least once every two hours," inmates were routinely kept in strait-
jackets for weeks at a time.[6]

He also made repeated escape attempts. In late August, he got as far as the bus station in Orangeburg before being picked up by orderlies sent out in search of him. A few months later, on November 17, he made it all the way to Manhattan. Once there, he proceeded directly to 44 Gramercy Park—the home of Dr. Fredric Wertham.

Bob had no trouble locating Wertham's apartment. For months, the psychiatrist had been conducting a cordial correspondence with his former patient, using his personal letterhead stationery. Wertham had even sent some snapshots of himself in response to a request from Bob, who planned to make a portrait bust of the doctor and present it to him as a gift.[7]

Apologizing for showing up so unexpectedly, Bob chatted aimlessly for a while before getting around to the point. He had run away from Rockland, he explained, because he "felt too restricted" there and was hoping that Wertham might "help him get work in a convalescent place." After spending some time convincing Bob that he would be better off back at the asylum, Wertham, who was scheduled to attend a psychiatric meeting that evening, asked him "whether he would go along with me and let me present him to the doctors as an instructive case which could be of benefit to other patients." Though Bob had mixed feelings about being treated "like a bug in a bottle," he consented.

Seated on the platform beside Wertham, Bob, who seemed cheerful to the point of giddiness once he found himself in the spotlight, readily fielded questions from the audience of about sixty psychiatrists, including a few of the city's most prominent psychoanalysts. He spoke openly and without hesitation about the most intimate details of his sex life, impressing the doctors with his candor. Asked about his attempted self-castration, however, he gave contradictory replies. At first, he declared that he had completely abandoned the idea. "I have come down to common sense. I realize I've been sick for years and that these ideas are impractical." At a later point, however, he suggested that, under certain circumstances, he might revert to his former behavior. "My whole mind was warped. If I get up against it again, I'll be that way again."

With Bob still present on the platform, the psychiatrists turned to a diagnosis of his case. After some debate, most concluded that Bob suffered from hebephrenia, a subtype of schizophrenia characterized "by foolish mannerisms, senseless laughter, delusions, and regressive behavior," and—like all forms of the disease—not susceptible to psychotherapy. Wertham, however, was inclined to disagree. He had come to believe that Bob was suffering from a mental condition heretofore unrecognized by the psychiatric community.

The essence of the syndrome was a "state of high emotional stress," caused by a profound psychological conflict or traumatic event in the patient's past. Eventually, the person becomes possessed by the delusion that he must commit an act of extreme violence as "the only way out." A definite plan takes shape in his mind. After a period of resistance, the urge to violence becomes overwhelming. Once he has carried out the act, his inner tension is relieved and he assumes "a superficial appearance of normality." At this stage, there is the potential for full "insight and recovery, with the reestablishment of emotional equilibrium." Without such "an inner adjustment," however—best obtained through psychotherapy—the patient is almost certain to experience a recurrence of the disease, "during which he is capable of anything."

At that point, Wertham was still in the process of refining his theory. Eventually, he would claim to have discovered a new "clinical entity" and would give it a name. Borrowing a term from Swiss psychiatrist Hans W. Maier, he would call it the *catathymic crisis*.[8]

The meeting lasted late into the evening. Afterward, Bob was taken to Bellevue's admitting office. He spent the night in the hospital before being bused back to Rockland the following morning.

He remained at the state asylum for another six months. For the most part, he was "quiet and cooperative," though he was still subject to periodic fits of unprovoked fury. On one occasion, for example, several recent graduates from the NYU medical school were visiting Rockland. Among them was a young doctor named Jeremiah Last. As they toured the facilities, they came upon Irwin working on a piece of sculpture. Struck by its craftsmanship, Last offered Bob a compliment. The words were barely out of his mouth when Bob, flying into a rage, threw down his tools and hurled himself with a roar at the startled doctor.

"I backed away," Last later recounted, "and it took several of my fellow students and an attendant to restrain Irwin. He kept roaring and shouting. He seemed to have unbelievable strength for a man of his build."[9]

The piece that Last had paused to admire was a plaster statue of a "strange faun-like" creature with the torso of a young girl, the "shaggy shanks of a mountain goat," and a face that bore a striking resemblance to Bob's. It was done so artistically that hospital authorities had it gilded and placed on permanent display at the entrance to the main building. In subsequent years, newspapers would make much of the bizarre piece as symptomatic of "the tormented mind of its creator." In an era when even the average tabloid reader was culturally literate enough to recognize the name of the ancient Greek satyr-god of the forests, punning headlines would describe it as a self-portrait of the artist as a "Psycho-Pan."[10]

Deemed "much improved" by his supervising psychiatrist, Dr. George Ettling, Bob was discharged from Rockland on May 16, 1934. Heading straight for Manhattan, he took a room at a cheap boardinghouse on West 66th Street. One week later, he paid another visit to Dr. Wertham. Though Wertham agreed that Bob's stay at the hospital "had evidently had a good effect on him," he was concerned about the sculptor's continued obsession with visualization and urged his former patient to keep in touch with him.[11]

Living off the money he had earned at Rockland from his artwork, Bob searched for a job that would utilize his sculpting skills. In early June, he was hired as an assistant by Gilbert Maggi, owner of Chelsea Realistic Products, a commercial sculpting firm on West 28th Street specializing in plaster display items. By all accounts, Bob was an exceptionally skilled and efficient worker and "was soon turning out little commercial statues faster than his employer."[12] With a seemingly secure job and a little extra money in his pocket, Bob decided to move out of his dingy room on the Upper West Side and into more congenial quarters. In early July, he returned to 240 East 53rd Street—the home of the Gedeon family.

The Snake Woman

NEARLY TWO YEARS had passed since Robert Irwin had last set eyes on Ronnie Gedeon. During that time, she had blossomed into a stunning young woman of seventeen. Headstrong and (as the tabloids never tired of reporting) "boy crazy," she had dropped out of high school after three semesters to pursue a career as a beautician, enrolling in one of the franchised "academies" operated under the name of A. B. Moler. A renowned figure in American tonsorial history, Moler had opened the world's first barber college in Chicago in 1893 and authored a number of standard textbooks in his field, including the 1911 *Manual of Beauty Culture*, the bible of the beautician's trade. His course of study, however—which encompassed not only the intricacies of the marcel wave, the cable twist, and the bob curl but also the treatment of various scalp diseases and facial blemishes—proved too rigorous for Ronnie, and after six months she quit the school, joining the ever-growing ranks of the unemployed.[1]

Out late virtually every night with a different boy, she clashed constantly with her Hungarian-born father, who railed against "this rotten American system where children laugh at their parents and start running wild before they cut their teeth."[2] On several occasions, after she brazenly ignored her curfew and returned home tipsy with drink, he resorted to corporal punishment.

For her part (as she confided to her diary), Ronnie saw her father as "spineless and irresponsible" and felt a desperate need to escape from the household. She found it in the spring of 1933, just after her sixteenth birthday, when she eloped with Bobby Flower, a family friend whose parents ran a bowling alley on East 15th Street. The marriage was annulled within months, and by early 1934, Ronnie was living back home. Shortly afterward—fed up with his daughter's disobedience and the way his wife always "took Ronnie's side instead of mine"—Joseph Gedeon moved out of the apartment and took up residence in a cubbyhole space in his upholstery shop on 34th Street.[3] He had recently decamped when Robert Irwin came to live at the Gedeons' home, a dilapidated three-and-a-half-story brownstone on East 53rd Street, divided into a basement apartment for the family and upstairs rooms for the boarders.

Bob was not immune to Ronnie's physical charms, which—since she often lounged around the premises in dishabille—he had ample opportunity to observe. To his mind, however, she was nothing but "a beautiful, brainless, fluffy thing."[4] He was far more attracted to her demure, sober-minded older sister, Ethel.

Following her own brief, ill-fated teenage marriage, Ethel had returned to school, taking a secretarial extension course at Hunter College in Long Island City. Having mastered the principles of stenography, she soon found a job at *Vanity Fair* magazine. Quick-witted, industrious, and possessed of a natural elegance, she was promoted within months to private secretary to Helen Norden, the magazine's managing editor (and mistress of its publisher, Condé Nast). Before long, Norden had grown so fond of Ethel that she began to invite her "along on her prowls through Café Society," where the working-class young woman mingled starry-eyed with "stage stars, society figures and a number of artists."[5]

From the moment of her annulment, Ethel had been courted

by a longtime acquaintance, an aspiring lawyer named Joe Kudner. Though fond of him, she found herself intrigued by the good-looking young sculptor who had returned to board with her family. Their relationship began in earnest when Bob came downstairs from his attic room one Monday evening to pay his weekly rent of four dollars and found Ethel alone in the living room of the Gedeons' high-ceilinged English basement.

"These come hard nowadays," she said with a rueful smile as he handed her the crumpled bills.

"They do now," he said. "But mark my words—my turn will come. I'm down now, but I'll be on top someday."

"By your sculpting work?" said Ethel.

"Certainly by my sculpturing work," Bob exclaimed. "I'm on the track of something right now that will make me eternally famous—I call it visualization."

It was, as Ethel later explained, the first—though by no means the last—time she heard of "this idée fixe of Irwin's."[6]

Impressed by some small pieces he had brought back with him from Rockland, she agreed to let him sculpt her head. While she posed for him in her living room, they engaged in lively (if largely one-sided) conversation about art, religion, and other of Bob's obsessive topics. In the following weeks, she accompanied him on a jaunt to the Metropolitan Museum, where he showed her his favorite statue, a full-size plaster reproduction of the Colleoni of Verocchio —an enormous equestrian statue depicting the Venetian mercenary-soldier Bartolomeo Colleoni, accoutered for battle and astride a huge stallion.

Steering "me past everything else in the West Hall—'that drivel,' he called it—Irwin told me to stop at the foot of the pedestal of the figure," Ethel recalled. "He made me look at it first dead on and close up." Then—speaking as if he himself had been to Italy and viewed the original monument—he continued: "This is the way it hits you in the open place in Venice, where it is gilded bronze. You come up right under it and get the feeling that horse is going to trample your brains out. And the feeling carries right in up to that head, as you step back." After pausing for a moment to contemplate the statue, he said in a tone that startled Ethel with its vehemence: "Just look at the way it flows. Why, it's more alive than nine-tenths of the fools who glance at it with dead eyes as they walk past and see nothing but a guy on horseback."[7]

Dazzled by his seeming erudition and his all-consuming devotion to art, Ethel, as she later admitted, was happy to play pupil to his master.[8] For his part, Bob "fell for her like a ton of bricks." Before long, he had convinced himself that Ethel was his soul mate and ideal visualization partner—a new and improved "edition" of his former fiancée, the Chicago dancehall girl Alice Ryan.[9]

Bob's fervent attentions to Ethel did not go unnoticed by Veronica. "Bobby is certainly making a play for my sister," Ronnie noted in her journal in late July. "I think he is out of his mind. He will never marry her if I have anything to do with it. I am going to take the matter up with mother. She will help me put the kibosh on it."[10] A few days later, Mary Gedeon—who knew of Bob's troubled history as a psychiatric patient but regarded him as "a decent fellow, honest in his personal and financial dealings, and pitifully alone in the world"—took him aside and, in the most tactful way possible, informed him that she "was anxious that Ethel have nothing to do with" him. Hastening to assure him that she herself had only the friendliest feelings toward him, she explained that she was simply thinking of her daughter's long-range comfort and security—that "she wanted Ethel to make a rich marriage."[11]

Bob was undeterred. Since his release from Rockland, he had been keeping in sporadic touch with Dr. Wertham, sometimes by phone, sometimes in person. In early August, he sought out the psychiatrist at Bellevue and spent the entire visit rhapsodizing about Ethel. When he declared his intention to marry her, Wertham "protested that he was acting too rashly." Much as he valued the doctor's opinions, however, Bob left the meeting unshaken in his resolve.[12]

Shortly afterward, while walking with Ethel along the 53rd Street pier, he blurted out a proposal. Ethel—who (so she claimed) had never felt romantically interested in Bob and had tired of his endless talk of visualization—gently broke the news that, while she hoped the two could remain friends, she had decided to become engaged to Joe Kudner. Bob was devastated. "I just went crazy," he confided in his diary. Two weeks later, he returned to the same East River pier, intending to drown himself. There were so many boats in the water, however, that he changed his mind, assuming that someone would come to his rescue.[13]

Another blow fell in October when he was fired from his job at Chelsea Realistic Products. Since his rejection by Ethel, Bob had become increasingly sullen—"a surly devil," as his boss, Gilbert Maggi described him. Fed up with his young employee's "moodiness," Maggi informed him one morning that he was letting Bob go. After handing him a severance check for twenty-five dollars, Maggi walked to the rear of the studio to fetch Bob's sculpting tools. As he was gathering up the implements, he suddenly "had the feeling that there was something behind him. Turning, he saw Irwin standing there with an insane glint in his eyes and, in his right hand, a meat cleaver that had sometimes been used to chip plaster."

"What the hell are you doing, Bob?" said Maggi.

"I'm going to split your head right down the middle," Bob snarled. "Then I'm going to fry your brains and have them for supper. You won't miss them. You never use them anyway."

Raising the cleaver, he took a swing at Maggi, who somehow managed to dodge the blow. "Galvanized into life-and-death action," the older man reached for "a pot of wet plaster nearby" and hurled it at Bob, hitting him in the face. As Bob "reeled drunkenly," Maggi got him in a bear hug, wrestled him out of the studio, tossed him onto the street, and locked the door.

"This score isn't settled!" shouted Irwin from the sidewalk. "I'll get you for this!"

But Maggi never saw Bob Irwin again.[14]

Over the next few months, Bob—like millions of his countrymen—found himself in desperate financial straits. With the unemployment rate near its Depression-era peak of almost 25 percent, he was forced to take whatever menial jobs he could find: elevator operator, coat-room attendant, dishwasher. None lasted more than a few weeks. By December, with his meager savings gone, he applied for Home Relief. On the day before Christmas, he received a welfare check for $19.10. Still obsessing over Ethel and plagued by suicidal thoughts, he visited Wertham, who "advised him as forcibly as I could to return to the state hospital." Shortly afterward, on January 11, Bob voluntarily recommitted himself to Rockland, where—with the exception of one abortive attempt to return to society—he would remain for nearly two years.[15]

After suffering so many setbacks and frustrations during his six-month sojourn in New York City, Bob saw Rockland as a kind of refuge—a place where "life would be easier for him" and he "could work on his sculpture without being bothered." Initially, however, he had trouble readjusting to institutional living. He found the confinement "more galling than ever" and was thrown into "despondency and despair" by his surroundings. "It is hard to live with people in an insane asylum," he bemoaned in his journal. "The diseased, the degenerate, the violent are my mess mates."[16] His mood grew even darker when, in late June, word reached him that Ethel had married Joe Kudner a few weeks earlier in a small ceremony in Manhattan.

It wasn't long before his "combative spirit" (as he euphemistically described his dangerously volcanic temper) got him sent to the violent ward. Drugged, straitjacketed, and strapped to a bed, he endured several "weary months of discipline and deprivation" before being returned to the general population. Apart from one other incident—when he was accused of "a sexual lapse or indulgence" with a young female patient—he remained generally quiet and cooperative for the remainder of his stay and was permitted the freedom of the grounds.[17]

Bob proved to be such a model patient that he was not only allowed to use sharp sculpting tools but also encouraged to teach a class in clay modeling at the newly opened children's pavilion, a facility for youngsters with "juvenile conduct disorders." At the dedication of the pavilion, attended by Governor Herbert Lehman and other state luminaries, several of Bob's pieces were on display, including a portrait bust of the governor himself, who—as Bob proudly noted in his diary—"took much interest in my sculpture."[18]

Another state official much taken with Bob's work that day was Clarence Low, president of the board of Rockland State Hospital and treasurer of the Democratic State Committee. Struck by a small bust Bob had made of President Roosevelt, Low arranged to purchase it for fifty dollars and have it displayed at the Democratic headquarters. To show his appreciation, Bob offered to make a bust of Low, who sent him several photographs to use as references.[19]

Though so comfortably ensconced in the asylum that he was not eager to leave, Bob was discharged on July 15, 1936, his condition having once again been judged "much improved" by his supervising psychiatrist, Dr. Ettling. Arriving in Manhattan later that day, he went directly from the bus terminal to the Gedeons' brownstone, where he learned that Ethel and Joe were residing in Astoria, Queens. That same evening, he paid the newlyweds a visit at their cottage, where he "presented to Mrs. Kudner the bust of her I had withheld out of mere spite. I told her that there was much of myself in the sculpture and now that she was married I did not want to bring back old memories."[20]

Six days later—unable to find a job and so heartbroken over Ethel that he "felt like jumping in the river"—Bob had himself readmitted to Rockland.[21]

He would remain there for another three months. During that time, to salve his emotional wound—"take the sting out of my breast," as he put it—he devoted himself to the creation of what he considered his masterpiece. Called *The Cobra*, the little sculpture was meant to symbolize what Irwin viewed as the essence of femininity. "So many women have the snake nature in them," he explained. "They lure men to death by their enchantments. They inspire to great heights and debase to great depths." The statue depicted a serpent with coiled tail, stubby body, and raised, hooded head that seemed to be swaying, as if under the spell of a snake charmer. Two things made the creature uniquely unsettling. It had an enormous pair of naked breasts and the face of a woman who wore an expression of postcoital bliss and whose features, as anyone who knew her would immediately recognize, were those of Ethel Kudner.[22]

14

Canton

A DECADE AFTER EMBRACING the freethinking philosophy of his intellectual hero, Robert Ingersoll—the "Great Agnostic"—Bob Irwin underwent a change of heart. "I got so filled up with religion during my youth that for years I wanted none of it," he explained. By the fall of 1936, however, he had developed a renewed "interest in the fundamentals of religion." Art and religion, he had come to realize, were "closely related," allowing us to transcend the suffering of the world by putting us in touch with an "unseen power," the divine source of all creation.[1]

For a while, Bob—like his father before him—grew obsessed with the teachings of John Wesley. In typical fashion, he would expound at length on Methodist doctrine to anyone within earshot. One listener much impressed with his evangelical spiel was a hospital attendant named Kenneth Iles, who worked at the new children's pavilion where Bob conducted his classes.

Before coming to Rockland, Iles had been a divinity student at the St. Lawrence University Theological School in Canton, New York, a village in the extreme northern part of the state, less than twenty miles from the Canadian border. In late summer 1936, he wrote a highly laudatory letter about Bob to the dean of the school, John Murray Atwood. Though Bob did not have a high school diploma, he was, as Atwood learned after contacting him directly, "better informed and better read than the majority of students." Since the school "occasionally had students with irregular educations who made good," Bob was accepted into the program on a nonmatriculated, trial basis. With the blessing of Rockland's superintendent, Dr. Russell E. Blaisdell, Bob, who was there on a voluntary basis, gave his ten days' notice of departure. On September 25, 1936, toting a couple of battered valises and a carton containing a few small sculptures, he headed north by bus to his new home.[2]

For much of his time in Canton, Bob's life was as normal and contented as it would ever be. He enjoyed his classes in religious education, homiletics, and Biblical literature, and impressed his instructors as an earnest and unusually well-read person. That Bob had spent time in an insane asylum "only made the professors more anxious to help him."[3] Far from being disturbed by his psychiatric history, they saw him as a sympathetic figure, a twenty-nine-year-old man seeking to rehabilitate his life through Christian service.

He found a room in a boardinghouse run by a couple named Hosley, who supplemented their income by keeping bees. To defray his rent, Bob lent a hand when the time came to harvest the honey. He also took on other odd jobs: delivering the *New York Times*, mowing lawns, shoveling snow.[4]

Deeply impressed with Bob's artistic abilities, one of his teachers, Dr. Angus MacLean—professor of religious history and future dean of the seminary—arranged for him to teach two classes in clay modeling, one for adults and one for children, who paid twenty-five cents per lesson. Since Bob's living quarters were too small to accommodate a work space, MacLean also "allowed Irwin to use his own home as a studio." Before long, Bob had become "an object of much admiration and curiosity" in the little community, invited to address the members of St. Lawrence Rotary Club, interviewed by a reporter for the *Syracuse Post-Standard*, and appearing on the local radio station to discuss "his own work and art in general."[5]

He also had a small but devoted circle of friends, including his landlord's wife, Mrs. Hosley, who developed such a keen "maternal affection for him" that, when her brother died in November, "she arranged for Bob to be given his clothing."[6] Among his fellow students, he became especially close to a well-to-do young man named Anders Lunde and a twenty-year-old from far humbler circumstances, Izzy Demsky.

A powerfully built, strikingly handsome nineteen-year-old, Demsky had endured a grim, Dickensian boyhood. One of seven children of poor Jewish immigrants who had fled the pogroms of Russia for the supposedly gold-paved streets of America, he had grown up in a hardscrabble section of Amsterdam, New York, where his father— a bitter, uncommunicative man given to outbursts of drunken rage —barely made a living as a junk peddler and ragman. Food was so scarce in the Demsky household that young Izzy was reduced to stealing eggs from a neighbor's chicken coop. To shield their ramshackle house from the cold, the walls were insulated with manure collected year-round from his father's dray horse. Every daily walk to school was a perilous gauntlet through neighborhoods filled with Jew-hating gangs.

Thanks to his native talents—and the patronage of an infatuated English teacher—Demsky flourished in high school, distinguishing himself in public speaking, acting, and essay writing. With money scraped together from various odd jobs—newspaper delivery boy, department store clerk, bellhop, waiter, factory hand—he managed to enroll at St. Lawrence. He found part-time work as a janitor and lived frugally, scrounging food from other students and renting a cubbyhole room in a cheap boardinghouse.

Between his studies, his menial work, and his athletic pursuits (he would become an intercollegiate wrestling champ), Demsky had little time for socializing. During his sophomore year, however, he bonded with Bob Irwin. "He was friendly, interested in boxing, and did odd jobs like me—a paper route, shoveling snow," Demsky later recalled. "I liked his sculptures and enjoyed talking to him." Bob did, however, have one glaring defect of character. Like Demsky's father, he "had a violent temper":

> He offered to buy a milkshake one day. I declined, because he didn't have much money either, and I figured going Dutch would be better. He insisted with such vehemence that I backed off and let him buy. He left school a little while later.

Less than two weeks after his departure from Canton, Bob Irwin would go from utter obscurity to nationwide notoriety. Izzy Demsky would always remember that tumultuous time in the life of the normally sleepy little college town. Twenty years later—long after he had changed his name to Kirk Douglas and achieved his own, far greater renown as one of Hollywood's biggest stars—he would conjure up memories of his old college friend while making *Lust for Life,* the biopic of Vincent van Gogh that earned Douglas one of his three Best Actor Oscar nominations. "I felt sorry for him, a talented artist at the mercy of incomprehensible forces," Douglas would write. "When I thought of Van Gogh, I thought of Bob Irwin."[7]

Bob took his classroom notes in a plain cardboard-bound notebook that also served as a sketch pad and journal. Its pages were filled with a hodgepodge of drawings, jottings, and clippings: freehand portraits of various acquaintances, rough sketches of future sculptural projects (among them a bust of Christ with devil's horns protruding from his forehead), biblical verses, obscene limericks, and a bizarre miscellany of newspaper items (including an advertisement extolling the virtues of Sears Roebuck toilets). There were also dozens of sporadically made diary entries, a considerable number of which referred to Ethel Kudner.

Though Bob had struggled to put Ethel out of his mind, he continued to brood over the woman he regarded as the paragon of her sex. Surrounded by "drawings of her various features, eyes, ears, nose, chin and full face," his entries are full of lovesick effusions. "God how I adore Ethel! Perfection. That's what she is. Absolute perfection. I could go out of my mind when I realize that she is married to someone else. It has made a shipwreck of me." The mere thought of other women actively repelled him. "Sex? It means nothing now!" he wrote. "I wouldn't even KISS anyone else now that Ethel is gone—forever." A later entry suggests that he had attempted to employ his powers of visualization to communicate with her telepathically. "Girl of my dreams! Can't you hear the still small voice in the night? Can't you hear me calling to you with words of adoration on my lips and a song of love in my heart?"[8]

Evidently determined to convey his feelings more directly, Bob made a trip to Manhattan in mid-December, three months after his move to Canton. Planning to stay with Mary and Veronica, he proceeded directly to their apartment. By then, the two women— along with Ronnie's pet Pekingese, Touchi—had moved out of their brownstone and found cheaper quarters in a shabby, six-story tenement a few blocks away, on the run-down fringe of Beekman Place. By sheer happenstance, Ethel was visiting for a few days, her husband having gone off on a business trip. Though not especially thrilled by Bob's unexpected arrival, she was cordial to him as always. Mary and Veronica, on the other hand, did little to conceal their annoyance at Bob for his unwanted attentions to Ethel.

Exactly what transpired during his brief visit to New York City is unclear, though one fact is well documented. By the time he returned to Canton, he had managed to convince himself that—all evidence to the contrary—Ethel had moved back in with her mother and sister because her marriage was in trouble.[9] This delusional belief was only one sign that his mental state, precarious at best, was growing shakier by the day.

He began to rant endlessly about visualization and the godlike powers it would grant him, including the ability to travel though time. To his classmate Albert Niles, he revealed his current attempts to "project his mind into the past" and observe "the conduct of historical figures" like his idol Napoleon. "I liked Bob," said Niles. "But he was emotionally and mentally unstable."[10]

At the same time, he began haranguing his fellow divinity students about a bizarre "scheme for religious revolution"—"a worldwide upheaval" that would "supplant Christianity" with a new spiritual movement he called "communistic religion."

"It was a confused theory," commented his friend Anders Lunde with considerable understatement. On one occasion, Lunde recalled, Bob took the stage during morning chapel services and launched into an impassioned speech about the need for a radical change in world religion—"but after his first few sentences, his rationality left him and with tears streaming down his face he walked from one side of the platform to the other in the grip of uncontrolled emotion." Afterward, as the assembly filed out of the chapel, Professor MacLean came up beside Lunde and whispered, "That boy is crazy."[11]

And then there were his increasingly frequent outbursts of uncontrolled anger, culminating in an episode that occurred in the third week of March 1937. The victim of Bob's fury on that occasion was a fellow divinity student named Leroy Congdon. Precisely what he did to provoke Bob is unclear. According to one account, he was visiting the children's art class Bob taught when he "tripped over a table and broke a piece of sculpture." Another source claims that Bob and his young pupils had constructed an elaborate model of Noah's Ark, and that—after borrowing a few of the animal figures to use in a puppet show—Congdon "returned some of them broken."[12] What is indisputably true is that, on the afternoon of Sunday, March 21, in front of the entire class, Bob flew into an insane rage at Congdon, spewing such vile curses and ugly threats that several of the students—including Professor MacLean's daughter, Susan, who was taking the class with her older brother, Colin—burst into tears. Then, before the flabbergasted Congdon could gather his wits, Bob hauled off and smashed him in the jaw.

When Angus MacLean got wind of the incident later that day, he called both young men into his office and asked for an explanation. As Congdon began to speak, MacLean saw that Bob was growing highly agitated and "warned him not to lose control of himself." His words had the opposite effect. With a crazed roar, Bob leaped from his chair and "went after Congdon," MacLean later testified. A powerfully built man who had served with the Canadian Army during World War I, MacLean "grabbed Irwin by the neck" and put him in a headlock "until he to promised to behave himself." Afterward, he "told Bob I could not have him working with the children when he was not emotionally dependable."

The following day, MacLean—"now deeply concerned with Irwin's behavior and mental condition"—brought him to see Dean Atwood. Bob "made wild charges against Congdon," Atwood recalled, "and accused Dr. MacLean of being 'against him.'" Atwood "tried to soothe" Bob and "suggested that he apologize to Congdon and forget the incident." Instead, "Irwin jumped from his chair, his eyes gleaming, and expressed his antipathy for Congdon in uncontrolled violent fashion." Then he stormed out of the office.

Two days later, on Wednesday, March 24, Atwood expelled Bob from the school for "instability." At the same time, he wrote a letter to Dr. Russell Blaisdell, superintendent of Rockland State Hospital, "stating that we were alarmed and raising the question of whether or not a man liable to such irrational and violent antipathy was not dangerous."[13]

How—or even whether—Blaisdell replied to this query is unknown. One psychiatrist who did have an opinion on the subject was Dr. Fredric Wertham.

Earlier in the year, Wertham had received an invitation to present a paper at a ceremony marking the twenty-fifth anniversary of his former workplace, the Phipps Psychiatric Clinic of the Johns Hopkins Hospital. The topic he chose was the so-called "catathymic crisis," the previously unrecognized mental disorder that, so he believed, accounted for certain acts of criminal violence. Without identifying him by name, he cited Bob Irwin as an example of an "unrecovered case"—a patient who had reached the stage of "superficial normality" but had not yet achieved the ultimate goal of full "insight and recovery." Without further intensive psychotherapy, Wertham declared, "a recurrence of the pattern of violence . . . could be predicted."

"This man is not cured," concluded Wertham, who would have the grim satisfaction of seeing his prognosis confirmed. "He will break out again in some act of violence against himself or others."[14]

Crisis

M ARY AND VERONICA'S DILAPIDATED brownstone on 53rd
Street might have seen better days, but it was positively palatial compared to their current place, a fourth-floor walk-up at 316
East 50th Street. Cramped and dimly lighted, with rear-facing windows overlooking a junk-strewn backyard, the apartment consisted
of three bedrooms—two hardly bigger than walk-in closets—a
bathroom, kitchen, and combination living/dining room. Despite
the limited space, the ever-frugal Mary continued to take in boarders. Such claustrophobic conditions—the two Gedeon women and a
renter sharing a small, dreary flat—might have been impossibly op-
pressive. What made the situation tolerable was the fact that Ronnie
was rarely at home.

In the evenings, she was out on the town with one of her many
male admirers. Her days were largely taken up with her flourishing,
if somewhat unsavory, career as a model.

She had gotten her modest start in the business thanks to Ethel,
who had invited her to a party where she met Helen Norden, Ethel's
boss at *Vanity Fair*. Impressed with Ronnie's looks, Norden intro-

duced her to Condé Nast, the magazine's publisher (and Norden's lover), who arranged for her to model for his daughter Natica, an aspiring artist.

Over the next few years, while dreaming of a career as a high-fashion model, Ronnie took whatever jobs she could find. Registering with the Hollywood Service Agency, she found sporadic work at trade shows, buyers conventions, and the like. Eventually, she discovered that she could find consistent and well-paid work as a "figure model," posing in the nude for amateur photography clubs. She had a firm, shapely body (her file at her modeling agency records her measurements as 5'8" in height and 126 pounds, with a 34" bust, 25" waist, and 35" hips) and, even more crucially, an utter lack of inhibition when it came to taking off her clothes.

In November 1935, she gained fleeting notoriety when she appeared "decoratively underdressed" in the annual stag show mounted by the New York Society of Illustrators at the Heckscher Theatre at Fifth Avenue and 104th Street—a benefit performance for struggling artists attended by eight hundred men, including such notables as cartoonist Rube Goldberg, famed illustrator Howard Chandler Christy, and Herbert Bayard Swope, first recipient of the Pulitzer Prize for reporting and former managing editor of the *New York World*. "Clad only in scanties," as one tabloid reported, Ronnie was "about to make her entrance in a skit called 'Nobody Makes a Pass at Me'" when the theater was raided by the police, who halted the show on the grounds of indecency. Five of the young female performers were taken into custody and charged with dancing in the nude, though Ronnie—thanks to her "silver-tongued eloquence"— managed to "talk herself out of her impending arrest."[1]

She reached the pinnacle of her career a year later when she began to pose for pulp true crime magazines. The 1930s were the heyday of these sensational publications. Fans of the genre could choose from more than one hundred titles—*True Detective, Master Detective, Startling Detective, Real Detective, Dynamic Detective, Daring Detective, American Detective, Official Detective Stories*, and dozens more. All offered garishly illustrated covers, generally featuring a half-naked beauty in mortal distress; interior black-and-white photos of both actual crime scenes and staged re-creations; and slick, well-researched stories with punchy tabloid titles ("Love Secrets of California's Rattlesnake Romeo!" "Pennsylvania's Sex Terrorist and the Horror in the Well!" "The Southwest's Pseudo-Maniac and the Singing Corpse!" "Crimson Trail of San Francisco's Gas-Pipe Killers!").

Beginning in the spring of 1936, Ronnie modeled for a number of these magazines—*Inside Detective, Front Page Detective,* and *Detective Foto*—almost always "in the semi-nude in an attitude of shame and humiliation." She was a cowering, scantily clad beauty threatened by a pistol-wielding thug in the story "Nine Mad Dogs," a negligee-wearing moll in "Pretty But Cheap," a half-naked victim in "I Am a White Slave." Her final appearance was in the April 1937 issue of *Inside Detective,* where her photograph—"cringing and shame-stricken," one arm flung over her face, the other raised to conceal her naked bosom—accompanied the story "Party Girl," an "exposé of a Boston vice ring smashed by the police." The issue hit the newsstands in the third week of March. Within days of its initial publication, that same picture—along with dozens of others—would be reprinted in newspapers throughout the country.[2]

On Thursday, March 25, 1937—one day after his expulsion from the St. Lawrence University Theological School—Robert Irwin set out by bus for Manhattan.

With nothing to keep him in Canton, he was hoping to move back to the city and was on his way to hunt for work. He had reason to feel optimistic. His friend Anders Lunde was engaged to a twenty-two-year-old socialite named Leonora Sheldon, whose brother William was affiliated with the American Museum of Natural History. A young naturalist who would gain renown as the world's leading expert on the American woodcock, William had recently returned from an expedition to Sichuan, China, where he had become the third person ever to shoot a giant panda. His specimen, mounted and displayed in a diorama of its natural habitat, was a prize of the museum.[3] Given Bob's experience at Thomas Rowland's taxidermy shop, Lunde was hopeful that his friend might land a job at the museum and had written to Leonora, who offered to do what she could on Bob's behalf.

Dressed in a dark-blue pin-striped suit, a threadbare Chesterfield overcoat—its black velvet collar in such sorry shape that he generally turned it up to conceal its worn-out nap—a yellow scarf, a tan fedora, and gray suede gloves purchased several days earlier from the J. J. Newberry store on Main Street in Canton, Bob embarked for the city around midnight. He carried two beat-up suitcases, one tied shut with a length of rope, and a few small sculptures in a cardboard box, including the portrait bust he had done of Clarence Low, the state official he had met the year before at Rockland. He left the rest of his possessions at the Hosleys' boardinghouse, explaining to his landlords that, depending on how his job search went, he would either be back in a few days or send a forwarding address.[4]

Arriving in midtown early on the morning of March 26—Good Friday—Bob went directly to Clarence Low's office at 103 Park Avenue to present him with the bust, which had been modeled on photographs Low had supplied. Bob apologized profusely as he placed the little statue on Low's desk. "It isn't any good," he kept saying, his voice so unsteady that Low feared he might burst into tears. "You should have posed for it, Mr. Low." Though Low secretly agreed—"the side view was all right but the front was not so hot," he later testified—he assured Bob that the statue was fine. Bob then launched into a tirade against the St. Lawrence Theological School, growing more agitated by the minute. "He talked wildly," Low would say afterward, "and he looked just as wild as he talked." Eager to get rid of Bob, Low made a show of looking at his watch and explained that he had a train to catch at Grand Central. As Bob accompanied him to the corner of Park and 43rd, he blathered nonstop about the job he hoped to get at the Museum of Natural History. "He talked like a maniac," said Low. Before they parted, Low "advised him to take the job and make a name for himself." He then shook Bob's hand and hurried into the station, "glad to get away."[5]

Bob's next order of business was finding a place to lodge. Knowing that there would be no space for him at the Gedeons' but eager to stay nearby, he scouted the neighborhood, finally settling on an attic room at 248 East 52nd Street, the brownstone home of a German-American couple, Charles and Matilda Ottburg. Identifying himself only as a "farmer from Utica," he handed over a week's rental—$2.50 plus a fifty-cent deposit on the key—and told his landlords not to worry about the daily upkeep of his room. "Don't bother to clean my room or make my bed," he said. "I'll do that all myself." He then lugged his belongings upstairs.

Besides a skylight, the room had a rear-facing window. Peering out, Bob saw that it commanded a view of the East 51st Street police station. He spent the next half hour or so settling in. Then he headed back outside, found a pay phone, and put in a call to an acquaintance, William Lamkie.[6]

For most of his fifty-eight years, Lamkie had been a model citizen. A graduate of Brown University, professor of municipal government at NYU, and member of the United States Shipping Board (precursor of the U.S. Maritime Commission) during the Great War, he had enjoyed an enviable life in a quiet Connecticut suburb with a devoted wife and two well-mannered sons. And then, in the spring of 1933, his life came unglued. For reasons he could never explain, he found himself committing a bit of small-time insurance fraud, claiming (falsely) that his car had been stolen and collecting five hundred dollars on his policy. When the insurance company discovered the scam, he was charged with perjury and second-degree grand larceny. In light of his sparkling résumé and spotless record, he was allowed to plead guilty to petit larceny and given a suspended sentence.

Not long afterward, he began to hear voices. Abandoning his family, he became a follower of the colorful cult leader Pierre Bernard, a.k.a. the "Omnipotent Oom," the self-made swami and yoga pioneer who had founded a "utopian Tantric community" on a seventy-two-acre estate (complete with a thirty-room Georgian mansion) in upstate New York. Within months of arriving at Oom's bucolic headquarters, Lamkie was arrested for sending viciously threatening letters to a former landlady. Adjudged mentally unsound, he was committed to Rockland State Hospital, where he met Bob Irwin.[7]

During the course of their shared two-year confinement in the asylum, the two became good friends and confidants, Lamkie deriving bemused fascination from Bob's quasi-metaphysical theorizing. Since their release, they had remained sporadic correspondents. By the spring of 1937, Lamkie was working as an industrial relations consultant and living with one of his two now-adult sons at 4039 43rd Street in Long Island City, a short subway ride away from Manhattan. It was there that Bob reached him by phone late on Good Friday afternoon.

They arranged to meet that evening for dinner at a Schrafft's restaurant in midtown. Bob arrived with a thick manila envelope that turned out to contain a manuscript he had been working on since his arrival at Canton: a handwritten fifty-page autobiography—"the highlights of my varied life and wide experiences with all kinds and classes of people," as Bob described it. Accompanying it was a typed, formal letter requesting, in effect, that Lamkie serve as Bob's ghostwriter: "You can take this sketch of my career, add to or subtract as you think fits the purpose," Bob wrote. "Take any liberty you think best. . . . This life story would of course appear over my signature and what you might add would be my words. You would be just expressing my thoughts."[8]

Exactly where Bob thought his autobiography would appear wasn't at all clear, though he obviously believed that there would soon be enough curiosity about his life story to merit its publication. He was determined that the world know the truth. "I'm damned sick and tired of being misunderstood," he nearly shouted. When Lamkie seemed reluctant to take on the project, Bob became violently agitated. "He was shaking," Lamkie said afterward. "He was irrational." Alarmed at Bob's emotional state, Lamkie relented. By the time he returned home a few hours later, manuscript in hand,

Lamkie was concerned that his friend was on the brink of doing something desperate. "I could see," he would report, "that everything was coming to a climax."[9]

After saying good-bye to Lamkie, Bob wandered aimlessly for a while. Drifting over to Times Square, he passed the entrance to Hubert's dime museum. A tawdry showplace located in the basement of a penny arcade, Hubert's was home to Professor Heckler's celebrated flea circus, along with an assortment of carnival freaks, sideshow performers, and celebrity has-beens, among them the African-American prizefighter Jack Johnson, one-time heavyweight champion of the world. With his love of boxing, Bob couldn't pass up the chance to see the legendary pugilist, now pushing sixty. Paying his fifteen-cent admission, Bob descended into the seedy underworld of Hubert's, where he listened to the nattily dressed Johnson recite—for the dozenth time that day—the tale of his epic 1910 bout with the "Great White Hope," Jim Jeffries. Afterward, Bob approached Johnson and asked permission to draw his portrait. The old fighter agreed to sit for him the following day. But Bob never returned for the appointment.[10]

Leonora Sheldon, the fiancée of Bob's friend Anders Lunde, had come down from Vassar for the holiday weekend and was staying with family friends, Mr. and Mrs. George Mullens, at their apartment on Riverside Drive. At 1:00 p.m. on Saturday, March 27, she and Bob met by prearrangement on a street corner near the Mullenses' home and walked to the American Museum of Natural History on Central Park West. There, Leonora introduced him to her brother, William, who had agreed to help Bob find work in the Department of Preparation and Installation, responsible for creating the museum's dramatic habitat dioramas. For unknown reasons, however, the job, as Bob later put it, "didn't pan out."[11]

Though badly disappointed, Bob—who could see that Leonora felt almost as crestfallen as he did—put on a cheerful face and asked her to come along with him to the Metropolitan Museum of Art, across the park on Fifth Avenue. Inside, he treated her to the same talk on his favorite statue—Verrocchio's Colleoni—that he had given Ethel. An amateur artist herself, Leonora was so taken with Bob's lecture that she agreed to meet him again the next afternoon for a more extended tour of the galleries.[12]

With severely limited funds and no job in the offing, Bob returned to his room at the Ottburgs' to fetch one of his sculptures, a small portrait bust of Marlene Dietrich. He then proceeded to the 42nd Street offices of *Stage*, "The Magazine of After-Dark Entertainment," as it billed itself: a slick, lavishly illustrated monthly devoted primarily to the professional doings of Broadway and Hollywood stars, along with current happenings in the worlds of popular music, radio, and dance.[13] Explaining to the receptionist that he was "seeking commissions to execute busts of actors for the magazine, Katherine Cornell and Cole Porter in particular," he was informed that the art director, Scudder Middleton, was away for the holidays and was told to try again next week.[14]

By the time Bob left the building, a terrible depression had descended on him. Heading east, he made his way toward the 53rd Street pier, where Ethel had once rebuffed his marriage proposal and where, two weeks after that shattering rejection, he had seriously considered throwing himself into the river. Now, once again, his thoughts turned to suicide.

As he crossed First Avenue, he saw something lying in the gutter —an old ice pick, dropped or discarded by an ice deliveryman. He snatched it up and slipped it into his coat pocket.

Seating himself at the edge of the pier, he stared into the river for a long time, trying to work up the courage to jump in. He was just about to take the plunge when he was vouchsafed a glorious vision. "The water turned light and was swirling all around like liquid light," he later recounted. "It was just as beautiful as can be." As he watched in mounting wonder, "the water of the river rose up and moulded itself into the form of Ethel. Her hair was gold." "I saw it," he declared, "just as clear as I see flesh and blood."

A tremendous exaltation suffused his spirit. He "had the distinct feeling that electricity and sparks were vibrating about his head and that lights were flashing all around." At that instant, he realized that his painful years of struggle to perfect his powers of visualization had led to this culminating moment. He was on the brink of attaining godhood, the ultimate goal of visualization. On the very weekend marking the Savior's resurrection, he himself was about to be transmuted into Jesus Christ!

Only one thing was lacking. He knew he "could not quite accomplish the role of Christ, without making a sacrifice, for a sacrificial rite was necessary to bring the wisdom of heaven upon earth." The problem, of course, was that, "while Christ went down into the grave and rose from the tomb in immortality," Bob worried that if he himself "went to the grave, which meant suicide by drowning," he might not rise again, in which case "all the principles for which he had worked for so many years would vanish."

The solution presented itself in a flash of inspiration. He would sacrifice Ethel. The internal pressure generated by her murder would be so intense that he "would be liberated from all the bonds of mortality and would arrive at the stage of Redeemer."[15]

Believing that Ethel was still living apart from her husband, he decided to seek her out at Mary and Ronnie's apartment a few blocks away. First, however, he went in search of an open hardware store. Finding one on Second Avenue, he purchased a small hand file. He then returned to his room at the Ottburgs', where he sharpened the ice pick he had retrieved from the gutter. Back outside, he walked the streets until nightfall, then turned his steps toward 50th Street.[16]

Part IV

The Mad Sculptor

Bloody Sunday

I T WAS ALREADY PAST NOON when Joseph Gedeon crawled out of his cot on Easter Sunday—no surprise since he hadn't gone to bed until after 3:00 a.m. He quickly performed his daily ablutions —scrubbed his face, brushed his teeth, trimmed his mousy moustache, splashed some water on his armpits. He couldn't take a shower since the sink and a toilet were the only bathroom fixtures in his living space—a screened-off corner of his workshop, barely big enough to accommodate his cot, a table and chair, a small woodstove, and a plywood closet he had built for his meager wardrobe. Still he felt relatively fresh, having bathed just two days earlier at his estranged wife's apartment.[1]

After affixing his pince-nez eyeglasses to the bridge of his nose, he donned a well-worn gray suit and checked himself in the full-length mirror attached to the outside of his bathroom door. The wall adjacent to the door was papered with Gedeon's extensive collection of cheesecake pinups, clipped from the pages of his favorite girlie magazines: *Beauty Parade*, *High Heel*, *Silk Stocking*. Then he shrugged on his overcoat and headed outside.

Despite the wintry weather, the streets were full of holiday strollers—men, women, and children resplendent in their Easter finery.[2] Heading east on 34th Street, he rounded the corner onto Third Avenue and ducked into Corrigan's Bar and Grill, where—except for a couple of brief interruptions—he had passed the previous evening from 7:00 p.m. until 2:55 a.m., just before closing time. He had drunk so many beers that he had staggered home in a state of semistupefaction. Even so, he had managed to roll the evening's highest score at skee ball—the popular, bowling-style arcade game that involved sending a small ball up an inclined ramp into holes ringed with rubberized targets. His winning score—310 points—was inscribed on a blackboard above the machine.

He found the proprietor, Calogero Parliapiano, behind the bar, collected his house prize from the previous night—one dollar—and ordered a celebratory schnapps. Somehow, in the course of that beer-soaked evening, he had misplaced his gray fedora. Parliapiano, however, hadn't come across the hat while cleaning up that morning, and no one had turned it in. Gedeon soothed his disappointment with another schnapps before leaving the bar. Outside, he headed for Second Avenue, on his way to Easter dinner with his family.[3]

Since separating from his wife four years earlier, Gedeon had maintained cordial relations with Mary, sharing holiday meals with her and their daughters and making occasional use of her bathtub. He had been up in her apartment just two nights earlier to enjoy a leisurely bath, the first he'd had in weeks. Afterward, they sat in the kitchen and came to a momentous decision. It was time for the two of them to reconcile. They would break the happy news to their children over Easter dinner.

Of course, Joseph wouldn't be able to move back in just yet since there was no space for him in the flat at present. Ronnie had turned over her little room to a visiting friend, Lucy Beacco, and was sharing the central bedroom with her mother. The other small bedroom was occupied by a boarder Mary had taken in five weeks before, a dapper little fellow Joseph knew only as "the Englishman."

Though Beekman Place was only a fifteen-minute stroll from

34th Street, Gedeon, still slightly hung over, opted for the Second Avenue El, arriving in his wife's neighborhood a few minutes before 2:00 p.m. He wasn't expected for another half hour, so—not wanting to show up unannounced—he found a phone booth in a cigar store and dialed the apartment. No one answered. Joseph, as he later explained, found that somewhat "odd" but "assumed his family was still at the Easter parade." He bought a few cigars to share with his son-in-law, Joe Kudner, then shopped for some small gifts for Mary and the girls: a potted lily and a two-pound box of chocolates. He still had some time to kill, so he ambled over to a newsstand and checked out the current issue of *Paris Nights*, another "spicy" magazine filled with bare-breasted beauties.[4]

At around 2:40 p.m., he strolled over to the building at 316 East 50th Street, rang the downstairs bell for his wife's apartment, and waited to be buzzed inside. He got no reply. He was still standing in the vestibule, wondering where Mary could be, when Ethel and Joe Kudner arrived, having driven in from Astoria, Queens. When Joseph informed them that no one appeared to be home, Ethel insisted that he try the bell again. Before he could push the button, one of the tenants emerged from the inner hallway. Holding the door open, Gedeon and the Kudners stepped inside.

Leaving Joe at the foot of the staircase with Ethel—who was wearing new Easter shoes that pinched her feet and didn't want to make the climb if no one was there—Gedeon headed up the four flights to apartment No. 16. The door, unlocked, swung open at his touch. He passed from the little entrance foyer into the darkened living room. Touchi, Ronnie's Pekingese, who usually bounded up to greet him, approached him nervously, ears flattened to his head, then tried to crawl beneath the davenport. Apart from the dog's whimpers, the apartment was utterly silent.[5]

Entering the kitchen, Joseph switched on the overhead light. The main dinner ingredients—a forlorn-looking pork loin and a bowl of uncut green beans—sat on the counter, uncooked.

With a growing sense of disquiet, Gedeon moved to the main bedroom. The double bed, shared by Mary and Ronnie, had not been slept in. The pillows were fluffed, the violet bedspread undisturbed. Everything was in order. As he scanned the room, however, his eye was caught by something peculiar: several chunks of what appeared to be a broken soap bar scattered on the carpeted floor.

Avoiding the soap, Gedeon stepped over to the door of the little bedroom on the left. The door was ajar. He pushed it open and peered inside.

Stretched faceup on the bed, completely naked, was his daughter Ronnie. Her complexion was a ghastly blue, her bulging eyes staring sightlessly at the ceiling. Ugly bruises ringed her neck. Even without touching her, Joseph could see that her body had gone stiff.

He backed away from the awful sight and hurried to the other bedroom. The Englishman's rigid corpse lay sideways on the mattress, a blanket covering him up to the shoulders, his blood-caked head resting on a pillow drenched in gore.

Swiveling on his heels, Gedeon rushed downstairs, where Ethel and Joe waited in the lobby. "They're all dead," he cried. "Murdered!" Aghast, Ethel and Joe followed him up to the fourth floor. While Kudner—face pale, lips drawn tight—viewed the two bodies, Ethel sat weeping in the kitchen. "Where's Momma?" she sobbed. Her father assured her that Mary must have escaped and gone for the police. "I'll go see," he said. Hurrying outside, he made for the East 51st Street station house a block away, while, upstairs, his son-in-law picked up the phone and dialed SPring 7-3100—the number of the NYPD headquarters.[6]

The first officers to arrive at the scene were Detectives Martin Owens and William Gilmartin of the Seventh Precinct. It was Gilmartin who discovered Mary Gedeon's corpse. Clothed in a green housedress, pink corset and brassiere, pink slip, and brown stockings, she was wedged beneath the bed that held the body of her daughter. It was clear at a glance that she, too, had been strangled. As with Ronnie and the boarder, her body was stiff with rigor mortis.[7]

By then, a cadre of detectives from the Homicide Squad—among them Charlie McGowan, Tony Fader, Ruddy McLaughlin, and Tom

Tunney (brother of Gene Tunney, former heavyweight boxing champion)—had shown up, along with Deputy Chief Inspector Francis Kear, Assistant Chief Inspector John A. Lyons, and Assistant District Attorney P. Francis Marro. Close on their heels came the acting chief medical examiner, Dr. Thomas A. Gonzales, and a battery of experts from the Police Research Laboratory.

While the crime scene photographers wielded their Speed Graphic cameras and the fingerprint men went to work on every surface that might possibly yield a telltale loop or whorl, Kear and his detectives scoured the apartment for clues. In a corner of the Englishman's bedroom, they found a man's right-hand gray suede glove, size 8¼ and "practically new." A pair of torn pink silk panties—clearly Ronnie's judging by their size—was jammed between the wall and the head of the bed on which her body lay. The rest of her garments—a fur coat, a dress, and a hat—were piled on the bathroom clothes hamper, at the foot of which lay her silk stockings and a pair of black suede pumps. A towel stained with dried blood had been carelessly tossed over the edge of the bathtub.[8]

Otherwise—except for the mangled bar of soap on the floor of the central bedroom—nothing was disturbed or out of place. The bureau drawers hadn't been ransacked, and the women's purses were untouched. Whatever the motive for the Easter Sunday Massacre (as the press would soon call it), robbery clearly wasn't it.

A preliminary examination of the bodies revealed that the boarder, a trim little man clad only in his undershirt and drawers, had received eleven stab wounds to the head with a sharp-pointed implement, "probably an ice pick." Gonzales later determined that the fatal wound, struck with an assassin's precision, had been delivered to the base of the skull, entering "just below the *foramen magnum*"—the opening through which the spinal cord enters the skull—and penetrating the brain.[9] From the position of the body and the undisturbed condition of the bedclothes, the Englishman—quickly identified as Frank Byrnes, a waiter at what the tabloids invariably referred to as the "swanky" Racquet and Tennis Club on Park Avenue—appeared to have been killed in his sleep.

Both women had "died of manual strangulation, the killer's hands applying such force that Mrs. Gedeon's thyroid cartilage was torn, while the girl's throat showed signs of hemorrhage in the larynx and muscles of the neck."[10] Judging from her badly bruised knuckles, Mary had put up a ferocious struggle. Until the women were autopsied, Gonzales couldn't say whether they had been raped, though in the case of Ronnie—her beautiful body sprawled naked on the bed, her slip ripped off, and her panties shoved behind the bed board— the answer seemed self-evident to investigators. Mrs. Gedeon's cotton drawers had also been torn away, and there were fresh scratches and abrasions on her upper thighs and genital area.

There were some clumps of mud scattered on the fire escape landing outside Byrnes's bedroom. At first, Kear took them as evidence that the killer had climbed onto the fire escape and slipped in through the unlocked window. Peering upward out the window, however, he discovered the source of the mud: a bunch of clay flowerpots on the fire escape directly overhead, damp soil oozing from the drainage holes in their bottoms. Since no mud had been tracked inside the apartment, Lyons concluded that the killer hadn't been on the fire escape after all.

There was only one other way that the killer could have entered: through the front door. Examining the lock, detectives found no signs of forced entry, indicating that the killer had been freely admitted to the apartment. That the Gedeons knew their killer was suggested by another clue—one that, in the words of the *New York Post*, added "a significant Conan Doyle touch to the grisly murders."[11] In the story "Silver Blaze," Sherlock Holmes and Dr. Watson travel to Dartmoor to investigate the disappearance of a famous racehorse and the apparent murder of its trainer. At one point, referring to the guard dog in the stable, Holmes draws the local inspector's attention to "the curious incident of the dog in the nighttime." When the inspector protests that "the dog did nothing in the night-time," Holmes replies, "That was the curious incident."[12]

The behavior of Ronnie's dog was equally significant to investigators. From the moment they had entered the apartment, the little Pekingese had put up such a shrill, persistent barking that the police finally summoned the ASPCA, which dispatched a special car to take the dog to a shelter. Neighbors confirmed that Touchi was an "annoying little animal" that "yapped its head off at strangers."[13] Not a single tenant, however, had heard the slightest sound from the dog on the night of the slayings, leading Lyons to the same conclusion reached by Sherlock Holmes—"that the midnight visitor was someone whom the dog knew well."[14]

One of the building's occupants, Cosmon Cambinias, did report hearing a suspicious noise on the previous night. According to Cambinias—who lived two floors below the Gedeons—he had just gotten into bed at eleven o'clock when he was startled by "a scream and the sound of a scuffle" from above. He went to his window and stuck his head outside, but all the "bedrooms on that side of the building were in darkness. The Gedeon apartment seemed silent as a tomb." Hearing no further noise, he "dismissed the incident" and went back to bed.[15]

Another tenant, an automobile mechanic named Charles Robinson who lived with his wife on the sixth floor, described a curious incident that police found potentially significant. "I got home about a quarter past two this morning," reported Robinson, "and when I got up as far as the fourth floor, I noticed that the door to the Gedeon apartment was open. As I passed it on my way up to my own place, I noticed the door was closing gradually, as if somebody was behind it, pushing it. I dunno, there was something about the way the door started to close that gave me the creeps, and I beat it to the sixth floor as fast as I could."[16]

While two of Lyons's men were interviewing the neighbors, the rest continued to search the apartment. Inside a drawer in the living room secretary, Detective Martin Owens found a dog-eared address book with a black imitation-leather cover. At virtually the same time, one of his colleagues came across a little volume, bound in tan fabric with a broken brass clasp, shoved in Ronnie's bedroom bureau among her lingerie. Its frontispiece bore the printed tile "Five Year Diary." Over this inscription, in a childish hand, she had written the word "My" and under it had scrawled her name.

Both items were immediately turned over to Inspector Kear. Thumbing through the address book, Kear saw that it was filled with names and telephone numbers, "mostly of men." The diary entries dated back to February 1932, when they mostly concerned Ronnie's tumultuous relationship with a young man identified only as "B." or "Bobby."[17]

Kear was still examining the diary when the telephone in the central bedroom rang. Detective Charlie McGowan, who was standing closest to the phone, picked up the receiver. The caller was a young man who asked to speak to Ronnie. Identifying himself as a police officer, McGowan got the name and address of the caller—Stephen Butter of 581 Lexington Avenue—then, telling him to stay put, hurried off to Butter's apartment, a short distance away.

Less than ten minutes later, the "tall, slim, frightened-looking" Butter, who knew only that he was "wanted for questioning," was escorted into the East 51st Street station, where a mob of newsmen was gathered at the entrance.[18] At his first glimpse of them, Butter realized that something dire had happened. It wasn't, however, until he spoke to Ronnie's grief-wracked sister, Ethel—who was seated beside her husband in the waiting area outside Inspector Lyons office—that he learned the shocking truth.

By then, Lyons himself had arrived from the crime scene and been joined by Police Commissioner Lewis Valentine. A rough-hewn former beat cop who "early concluded that cracking jaws and flattening noses were the only means of impressing law and order upon bums," Valentine had spent years fighting graft in the department as the head of the confidential squad, a precursor of the Internal Affairs bureau. Though he won many promotions, he made even more enemies, and ultimately found himself demoted and exiled to the wilds of Brooklyn. It wasn't until 1934 that his "stubborn honesty paid off" and he was appointed commissioner by the reforming Mayor Fiorello La Guardia. His reputation as a two-fisted, tough-as-nails lawman was sealed shortly thereafter when, spotting a well-dressed suspect in a lineup, he roared at his men: "That velvet collar should be smeared with blood. I don't want those hoodlums coming in looking as if they stepped out of a barber's chair. From now on, bring 'em in mussed up!"[19]

Knowing Valentine's reputation, Butter feared he might be subjected to some "roughshod treatment" at the hands of his interrogators. The commissioner and Lyons, however, saw at once that the young man was no triple murderer and—perceiving how distraught he was—took care to conduct their questioning in a "polite, almost apologetic" way.[20] As a clerk transcribed his statement, Butter—the last person besides her killer to have seen Ronnie Gedeon alive—provided a detailed account of her final evening.

A twenty-three-year-old messenger for a Wall Street brokerage house, Butter lived at home with his parents and younger sister, who had driven upstate to their rural retreat in South Cambridge, New York, for the holiday. His best friend, Lincoln Hauser, had also gone away for the weekend, though not before asking Stephen to "keep an eye" on the girl he was dating, the beautiful blond artist's model Ronnie Gedeon. Stephen had arranged for Ronnie and her best friend, Jean Karp, to come over to his place on Saturday night for dinner and, to make it a foursome, had invited a pal of his own, Frank Schlenner. When Ronnie arrived at just before eight, however, she was alone, Jean having come down with a severe head cold.

The trio spent the evening drinking beer and gin, dancing to radio music, and enjoying a spaghetti dinner prepared by Ronnie. At around 2:00 a.m., Schlenner took his leave, explaining that he had "promised to take his mother to an early mass downtown." Throwing on their overcoats, Butter and Ronnie headed over to the Monte Carlo Bar and Grill at 145 51st Street for a couple of gin highballs. At 3:00 a.m., closing time, he walked her home, escorted her upstairs, and—after making plans to call for her at ten the next morning and take her to mass at St. Patrick's Cathedral—headed back to his apartment. He had neither seen nor heard anything unusual when he left her at her door. On Sunday morning, he had shown up at her building as arranged, but when he rang the downstairs buzzer no one answered. Puzzled, he returned to his own apartment and dialed her number at intervals until just before 3:00 p.m., when Detective Owens picked up the phone.

The interrogation lasted until 9:00 p.m., when Butter was informed that he was free to go. Physically exhausted and emotionally spent, he made his way onto the street, where he was besieged by reporters clamoring for a statement. "Gee, it's tough," Butter managed to say. "We had a swell time Saturday. Veronica was a swell kid."[21]

Butter's warm opinion of Ronnie was seconded by her former husband, Robert Flower, the "Bobby" who figured so prominently in the early parts of her diary. Traced to a bowling tournament at the 212th Street Armory, where he was operating a hot dog stand, the "tall, thin, good-looking young man" struggled to control his emotions as he spoke about his murdered ex-wife.

"I don't know why anyone would want to kill Ronnie," he said hoarsely. "She was a sweet kid and never hurt anyone in her life. It doesn't make sense. There's no reason for anything like this to happen to her."

Asked about their failed marriage, Flower made it clear that he harbored no ill will toward his ex-wife. "When we got married she was just a kid," he told his interrogators. "I guess neither of us knew what it was all about. We got along pretty well but I guess she didn't want to be tied down. She wanted good times and going places and I just didn't have the money. After a while we talked things over and decided our marriage wasn't a go. Ronnie sued for annulment on the grounds that she was a minor at the time of our marriage. We stayed good friends and I tried to see her once in a while. The last time I saw her was about three weeks ago. We went to see *Lost Horizon* at the Music Hall."

He paused for a moment, as if to get hold of himself, and then, in a voice quivering with grief and fury, said: "I hope they find the son-of-a-bitch who did it and send him to the chair."[22]

Brought to the police station for questioning a short time later,

Frank Schlenner—the young man who had partied with Butter and Ronnie on the night of the slayings—confirmed his friend's account, as did Linc Hauser, who had hurried back from his father's vacation home in Saratoga Springs. Fetched from her home in the Bronx, Ronnie's best friend, Jean Karp, was so overcome with grief that she could barely speak. Police learned that she had intended to stay overnight at Ronnie's place following the dinner at Butter's apartment. Had she done so, she undoubtedly would have met the same fate as her friend. She had escaped murder (as one tabloid put it) "only because of the beneficent accident of a severe cold."[23]

Adrian Gregory, a coworker of Frank Byrnes's at the Racquet and Tennis Club, shed some light on the Englishman's movements on the last night of his life. The "pint-sized" waiter—who had come to America from his native Liverpool in 1924—had left work at around 8:40 that evening. He had tried to "borrow a couple of bucks" from Gregory to attend the employees' annual dance at the Hotel McAlpin that evening. Failing to get the money, Byrnes returned to his rented room and apparently went straight to bed.[24]

These interviews—combined with Dr. Gonzales's preliminary medical findings and the detectives' own methodical study of the crime scene—allowed Kear to provide reporters with a tentative reconstruction of the murders:

> Byrnes was the first victim slain as he slept. Subsequently, Mrs. Gedeon returned home. The killer had apparently been lying in wait for her. As she entered the house, she was attacked, dragged into the bedroom and criminally assaulted. The strangulation and the assault were apparently simultaneous. The body was pushed under the single bed in the room adjoining the 'master' bedroom. When Miss Gedeon came home she apparently stepped into the bedroom to the left of the entrance and partially disrobed. Evidently she did not want to awaken her mother. Leaving her clothing on the hamper in the bathroom, she then walked across the living room. As she entered the other bedroom, the murderer attacked her. The girl was clad only in her chemise. This was ripped off during the vio-

lent struggle that followed. It seems the killer must have begun strangling the model immediately. After the murder, the body was dragged to the small chamber adjoining the large bedroom and dumped on the single bed. Then the killer opened the front door and slunk into the night.[25]

Based on the evidence gathered up to that point, it was a perfectly plausible scenario. In almost every particular, however, it would prove to be wrong.

The Party Girl

A T A TIME when New Yorkers were routinely treated to such tabloid headlines as "RUM-CRAZY RIPPER CARVES DRUNKEN WOMAN TO DEATH," "GIGOLO CONFESSES TO TORSO MURDER," and "LOVER SLASHES SWEETHEART WHO SPURNED HIM," the slaying of the two Gedeon women and their boarder might have been expected to provide the public with some fleeting diversion at best. A rare combination of ingredients, however—a kind of perfect storm of prurience—raised the triple murder above the usual crime-and-scandal-sheet fare, turning it into what *Newsweek* magazine proclaimed "the best story in Manhattan tabloid history, everything that sensational journalism could ask for."[1]

There was, to begin with, the person of Ronnie Gedeon, the ideal tabloid victim: a stunning twenty-year-old model, strangled, stripped naked, and (so early reports insisted) sexually assaulted on the bed beneath which her murdered mother's body lay. The corpses of the two women, along with that of Frank Byrnes, had been transported to the morgue at Bellevue, where autopsies were scheduled for late Monday morning. As Dr. Gonzales made clear, there was no way of telling whether the women had been raped until the post-mortem examinations were completed and vaginal swabs analyzed. Unconstrained by anything as trivial as mere fact, however, the tabloids lost no time in attributing the murders to the era's leading boogeyman, the sex maniac.

"ART BEAUTY, MOTHER SLAIN BY SEX-FIEND" read the headline of Monday's *New York Evening Journal*, which—blithely ignoring the words of caution issuing from the medical examiner's office —informed readers that "there was no doubt in the mind of investigators that a maniacal sex factor figured in the murders." A half-page cartoon in the *Journal* showed a young female labeled "American Womanhood" opening her apartment door to be confronted by the towering shadow of a monster labeled "Sex Murderer." Another, on the editorial page of the same paper, depicted a drooling thug in a cap labeled "Sex Fiend Killer" moving a skull-shaped playing piece over a checkerboard labeled "American Homes." Other newspapers referred to the perpetrator as a "sex-poisoned beast," a "sex-maddened strangler," and a "sex-crazed lunatic" who violated his victims' bodies "before or after death."[2]

Dispensing with any pretense of journalistic objectivity, Monday's *Daily News* delivered its front-page story of the crime—"a blood-chilling episode of insensate lust and death"—in the pulp-fiction style of a dime store whodunit:

> It was dark as pitch—but the darkness was alive with danger. The clock struck 3. Veronica Gedeon turned the key in the lock of her Beekman Hill apartment. The silence was heavy. Touchi, her pet Pekinese, didn't run to greet her. That was strange. Veronica, who was 20, closed the door behind her in her five-room suite at 316 E. 50th St. A hand shot out of the darkness. It closed around her throat. Its powerful fingers pressed tighter —tighter.
> Her assassin dragged the girl—who had been a prize beauty

and an artist's model—toward her bedroom. The pressure on her throat became unendurable. Her lungs burst. She ceased to struggle. She was dead.

Then the strangler stripped her of her clothes.[3]

The morbid fascination provoked by the crime was made even greater by its setting. Not a single tabloid failed to note the connection among the Vera Stretz case, the Nancy Titterton bathtub murder, and the current atrocity, all of which had taken place within a few blocks of one another in the ostensible haven of Beekman Place. The parallels between the Titterton slaying and the Gedeon murders seemed especially striking. Both crimes had occurred on Easter weekend exactly a year apart. And both had been discovered by men who worked as upholsters—John Fiorenza in the Titterton case and now the estranged husband and father, Joseph Gedeon.[4]

What truly elevated the killing of Ronnie Gedeon above the common run of criminal sensations, however—and endowed her with a celebrity she had never enjoyed in life—was something unparalleled in tabloid publishing: a profusion of photographs of the lovely young victim posing provocatively in various states of undress. Within hours of the first published reports of the slaying, a freelance photographer named J. Jay Hirz telephoned the city desk of the *Daily News* to say that he was in possession of several dozen "figure studies" of the slain model that he was willing to part with for ten dollars apiece. Before long, other amateur shutterbugs—members of private "camera clubs" who forked over five dollars an hour to take pictures of naked women—emerged from the woodwork to peddle their own lascivious "art photos." By Monday evening, the late editions were already running nude pictures of Ronnie, discreetly retouched with gauzy, airbrushed veils. On the following day, the *Daily News* alone featured nine photos of the "prize beauty," either seminude or in a negligee. "As a murder mystery, it was a natural," *Time* magazine observed in a piece about the case. "As a picture story, it was a Roman holiday."[5]

Other photographs, reproduced from the true crime magazines

she had modeled for, gave an additional lurid twist to the story. Under headlines reading "Prophecy of Murder," "Shadows of the Doom to Come," and "Act that Turned Real Off-Stage," a terrified-looking Ronnie—dressed in skimpy undergarments or half-open kimonos—was shown trussed up with ropes, falling to her knees with a gun to her head, or cowering at some unseen attacker. The accompanying captions were all variations on the same portentous theme: the eerie way in which the pictures seemed to foretell her terrible fate. "When Veronica Gedeon posed for this photograph just a year ago to illustrate the cover of a magazine, she had no inkling that she, too, would be the victim of circumstances she was portraying," said the *Journal*. "Veronica Gedeon is here shown registering horror for a recent magazine illustration. Is this the way she gazed on her doom in her home early Easter morning?" wrote the *News*. "A year ago, the beautiful Veronica Gedeon took this terror-stricken pose to illustrate a story in *Inside Detective* magazine. Twelve months later she was again the shrinking beauty. But this time her attacker was not acting," intoned the *Mirror*.[6]

Acquaintances of Ronnie, incensed at seeing her pictured as "a wild girl with wild ways" who "met with a wild fate," rushed to her defense. She was "definitely a person of the proprieties," said her best friend, Jean Karp, who informed reporters that, in recent months, "Ronnie had taken a deep interest in the Bible, reading it for literary not religious reasons." Another good friend, Bobby Haenigsen—wife of cartoonist Harry Haenigsen, creator of the popular comic strip *Penny*—affirmed that "Ronnie was a fine girl. She and her mother were very devoted to each other. They were more like sisters than mother and daughter." The illustrator Saul Tepper, who had occasionally employed her as a model, described her as "a swell kid with a beautiful smile. She never impressed me as the kind of a girl who could become involved in any kind of a tragedy. She was so gay and light-spirited. I never saw her moody or temperamental. From what I saw of her I got the impression of a gay, good-natured girl who seemed to get a lot of fun out of life." Even West Peterson, editor of *Inside Detective*, the true crime magazine Ronnie had repeatedly posed for, chimed in with a testimonial. Veronica, he declared was "'decent' in every sense of the word . . . an honest girl from a family in straitened circumstances who was trying to earn her own living with the natural talents with which she was endowed. She was not 'cheap.' She did not sleep with men so that they would give her money. Had she not chosen to be a photographers' and illustrators' model, she might have been another stenographer, a sales girl, or a nurse. She had the intelligence to succeed in any of these callings."[7]

Offsetting these heartfelt tributes, however, was a deluge of rumors that cast Ronnie's character in a highly dubious light. Her "little black book" reportedly "bulged with the phone numbers" of her many boyfriends, a number of them "important Wall Street men with private numbers and public wives." Reportedly, she "was once employed at the Man About Town nightclub, 15 West 51st Street, but was discharged after getting into a brawl in which she received a black eye." There was her bare-breasted appearance in the notorious November 1935 Society of Illustrators burlesque show. And even darker stories soon emerged. Though quick to justify her behavior as an act of financial desperation, West Peterson felt compelled to reveal that Veronica had once "posed for a film taken by an unscrupulous photographer to be unreeled at bawdy stag parties." And shortly after the murders, the gossip king Walter Winchell, the nation's most powerful newspaper columnist, wrote that Ronnie had recently suffered "a sorta breakdown" from "too much whoopee." Though the message was coded, anyone fluent in Winchell's inimitable style—his "slanguage," as he called it—understood that he was referring to an abortion (a fact quickly confirmed when detectives tracked down the physician who had performed it).[8]

Still, it wasn't Winchell or any other professional scandalmonger who was most responsible for fueling the public perception of Ronnie as a promiscuous party girl. It was her father.

At around 4:00 a.m. Sunday, following a continuous twelve-hour grilling, Joseph Gedeon emerged from the East 51st Street station and found himself surrounded by a mob of newspapermen barraging him with questions. Announcing that he needed to get back to his upholstery shop—he had a "rush job" to finish, he explained, and had "already lost a day of work"—he made for the Second Avenue El with the reporters at his heels. Back at his shop, having refused to utter a word during the brief train ride, he locked himself inside and set about "reupholstering an overstuffed fan chair in green horsehair velvet for a client on the Upper East Side." He was too exhausted to concentrate, however. Throwing himself onto his cot, he dozed fitfully for a few hours, awakening shortly before 8:00 a.m. Thinking he might feel better if he had something in his stomach—more than twenty-four hours had elapsed since his last meal—he headed out to a greasy spoon on 34th Street called the Willow cafeteria but found himself unable to eat. He drank two cups of coffee, then returned to his shop.[9]

Waiting for him on the sidewalk were five detectives led by Captain Frank Curry, who was armed with a search warrant. Gedeon unlocked the door and let them inside. No sooner had they entered than Curry spotted a set of upholstery needles, a few more than eighteen inches long, lying on Gedeon's workbench. At a nod from the captain, one of his men confiscated them all.

"How am I supposed to get any work done without my tools?" asked an irate Gedeon.

When Curry replied that the needles would be returned just as soon as the crime lab was done with them, the old man stormed out of the shop, elbowed his way through the milling crowd of reporters, and hurried to the apartment of a friend named Herman a few blocks uptown, where he spent the next few hours spewing epithets at the police and imbibing schnapps.[10]

When he returned to his shop at around 1:30 p.m., the detectives were gone, though a handful of reporters were still gathered at his doorstep. His tongue loosened by the alcohol, Gedeon invited them inside. Perched on the edge of his cot, he lit a cigarette and began to hold forth, while the newspapermen took note of the squalid condition of his "dismal little cubicle," paying particular attention to the "pictures of bare-breasted women tacked to the wall," the "cheap 'art' magazines filled with nude photographs" stacked in a corner of the room, and, on a wooden shelf above his bed, books of mail-order erotica like Dr. La Forest Potter's *Strange Loves: A Study in Sexual Abnormalities* ("A startling, provocative disclosure of fantastic, strange amatory curiosities among savage and civilized races!").

Gedeon was indignant about the way police had treated him. "They took my fingerprints, I don't know why," he growled. "They even took the stuff from under my fingernails."

They'd also made him empty his pockets. "They found some nude pictures," he blithely told the reporters, who were busily scribbling away in their notepads. "French postcards. When they asked me about them, I said, 'Why shouldn't I have them? I'm a grown man and it's all right to have those pictures with me.'

"One time," he continued, "one of the detectives called me a liar. I said to him, 'You're a liar, too. I suppose if I took off my glasses, you'd hit me. Well, I'd hit you right back.'"[11]

Asked by the reporters about his alibi, Gedeon repeated the story of his evening at Corrigan's, crowing about his triumph at skee ball and wondering aloud about his misplaced hat. To a man, the reporters were confounded by the little upholsterer's demeanor—his apparent indifference to the horror that had befallen his family. "Gedeon's reaction to the tragedy is impersonal, detached," observed the *Journal*. "He is as ready to talk about his bowling score on the night of the killing as he is about the deaths of his wife and Ronnie. He seems more concerned with the disappearance of his gray hat than with the loss of his loved ones."[12]

Equally startling were the things he had to say about his younger daughter. "Ronnie was wild and willful," he declared. "She made suckers out of lots of men. Believe me, I know how she was. She would lead a guy right on, right up to the point of—whatever you want to call it—and then give him the horse laugh. She would tease men that way. Maybe she did that to some guy and got him so worked up and nuts that he killed her for it. Girls like Ronnie don't realize you can't treat a man that way."[13]

When asked if he thought the killer might have been someone romantically involved with his wife, Gedeon dismissed the idea with a sneer. "I don't think my wife would be attractive to other men. She was a very cold woman, the coldest I ever knew. But," he added with a shrug, "there's no accounting for taste."[14]

By then, he had grown weary of answering questions. With an impatient wave of the hand, he dismissed the reporters, who went off to file their stories about the bizarre little man who, in blaming his daughter's terrible death on her own reckless sexual behavior—"the exuberant employment of her charms," as one newspaper put it— had left her "without a shred of reputation."[15]

At roughly the same time—about half past three on Monday afternoon—Dr. Gonzales was completing his autopsies on the victims. Remnants of spaghetti in Ronnie's stomach confirmed Stephen Butter's account of her final evening, as did the large quantity of alcohol in her stomach, blood, and brain. Mrs. Gedeon's stomach contained the remains of "a hearty dinner of cabbage, green vegetables, and potatoes, only partially digested when she died." The "arrested state" of this meal suggested that she had been killed sometime between 10:00 p.m. and midnight, lending "mute corroboration to Cosmon Cambinias' story of the cry in the night."[16]

Despite the cuts and bruises around Mary Gedeon's genitalia and signs that Ronnie had recently engaged in sexual intercourse, Gonzales could find no definitive evidence that either woman had been raped. The tabloids, compelled to abandon their characterization of the killer as a sex-maddened fiend, scrambled to come up with a catchy new nickname, finally settling on the "Phantom Strangler of Beekman Place."[17]

One small discovery—reported by the tabloids in typically overheated fashion as "human flesh and hair clawed from the strangler"— consisted of two very fine, almost colorless hairs, microscopic in size, along with some equally tiny bits of skin found beneath Mary Gedeon's fingernails. These—along with Frank Byrnes's pillowcase, which bore a bloody palm print—were turned over to the "scientific sleuths" of the Police Crime Laboratory at the Poplar Street station in Brooklyn. Under a headline reading "STRAND OF HAIR + BIT OF SKIN MAY = ELECTRIC CHAIR," the *New York Evening Journal* ran a story acknowledging that the tiny hairs and "minute particles of skin" taken from Mrs. Gedeon's fingernail scrapings were exceptionally "meager clues" but pointed out that the clues that led to the solution of the Nancy Titterton murder—a length of twine and a single strand of horsehair—were "equally meager." In the end, however, analysis showed that the hairs and skin had come from Mary Gedeon herself, while the bloody palm print had been left accidentally by Dr. Gonzales during his examination of Byrnes's body at the murder scene.[18]

By Monday, seventy-five detectives from the homicide, gang, and Broadway squads were at work on the case, checking out the nearly 150 names found in Ronnie's address book, along with every person who had ever boarded with the Gedeons. Searching for anyone who might have been harboring a grudge against one of the victims, investigators soon learned of a man named James Fetton. A few years earlier, when Mary was still in possession of her brownstone on East 53rd Street, she had applied for home improvement funds to the federal loan association where Fetton worked as an appraiser. When he tried to shake her down—threatening to turn in an unfavorable report unless she came across with a valuable necklace she owned—she filed a formal complaint. Convicted of attempted extortion, Fetton ended up serving a ninety-day sentence and had been heard to issue threats against the woman who had put him behind bars. Tracked down and questioned by police, however, he turned out to have an alibi "tight as a drum."[19]

Other suspects were identified and quickly dismissed—an intern at nearby Midtown Hospital said to have been in love with Ronnie; a male singer at the Man About Town nightclub, where she had briefly worked as a hostess; a "William College student" she had gone out with a few times.[20]

For a while, attention shifted to the third and most enigmatic of the victims, Frank Byrnes, described by Inspector Lyons as a "man of mystery." Information gleaned from his relatives in Liverpool revealed that he had come to America about thirteen years earlier and worked at a variety of jobs, including "butler to a Park Avenue millionaire and cocktail shaker in a Manhattan club." He was reputed to be a ladies' man, as well as an inveterate racetrack gambler. The latter habit—if true—raised the possibility that Byrnes had been the real target of the killer, perhaps after welshing on a bet. There was also speculation that Byrnes and Mary Gedeon had been targeted for death by a "former intimate friend" of the "still-attractive matron"—a "huge Hungarian" named John Pattanlyus who, "suspicious that the suave, well-educated Englishman was a rival for Mrs. Gedeon's attentions," had slain them both in a fit of insane jealousy, then killed Ronnie when the young model returned home and stumbled on the murder scene. In the end, however, these theories led nowhere.[21]

It was Ronnie's best friend, Jean Karp, who provided what appeared to be the most promising lead. Too overwrought to supply much coherent information in the immediate aftermath of the murders, she was questioned again on Monday. This time, she mentioned a man who instantly found himself on the front page of every tabloid in town: a sometime chauffeur named Georges "Frenchy" Gueret.

A colorful character who, even when unemployed, paraded around in a chauffeur's uniform, complete with jodhpurs and leather puttees, the Parisian-born Gueret conformed in every respect to the popular stereotype of his countrymen. A self-proclaimed connoisseur of good food, fine wine, and pretty women, he spoke, after seventeen years in this country, with a thick French accent. His preferred headwear was a woolen beret, though he also owned a straw boater hat of the type favored by his idol, the Gallic troubadour Maurice Chevalier, whose syrupy ballads he was fond of performing at dinner parties.

Investigators quickly discovered, however, that the debonair "Frenchy"—who had boarded at the 53rd Street brownstone with

Vera Stretz and her attorney, Samuel Leibowitz, prepare to leave the courtroom following her acquittal.

Nancy Titterton.

All of the images appear courtesy of the author's private collection unless otherwise noted.

Robert Irwin.

In addition to her magazine modeling, Veronica Gedeon frequently posed for members of amateur "camera clubs."

"The Mad Sculptor" at work. *(Reprinted by permission of the* New York Daily News*)*

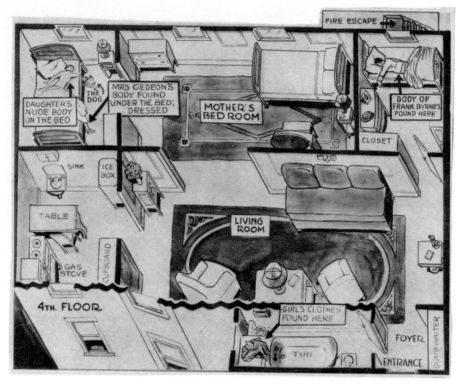

Layout of the Gedeons' apartment.

A detective examines the blood-soaked bed where boarder Frank Byrnes was slain.

Police remove the body of Ronnie Gedeon from her Beekman Place apartment building.

Bob's portrait bust of Ethel.

Following her murder, dozens of amateur shutterbugs peddled their nude photographs of Ronnie to the tabloids, which printed them with discreetly placed, airbrushed veils. This is one of the rare unretouched versions.

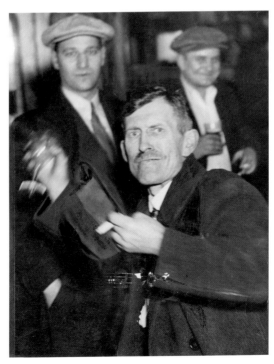

Joseph Gedeon takes aim with a beer glass at a tabloid news photographer.

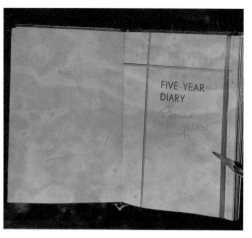

Ronnie's ex-husband, Robert Flower, kneels at her casket.

Ronnie's diary. Her entries about "Bob," originally assumed to refer to her ex-husband, helped detectives identify her killer.

This portrait of Bob was distributed around the country via police circulars, newspapers, and magazines—including *Inside Detective*.

The Statler Hotel in Cleveland, where Bob found work under the pseudonym "Bob Murray."

Bob's sketch of Henrietta Koscianski.

Henrietta identified Bob while reading the cover story in the July 1937 issue of *Inside Detective* magazine.

Detective Frank Crimmins escorts Bob from the plane that brought him back to New York City from Chicago.

Dressed in the dapper white suit he demanded as part of his surrender agreement, Bob is led to court for his arraignment.

Ethel Kudner leaves the grand jury room in the company of her lawyer.

Samuel Leibowitz, "the Great Defender," prepares for business.

Wayne Lonergan displays the charms that won the hearts of both Patsy Burton and her father, Bill.

Mary and Ronnie shortly before their move to the 51st Street flat—had a darker side. He had a police record: an arrest on a petty larceny charge that had earned him a short stint in jail. More to the immediate point were the accusations leveled by Jean Karp: that Frenchy had "quarreled bitterly" with Mary Gedeon over some money issues and "made a nuisance of himself" to Ronnie with his unwanted attentions. He also fit the police profile of the killer in another way: as an inmate of the Gedeons' home, he would have been known to the Pekingese, Touchi.[22]

Early Monday, Frenchy was picked up for questioning at the East 53rd shop of shoemaker Ballo Torregraso, where he was "doing a paint job in exchange for some lounging privileges." Shortly afterward, Detective Frank Crimmins and John B. Kaiser—"crack operatives of the Seventeenth Squad"—were sent to his rented room at 201 East 50th Street, a block and a half from the Gedeon apartment. When a search of his living quarters turned up two badly blood-stained handkerchiefs, the tabloids lost no time in declaring the case cracked.

"HOLD 'FRENCHY' IN MURDER OF 3," trumpeted the *Mirror*. "SEIZE CHAUFFEUR IN MODEL'S MURDER," blared the *News*. The situation grew even grimmer for Frenchy when he told his interrogators that he had spent part of Easter weekend at the home of his friend Charles Mocoro. Sent to Mocoro's room at 987 Second Avenue, detectives found four ice picks, one bearing what appeared to be blood stains. Lyons and his colleagues had already begun to entertain the theory that the triple slaying was committed by two men, a possibility that would resolve one of the more puzzling aspects of the case: "how a single murderer could overcome both Mrs. Gedeon and Veronica without disturbing the apartment more than was done." Mocoro quickly found himself in custody.[23]

The excitement over the ostensible solution to the crime was short-lived. Both men proved to have airtight alibis. The bloodstains on Frenchy's handkerchiefs were the result of his chronic and copious nosebleeds, while the stains on Mocoro's ice pick turned out to be rust. Swarmed by reporters as he left the police station, Frenchy brushed off the notion that he might do harm to either Gedeon woman and offered a theory of his own.

"I never fight with anybody," he proclaimed. "I am a gentleman. I have never caused trouble for anybody, especially any woman. To Ronnie I was like the papa. The uncle. We were friends. No, I did not kill Ronnie Gedeon, that beautiful girl. No, I did not kill her good, hard-working mama nor this lodger of theirs, a man I do not know from Adam."

"Then who did?" asked a reporter.

"I tell you," said Frenchy. "Mama Gedeon was a very stingy woman. Somebody killed her for her money. The other two were killed because they hear or see something."[24]

With his most promising suspects cleared, Lyons offered a somber assessment to the press. "We are up against a stone wall and will just have to keep working on in the dark until we get something we can sink our teeth into," he declared, mixing his metaphors in a way that might have seemed amusing under less tragic circumstances.[25]

One man who claimed to have some knowledge of the culprit was the Reverend Gerald L. K. Smith. A silver-tongued hate-monger who preached racism, anti-Semitism, and other forms of bigotry, Smith—over the radio, on the lecture circuit, and in the pages of his monthly magazine, *The Cross and the Flag*—called for the forced shipment of America's "black savages" to Africa, the deportation of its Jews to Russia, and the "halt of immigration by Asiatics," all in the service of purging the country of its insidious non-Aryan elements. He also railed ceaselessly against the "Bolshevik menace," also known in his parlance as "Christ-hating Muscovites."

On Monday evening, the day after the massacre, Smith delivered one of his rabble-rousing diatribes to the Men's Club of St. Stephen's Protestant Episcopal Church in Brooklyn, in the course of which he referred to the dominant news story of the day. "I charge that the crime which was committed in Fiftieth Street in Manhattan, the murder of Veronica Gedeon, artists' model, and two others, was committed by a sex-mad maniac," he thundered, "part of the atheistic Communistic lawlessness which is gnawing at our social structure." Reporting on his speech the following afternoon, the *Post* took an appropriately derisive tone. "Now we know the reason for the current wave of revolting sex crimes in New York City," the paper jeered. "The Communists are to blame."[26]

One person the police were much interested in talking to was Lucy Beacco, the visiting friend of Ronnie's who had been staying in the little bedroom where the bodies of the two Gedeon women were found. From a letter they discovered atop her bureau, investigators learned that she had gone to spend the Easter weekend with friends in North Adams, Massachusetts.

Brought back to Manhattan late Monday afternoon, she was questioned by the police, then escorted to the crime scene by Detective Martin Owens, who instructed her to take a look around and tell him whether anything was missing. Aside from the sheets and pillowcase removed by the crime lab technicians, everything appeared to be where she'd left it. She was just about to leave when something caught her eye.

"Wait a minute," she said, pointing to the bureau. "I had a clock on there."

"When did you last see it?" asked Owens.

"Friday night when I left for Massachusetts."

"You sure?"

"Yes, absolutely," said Beacco.

Asked to describe it, the young woman said it was "a cheap clock, a Baby Ben. It didn't cost more than two or three dollars." Why anyone would bother to steal it was a mystery.[27]

Murder Sells

B Y TUESDAY, THE TABLOID COVERAGE of the case had already reached a frenzied pitch, with the *News* devoting nine full pages to the story. Treating the tragedy as pure pop entertainment, the paper bestowed a snappy title on the crime—"The Murder of the Artist's Model," New York's most thrilling "Drama of Death." Under the headline "THE CAST IN 'THE MURDER OF THE ARTIST'S MODEL,'" it even ran a Hollywood-style credit list, as though the principal figures in the case, including the victims, were merely actors playing roles in a movie melodrama:

> THE MODEL—Veronica Gedeon
> THE ROOMER—Lucy Beacco
> THE MOTHER—Mrs. Mary Gedeon
> THE LODGER—Frank Byrnes
> THE BOYFRIEND—Stephen Butter
> THE FATHER—Joseph Gedeon
> THE BEST FRIEND—Jean Karp
> THE KILLER—?[1]

So unbridled was the tabloid's "wallowing treatment of the murders" that—in response to a barrage of letters from indignant readers objecting to its focus on "morbid sensationalism"—*Daily News* publisher Joseph Medill Patterson was moved to defend his newspaper's policy in a remarkable editorial. Titled "What Is the Best Story?" and accompanied by a pair of photographs—one of U.S. Supreme Court Chief Justice Charles Evans Hughes, the other of a half-naked Veronica Gedeon—the editorial contrasted the *News*'s cursory mention of an important Supreme Court decision handed down on Monday with its lip-smacking coverage of the Gedeon murders.

Acknowledging that "the Supreme Court story was historically more significant," Patterson nevertheless argued that his managing editor made the right decision by playing up the Gedeon tragedy. "Look at this murder story as a story," he argued:

> The murders themselves were grisly and mysterious enough. But also they were committed against a background of light living and light loving, family complications, bootlegging, shadowy married friends of the victims, etc. Mystery story writers —Agatha Christie, Rex Stout, the late Conan Doyle, or Edgar Allan Poe himself if he were alive—would revel in such an assortment of raw materials for a murder plot. And the resulting novel, play, or movie would sell. Murder sells papers, books, plays, because we are all fascinated by murder. It is a part of life —the most fatally intriguing part. And this is a murder story in real life. . . . Perhaps people should be more interested today in the Supreme Court than in the Gedeon murder, but we don't think they are.[2]

Two days later, as though to thumb its nose at snooty critics who condemned it for pandering to popular taste, the paper proudly ran a letter from a typical reader that perfectly validated Patterson's point:

> I ain't much of a hand at writing because my kids only a year ago taught me to write. But I want to tell you that I think your

paper is darn good. I learnt to read from *The News*. I like them pictures of the beautiful murdered model and I tear them out of the paper and hang them on the wall. My wife gets mad, but ha ha. And them people who says your paper is not good is nuts, ha ha. —Delighted Customer[3]

For its part, the *Mirror* played up the human-interest angle by running a voyeuristic *True Confessions*–style feature supposedly penned by Veronica's boyfriend, Lincoln Hauser. Titled "Ronnie's Fiancé Tells Love Tale," the five-part series promised titillating revelations by the person who knew the "slain beauty" more "thoroughly" and "intimately" than anyone else.

While portraying the "slain artist's model" as a "sweet kid" who brought "dainty foods and flowers" to hospitalized friends, "loved the pageantry of the church," avidly read "the classics and fine poetry," and longed for "a home, children, and an orderly life," the ostensible memoir mostly dished up juicy innuendoes about her life as a party girl. Ronnie "played the field and she played it recklessly and enjoyed every minute of it." She "had a closet full of clothes. Some she bought herself and some were bought for her. A well-known insurance man frequently bought her beautiful gowns and accessories." She "knew dozens of headwaiters by their first names. Sometimes her escorts were middle-aged men. She would come home sometimes at six or seven o'clock in the morning after a night in the finest clubs and hotels in the city." In the studios where she posed in the nude, she met "prominent men and women and would be asked to join them in wild parties. Sometimes she went and sometimes she did not. She wanted to quit but invariably she would say that there was some kind of an excitement about it that she couldn't shake off. She knew that it was the wrong thing to do but there was no way to get her to stop."

In the end, Hauser's purported memoir was an epitome of tabloid cynicism, serving up sexual titillation under the guise of moral instruction: the cautionary fable of a good-hearted but unconstrained young woman who "played the field and played it recklessly" and paid the ultimate price for her promiscuous ways.[4]

Tabloid publishers weren't the only ones to indulge in the crass exploitation of the Beekman Hill tragedy. On the same day that Patterson's editorial appeared, city newspapers began running an advertisement by the Segal Lock and Hardware Company. Beneath the bold-type warning "IT CAN HAPPEN TO YOU!," the ad showed a picture of the lock maker's patented "jimmy-proof" dead bolt and a newspaper clipping headlined "TRIPLE MURDER IN GEDEON FLAT."

That the perpetrator of the Easter Sunday Massacre was no homicidal intruder but (as authorities had made clear from the start) an acquaintance of the Gedeons made no difference. Throughout the city —but particularly in Beekman Place and adjacent neighborhoods —locksmiths reported doing a "land-office business." In a single day, Charles Negroponte, who ran a shop at 204 East 50th Street and whose "normal sales averaged six or so daily," sold "seventy-five new locks." His merchandise was moving even faster than it had a year earlier, after the neighborhood's previous atrocity. "When Mrs. Titterton was killed, things got good," said Negroponte. "We never expected to see days like that again." Compared to the "swell business" he was doing now, however, Negroponte viewed the "post-Titterton rush as a mere flurry."[5]

On Tuesday afternoon, police announced that Dr. Erasmus Hudson —a New York physician and fingerprint expert who had gained national renown for his work on the Lindbergh baby kidnapping case —had managed to raise a bloody thumbprint from the bathroom door of the Gedeons' apartment by means of his pioneering silver nitrate technique. Specialists from the Bureau of Criminal Identification at police headquarters were in the process of comparing the print to those taken from the many individuals who had already been called in for questioning. Kear and his cohorts were particularly eager to see if the telltale print matched up with the thumb mark of the man who was rapidly becoming their prime suspect: Joseph Gedeon.[6]

As much as anything else, it was Gedeon's weird indifference to the murders that had piqued the suspicions of the detectives. His bizarrely blasé behavior was on full display on Tuesday. Even as the bodies of his wife and daughter were being transported from the Bellevue morgue to James McCabe's funeral parlor on West 90th Street—where a crowd of morbid curiosity seekers was already gathering on the sidewalk for a glimpse of the celebrity corpses—the little upholsterer was pursuing his daily routines as if nothing out of the ordinary had occurred.

Emerging from his shop at around eight in the morning, Gedeon —trailed by a mob of reporters and a pair of detectives assigned to keep watch on him—strolled to Diamond Dry Cleaners at 547 Third Avenue, where he dropped off a gray topcoat to be sponged and pressed. He then proceeded to the Willow cafeteria on 34th Street, stopping first at a corner newsstand to pick up the morning tabloids.

Seating himself at a table, he flirted with the waitress as he put in his usual order of oatmeal and coffee, then settled back with the papers, pursing his mouth in apparent distaste as he pored over the many photos of his scantily clad daughter. From surrounding tables, reporters began peppering him with questions. Asked if he had any theories about the killer, he replied without hesitation.

The culprit, he declared, was "a married millionaire who wanted to have an affair with Ronnie. I don't know his name. I just know he came from Boston. He offered Ronnie a big car, an apartment, and jewelry if she would sleep with him. But she turned him down. I believe his frustration caused him to do it. Not that he killed her himself. He must have hired someone else to do it."

How, someone asked, could he take the tragedy so calmly?

"I'm a fatalist," he replied with a shrug. "Also a naturalist. I take things naturally. Everything occurs because of causation. Whatever happens has to happen, and so why get excited about it?"[7]

There were, of course, certain things that did upset him. He lamented the fact that his wife carried no life insurance. "She always told me she didn't want anyone to profit her death. I thought differently," said Gedeon. "My idea is that a man and wife should be insured in each other's names for the benefit of the domestic partnership."

Still, he wasn't overly concerned about his finances. "A girl with five thousand dollars wants to marry me right now," he explained. "But she's ugly. I couldn't marry an ugly woman. My idea of the right wife for me is a woman between thirty-five and forty, pretty and full of pep, but with good sense. I wouldn't care whether she was a blonde or brunette."

Gedeon continued to chat away merrily until one of the reporters began to press him on his alibi. "That's enough," he growled, leaping from his chair and bolting from the restaurant. After a quick trip by cab to McCabe's funeral parlor—where he dropped off the burial clothes that Ethel had tearfully picked out for Mary and Ronnie—he returned to his shop and locked himself inside.

Shortly afterward, a group of his friends showed up, all fellow Hungarians, including Paul Nadanyi, editor of the local Hungarian newspaper, the *Daily Népszava*. After a few glasses of schnapps, Gedeon agreed to be interviewed by Nadanyi. His "mood fluctuating from gloom to belligerence," he blamed his travails on his wayward daughter and overindulgent wife. As for the police, who clearly still had him under surveillance, he expressed nothing but defiance: "The cops can't break me," he said, shaking a fist. "I have seven lives."[8]

From the sidewalk below his second-story shop, reporters called up to Gedeon that his alibi had been shaken. Going to the door, he was told that the owner of Corrigan's Bar and Grill, Cal Parliapiano—who had originally corroborated Gedeon's account of his whereabouts at the time of the murders—had "changed his story and now says he's not sure you *were* in his place all the time you said you were." Though the barkeep had seen Gedeon at the skee ball machine twice that evening—when he arrived for work at

7:00 p.m. and when he left around midnight—he couldn't say for certain "whether he was there all during the intervening hours."

Hearing this news, Gedeon erupted into "geysers of wrath." "You're lying, he's lying or you both are crazy as hell!" he screamed. Gathering up his buddies, he shoved his way through the clamoring mob and made his way to the curb, where he and his friends piled into a taxi and took off.

They spent the next five hours drinking schnapps and playing gin rummy at his friend Herman's apartment. At around ten, Gedeon felt in the mood for his favorite pastime. Taking a cab to Radio City Bowling and Billiards, across Sixth Avenue from the Music Hall and open twenty-four hours, they bowled merrily all night, Gedeon using his usual sixteen-pound ball and racking up consistent scores in the 200-to-225 range.

They were still going at it at seven in the morning when a bunch of reporters—tipped off about Gedeon's location—burst into the place. Making their escape, Gedeon and his friends took a cab to the Beekman Tavern on Second Avenue and 50th Street, around the corner from his deceased wife's apartment. "Done up like a Bavarian beer garden," it had been Mary's favorite watering hole.

Taking a table in back, they lit cigarettes and ordered beers. Gedeon was just starting on his second glass when the newspapermen showed up. One of the photographers—John Reidy of the *Mirror*—pointed his Speed Graphic at Gedeon. His face a mask of rage, the little man flung the contents of his glass at Reidy, then cocked his arm and—as the cameraman pressed the shutter button—hurled the glass itself.

A melee erupted. Chairs were thrown, beer steins shattered, punches exchanged. As he scuffled with Reidy, Gedeon's pince-nez eyeglasses were knocked to the floor and trampled to pieces. Finally, a pair of beat cops rushed in and put a halt to the fracas.

Gedeon was escorted back to his shop, where a "fresh batch of newshounds—the day shift—was waiting." Standing on his stoop, the little upholsterer—his clothes and hair disheveled, his glasses gone—hurled curses at the reporters and gestured his contempt by drawing a finger across his throat. Then he disappeared inside, bolted the door behind him, stripped off his clothes, and—exhausted from his long night of carousing—collapsed on his cot.

He managed only three hours of sleep. Shortly before 11:00 a.m., he was awakened by a pounding on his door. It was Detective Sidney Lecher, sent there with orders from District Attorney William C. Dodge to bring Joseph Gedeon in for another round of questioning.[9]

To the disappointment of the police, who were hoping that the bloody fingerprint found on the bathroom door of the apartment would tie Gedeon to the killings, the crime lab experts had been unable to come up with a match. Despite the lack of physical evidence against him, however, investigators were increasingly convinced that Ronnie's father was the culprit. Apart from his bizarrely unfeeling behavior in the wake of the killings, there was the revised testimony of Cal Parliapiano, which had punctured a hole in the upholsterer's supposedly "airtight alibi." Gedeon's skee ball partner that night, a linotype operator named Thomas Kelly, could only "swear to his presence from midnight to closing, while the bartender, Eddie Murray, didn't remember seeing him at all. 'It was one of the busiest nights we ever had. They were lined up two deep at the bar.'"[10] That left a gap between 7:00 p.m. and midnight when Gedeon's whereabouts could not be independently confirmed. Nor could anyone testify to his movements after 3:00 a.m.

There was also the matter of his clothing. Several patrons of Corrigan's had told detectives that they recalled seeing Gedeon in a shabby brown suit on the night of the killings. Since Sunday, however, he had been wearing a gray-checked jacket and pants, leading police to suspect that "the brown suit might have been discarded because it had been stained with blood."[11]

Casting Gedeon's character in a particularly unsavory light was his supposed sexual degeneracy. In the tabloids, he was now routinely described as "a student of erotica"—"a French postcard fancier" who lived in a "sleazy bower of love shelved with risqué books," used "pictures of naked women to satiate his queer animal desires," and had deserted his wife "in favor of solitude and sex practices more bizarre than the marriage bed." Retained by the *Daily News* to provide expert commentary on the unfolding case, Dr. Carleton Simon—former Special Deputy Police Commissioner of New York and author of such works as *Homosexualists and Sex Crimes, The Menace of Dope,* and *The Negro Criminal*—flatly declared that "Gedeon's behavior is certainly not that of a normal man." The evidence? "He likes to read about sex and treasures photographs of nude women."[12]

Certainly he had the physical strength to perpetrate the murders. Though he was slight of stature with a "mousy appearance," he had developed enormously powerful hands, partly from years of "pulling cloth and leather" in his upholstery work, partly from his addiction to bowling (he boasted of routinely playing seventy games in a single night). His favorite parlor trick was bending a beer-bottle cap in half between his thumb and forefinger.[13]

As for a motive, the current thinking among the members of the Homicide Squad was that—having discovered "that Mary Gedeon and roomer Frank Byrnes had a relationship that transcended the conventional"—Gedeon had "killed his wife and Byrnes in a fit of jealousy and added Ronnie because his disapproval of her way of life amounted to a fixation."[14]

Determined to wrest a confession from "the extremely odd little man," investigators proceeded to subject him "to a grilling of such intensity as had seldom, if ever, been equaled in any New York homicide investigation."[15] Sequestered in a "bare and forbidding" room on the third floor of the East 51st Street police station, Gedeon was seated on a hard-backed wooden chair, a blazing light trained on his face. Working in teams, his interrogators—including at times Assistant District Attorney P. Francis Marro, Deputy Police Commissioner Harold Fowler, Deputy Chief Inspector Kear, and District Attorney Dodge himself—pounded away at him for hours on end. Occasionally, the pounding was more than verbal. Like other suspects subjected to the third degree in those days, Gedeon ended up with some ugly contusions.

Right from the start, his questioners made it clear that they no longer believed his alibi. "You claim you were in Corrigan's the whole time," said Kear. "But now the bar owner says he only saw you there at seven p.m. and at midnight."

Gedeon was unfazed. "He was busy that night. Maybe he didn't see me continuously. But I was there in the crowd." As for the people who said he was dressed in a brown suit, "they're mistaken," said Gedeon. "I had on this same gray suit as now."

At one point, Kear produced the gray suede glove found at the murder scene and asked Gedeon to try it on. Though it fit easily, the upholsterer insisted that it wasn't his. "I'm a poor man," he said. "I haven't owned any gloves for two or three years."

"Considering that your wife and daughter have been horribly killed, you've shown little grief," said Kear.

"I'm always that way," Gedeon answered. "Things hurt me deep, but inside."

"You didn't love your wife?"

Gedeon's answer was harsh. "She was an ignorant woman. She didn't know how to bring up her children. But I wouldn't kill her."

"Did you love Veronica?"

"She was never dutiful to me," Gedeon replied. "I paid twenty dollars for the *Book of Knowledge* when she was little. She wouldn't study it. All she wanted to do was go to movies. But Ethel, my other daughter, she read the book. She was a good girl."

Despite the medical examiner's finding that neither woman had been sexually assaulted, the interrogators returned again and again to Gedeon's supposedly aberrant psychology, the main symptoms of which were his unabashed interest in sex and the pleasure he derived from pictures of bare-breasted women.

"You are a student of erotica, are you not?" asked Assistant DA Marro.

"I have pictures of naked women in my room and books on unusual sex practices," Gedeon admitted. "But that wouldn't make me commit murders," he sensibly added.

"Why do you have a full length mirror attached to your bathroom door?" he was asked.

"Oh, I am very much interested in nature."

"You mean you're interested in nude women?"

"Well, that's a part of nature. Yes, I like to see them."

"Why is the mirror on the door?"

"Well, I like to make love to women and to be able to see how they look when I kiss them. I love all nature—anything that is beautiful. Not only women but trees, flowers, birds."

"You don't regard yourself as being abnormal in your attitude towards women?" Marro pressed.

"No," Gedeon insisted. "I'm not abnormal at all. I'm just a man who appreciates life."

"Why have you got all those pictures of nude women around your room?"

"What's so odd about that?" asked Gedeon. "They aren't nasty pictures. They are out of art magazines."

"You have some peculiarities about the relations of men and women, haven't you?" Marro persisted.

"Well, I think there is always a conflict between the sexes. Women want to dominate men, but men shouldn't let them do that."

"You mean it's the business of men to control women?"

"If you don't control them," said Gedeon, "they take advantage of you."

"What did you quarrel with your wife about when you and she separated?"

"Nothing in particular," Gedeon said. "They were not respectful to me at home. So I said, 'All right, I'll leave. You live your own life and I'll live mine.'"

"You didn't hate your wife?"

"No."

"Did you love her?"

"Well," said Gedeon, "she was my wife."

Hour after hour, the cross-examination went on. For all the effort to break him, however, the little upholsterer stood firm.

"You're making a terrible mistake," he kept repeating. "I didn't do it. I wouldn't kill my family."[16]

Despite his denials, authorities remained convinced that it was only a matter of time before Gedeon cracked. Emerging from the isolated interrogation room late Wednesday afternoon, District Attorney Dodge was surrounded by newsmen. "I can state positively that we have a definite suspect," he said with a grin.

"Though he refused to comment further," the *News* reported, "his implication was obvious that the police were ready to break 'The Murder of the Artist's Model.'" Screaming headlines in the tabloids left no doubt that Joseph Gedeon was about to be charged with the atrocity: "HOLD FATHER OF MURDERED MODEL," "POLICE TIGHTEN NET ON SLAIN MODEL'S DAD," "GEDEON'S ALIBI TORN BY GAPS," "GEDEON FACES ARREST." One paper went so far as to publish a close-up of the little upholsterer's eyes under the caption "EYES OF A MURDERER," while the front page of the *Mirror* carried the photo of Gedeon—his face contorted with rage —about to hurl his beer glass at the cameraman.[17]

Gedeon's situation looked even grimmer when, shortly after Dodge made his announcement of an imminent break in the case, a team of detectives was dispatched to the upholsterer's shop to search for several items. One was the mate to the incriminating gray glove. Another was the brown suit Gedeon had reportedly been wearing on the night of the murder. The third was the ostensible weapon used to kill Frank Byrnes: what the tabloids, in their typically inflammatory style, had taken to calling the "Gedeon Death Needle."

After the *News* ran a picture of the varying sized needles confiscated during the initial search of Gedeon's workplace, an upholsterer named Sam Kross got in touch with the police, having spotted something strange in the photograph. According to Kross, Gedeon's supposedly complete set lacked a vital component: a twelve-inch "regulator" (as the needles are known in the trade). Questioned about the absent tool, Gedeon could only say that he must have lost it.[18]

Despite a concerted effort that included the Department of Sanitation—which was enlisted to search "all the sewers in the area bordered by Forty-eighth and Fifty-third Streets from Third Avenue to the East River"—the vanished foot-long "regulator" was never found. Nor did the police turn up the missing glove. They did find a threadbare brown suit jacket, but Gedeon dismissed it with a snort as an "old rag" he hadn't worn in years and insisted that he had no idea where the matching vest and pants were, having discarded them long ago.[19]

Quite unexpectedly, police found something else besides the old jacket while ransacking Gedeon's premises: a nickel-plated .38-caliber revolver loaded with two bullets and buried in a box of horsehair in a corner of his workroom. Taken to his shop and confronted with the weapon, Gedeon spun a wildly improbable tale, claiming that, on the steamship that brought him from Hungary twenty-nine years earlier, he had met a man who "gave me the gun and asked me to hold onto it for him." Nearly three decades later, Gedeon was still waiting for its rightful owner "to call for it."

As for how it came to be hidden in the horsehair, the little man explained with a smirk that he had kept it in his bureau drawer until recently, when a "big, blonde hustler" dropped in to keep him company one night and happened upon the pistol. "So I hid it, figuring that trouble might come of a girl like that knowing where there was a loaded gun handy."[20]

Since Gedeon had initially denied owning a gun, "detectives were elated at having caught him in such a definite lie," the *New York Post* reported. They were happy for another reason, too. By then, the upholsterer had already endured a brutal twenty-four-hour interrogation. Without formally charging him with a crime, police couldn't hold him indefinitely. Since the gun was unlicensed, however, Gedeon was now subject to arrest for violating New York State's Sullivan Act, a felony punishable by up to five years in jail.

He would be formally charged with the crime on Thursday evening. Before that happened, however, his inquisitors—partly out of basic human decency, partly in the hope that the emotional stress of the occasion "might break the stoicism with which he had thus far resisted their efforts"—granted him permission to attend the funeral of his wife and daughter.[21]

Bundled into a police car with four detectives, Gedeon was driven uptown to West 90th Street, where a mob of the morbidly curious —estimated at between three and five thousand people—thronged the sidewalks outside McCabe's funeral parlor. Others watched from the surrounding rooftops, fire escapes, and apartment windows. When the police car pulled up and the wizened little man climbed out, a shout went up: "There he is! There's Gedeon!" Shielding his face with his hat, he was hustled through the surging mob by his police guards.

Inside the chapel, the air was heavy with the scent of dozens of wreaths, including one from the Society of Illustrators, "in whose show," as the *News* helpfully reminded its reader, "Ronnie had a part when it was raided by police for indecency." Other floral tributes were from "artists for whom Veronica had posed, from fellow models, and from her many boyfriends."[22]

The bodies of mother and daughter lay head to head in open satin-lined coffins. Ronnie wore a white satin gown with an orchid corsage pinned to her left shoulder. Mary was garbed in blue satin with a corsage of roses and lilies of the valley. Each had a rosary placed in her right hand.

The little chapel was crowded, though mostly with news photographers and "determined curiosity seekers" who had managed to wangle their way inside. There were only a handful of actual mourners: Ronnie's ex-husband, Bobby Flower; her supposed fiancé, Lincoln Hauser, and his pal Stephen Butter; her two closest friends, Jean Karp and a model named Sarilla Bell (who had also taken part in the notorious Society of Illustrators stag show). Ethel was in such a state of collapse that she had to be taken into another room. Her husband, Joe Kudner, sat through the brief service with his parents at his side.

After asking the detectives to clear the room of strangers, Gedeon cast a brief glance at Veronica, then stood beside his wife's bier for several minutes before seating himself in a folding chair behind his son-in-law. He sat dry-eyed through the service, conducted by the Reverend Father Joseph Daley of the nearby Church of St. Gregory the Great. "Enter not onto judgment of thy servants," intoned the priest. "From the gate of hell deliver their souls. . . . Eternal rest grant unto them, O Lord."

When the prayers were completed, Gedeon stepped forward, glanced first at Mary, then at Veronica, and hurried back to his seat. If police were hoping that the sight of his murdered wife and daughter would cause him to crack and spill out a confession, they were disappointed. The little upholsterer remained utterly calm, in marked contrast to the emotion displayed by Joe Kudner and the trio of young men who had known and loved Veronica—Bobby Flower, Linc Hauser, and Stephen Butter. Each of them leaned over the casket and kissed the corpses. There were tears in the eyes of the three young men, while Kudner wept openly.

Fifteen policemen struggled to hold back the crowds as Gedeon emerged from the funeral parlor and was hustled into a waiting squad car. Another smaller crowd of morbid spectators—this one numbering an estimated three hundred people—was waiting at St. Mary's Cemetery in Yonkers, where the two caskets were to be buried, one on top of the other, in a grave owned by Ethel Kudner.

Officiating at the burial was the mortician, James McCabe, who led the mourners in the Lord's Prayer and three Hail Marys. As Gedeon watched the bodies of his wife and daughter disappear into the earth, he finally lost his "expressionless calm." Bursting into tears, he stumbled toward Ethel, who sat weeping in a wooden folding chair.

"Oh, Father! Father!" she cried, stretching out her arms and drawing him into the chair beside her. As he laid his head on her shoulder, his body convulsed with sobs, she threw her worn raccoon coat partly over him and held him in a close embrace. They sat there, weeping, until the brief service was over.[23]

Immediately after the burial, Gedeon was returned to the East 51st Street police station, where he was grilled for another six hours before being formally placed under arrest for the gun charge. Driven downtown to police headquarters, he was fingerprinted and placed in Cell No. 1, his shoelaces, necktie, and belt confiscated as a routine precaution against suicide. Apart from the respite to attend the funeral, he had endured thirty-three hours of brutal, nonstop interrogation and—except for the brief, aborted doze following his night-long carouse with his friends—had gone without sleep for more than two days. Though a large, metal-caged ceiling light glared directly overhead, Gedeon fell into a profound slumber the moment he stretched out on the cot.

Awakened at 5:25 the next morning, he was given some coffee and cake, which he devoured with relish. At promptly 9:00 a.m., wearing his neatly buttoned double-breasted overcoat and a green hat cocked at a jaunty angle, he was brought upstairs to the lineup room, where he stood on the brightly lit platform and freely confessed to the unlawful possession of the handgun. Back to his old defiant self, he wore a disdainful smirk throughout the proceedings. Before leaving the stage, he topped off his performance by bowing deeply to his police audience and saluting them with a sardonic "I thank you—gentlemen."

Brought into Felony Court for his preliminary arraignment, he was allowed a brief consultation with his lawyer, Peter L. F. Sabbatino, a former assistant district attorney retained by Ethel. Seated on a court bench, Gedeon described, with accompanying gestures, the third-degree treatment he had received at the hands of the police: how they had yanked his ears, bent his arms nearly to breaking over the back of his chair, slugged him in the stomach, and battered him about the face and head.

Sabbatino's adversary that morning was the man now occupying his former position, Assistant DA Raymond Leo. Appearing before Magistrate Michael Ford, the two lawyers got involved in a battle that quickly "approached the fisticuffs stage." Describing the upholsterer as a "possible suspect in the triple Gedeon murders," Leo asked the judge to set bail at $15,000. Sabbatino sneered that the police were "barking up the wrong tree." Since his client had no criminal record and was there on a mere misdemeanor charge, Sabbatino demanded a nominal bail of fifty dollars.

When the judge sided with the prosecutor and set bail at $10,000, Sabbatino erupted. "Your Honor," he said, "my client has been subjected to the third degree. They used the old back room tactics on him. He was kicked and pulled and dragged and slapped for hours. He's a mass of bruises." Acceding to Sabbatino's demand, Magistrate Ford ordered an immediate physical examination of the prisoner by three court-appointed MDs: Gedeon's personal doctor, Barnett Dobrow; Ralph J. Carotenuto, the Tombs' resident physician; and Dr. Perry Lichtenstein, who was attached to the DA's office.

Informed of Sabbatino's charges, Police Commissioner Valentine brushed them off. "I don't believe it," he told reporters. "It's the usual allegation of an attorney whose client is in serious trouble. At the beginning of the investigation, I instructed Assistant Chief Inspector John A. Lyons to see that no one laid a hand on Gedeon. He's the victim of a double hernia and a frail little man."

Asked about the visible bruises on Gedeon's face, the commissioner had a ready response. "I'm told the suspect's injuries were inflicted when he bumped into a swinging door at the East 51st Street Station. And the old fellow was mixed up in a number of brawls with photographers when he was out of police custody.

"His eyeglasses were smashed in one of those brawls," Valentine added, "and it was the *police* who chipped in to buy him the new glasses he wore in court. That was done out of pity. The old man was staggering around blind as a bat."[24]

Though Gedeon still topped the official list of suspects and the tabloids continued to bay for his blood, not everyone was convinced of his guilt. One doubter was John Shuttleworth, editor of *True Detective* magazine. On the morning of the little upholsterer's arraignment, Shuttleworth asked one of his writers, Frank Preston, to "check with Gedeon's neighbors. See if they know anything about his movements on Saturday night."

It didn't take long for Preston to track down thirty-one-year-old Anthony Rocco at a smoke-filled pool hall below street level in the East 20s. After some prodding, Rocco, a former amateur boxer who occupied a tiny flat above Gedeon's workshop, admitted that he had seen the upholsterer on Sunday morning at five minutes past 3:00 a.m.

"I was coming home late from a party and he was just reeling in," Rocco recalled. "He looked to be pretty drunk. I said 'Good morning' just as he was putting his key in the lock. He mumbled back, 'Good morning.' I saw him go into his room and I went upstairs."

When asked how he could be "so sure about the time," Rocco explained that he "always set my alarm clock by my wrist watch and when I got upstairs it was exactly seven minutes after three."

"Why haven't you told the police about this?' asked Preston.

"Because I didn't want to get into a jam," Rocco said.

After convincing the ex-pug that he had nothing to worry about, Preston rushed him down to the Centre Street headquarters, where Rocco related his story to the police, corroborating Gedeon's alibi that he had returned straight home from Corrigan's on the night of the murder.[25]

Later that afternoon, Sabbatino was back in court, brandishing the report of the three physicians, who had found unmistakable signs that Gedeon had in fact been manhandled during his thirty-three-hour ordeal. The little man's "injuries included abrasions to the lower jaw, scratches behind the right ear, a black-and-blue left ear, abrasions and contusions above the right eye, and black-and-blue marks on the chest and back of the neck."

"My client has been brutally beaten," Sabbatino angrily declared. "I want him released on low bail so I can get him to press charges against those responsible. The gun charge is not connected in any way to the murders. This man is being railroaded. The police and the district attorney have no case whatsoever."

Sharing the lawyer's indignation over the evidence of police brutality, Magistrate Ford cast a baleful eye on Assistant DA Leo. "I set high bail because of the Prosecutor's statement that this man is a murder suspect. Shall I treat him as a murder suspect or merely as the possessor of a gun?"

"If Your Honor wishes to reduce bail," a sheepish Leo replied, "we are willing. There is no issue here except violation of the Sullivan law. We withdraw all reference to murder in connection with this man."

With that, Magistrate Ford reduced the bail to one thousand dollars. A few hours later, after bondsman Louis Topper put up the bail, Joseph Gedeon swaggered out of the front entrance of the Tombs with his lawyer beside him.

The next morning, Saturday, April 3, New Yorkers who, for nearly a week, had been assured by the tabloids that it was only a matter of hours before Joseph Gedeon confessed to the murders of his wife, his daughter, and a total stranger were jolted by bombshell headlines: "GEDEON FREED," "GEDEON OUT OF JAIL," "LOW BAIL SETS GEDEON FREE!"[26]

That same day Frank Byrnes, the pitiful bit player in the city's hottest melodrama, went obscurely to his grave in St. John Cemetery in Queens. In contrast to the hordes that had turned out for the funeral of the glamorous star, only eight mourners showed up: two distant relatives and a half dozen friends from the New York Racquet and Tennis Club.

The interment was a sadly perfunctory affair. Still, the tabloids did their best to wring as much pathos as possible from the occasion. That Byrnes was laid to rest in a plot belonging to George Longfellow, a "remote relation by marriage," seemed sadly appropriate to the *Mirror*'s reporter, who observed that the little Englishman's "history as a lodger in other folks' home was rounded out by his burial in other folks' cemetery plot." The writer for the *News*, meanwhile, pointed out that Byrnes—who reportedly pined for his native England—had ended up in a cemetery whose "grounds were bright with reviving green, the green that reminds homesick Britons of England in the spring."

Interviewed by reporters following the burial, George Longfellow described his relative as a man who was not only an exceptionally heavy sleeper but also partially deaf. "Byrnes would fall into a deep slumber the minute he hit the bed," said Longfellow. "And he had been hard of hearing for years." The statement shed light on one of the nagging mysteries in the case: why Frank Byrnes had not been awakened by Mary Gedeon's death struggle.[27]

Rumors that the forty-five-year-old Mary had been romantically involved with a "mysterious stranger"—a man she had introduced to several friends as her "new husband"—sent police on a futile hunt for the "second Mr. Gedeon" (as the tabloids dubbed this phantom). Her daughter's seemingly endless string of boyfriends also came in for renewed scrutiny. According to the papers, detectives were now seeking "a young army officer who gave Ronnie her first taste of high society life at a Waldorf-Astoria military ball a year ago"; a married art patron and a professional athlete, each suspected of being the father of her aborted child; and the "Boston playboy millionaire whom they had formerly regarded as a figment of imagination created by the eccentric upholsterer to divert suspicion from himself."[28]

Even as the tabloids were describing these latest developments, however, police were hard on the trail of an entirely different suspect. Hoping to lull him into a false sense of security, they had been conducting their investigation with such secrecy that even many officers assigned to the case knew nothing about it.[29]

It was Ronnie's dog-eared five-year diary that had first alerted them to his existence. Since the discovery of the little volume in her bedroom bureau, investigators had been poring over the nearly fifteen hundred entries dating back to 1932.

References to "Bobby"—her ex-husband, Robert Flower—dominated the early parts of the diary, where he was described as "the most lovable creature," her "first love and also my last," a young man she was "crazy about" and would "do anything for." The name appeared again toward the end of the diary. These entries, however, had a weirdly "sinister tenor." Now, Bobby was obsessed with Ronnie's older sister. He was "out of his head." His pursuit of Ethel had turned into a kind of stalking. "I am afraid of B.," wrote Ronnie. "He has been hanging around the house since Ethel handed him a large dose of ozone."

The dramatic shift in Ronnie's feelings about Bobby puzzled investigators until it occurred to them that she was talking about two different men.

Early Wednesday morning—around the time that Joseph Gedeon was being taken to the police station to begin his grueling interrogation—Detective Martin Owens drove out to Astoria, Queens, to question Ethel Kudner. Told about her sister's diary, Ethel confirmed that the later entries referred not to Bobby Flower but to an ex-boarder at her mother's brownstone.

"But he couldn't have anything to do with this," she quickly added. "He isn't that kind of person. He's an exceptionally talented sculptor. His heart is in work."

"Why don't you let me be judge of that?" said Owens. "Now tell me. What's his full name?"

"Irwin," said Ethel. "Robert Irwin."[30]

Prime Suspect

F OR BOTH THE NEWSMEN assigned to the case and the public at large, the announcement was a bolt from the blue. Early
Monday morning, April 5, Acting Lieutenant Thomas Martin of the
Homicide Squad called a news conference at the East 51st Street police station, where he distributed a photograph of a clean-cut, good-
looking young man staring intently at the camera.

"We now have a definite suspect in the Gedeon murder," said
Martin. "His name is Robert Irwin. We are more interested in him
than in any other man we've questioned in this case."[1]

In the days since Ethel revealed the identity of the second, highly
volatile "Bobby" in her slain sister's diary, investigators had uncovered virtually all the key facts about Irwin's life: his fanatically religious upbringing, his stints in reform school with his delinquent
brothers, his time in Hollywood, his studies with Lorado Taft, his
attempt at self-emasculation, his two periods of confinement at the
Rockland State Hospital, his work as a taxidermist, his recent expulsion from the St. Lawrence University Theological School.

They knew about his "explosive personality," his pattern of erupting into terrifying outbursts of violent rage, his efforts to "achieve supreme superiority in sculpture" by bottling up his "love urges." With one hundred detectives assigned to the case, they had traced his movements from Canton to Manhattan on Good Friday, spoken to Clarence Low and Leonora Sheldon, and located the Ottburgs' boardinghouse, where they learned that Irwin had skipped out sometime in the middle of Saturday night, leaving behind his gray fedora, an empty cardboard carton, and a box of table salt.[2]

Besides putting together a compelling circumstantial case, they had found more concrete evidence. Dispatched to Canton, a pair of detectives had quickly tracked down Pauline Dishaw, the salesgirl at the J. J. Newberry department store who had sold Irwin a cheap pair of gray suede gloves, identical in style, size, and material to the one found at the murder scene. In Irwin's room at the Hosleys' boardinghouse, where he had left some of his belongings behind, they also turned up his notebook. There, among his paeans to Ethel's perfection, he had vented his bitterness toward the two women he blamed for coming between him and his beloved. "If only Ronnie and Mrs. G. hadn't interfered!" he had written. "How I hate Ronnie and her mother for what they have done to me!"[3]

These entries strongly suggested that Irwin had a clear-cut motive for the killings: "to revenge himself on Mrs. Gedeon and Veronica for having broken up his romance with Ethel," as the *New York Times* reported. Certainly he had the physical strength to commit the strangulations, with powerful hands developed from his years of molding clay and wielding a mallet and chisel. Police had also been informed by several of Irwin's acquaintances that he "habitually carried" an eight-inch-long sculptor's tool "with a sharp point and taped handle"—presumably the weapon "with which Byrnes was stabbed."

They even had a theory linking Irwin to the oddly shaped piece of soap found on the floor of the Gedeons' living room. Beginning in 1925, Procter & Gamble had sponsored an annual soap-carving contest, awarding major prizes to the best original works of art sculpted from Ivory soap. The contest—whose winners were judged by a committee of eminent sculptors, including Lorado Taft —turned the hobby of soap carving into a nationwide craze. By the early 1930s, annual submissions totaled well over five thousand little soap statues: everything from nude torsos to nativity scenes, Greek mythological heroes to Hollywood celebrities, circus animals to Civil War battle scenes.

To several of the detectives at work on the Easter Sunday murders, the chunk of soap on the Gedeons' living room floor, when viewed from certain angles, resembled a woman's face. With Irwin now identified as the prime suspect, the theory quickly circulated that, after killing Mrs. Gedeon and Frank Byrnes, the sculptor had whiled away his time as he waited for Ronnie's return by carving a little bust of Ethel from a bar of bathroom soap.[4]

Ethel herself remained unconvinced of Bob's guilt. Waylaid by reporters outside the midtown ASPCA, where she had gone to retrieve her sister's Pekingese, Touchi, on Monday morning, she repeated the opinion she had expressed to Detective Owens. "I cannot believe that Irwin is the man who killed my mother and sister." Dr. Russell Blaisdell, superintendent of Rockland State Hospital, was equally emphatic. While it was true that Bob had "trouble controlling his emotions, and a vicious temper," Blaisdell told reporters, "this temper of his cooled off in a flash. After an outburst, he was extremely remorseful.

"I just can't visualize him as being connected with the Gedeon murders," the psychiatrist continued. "The Gedeon murders were done by a crafty fiend who lay in wait. Irwin never could have lain in wait. He wouldn't have been able to control himself. And if he *had* done such a thing, he would have been sorry afterwards. He wouldn't hide. He would try to find someone to unburden himself to."[5]

The police, however, had no doubt that Irwin was their man. "We have enough evidence linking Irwin to the crime scene to get a Grand Jury indictment and send the man to the chair," Chief Inspector Lyons told the press on Monday afternoon. That same evening, Police Commissioner Valentine ordered all New York City police precinct commanders to post men "at all bridges and tunnels leading from the city and at all bus, railroad, airplane and ferry terminals." At the same time, he issued a Teletype alarm to seven states besides New York—New Jersey, Connecticut, Pennsylvania, Ohio, Delaware, Rhode Island, and Massachusetts:

> Arrest for triple homicide this city. Robert 'Bob' Irwin, last known address 36 State St., Canton, N.Y. He is of U.S. nativity, 29, five feet nine, 140 pounds, stocky build, dark-blond wavy hair, high forehead, eyes squinty.
>
> When last seen was wearing black overcoat with velvet collar, tan fedora hat, light scarf.
>
> Suit may be black with penciled stripe or bluish gray with pin stripe; black shoes, size 8, which were made in Canada; medium blue shirt with black stripe, made by the New Way Process Co. of Pennsylvania.
>
> Irwin is a sculptor, but may be employed, or seek employment, in taxidermy work or decorative flower establishments. Kindly make inquiries at art clubs and such places where he might seek employment.
>
> Lodges in cheap rooming houses and was formerly an inmate of the Rockland State Hospital Insane Asylum. May be hitchhiking to Philadelphia, Pa. or Washington, D.C. Also check morgues for suicides and give this case the necessary attention.[6]

For a solid week, Ronnie Gedeon and her eccentric, "eroticminded" father had been the headliners in "The Murder of the Artist's Model." With the announcement that her killer had been positively identified, all that changed overnight. To be sure, the sensationalistic papers continued to milk Ronnie's life for every last prurient drop. When police released excerpts of her diary to the press, the *Daily Mirror* ran a story headlined "Slain Model's Diary Bares Love Secrets," claiming that the little volume was "pulsating with the life and love that stirred" within the lovely young model. Even this story, however (which turned out to consist of such "pulsating" entries as "Dear Diary, I am crazy about a certain boy named Bobby" and "Went out last night and nearly fell asleep, I was so bored"), was relegated to the inside pages.[7]

It was her killer who would now dominate the front pages. Just as the doomed, fast-living Ronnie seemed tailor-made for the sensationalistic press, Robert Irwin was a tabloid editor's dream: a talented artist and aspiring seminarian whose long history of bizarre behavior had culminated in the "Easter Sunday triple-murder orgy." Tabloid scribes tripped over themselves in their rush to coin lurid epithets for the latest criminal sensation: "the sex-tormented artist-theologian," "the sex-tortured madman," "the religio-sex maniac," "the erratic and erotic sculptor." It was a writer for *Daily News* who came up with the winner, the nickname by which Robert Irwin would become known in the annals of American crime: the Mad Sculptor.[8]

Manhunt

W ITH IRWIN'S PHOTOGRAPH SPLASHED across the front page of virtually every newspaper in the East and an estimated twenty thousand law officers on the lookout for him from Maine to Maryland—"the greatest manhunt since the kidnapping of the Lindbergh baby"—police were confident that he would be apprehended within a matter of days. In New York City alone, several hundred detectives were detailed to the search. Under the theory that he was "down to his last dollar," a dozen officers from the East 5th Street station scoured the dives, missions, and municipal shelters of the Bowery, that squalid "street of forgotten men" where, police theorized, "the panicky fugitive might desperately hope to pass unknown and unregarded." Others combed the "flophouse districts on upper Third Avenue, on East 23rd Street, on Eighth Avenue in the 20s, and on lower Fulton St., Brooklyn." Police were also dispatched to Bellevue and other city hospitals on the chance that he had checked himself into a psychiatric ward.

As with every highly publicized manhunt, there were countless sightings of the fugitive. In Manhattan, he was seen panhandling on the Lower East Side, dining in a bar and grill on Rivington Street, staying at a cheap lodging house in Hell's Kitchen, and "dancing stark naked on a fire escape." Anonymous tipsters from around the country claimed that he was staying at a hotel in Atlantic City, hitchhiking in the Poconos, shopping for jewelry in Baltimore, skulking around the campus of Vassar College, begging for a handout from fraternity members at Rutgers University, riding a boxcar to Hollywood, driving a stolen car to Cape Cod, and stowing away on a ship carrying volunteers for the Spanish Civil War. He was also supposedly spotted in Astoria, Queens, presumably on his way to the home of his obsessive love interest, Ethel Kudner. Taking no chances, authorities persuaded her to abandon her residence and go into seclusion at an undisclosed location under twenty-four-hour police guard.

Ethel's father had his own novel theory about Irwin's whereabouts. Early Tuesday morning, Joe Gedeon and his attorney, Peter Sabbatino, were back in court for a hearing on the gun possession charge. When Sabbatino requested a month-long postponement, District Attorney Dodge offered no objection. As various commentators dryly noted, this sudden agreeableness on the part of the prosecutor was a barely adequate form of atonement for Gedeon's outrageous mistreatment—the legal equivalent of beating up a man for an offense he didn't commit and then, after realizing your mistake, shaking his hand and saying, "No hard feelings." Following the brief proceedings, Gedeon spoke to reporters about Irwin. "I think he's the man, all right," said the little upholsterer. "He's very clever. And he's also extremely adept at making wonderfully life-like masks. If you ask me, I think he'll try to disguise himself with a mask of some kind and go parading around the streets while detectives hunt him."[1]

A less fanciful possibility was advanced by Commissioner Valentine. "Irwin is a psycho case," he told reporters, "and we're afraid he'll commit suicide the moment he feels we're getting close to him." Not long after the commissioner issued this statement, a young man resembling Irwin threw himself from a window of the Hotel Montclair on Lexington Avenue and 49th Street, leaving behind four dollars to cover his bill and a note to the manager apologizing for "the publicity that my action will cause you." Two men were brought to the Bellevue morgue to view the body: John Stuart, who had once roomed with Irwin at the Gedeons' brownstone, and Alexander Ettl, owner of the sculpture-casting firm where Bob had briefly worked in the fall of 1930. Both announced that the young suicide was not Irwin.[2]

Ettl, who theorized that Bob might have stabbed Frank Byrnes to death with a sharp-pointed sculptor's gauge, was featured in the *Mirror*'s center-page photo spread, posing with one of the implements. He wasn't the only acquaintance of Bob's to get his picture in the papers. In the coming days, the tabloids would run photographs of anyone their reporters could track down who had some connection to the case: Irwin's former art students at St. Lawrence University (including the two children of Professor Angus MacLean); Benjamin Hosley, the Canton beekeeper at whose home he had boarded; Leonora Sheldon's fiancé, Anders Lunde, and her panda-hunting brother, William; Bob's New York patron, Clarence Low; Pauline Dishaw, the salesgirl who had sold him the gloves he wore on the night of the murders; Gilbert Maggi, his boss at Chelsea Realistic Products, who, after firing Bob, found himself confronted by a cleaver-wielding madman; Leroy Congdon, the divinity student who had been attacked by Bob for no good reason, leading to the latter's expulsion from theology school; and Arthur Halliburton, his old housemate in Chicago, who had also been on the receiving end of one of Bob's insane outbursts—"the most brutal beating I have ever known anyone to receive," as he described it to reporters.[3]

Halliburton's recollection of his assailant as a "screaming maniac" contributed to the tabloid depiction of Bob as a monster of supernatural dimensions. "IRWIN PICTURED AS A WEIRD 'DR. JEKYLL AND MR. HYDE,'" blared one headline. "Combined in the sex-tormented psychopath, police found the contradictions of wild lust and the rigid asceticism of a religious fanatic," read the accompanying story. "Sometimes he was the perfect gentleman, as when he squired about New York just a few hours before the slaying pretty Leonora Sheldon, Social Registerite and amateur artist. At other times, caught in a maelstrom of perverted lust, he was portrayed as a demon with homicidal tendencies." His "diverse personalities" were very much in evidence at Rockland, where, according to one unnamed source, he would transform in an instant from "a tractable, even likable patient" into a raging madman "swept away by demoniac furies—fighting attendants with a giant's strength, shrieking threats to kill and maim those who attempted to check the wild flights of fancy in which he picture himself as a superman."[4]

Another article, citing the opinion of Dr. Mortimer Sherman, former chief alienist at Kings County Hospital in Brooklyn, described Irwin as a "Sadistic Gorilla Man." Sherman's diagnosis was based on the photograph of Irwin distributed by the New York City Police, a picture in which Bob, neatly dressed in jacket and tie, head slightly cocked to one side, wears a studious expression on his clean-cut, boyish-looking face. Sounding less like a twentieth-century psychiatrist than a practitioner of nineteenth-century physiognomy—the quack pseudoscience of deducing a person's psychology from his or her facial characteristics—Sherman opined that Bob's slightly knit eyebrows were "slanting downward in Satanic fashion." His nostrils (perfectly shapely to an objective eye) were "upturned in an animal snarl." His mouth—in actuality rather delicately shaped, with a full, almost feminine lower lip—was a "straight slit that shows the snarling animal." These "face characteristics," Sherman declared, "show him subject to abnormal types of sex called sadism in which lusts of pleasure and pain are the primary elements of the sex life."[5]

The same photograph of Bob, with a trim little moustache airbrushed onto his face, was used to draw a parallel between the Mad Sculptor and one of the country's most notorious criminals. Juxtaposing this doctored photo with a strikingly similar portrait of America's former Public Enemy No. 1, the *Daily News* ran a piece describing Irwin as the "crime-twin of John Dillinger"—"a Dillinger of Sex." This time, the paper's go-to expert was Dr. William Moulton Marston, a noted psychologist who, a few years later, would enter into pop culture lore as the creator of the comic book character Wonder Woman. According to Dr. Marston, the two killers were "similar in almost every external respect. Both have the same bulging foreheads, distended nostrils, heavy-lobed ears, and thinning hair." His "microscopic study" of the two faces showed conclusively that "Irwin's murders for sex" were "the twin of Dillinger's murders for money."[6]

Another psychiatrist, who had supposedly treated Irwin at Bellevue, reinforced the characterization of the fugitive as a creature from a grade-B horror movie—"a night-prowling, gorilla-fisted rover." Irwin "paced his detention cell ceaselessly with a rolling lumbering gait, slightly hunched over," this unnamed doctor was quoted as saying. "He napped fitfully through the days and only came fully alive by night when he was in a frenzy to get away."[7]

Though close-up, page-one photographs of Bob's hands showed him to be not "gorilla-fisted" at all but possessed of long, tapering fingers, tabloid readers were assured that his years of sculpting in clay had endowed him with superhuman power. "His hands appear delicate but are deceiving in their strength," one paper noted. "When the black lightning from the half-world of madness strikes his twisted brain, those hands become infused with the power of five men—and death is at his fingertips!" Any frustration of his desire might provoke his "murderous rage." In the throes of one of his "ungovernable tantrums," his "long strong fingers" would "invariably lunge for his victim's throat."[8]

A different, though no less sinister picture of Irwin—portraying him not as a raging madman but as a coldly calculating psychopath —was painted by Bryan Bishop, a journalist who had spent time in Rockland several years earlier after suffering a nervous breakdown. According to Bishop, Bob had himself committed to Rockland as part of a diabolical scheme to commit the perfect murder. "Even in those days," Bishop recalled, "he was plotting revenge against Ronnie and her mother. He spoke about it constantly. The key to getting away with the crime, he said, was to get yourself into an asylum. That way, there was no need to worry. Once you were branded as insane, you could never be convicted like other men." To various observers, the reported discovery of a collection of newspaper clippings on the Nancy Titterton case in Bob's lodgings at Canton was proof that he had long been planning his own Beekman Place murder.[9]

With this monster on the loose, no one was safe. "NEW KILLINGS BY SCULPTOR FEARED," ran a headline in Wednesday's *Evening Journal*. Under the theory that the penniless fugitive might resort to panhandling, police warned the public to beware of any beggar matching Irwin's description. "If such a panhandler asks for a dime on the street, it's wisest to give him the dime—and look for the nearest cop," officials advised. "It may cost you your life to refuse. It is not beyond reason to imagine Irwin, begging from three or four persons and being turned down by all, having a homicidal outburst. Do not attempt to subdue this man without armed help."[10]

The relentless newspaper portrayal of a city haunted by a homicidal "night-prowling" madman had the inevitable result. "Night and day, hysterical pleas for help have been flooding police telephones," the *Evening Journal* reported. Virtually all the calls came from single women, who had remarkably similar stories to tell. Preparing for bed, or lying awake under the covers, or on the brink of dozing off, they would suddenly become aware of a menacing presence and look up in horror to see a sinister man peering at them from the fire escape, or trying to climb through the window, or standing beside their beds with clutching, outstretched hands.[11]

On Saturday, April 10—five days after police first identified Robert Irwin as their number one suspect—Commissioner Valentine announced to reporters that he was "confident that Irwin will be apprehended in a reasonable time." So certain was the commissioner of the Mad Sculptor's imminent capture that he cancelled a print order for an additional twenty thousand wanted circulars "because Irwin will be in our hands before the circulars are needed."[12]

Despite this and similarly sanguine pronouncements, however, Irwin continued to elude the police. Each day brought new headlines placing him in different parts of the country: Columbia, South

Carolina; Scranton, Pennsylvania; Steubenville, Ohio; Kalamazoo, Michigan; Kenosha, Wisconsin. On Sunday, April 11, the *New York Times* reported that police in Utica, New York, had received a suicide note signed "Robert Irwin." "I am sick of the whole business," it read. "I think several cops recognized me. I am going to end it all. Please send my clothes to the Rockland State Hospital." Two days later—claiming that "police have officially turned the manhunt for Irwin into a woman-hunt"—the *Mirror* floated the theory that Irwin was making his way to the West Coast as "a female impersonator." "During his school days, Irwin took part in amateur dramatics and was reported to be exceedingly clever in makeup," read the story. "The regular features of his face, moreover, would aid him passing as a girl."[13]

Though Commissioner Valentine and his subordinates failed to see the humor in the situation, one editorial wag was inspired to remark on the countless cross-country sightings of Irwin in a mocking bit of doggerel:

> The police have a tip that he's sailed for Peru,
> Information received puts him in Utah, too.
> They're dragging the river and combing all Queens
> With a net. He's in Armonk, likewise New Orleans.
> An important anonymous telephone call
> Says "He's here" merely "here" and no address at all.
> East Side and West Side, the town all around
> Persuasive, ubiquitous, and yet unfound
> Is this fellow distinguished by having the quaint
> Gift of being at once several places he ain't.[14]

That the police were becoming increasingly desperate in their efforts to track down the nation's most sought-after fugitive became painfully clear when John C. Tucker, a Jersey City hypnotist who claimed to have "helped solve several important cases," offered to assist in the manhunt. Tucker proposed to enter the Gedeon apartment with an aide, a fellow New Jerseyan named Hale Haberman.

Tucker would then put Haberman into a trance "and, presto, the whereabouts of suspect Robert Irwin would be revealed through the aide in a twinkling." Though Assistant Chief Inspector Lyons was ultimately prohibited from availing himself of the hypnotist's services, his initial impulse was to give Tucker a chance. "It can't do any harm," he told reporters.[15]

Lyons also raised some eyebrows when he made what amounted to an offer of immunity to Irwin in return for his surrender. "The man is stark mad," Lyons told a group of reporters. "He'll never be indicted or go to trial for this crime. It makes no difference whether he committed three of three hundred murders as far as the State is concerned. It's no longer a criminal matter; it is simply a medical case. All we want now is to safeguard the public. He's a danger to the community wherever he might be."

Joining the effort to secure Irwin's surrender, Dr. Russell Blaisdell, superintendent of Rockland State Hospital, issued a public appeal to his former patient:

> In view of what has been published in the newspapers and broadcast over the air, your disappearance and continued absence are looked upon with grave suspicion. It is much to your interest to come forward and give an accounting of your movements. As one who has always befriended you and had your interest at heart, I advise and urge you to go immediately to the police or communicate with me at this hospital.

But Blaisdell's plea, like the bait dangled by Lyons, did nothing to lure Irwin out of hiding.[16]

In the struggle for newsstand supremacy, the *Daily News* scored a major coup over its tabloid rivals with the serialized publication, beginning Monday, April 12, of "Robert Irwin's Own Life Story." The autobiography had been acquired from Bob's old Rockland friend, the former Oom cult member William Lamkie, who had shown up at the paper's offices a week earlier with his lawyer, Ellis Bates, offering Bob's manuscript for sale. Appearing in installments over five successive days, the "self-searching record of the young sculptor's emotions, desires and ambitions" (as it was touted in the paper) is a revealing document.

In Irwin's telling, his life was a courageous struggle to surmount the hardships and deprivations of his past: his philandering evangelist father; his neglectful, fanatical mother; his "drab, insecure childhood"; his consignment to reform school, where his "instinctive love for art first asserted itself." Possessed of "the urge to be on my way to greener pastures," he embarked on the adventurous life of a picaresque hero.

After drifting "from pillar to post"—"living in the jungle where beast ate beast and only the fittest survive"—he was led by his "guiding star" to the Hollywood studio of Carlo Romanelli, "under whom I spent two years of intensive and profitable study." Eventually, when "the desire for more worlds to conquer got the better of me," he left for Chicago to work with Lorado Taft. The "nation's outstanding sculptor" took such a shine to the young artist that he found a place for Bob at the home of his stepmother. Shortly afterward, Arthur Halliburton came to live there, too. Bob describes his assault on Halliburton, though in his version, his housemate at Mrs. Taft's was entirely to blame. "A highbrow type," Halliburton (according to Bob) flaunted his "social superiority" by snidely remarking on "some of my crude habits, or what he considered them." As a result, "we had a brawl" that "gave me a chance to show my *physical* superiority."

Bob's struggles to pursue the "sacred cause" of his art during the difficult years of the Depression made him "open to all sorts of fears and worries." How, he asked himself, "can I become a great sculptor, as I have led myself to believe?" Concluding that "the instinct to propagate" was the "most diverting factor," he ended up in Bellevue after attempting to "deprive myself of sex urges." There he found himself "in the psychopathic ward with people who"—unlike himself—"had actually gone mad."

Following his transfer to Rockland, he was able to meditate on all sorts of mysteries and profundities that he shares in his memoir:

> I can understand how the reproductive organs in Vedic liter-ature symbolize the creation of life. The normal expression means greater health, greater intellect, a finer spirit. The ane-mic figures of the saints must have been done by suppressed, sexless creatures or those indulging in unnatural practices. . . .
>
> What makes a homo-sexual? Probably many factors. If I had money, I would finance a scientific study to get at the basis and with that we might get everybody back on the beaten track. Does art make people veer in that direction? For instance, Os-car Wilde and many another genius? Do lesbian women make good wives might be another good question to propound. . . .
>
> In a world of plenty for everybody there is not enough to go round. My simple wants are not too much to expect, but mate-rialism and art don't go together. If I labor, I long for my art. If I model, I starve. . . . Why is it so? The philosopher might say it is all part of the game and one should take it in stride like the runner as part of the next step. The Yoga would say it was all an illusion.

The narrative takes him all the way through his decision to enter the St. Lawrence University seminary, his "encounter with a fellow theological student for breaking my models," his dismissal by Dean Atwood, and his imminent departure for the "big city."

Bob's autobiography is certainly no literary masterpiece. It is crammed with clichés and stilted Victorian language. "Mother's re-ligion was the consolation from all the woes that flesh is heir to," reads a typical passage. "Day by day, one step at a time, was her plan. She never doubted the Lord would provide. There was always the silver lining, no matter how dark the cloud." Still, it is clearly the work of a bright and literate person. For all its flagrant rationaliza-tions, rambling digressions, and delusions of grandeur, it is hardly the work of the raging lunatic portrayed in the press. Only one passage strikes an ominous chord. After casually noting that he had "done a bust of Ethel," Bob ruminates on the "snake nature" of women. Then, in words whose chilling import was clear only in retrospect, he adds: "There is something worse than the serpent's sting. To be jilted and spurned by one for whom one cares sears the very soul and makes the world go black."[17]

While not completely discounting the possibility that Irwin had fled westward, Commissioner Valentine remained convinced that the sculptor was holed up somewhere in the metropolitan area. "New York City is the greatest hideout in the world," he declared at a news conference on Tuesday, April 13. "Despite the fact that we're getting tips from all over the country, I've always believed he's right here." Anyone "sheltering or harboring" the fugitive, he reminded the public, was "himself committing a felony."[18]

Believing that the cash-strapped Irwin might "demand a cut of the sale of his life story," Valentine ordered a pair of Homicide Squad detectives to keep surveillance on William Lamkie. Other police officers, disguised as uniformed security guards, were posted in the exhibition halls of the Metropolitan Museum of Art under the theory that "Irwin will be driven by irresistible artistic need and impulse to visit the galleries." According to a story in the *Mirror*, police were also keeping watch over artists' supply shops in lower Manhattan after getting wind of a macabre rumor that Irwin was "barricaded in a Greenwich Village studio at work on a sculptural masterpiece which will be his farewell to the world . . . a post-mortem likeness in stone of Ronnie Gedeon."[19]

On the evening of Wednesday, April 14 — in what most newspaper commentators saw as an act of desperation — police made a major sweep of the Bowery, rounding up forty-three young, bearded derelicts and hauling them into Night Court, where Magistrate Leonard McGee, acceding to the request of Commissioner Valentine, sentenced all of them to five days in jail on vagrancy charges. The sentences were meant to give the police "ample time to peer behind the whiskers of the captured derelicts, take their fingerprints, and study their physical characteristic to make sure none of them might be Irwin."

Once again, the cops came up empty-handed. "POLICE ADMIT IRWIN CLUES ARE EXHAUSTED," read the headline in the next day's *Evening Journal.* The accompanying story quoted Captain William T. Reynolds, in charge of the Fourth Detective District, who acknowledged that the manhunt had reached a dead end.

"All the leads we have had were washouts," said a dispirited Reynolds. "We are stumped in our search for Irwin."[20]

Though one of the few New York City detectives not assigned to the manhunt, John J. Whalen—currently detailed to the Grand Jury Squad under Captain Barney Dowd—had been following the case closely in the newspapers. From reading interviews with the Ottburgs—Irwin's landlords at the time of the murders—he knew that the sculptor had arrived in the city with a pair of beaten-up suitcases, one tied shut with a piece of rope.

As he later explained to reporters, Whalen began to wonder "what I would do if I were in Irwin's position." To begin with—contrary to what Commissioner Valentine believed—he would leave the city as quickly as possible. He "pictured himself trying to get out of town, lugging two heavy suitcases and lacking enough money to travel by taxicab." The "most natural thing," he concluded, "would be to go to a railroad station and check the bags."

Before joining the NYPD a decade earlier, Whalen had worked as a baggage clerk in the checkroom of Grand Central Station and knew that pieces of unclaimed luggage sometimes offered up "fertile secrets for the police." Among the items found during his time there were "a number of revolvers, a complete opium layout, several large quantities of silverware, and two stillborn babies."

With Captain Dowd's permission, Whalen immediately set about examining "every piece of luggage in the checkrooms at Grand Central, Penn Station, and at bus and subway lockers." Though he initially came up empty-handed, he couldn't shake his conviction that Irwin had stashed his bags somewhere before taking flight. "How a fugitive from justice could openly carry a suitcase which had received so much publicity was beyond me," he explained.

Returning to Grand Central and enlisting the help of a baggage clerk, he went through the checkroom again. His persistence paid off. At roughly 8:45 p.m. on April 26, 1937, Whalen came upon a pair of battered suitcases, one held shut with a knotted old belt. Among the contents were an artist's sketchbook bearing Irwin's name, a box of business cards printed with the inscription "Robert Irwin, Sculptor," various newspaper clippings on the Easter Sunday Massacre, and a cheap Baby Ben alarm clock promptly identified by Lucy Beacco as the one taken from the tiny bedroom where the bodies of Ronnie and Mary Gedeon had been found.

Though the clock was a particularly important find—the first piece of physical evidence directly linking Irwin to the crime—the recovery of the suitcases would play no role in his capture. It did, however, confirm Detective Whalen's intuition. Commissioner Valentine was wrong. Robert Irwin, the Mad Sculptor of Beekman Place, had fled the city.[21]

Part V

The Defender

Murder in Times Square

B Y THE TIME DETECTIVE WHALEN embarked on his search for the missing suitcases, the tabloids had run out of stories to report — or invent — about the Easter Sunday triple slaying. Happily for lovers of lurid homicides, mid-April brought a juicy new murder that — while not quite up to the sensationalistic standards set by the Irwin case — provided the public with a week or so of morbid titillation.

A few minutes before two o'clock on Sunday afternoon, April 18, Miss Moya Engels, a nightclub performer known for her Hawaiian hula-hula act, arrived at the WOV radio station building, just east of Times Square, where she had reserved rehearsal space to practice a new routine. The door to the third-floor studio she had engaged — No. 306 — was closed but unlocked. No sooner had she stepped inside than she froze in confusion. On the opposite side of the twenty-five-by-forty-foot room, a pair of woman's feet, shod in black oxfords, protruded from beneath the gray rayon wall-curtains used as soundproofing. "I thought the girl had fainted from dancing," Engels later told reporters. "She was groaning and breathing heavily. Then I pulled aside the drapes and looked at her." At her first glimpse of the woman, Engels let out a scream and ran from the studio to seek help.

Summoned by the elderly elevator operator, Paul Klein, two radio patrolmen, Officers Walter Rowley and George H. Stevenson, arrived on the scene within minutes. The beautiful chestnut-haired victim, still clinging to life, had been savagely bludgeoned with a claw hammer that lay on the floor a few feet from the entrance to the studio. She was rushed to Roosevelt Hospital, where she managed to survive for another six hours before succumbing to her injuries — "a compound fracture of the skull and lacerations of the brain," according to the findings of Assistant Medical Examiner Milton Helpern.

From her Social Security card and other items found in her purse, her identity was quickly established: Julia Nussenbaum, twenty-four years of age, originally of Bridgeport, Connecticut, currently residing at 439 West 123rd Street with a roommate, Miss Dorothy Hunkins. Within a short time, investigators had uncovered other key facts. A graduate of the Juilliard School of Music and an accomplished concert violinist, Julia had traded the symphony hall for the vaudeville stage two and a half years earlier. Adopting the stage name Tania Lubova, she had joined an eight-member troupe, consisting of five musicians and three dancers, that had enjoyed considerable success on the midwestern Orpheum Circuit. More recently, she had teamed up with an accordionist-singer named Maria Montiglo. They were scheduled to leave the next day for a two-week engagement at the Esquire, Toronto's best-known nightclub.

According to her roommate, someone had telephoned Julia late Saturday night, asking her to be at the Times Square rehearsal studio at ten o'clock Sunday morning. Dressed in a rose-patterned blue dress and gray-blue spring coat and carrying her seven-hundred-dollar violin in a zippered leather bag, she had left the apartment at around 8:45 a.m.

The elevator operator Paul Klein told police that, at roughly 9:45 a.m., he had taken a tall, powerfully built man up to the third floor and seen him head down the narrow hallway to the studio. Julia had arrived around ten o'clock. About fifteen minutes later, the man rang for the elevator and descended to the street. Klein had noticed nothing strange about his behavior. Silence fell on the building until, four hours later, Moya Engels showed up.

From a telltale track of blood that ran in a sweeping curve across the floor of the studio, police were able to reconstruct the crime. Evidently, Julia, still wearing her coat and hat, had seated herself on one of the wooden chairs near the south wall of the studio, placing her violin case on the floor beside her. She and her assailant, clearly someone she knew, had talked for a few minutes. Suddenly, without warning, he had produced the claw hammer and delivered a savage barrage of blows to her forehead. Bleeding profusely, she had crumpled to the floor. In a frenzied attempt to hide her body, he had dragged her to a little dressing room on the opposite side of the studio but, finding it locked, had hauled her toward the drapes and shoved her beneath them.

From interviews with the dead girl's stricken father and other family members and friends, police quickly identified a suspect: thirty-one-year-old Mischa Ross. Born Mischa Rosenbaum in Danitzer, Russia, not far from Kiev, Ross, a talented mandolin player, had come to the United States with his brother Zachary in 1925 as part of a touring Russian orchestra. They had settled in New York after obtaining forged birth certificates indicating that they had been born in Montreal. In 1931, while playing in an orchestra in a Catskills hotel, he had romanced the adolescent daughter of the owner, Nathan Nessolovitz. The two were married and had a daughter, Adele. Three and a half years later, Ross deserted his family and moved into the Hotel Normandie on West 46th Street, while his wife and child went to live at his father-in-law's house in the village of Woodridge, not far from Monticello, New York. Ross visited them occasionally when not on tour.

It was Ross who put together the vaudeville troupe that Julia had joined in early 1935. Traveling in her company throughout the Midwest, he had fallen in love with the beautiful young violinist. Ap-

parently Julia was receptive to his "amorous advances" until she discovered that he was still married, at which point she broke off their
affair. She remained friendly with him, however, and allowed him to
serve as her theatrical agent. For his part, Ross had continued to ob-
sess over Julia. Interviewed by Homicide Squad detectives who had
come to inform him of his daughter's death, Julia's anguished father
told a story of increasing harassment by Ross.

"Julia didn't know what to do," Nussenbaum said between sobs.
"The man kept continually making advances to her. I went to New
York with my brother-in-law and asked him to please leave Julia
alone if he really loved her. When I told him that Julia would never
marry him, he said that 'only over my grave will she marry anyone
else.'"

Just a few hours after a five-state alarm was sent out, State Troopers W. M. Lewis and Edward Smith picked up Ross at his father-
in-law's house. Drunk to the point of stupefaction, he was locked
up overnight in the Sullivan County jail without his tie, belt, or
shoelaces. The next morning, as tabloid headlines trumpeted the
city's latest crime sensation—"MURDER IN THE RADIO STUDIO,"
"TIMES SQUARE HAMMER SLAYING," "BLUDGEONING DEATH
OF THE BEAUTIFUL VIOLINIST"—Detectives Bradley Hammond
and John J. Quinn of the NYPD drove him back to Manhattan.

Bleary-eyed, disheveled, and still barely coherent, Ross screamed
hysterically while being booked. When newspaper cameramen tried
to take his picture, he threw himself facedown on the floor at the
feet of District Attorney Dodge, who was photographed looking visibly embarrassed as he stood over the sobbing, prostrate prisoner.
Under an intense grilling by Dodge and others, Ross admitted that
he "might have hit Julia to defend himself," though he claimed to
have virtually no memory of the events. "I remember seeing the elevator operator on my way to Room 306," he said. "Julia was there.
As to who was there first, I can't remember because I'd been drinking. I remember that Julia and I were alone and that she argued with
me. She hit me with a stick. I don't remember what kind of stick but
I must have taken it from her and hit her with it. I don't remem-

ber hitting her. The next thing I remember I was on a bus and I fell asleep. I don't remember how I got to Woodridge, my wife's home, but I got there. I don't remember anything until I woke up in jail in Monticello."

It wasn't until the close of the interrogation that Ross was told that the girl had died six hours after the discovery of her body. He uttered a terrified shriek and babbled, "No! No! My God, I didn't kill her. I'd never do anything like that to Julia. She was always so good to me, so kind, so gentle." Sobbing her name over and over, he was placed in the "suicide cell" overnight.

By then, police knew that the soundproof studio where Julia was attacked had been reserved that Sunday morning by a man named Ross. Convinced that the crime was a coldly premeditated act—that the beautiful young violinist "was deliberately lured to the rehearsal room so that she might be killed in the Sunday morning quiet of a deserted office building"—Dodge announced on Monday afternoon that he would "go before the grand jury as promptly as possible and ask for this man's indictment for first degree murder."[1]

Ross's lawyer, Joseph Perlstein of 1440 Broadway, specialized in theatrical contracts, not criminal defense. With Mischa facing the death penalty, his brother Zachary immediately turned to the man who had represented one hundred thirty clients charged with first-degree murder and saved every one from the electric chair: Samuel S. Leibowitz.

When Ross was arraigned in Homicide Court on Tuesday, April 21, Leibowitz was at his side. Following the proceedings, the Great Defender spoke to reporters. His comments made it clear that he intended to pursue the time-honored tactic of smearing the female victim. Far from being a sexually obsessed stalker, Ross—so Leibowitz suggested—was a loving husband and father whose marriage had run into trouble and who wanted nothing more than to reconcile with his wife. When, during their fateful encounter on Sunday morning, he informed Julia that he was ending their affair and returning to his family, the beautiful "love thief" had flown into a jealous rage and set upon him in a frenzy. Her death was the tragic outcome of the violent altercation she herself had provoked. "It's an old, old story," said Leibowitz, "that a woman cannot steal another woman's husband without flirting with death."

Informed of Leibowitz's remarks, Julia's family—just returned from her burial at a Jewish cemetery in Fairfield—responded with outrage. "He won't get away with that," said her sister, Mrs. Edith Schnee, her voice shaking with indignation. "Ross was Julia's booking agent and accompanist, that's all. Their relationship wasn't even platonic. She could scarcely endure his presence and spent most of her time trying to get him to let her alone."

Apprised of these remarks, Leibowitz issued a clarifying statement that did little to appease Julia's family. "I do not want to be misunderstood as condoning the killing of a human being if the same was done unlawfully," he said. "The relationship between the parties, such as it was, does not justify the taking of human life unlawfully. Nor do I want to paint this unfortunate girl as a sinner and the same time my client as a saint. However, it has been my observation that these triangle affairs eventually lead to tragedy. No woman, or man for that matter, can court another's spouse without inviting disaster."

Whatever hope Leibowitz entertained of convincing a jury that Ross hadn't planned Julia's murder in advance was severely undermined on Tuesday afternoon, when James Cockerell, superintendent of the Hotel Normandie, identified the murder weapon as a hammer stolen from his tool chest the morning of the killing. He had left the tool chest on the floor beside a public telephone booth in the hotel lobby while he went off on an errand. As Cockerell headed out, he had noticed someone walking by the phone booth—Mischa Ross.

By the time Ross came to trial on Monday, June 7, it was clear that escaping the chair was the best he could hope for. At Leibowitz's urging—and with the consent of District Attorney Dodge—he pleaded guilty to the lesser offense of second-degree murder, carrying a penalty of twenty years in prison to life. Afterward, "his eyes sparkling with unconcealed happiness at being permitted to dodge a trial for first-degree murder," he was taken into the adjoining jury room, where he calmly described to reporters how he had killed Julia Nussenbaum.

"I didn't think I loved her," he said. "She was in love with me, though. She knew I was married but she loved me."

On the evening before the killing, he continued, a friend gave him a bottle of sweet red wine. The next morning, "I drank the whole bottle. It made me sort of light-headed."

As he started to leave the hotel for the studio, where he and Julia had arranged to meet, he spotted the hammer in the tool chest beside the telephone booth. "I took it with me," he said, "more for a joke than anything else, I guess."

As soon as he and Julia met in the studio, they started arguing. They had quarreled frequently, he explained, "and always because I wanted to leave her and go back to my wife." "She got very excited," said Ross. "She slapped me. I told her if she felt that way, she should go ahead and kill me. I gave her the hammer. She hit me on the left shoulder and arm. I took the hammer away from her and hit her back. I don't know how many times.

"She fell to the floor. I don't remember striking her after she fell. Maybe I did. I don't know. I don't remember trying to hide the body like the police say I did. I was in a daze. You fellows know how badly a whole bottle of wine will make you feel.

"I didn't think she was dead. I left her there on the floor and went away. The next thing I remember I woke up in my father-in-law's home in Monticello."

Asked by a reporter if he felt sorry for the slaying, Ross replied, "Naturally."

Two weeks later at his sentencing, Ross stood weeping self-pitying tears while Leibowitz appealed to Judge Saul S. Streit for clemency: "I don't think this man went there with murder in his heart. They had a quarrel and he lost his head. There was a genuine affection between them for two years. A life sentence would not serve any purpose. He is not a criminal at heart. It was a crime of passion."

Judge Streit, however, was unmoved. Referring to the prisoner as a "heinous, brutal murderer," he scoffed at Ross' contention that Julia had struck him first with the hammer. "I can't see why he brought the hammer here in the first place, or why he struck her from eight to twelve blows with it. I think there's sufficient evidence here for a jury to find him guilty of murder in the first degree."

With that, Judge Streit handed down a sentence of thirty-five years to life.

It was not the outcome Ross had hoped for. "I didn't expect to get more than twenty years to life," he groused as he was led from the courtroom. For Samuel Leibowitz, however, the case only added to his reputation as the greatest criminal defense attorney of his time —the man who had never lost a client to the chair.[2]

Henrietta

S ITUATED AT THE CORNER of Euclid Avenue and East 12th
Street in downtown Cleveland, the Statler was one of the city's
finest hotels, each of its seven hundred rooms equipped with such
state-of-the-art amenities as a "private bath with anti-scald device,
running ice-water, electric closet light, and a thermostat which keeps
the temperature at any point desired by the guest" (as one advertisement touted). A popular site for business conventions, wedding re-
ceptions, and charity balls, it was also the favorite gathering place for
the Cleveland mob, which not only rented rooms there for its secret
initiation ceremonies but also, in 1928, held a historic event on the
premises: the first summit meeting of organized crime leaders from
around the country, among them such Mafia bigwigs as Joe Profaci,
Vincent Mangano, and Pasqualino "Patsy" Lolardo. For any hotel employee, from kitchen helper to concierge, a job at the Statler
meant "working within the elite of the service industry."[1]

One of those employees was Henrietta Koscianski. A buxom,
black-eyed nineteen-year-old whose face—apart from her blocky,
deeply cleft chin—had a delicate prettiness, Henrietta was the

daughter of poor Polish-American parents who had struggled to send her through high school. She had gone to work immediately after graduation, toiling at various menial jobs before finding a steady position at the Statler. She worked as a pantry maid, preparing vegetables and making salads, desserts, and cold dishes for thirteen dollars a week, most of which went to the support of her family.

In the spring of 1937, Henrietta had been at the hotel for a year and a half, long enough to know most of her fellow employees, at least by sight. Sometime in early May, she noticed a new face among the workers: a young man of medium height with dark, wavy hair and a nice-looking face. He had been hired as a dishwasher, then worked for a few weeks as busboy before being promoted to bar boy in the grillroom, responsible, among his other duties, for keeping the bar stocked with clean glasses and ice and for fetching the bartenders their meals. His name — so he said — was Bob Murray.

A conscientious fellow — described by his supervisor, Mike McNeeley, as "the best worker I ever had" — Bob was much admired by his peers for his artistic ability. During lunch breaks, he would sit at a table in the employees' cafeteria and sketch deft little portraits of the hotel help that he sold for twenty-five cents each. He was known to be "polite and easy-going," though he could also "flare into sudden and unexpected fits of anger." On one occasion, he came close to beating up a busboy named Andy Petro over some trivial disagreement. Only McNeeley's intervention saved Petro from a thrashing.[2]

Sometime in mid-June, Henrietta caught Bob's eye. He began hanging around the kitchen during the after-dinner lulls, chatting away about art and religion and so many other subjects that Henrietta often had trouble following his conversation. At one point, much to her surprise, he asked her on a date. She turned him down gently, explaining that she "didn't know him well enough."

On Wednesday, June 23, Bob offered to sketch Henrietta's portrait for free. Having heard so much about his artistic talents from the other workers, she readily agreed. She seated herself at the counter while he perched on a nearby stool and began to draw. While he worked, he told her that he "used to earn his living going from house to house, making sketches of people," though he didn't say where or when. He took only ten minutes to finish his picture, a flattering profile view of Henrietta that captured her pert nose, pretty mouth, large dark eyes, and fashionably marcelled hair.

Not long afterward, her night shift over, Henrietta took the service elevator up to the thirteenth-floor employees' dormitory, where she shared a room with a maid named Dorothy Kresse. Though it was nearing midnight by the time she got ready for bed, Henrietta was still wide-awake. She asked if Dorothy had anything to read. As it happened, Dorothy had just purchased the current issue of one of her favorite magazines, *Inside Detective*. She tossed it over to Henrietta, who quickly became absorbed in the true detective magazine.

Its cover was characteristically lurid. Against a blood-red backdrop, a beautiful young woman, her silk nightgown slipping from one shoulder to expose most of her left breast, cowered on a bed while a pair of clutching male hands reached down for her throat. "VERONICA GEDEON — MODEL FOR *INSIDE DETECTIVE* IS MURDERED!" screamed the headline.

The accompanying story, written by the magazine's editor, West F. Peterson, paid tribute to Ronnie Gedeon as an altogether decent, considerate young woman who, despite her great beauty, never put on airs. "All who encountered Ronnie through business liked her," Peterson wrote. "She always had a smile for the receptionist, she never 'ritzed' the office boy. At Christmas, when one of the staff was ill, she chipped in to buy the convalescent a present. . . . Members of the art department, who knew her best, said she was fun-loving, conscientious, generous, and altogether likable.

"For this reason," the article continued, "the news of her sudden and altogether horrible death came as a shock almost too staggering to be credible. And it is only natural that *Inside Detective* is taking a personal interest in the solution of the mystery and the capture of the killer."

After summarizing the case, Peterson concluded by presenting what he described as "the most unusual cash reward ever offered in my years of observing real-life detective dramas":

The publishers of *Inside Detective* have offered a one thousand dollar reward to be given to the detective or private citizen who does most toward obtaining the detection, apprehension, and conviction of the killer or killers. . . .

If Robert Irwin is not captured at the time of publication of the current issue, *Inside Detective* readers are urged to watch for the young artist who is admittedly affected with a social disease, and whose alleged mania to kill springs from a religio-sexual complex which, in the past, caused him to be committed to institutions for the insane. . . .

Anyone turning in Robert Irwin will automatically be considered a leading candidate for the *Inside Detective* reward money.

STUDY IRWIN'S PHOTOGRAPH!
NOTE IRWIN'S CHARACTERISTICS!
REMEMBER THAT IRWIN MAY BE ANYWHERE — AND
THAT HE MAY BE MASQUERADING IN FEMALE ATTIRE!

Watch for Robert Irwin, if, at the time this magazine is on sale, you have not already read of his capture, dead or alive. Notification of his apprehension should be wired or telephoned to The Editor, *Inside Detective* Magazine, 140 Madison Avenue, New York.[3]

The article was illustrated with more than a dozen photographs, some of Ronnie's titillating poses for the magazine, a few of Joseph Gedeon, one of Ronnie's Pekingese, Touchi ("The Only Murder Witness"), and, very prominently, the widely circulated portrait of Robert Irwin, the "Hunted Maniac."

Henrietta stared for a long time at Irwin's photograph. To her eyes, the fugitive looked strikingly like Bob Murray. She showed the picture to Dorothy, who laughingly agreed that the mad killer bore a resemblance to "our Bob." Henrietta thought it would be fun to tease Bob about it the next time she saw him. Then she turned off the light and went to sleep.[4]

It wasn't until Friday evening, June 25, that she saw Bob again, when he showed up in the kitchen to fetch some ice for the bar and came over to chat. After a few minutes of small talk, Henrietta, a playful lilt in her voice, asked, "Say, Bob, what's your last name again?"

His eyes narrowed slightly. "Murray," he answered. "Why?"

"Ever hear of Robert Irwin?" she asked.

His reaction startled her. Spinning on his heel, he muttered a barely audible "no" and strode from the kitchen.

"I couldn't believe it," Henrietta later recalled. Could it possibly be that her friend Bob Murray really was the infamous Mad Sculptor? "Looking back now, I think I didn't want to believe it."

Her suspicions fully aroused, Henrietta hurried to her room for the detective magazine, which she showed to a half dozen of her fellow employees—her boss Alice Barnes, stewards Larry Guardini and John Konya, desk clerk Manuel Meridas, waiter captain William Peters, and the night manager, Louis de Clairmont. All saw the resemblance at once. At approximately 12:25 a.m., Clairmont called the police. A squad of detectives arrived within minutes. Inside the grillroom, they learned that the bar boy calling himself Bob Murray hadn't been seen since he had been sent to the kitchen for ice. A search of the building turned up no sign of him.

From his employment application, they learned that he was living at the Lake Hotel, a cheap hostelry on Ninth Street where rooms could be had for $1.50 a week. Racing to his room, they found signs that it had been vacated in a hurry. Among the scattered items left behind was a batch of tabloid clippings on the hunt for the Mad Sculptor.

The next morning, early editions of newspapers throughout the country plastered the story on their front pages: "IRWIN FOUND IN OHIO, ESCAPES," "IRWIN SPOTTED IN CLEVELAND, ESCAPES POLICE NET," "GIRL SPOTS IRWIN IN CLEVELAND; HE FLEES," "IRWIN ELUDES CLEVELAND POLICE AFTER GIRL RECOGNIZES FUGITIVE."[5]

After sending out an eight-state alarm and assigning 187 men to the case, Cleveland Chief of Police George Matowitz held a news conference to offer his opinion. "I think Irwin probably went out on a freight train or aboard a tramp steamer or an ore freighter. It was by some hobo route—we are sure of that."

Shown Irwin's picture, however, several ticket clerks at the Greyhound bus terminal said that it closely resembled a man who had boarded a 1:20 a.m. bus for Chicago.[6]

The Front Page

C LEVELAND HAD NEVER BEEN Bob's original destination. In fact, for a week after the massacre, he had made no attempt to flee at all.

From the moment the killing was over, he had felt perfectly at peace with himself—"as calm as I've been in my life before." Without bothering to check if the apartment door was locked, he had gone into the bathroom to wash up. He then spent a leisurely hour rummaging through drawers, searching in vain for some photographs of Ethel. He came across Ronnie's diary but had no interest in it.

In the bedroom where Ronnie and her mother lay, he grabbed the little alarm clock, its glowing, hypnotic face faded now in the dawning Easter light. Given the nasty scratches on his cheeks, he knew he'd have to keep out of sight for a few days, so he went into the kitchen and stuffed a paper bag full of provisions. Then, retrieving the ice pick from the side table where he'd placed it, he left the apartment and headed back to the Ottburgs' house on 52nd Street.

There was no need to hurry. It was 6:30 a.m. and the Sunday streets were deserted.

Upstairs in his room, he discovered that one of his gloves was missing. He realized right away that he must have left it in the apartment, but going back for it seemed like too much of a bother. Stripping off his clothes, he climbed into bed and slept all day.

He awoke to the shouts of newsboys, crying their extras in the streets below. For the next week, he stuck mostly to his room, venturing out only after dark to buy a paper from a late-night newsstand. During the day, from his rear-facing window, he watched the constant commotion at the 51st Street police station—the mob of reporters milling on the sidewalk, the comings and goings of detectives and squad cars. A couple of times, he even caught a glimpse of Joe Gedeon being hustled through the crowd into the station house.

Very late one midweek night—when the tabloid witch hunt against Gedeon was at its height—he had chanced a trip to a twenty-four-hour eatery, the Surrey Cafeteria on Third Avenue and 54th Street. He was seated at the counter, finishing his hamburger, when the fellow beside him looked up from his newspaper and, nodding toward a photograph of the little upholsterer, said, "Do you think the old fellow is guilty?"

"I don't know," he answered with a shrug. "You never can tell." Then he hurriedly paid his check and left.

He had made up his mind that, if Gedeon were charged with the murders, he would turn himself in. He liked the old man and, as he later told people, "wouldn't have let him go to the chair." He prayed things wouldn't come to that, though. His hope was that "it would end by throwing suspicion on some unknown lover of Ronnie and that the lover would not be found."

It wasn't until a full week after the murders that he figured it was time to leave town. Late Sunday afternoon, April 4, he checked his bags at Grand Central Station and took a train to Philadelphia. He stayed there until Monday morning when, passing a newsstand, he saw a headline reading "MAD ARTIST WANTED."

He knew at once who had fingered him to the cops: that son-of-a-bitch William Lamkie, a man he had regarded as one of his closest friends. He vowed to get even with him one day.

He still had the ice pick in his coat pocket. He tossed it into a trash can and, around 10:00 a.m., hopped a bus for Washington, D.C.

He spent all Monday afternoon walking around the city, strolling to the White House and visiting the National Gallery. With his face plastered all over the front pages, he assumed he'd be arrested any minute and was surprised when no one recognized him. During his entire time as America's most wanted fugitive, he made no effort to alter his appearance and was much amused by the newspaper stories describing him as a "master of disguise" who might be going around in female clothing.

After his afternoon of sightseeing, he made his way to the freight yards. He "had done a lot of bumming," he explained afterward, "but had no freight car experience. I decided to go whatever way the freight went." He found a vacant boxcar, climbed inside, and went to sleep.

When he woke up the following morning, Tuesday, April 6, the train was moving and he had company—"a regular bum who gave me all sorts of tips." The two traveled all the way to Willard, Ohio, where Irwin got off. From there, he hitchhiked to Akron, then caught another ride to Cleveland, arriving there on Thursday, April 8. He had settled into his new life pretty comfortably by the time that pantry girl, Henrietta Whatsername, recognized him.[1]

He had hurried from the kitchen and kept on going until he reached his hotel. He knew he couldn't stay on the run forever. His arrest was inevitable—probably sooner rather than later, now that he'd been recognized. Why not make a splash by giving himself up? Not to the cops but to someone who appreciated his importance, who had once called him a "mad genius" on his nightly broadcast— America's most popular newspaper columnist and radio commentator, Walter Winchell.

Quickly gathering his belongings, he made straight for the bus terminal, only to find that he was two bucks short of the twelve-dollar fare to New York City. So he bought a one-way ticket on the next bus to Chicago.

Now, seated by a window in the sleek, blue-and-white Super Coach, he debated his next move. It suddenly occurred to him that he could make good money by turning himself in to a newspaper—certainly more than that double-crosser Lamkie had gotten for peddling his life story to the tabloids.

It was 6:30 Saturday morning when he arrived in Chicago. He spent a few hours wandering around Lake Shore Drive and the Loop. Spotting a movie marquee announcing an exclusive newsreel of the June 22 Joe Louis–Jim Braddock heavyweight match, he bought a thirty-five-cent ticket and, after taking in the footage of the bout, stayed to watch the main feature, *Wings Over Honolulu*, starring Ray Milland and Wendy Barrie.[2]

Afterward, he found the nearest drugstore, shut himself inside the rear telephone booth, and dialed the number of the *Chicago Tribune*. Connected to the city editor, he identified himself as Robert Irwin and was answered with an irate "Take it somewhere else, buddy. I don't have time for monkey business." When the editor slammed down the phone, Bob slipped another nickel into the coin slot and called the *Chicago Herald and Examiner*.[3]

Created from the merger of two Chicago newspapers, Hearst's *Herald and Examiner* was famed for its old-school, bare-knuckled journalism. Its no-holds-barred approach was epitomized by night city editor Frank Carson. In 1920, for example, following a sensational murder-suicide involving the head of a prominent Chicago advertising firm and his mistress, Ruth Randall, Carson managed to steal a pivotal piece of evidence—Randall's diary—from the safe at police headquarters. He then copyrighted it and announced his plan to publish it in sections over the course of a week. When authorities howled that Carson was preventing the coroner's jury from seeing the diary, he "cheerfully announced that the jury was not going to be deprived of the document—they could read it in the *Herald and Examiner* in daily installments."[4]

Carson's crime reporters were equally brazen, going to any

lengths necessary to secure a scoop, from impersonating police officials to buddying up to murder suspects. It was partly by befriending Carl Wanderer, for example, that *Herald and Examiner* reporter Charles MacArthur helped crack one of Chicago's most notorious homicides. A heavily decorated World War I veteran, Wanderer had just returned from a movie with his pregnant wife, Ruth, on the night of June 21, 1920, when a gun-wielding vagrant accosted them in the vestibule of their apartment building. According to his account, when the "raggedy stranger" opened fire on Ruth, mortally wounding her, Wanderer drew his own pistol and shot the man dead. Wanderer was hailed as a hero until MacArthur, working with his crony Ben Hecht, a reporter for the rival *Chicago Daily News,* began to notice discrepancies in his story. Ultimately MacArthur and Hecht managed to wrest the truth from Wanderer, who confessed that the "mugging" was part of a byzantine plot to murder his wife so that he could run off with his homosexual lover.[5]

MacArthur and Hecht would later immortalize their freewheeling days as Chicago crime reporters in their smash Broadway hit, *The Front Page.* In that 1927 play, an escaped murderer turns himself over to Hildy Johnson, ace reporter for the *Herald and Examiner,* who keeps the fugitive hidden from the police and other newsmen so that he can get the exclusive scoop on the story.[6]

With Robert Irwin's phone call to the *Herald and Examiner* on the afternoon of Saturday, June 26, life—as the saying goes—was about to imitate art.

Having been dismissed as a hoaxer when he tried the *Tribune,* Bob took a different tack when he reached Harry Romanoff, Frank Carson's successor as city editor of the *Herald and Examiner.*

"I'm a friend of Robert Irwin, who is wanted in New York for the Gedeon murders," said Bob. "He wants to give himself up. What kind of deal can you make with him?"

"I'd have to know more about it," Romanoff calmly replied. "Obviously no deal can be made over the telephone. We'd have to talk it over with you face to face."

"That can be arranged," said Bob. "I'll meet your representative at 2:30 near the fountain at the south end of the Art Institute."

At the appointed time, reporter Austin O'Malley arrived in Grant Park and headed for the designated rendezvous spot: Lorado Taft's celebrated sculpture *Fountain of the Great Lakes*. Gazing up at the grouping of five graceful nymphs was a slender young man in a well-worn gray suit and gray fedora. O'Malley recognized him at once as Robert Irwin.

After introducing himself, O'Malley led Bob to Michigan Avenue and hailed a cab. Minutes later, they were seated in the office of Managing Editor John Dienhart. Within an hour, Bob had signed a contract that began:

> Universal Service agrees that if the undersigned Robert Irwin proves to the complete satisfaction of the police authorities that he is the Robert Irwin now wanted by the New York police in the Gedeon case and upon fulfillment of the terms of the agreement, a sum of $5,000 will be paid to the undersigned.

For his part, Bob agreed to provide a complete signed confession for exclusive publication by the Hearst syndicate and to "refrain from giving interviews to any newspapers other than the Hearst press for a term of two weeks."[7]

Accompanied by Dienhart, O'Malley, Romanoff, a cameraman, and a stenographer, Bob was then whisked off to a room at the Morrison Hotel. After a bath, a shave, and a room-service meal, he seated himself in an armchair and lit a cigarette. With a captive audience hanging on his every word, he settled back and launched into a rambling monologue. He related his entire life story, philosophized at length about art, immortality, and religion, and expounded on his theory of visualization ("my contribution to civilization," as he called it).

Stifling their impatience, Dienhart and his colleagues kept prodding him to focus on the matter at hand: the Easter Sunday murders. Finally, he gave them their money's worth.

Confession

"THAT NIGHT I SAID TO MYSELF I am going up there and killing Ethel," Bob told his rapt listeners. "I never intended to get anybody but her. I thought that after killing Ethel then they would kill me in the chair, but I didn't care.

"Then I said to myself that after being in the nut house all your life, you can't go to the chair. You might, but the chances are that you won't. They'll put me in the nut house again and then I'll be there all the rest of my life and catch up with myself in a spiritual way."

After sharpening his ice pick, he had walked to the apartment building at 316 East 50th Street, arriving at around nine that Easter eve. No one answered when he pressed the downstairs buzzer. He waited on the sidewalk for nearly an hour before he saw Mary Gedeon approaching. Surprised—and not entirely pleased—to see him, she nevertheless invited him upstairs.

"Mrs. Gedeon did not want me to have anything to do with Ethel," Bob explained. "Outside of that she was always very friendly to me."

Mary had been out for much of the day and was dead tired. Sinking into a chair at the kitchen table, she asked if he would walk the dog. Bob was happy to oblige, taking Touchi for a stroll around the block.

Back upstairs, he joined Mary in the kitchen. The last time he had visited the apartment, back in December, Ethel had been staying with her mother, and Bob had gotten it into his head that she and Joe Kudner were separated. Assuming that she was "out having a good time," he did his best to stall until she returned. Pulling out his little pad and a pencil, he began to draw Mary's portrait. "I took just as long as I could on that picture, and all of the time I was feeling her out about Ethel."

Bob was still sketching when the little Englishman Frank Byrnes showed up. He and Bob shook hands and exchanged a few pleasantries before Byrnes retired to his bedroom and closed the door.

He had been there for more than an hour when Mary, who still had some holiday preparations to attend to before she went to bed, said, "Bob, Ethel isn't here and it's very late."

"I am going to stay here until I see Ethel," Bob replied.

Mary, her patience at an end, half rose from her seat and yelled, "Get out of here, or I'll call the Englishman."

Bob went mad.

"At that moment," he related, "I hit her with everything I had. She fell back on the floor with her legs back over her head. I grabbed her by the neck. I was astonished at the fight she made. She had plenty of life in her. She scratched my face like nobody's business.

"I had Mrs. Gedeon by the throat and I never let loose of that throat for twenty minutes. Finally her arms dropped back limp and her shoulders sagged to the floor.

"All the time this damned Englishman was in the next room just ten feet away. She died right in the front of that room, just ten feet away. She put up a hell of a fight. I can't understand why she didn't bring the whole town down on us."

At this point in his narrative, Bob revealed a detail so obscene that it was censored from all published versions of his confession.

Made even more shocking by the matter-of-fact tone in which he divulged it, it explained the injuries that Medical Examiner Gonzales had found on Mary Gedeon's genital area.

Mary Gedeon had, in fact, been sexually violated. But not by Robert Irwin.

"While I had her on the floor," he recalled, "the dog put his nose to her private parts. I continued to choke her for about twenty minutes before I was sure she was lifeless. I wanted to degrade her as low as I possibly could, so I pulled her garments from her body and allowed the dog to ravish Mrs. Gedeon."[1]

"My face was badly scratched," Bob continued after a momentary pause. "My hands were full of blood. I smeared it on her, on her face and on her breast. Then I threw her in the bedroom under the bed." When Touchi crawled in after his mistress, Bob thought of killing the animal, too, but refrained "out of pity."

He was still convinced that Ethel would show up. He had no intention of leaving until he had "done what I had come to do. I had to keep waiting for Ethel. She was the one I felt I must kill. I simply had to wait for her to finish what I had planned."

He realized that Ronnie might arrive first. He had no desire to kill her. "She was beautiful, and I hate to destroy beauty. I said to myself if Ronnie comes in first, I can tie her up and leave her." He had read somewhere that a bar of soap wrapped in a rag made an effective blackjack, one that "would stun but nothing more. So I went in the kitchen and got some ordinary soap and made a blackjack out it with a washrag." He would later be amused to read in the tabloids that he had used the soap to carve a small sculpture of Ethel.

At about 3:00 a.m., he heard Ronnie enter after saying a laughing good night to someone in the hallway. She went directly into the bathroom, while he waited in the darkness of the little bedroom where he had concealed her mother's corpse. "She stayed in there the longest time," Bob related. "I thought she was never coming out."

It was already after 4:00 a.m. when Ronnie suddenly entered the bedroom. Bob—who had been lost in thoughts of Ethel and hadn't heard Ronnie leave the bathroom—hurriedly "let her have it" with the blackjack. "The soap went all over the floor," he said. "It didn't have the slightest effect. I can well believe that she was drunk because she didn't put up any fight at all."

Grabbing her by the throat, he dragged her onto the bed. "I held her the longest time, just tight enough so that she could breathe," he explained. "There were moments when the pressure was relaxed enough so that she could speak a few words but not loudly."

Disguising his voice, he asked her where Ethel was. Ronnie answered that she was at home with her husband, Joe Kudner.

"I gave it up and I didn't know just what in God's name I would do," said Bob. "I wanted to let Ronnie live if I could. We were always pals. I suppose she thought I was going to rape her. She said, 'Please don't touch me. I just had an operation and the doctor said if I have intercourse, I could die.' I had no such thought in mind. So I kept holding on—just light enough to prevent noise, not tight enough to kill."

He estimated that he had kept his grip on her for around two hours, though he had little sense of the passage of time. "When you get in a mix-up like that," he said, "you don't think about what you are doing, and time means nothing. The whole night passed to me like a blue daze."

Finally, her voice weak and tremulous, Ronnie said: "Bob, I know you. You are going to get in trouble if you do this."

Those words were her death sentence.

"The minute she used my name," Bob said calmly, "I clamped down on her and choked her until she was lifeless. She immediately became the most repulsive thing I have ever seen in my life. It was like blue death, just oozing out, a spiritual emanation just oozing out.

"I turned on the lights and ripped off her chemise, leaving her on top of the bed, her mother's body underneath." He then put out the lights and left the room.

It was daybreak by then. Knowing that Frank Byrnes could identify him, he "went in and fixed the Englishman" with the ice pick he had intended to use on Ethel. "I struck him the first time in the temple, so far as it would go. The pick was about six inches long. The poor fellow lay there twitching but did not bleed. I had to hit him eleven times.

"After I put him out of his misery, I went in and took a little clock. The last thing I said to myself was: 'Buddy, you did it!'"

Up until that moment in Bob's recitation, no one had interrupted him. Now, however, Dienhart asked how he felt about the murders.

"I'm certainly sorry I killed all three of them," Bob said offhandedly. "There was only one I was after, and that was Ethel. I don't know whether it was hate or love that made me want to kill her. If she had come in first, I would have killed her and nobody else. I don't think I would have marred up her features, as I only wanted to stab her once with the ice pick, and one little hole wouldn't show."

And what did Bob expect to happen to him now, Dienhart asked.

"Whatever is coming to me, I'll take," Bob answered with a smile. "If I don't get the chair and I go to an institution, I'll use my money to hire someone to work for me to drill me in visualizing. I want to develop myself.

"Even if I die, that won't be the end of it. That cycle comes back. These people I killed aren't lost. Theirs are borrowed lives, and if I live I will reap them. I only meant to borrow one life. I will repay these lives by developing that power of visualizing, which is the next step in the evolution of the human race."[2]

Celebrities

T HE NEWS BROKE at ten o'clock Saturday night when the five-
star final edition of the *Herald and Examiner* hit the stands.
"IRWIN SURRENDERS HERE; CONFESSES KILLING MODEL!"
screamed the headline in letters three inches high. A self-congratu-
latory front-page item, four columns wide, boasted of the scoop as
"by far the most notable newspaper achievement of the year."

Within minutes, a squad of detectives descended on the *Herald
and Examiner* building on Madison Street, while reporters from rival papers "staked out the exits and climbed onto an elevated railroad trestle that commanded a view of the newsroom." Bob, however, was nowhere to be found.

Sequestered inside his room at the Morrison Hotel—where he
would be kept incommunicado until the Hearst syndicate was ready
to hand over its prize to the authorities—he ate a hearty dinner and
passed some time playing gin rummy with Austin O'Malley and a
few of the other newsmen. At one point, someone asked him what
he planned to do with his five thousand dollars. Bob replied that he
intended to use most of it to "help his two brothers," Vidalin and

Pember. Both were currently behind bars—Vidalin in Washington State Penitentiary for armed robbery, Pember in Oregon State for "assault with intent to rob." Once they were released, they would be able to use Bob's money to get a new start in life.

While commending Bob on his generous impulse, O'Malley suggested that he might "better spend the money for his own defense." With five thousand dollars at his disposal, Bob could afford the best lawyer around.

"Maybe," said O'Malley, "you can get Samuel Leibowitz."[1]

Having received what he regarded as a reliable tip that Robert Irwin was hiding in Hoboken, New Jersey, Police Commissioner Valentine had initially dismissed the reports that the Mad Sculptor's trail had been picked up in Cleveland. The news coming out of Chicago, however, changed his mind in a hurry. By Sunday morning, June 27, he had reached an arrangement with representatives of the Hearst organization. Two New York City detectives, Martin Owens and Frank Crimmins, would leave immediately for Chicago by chartered plane. They would be accompanied by reporter Ray Doyle of the Hearst-owned *Daily Mirror*. Irwin would be delivered directly into the custody of Owens and Crimmins. In exchange, Doyle would be "the only reporter present at the surrender."[2]

The surrender was arranged for 1:30 p.m. at the office of Cook County Sheriff John Toman. At the designated time, Irwin appeared with his escorts from the *Herald and Examiner*. He was dressed in a natty summer outfit that he had demanded as part of his deal with the paper: white Panama hat, white linen suit, white shirt, blue tie, and two-tone, black-and-white shoes. Looking "well rested and thoroughly at ease," he calmly signed a waiver of extradition. Detective Owens then took possession of the prisoner and made ready to return to the awaiting plane. Before leaving the sheriff's office, he placed a courtesy call to Chicago's Chief of Detectives, John L. Sullivan, formally notifying him of Irwin's surrender.

It was immediately clear that Sullivan had no intention of letting the New York City police reap all the glory for the capture of America's most high-profile fugitive. Demanding to see the official arrest warrant, he ordered Owens to stay put. Minutes later, a squad of Chicago police officers burst into the sheriff's office and took Irwin into custody.[3]

With Owens and Crimmins beside him and his press retinue following close behind, Irwin was driven to Chief Sullivan's office, where—much to the chagrin of the two New York City detectives—it was discovered that the arrest warrant had been made out for "Arthur Irwin." A wire was immediately dispatched to Commissioner Valentine, requesting an amended document.

While awaiting a reply, Sullivan—determined to grab as much attention as possible before relinquishing Irwin—staged an elaborate charade for the benefit of the press. Before an audience of fifty newspapermen and an equal number of police officials, Bob—smiling, joking, and generally basking in the limelight—was paraded through the booking process. After being fingerprinted, he was told to remove his jacket so his physical measurements could be taken, a standard procedure in the Chicago PD, which had never fully abandoned the Bertillon system of "anthropometric identification" it had adopted in 1888.

"Say, old man," said the officer recording his statistics, "you look as though you're in good shape."

"You bet I am," Bob said, puffing out his chest. "I always keep myself that way."

A few minutes later, when one of the spectators offered another flattering comment about his physique, Bob struck a preening pose and said, "Sure, I'm proud of it."

Police matrons and female clerks kept popping into the room to steal glimpses of the celebrity killer. They emerged like starstruck schoolgirls, burbling, "How good-looking he is . . . What a lovely boy . . . Hasn't he got nice hair . . . How could he have done such a thing . . ."[4]

Manacled to Detective Charles Moore, Bob was then placed in the weekly police lineup, along with eight other men arrested on minor charges. Told to turn this way and that on the floodlit platform so the audience could view him from all sides, he obeyed with "a jaunty, unconcerned air." When Chief Sullivan asked if he understood why he was there, Bob grinned and said, "Sure. A trip to New York."

Only once did he lose his composure. As he stepped from the lineup, a news photographer reached out and snatched Bob's Panama hat from his head to get a better picture of his face. "What the hell do you think you're doing?" screamed Bob, lunging so violently at the man that Detective Moore, still handcuffed to the prisoner, was thrown off balance. For those witnessing the scene, the moment was a revelation—a dramatic display of "the swift flow of emotion that made him such a dangerous character."[5]

By the time Bob was led back down to Chief Sullivan's office, he had regained his aplomb. By then, a corrected warrant had been wired from Chief Valentine. Officially transferred into the custody of Detectives Owens and Crimmins, Bob was driven to the Chicago Municipal Airport in Cicero, where an estimated crowd of four hundred gawkers—most of them women—were waiting to see him off. At precisely 5:32 local time, Bob and his entourage—now consisting of the two New York City detectives, a pair of Chicago policemen, Ray Doyle of the *New York Daily Mirror*, and three other Hearst reporters—took off in a specially chartered, twenty-one-seat American Airlines passenger plane, the *Arkansas*, flagship of the line's fleet.[6]

During the four-hour flight, Bob—whose handcuffs were removed upon boarding—devoured a meal of sliced chicken, tomato salad, nut bread, and coffee; chain-smoked an entire pack of cigarettes; chatted pleasantly with stewardess Bernadette Anderle; and calmly answered questions posed to him by Detective Crimmins.

He grew visibly agitated only once—when Crimmins asked why he "stole that clock from Ronnie Gedeon's bedroom the night she was killed."

"Do you know," Bob said with a grimace, "that's the one thing

I'm ashamed of—stealing that clock. To kill is one thing. But to be a sneak thief—ugh!"

"So why did you do it?" Crimmins pressed.

Bob blinked nervously. "The clock was in front of me as I strangled Ronnie. Its dial shone. It looked like two green eyes. It fascinated me."[7]

Even before the plane landed in New York, Ben Hecht and Charles MacArthur had been contacted by reporters struck by the uncanny parallels between their hit show *The Front Page* and the events that had just played out in Chicago. Both men reacted with high amusement. Recalling his own brazen exploits as a crime reporter for the *Herald and Examiner*, MacArthur was gratified to see that the paper still retained its old scrappy spirit. "After I left, it seemed to calm down," he said. "I thought it had reformed. As an alumnus, I'm delighted it has not."

As for Hecht—by then the highest-paid screenwriter in Hollywood—he conveyed his delight in mock indignation. "We ought to sue the *Herald and Examiner* for plagiarism!" he exclaimed to reporters. "They stole our plot! Our best plot!"[8]

A mob of several hundred curiosity seekers, kept back from the landing strip by more than two dozen police officers, was waiting at Floyd Bennett Field in southeast Brooklyn when the *Arkansas* touched down shortly before midnight. Handcuffed to Owens, Bob —looking somewhat rumpled but chipper as ever—stepped off the plane and waved cheerfully to the crowd before being bundled into a police automobile. Preceded, flanked, and followed by a cavalcade of motorcycle patrolmen and squad cars, he was sped to police headquarters on Centre Street, hustled through a rear entrance to avoid the horde of newsmen gathered in front, and led directly to Assistant Chief Inspector Lyons's second-floor office.

Besides Lyons, a group of high officials was assembled in the room, among them Commissioner Valentine, District Attorney

Dodge, Assistant DA Miles O'Brien, Deputy Chief Inspector Francis Kear, and Captain Ed Mullins. Much to their frustration, the normally voluble prisoner suddenly clammed up, refusing to answer any questions or to verify the confession he had made in Chicago. Staring defiantly up at Dodge, he said, "You can beat the Jesus out of me, you won't make me talk."

"We don't do things like that here," the DA answered with a tight smile.

Owens, also present in the room, had a theory about Bob's stubborn silence. "He thinks his contract with the *Herald and Examiner* is so binding that he can't make a statement to anybody," Owens said to the others. "Otherwise he'll forfeit the five thousand dollars."

Turning to Bob, he said, "The contract says you can't give your story to other newspapers. It doesn't mean you can't talk to the District Attorney or the police."

"All we want to know," said Dodge, "is whether the confession you signed in Chicago was a true confession."

Bob, however, would not be cajoled into talking. The "atmosphere in the room is too hostile," he said. He insisted on having "at least one friendly face" present. When asked whom he had in mind, Bob replied without hesitation: Dr. Fredric Wertham.[9]

The phone had been ringing for a while before it roused Wertham from his sleep. Gazing at the bedside clock with bleary eyes, he saw that it was half past three in the morning. He lifted the receiver and gave a groggy hello.

"Is that you, doctor?" said the voice on the other end.

"Yes, this is Dr. Wertham."

"Don't you recognize me? It's Bob."

Wertham was stunned into momentary silence. "Where on earth are you?" he asked when he regained his voice.

"Down here in police headquarters with Commissioner Valentine and the district attorney and a lot of other police officials."

Half believing that the call was a hoax, Wertham asked to speak to one of the officials. Almost at once, someone got on the phone and identified himself as Inspector John Lyons.

"Bob insists that he has to talk to you," said Lyons. "Commissioner Valentine would appreciate it if you would. He'll send his own car to fetch you."

Wertham asked for a few minutes to get ready. By the time he had washed, shaved, and thrown on his clothes, the police car was waiting for him.

Minutes later he was ushered into a side entrance of the Centre Street headquarters. Inside a second-floor conference room, he found Bob standing in front of a long table whose seats were occupied by "about fifteen of the highest officials of the police department and the district attorney's office."

At his first glimpse of the psychiatrist, Bob broke into a broad grin. "Not often in my life," Wertham said afterward, "have I seen a man so pleased to see me."

Obtaining permission from Commissioner Valentine to confer in private, Wertham and Irwin were led into the corridor, where they stood in a corner and spoke in hushed voices, Bob "talking excitedly" and "looking around to make sure that no one was listening."

"What's happened won't make any difference between us, will it?" he asked with a catch in his voice.

"Absolutely not," Wertham assured him. "Everything is as before between you and me. But why on earth didn't you come to me before Easter and tell me you felt so badly again?"

"Oh, let's leave those old things," Bob said. Then, "with arms and hands gesticulating," he began "talking a blue streak," relating everything that had happened since he'd arrived at headquarters.

"I wouldn't talk to them before you came, but they were very nice about it," he said. "They gave me a salad with lettuce and tomatoes. I'm crazy about tomatoes. They didn't even beat me up."

"High police officials never beat people up," Wertham said dryly. "They have cops for that. That just shows what serious trouble you're in now."

Trying to impress upon Bob that he was in an "awful mess" and that his refusal to talk only made him look guiltier, Wertham urged him to break his silence.

"You don't have to tell them the whole story," he said. "But you seem to have talked a lot to reporters in Chicago. So tell them something here, just to satisfy them. Your life is in terrible danger."

"You know that I was sick," said Bob.

"Were!" exclaimed the doctor. "You *are* sick. And all you have to do is be yourself. That is your only chance. I promise you I'll do anything I can for you, whatever happens."

Though reluctant to speak without a lawyer present, Bob allowed himself to be convinced. Returning to the conference room, he took a seat, lit a cigarette, and began to talk, confirming all the details of his Chicago confession. For the most part, he recounted the tale in a calm, untroubled way, though he grew intensely agitated at several points. While he showed no emotion when describing how he'd torn off Mary's underwear so the dog could get at her genitals, he flew into a rage when the district attorney asked if he had raped Ronnie, taking the query as "a horrid accusation."

At another point, when Commissioner Valentine asked if he felt any remorse, Bob became wildly excited.

"Yes, but I believe those lives are not lost, they are borrowed and I can repay them," he said, eyes glinting.

"What do you mean by that?" asked Valentine.

"I don't believe anything is lost and that all life is only a part of the Divine Life," said Bob. "I think that the progress of evolution is from the material to the mental or spiritual plane and I think that visualizing, developing the faculty of visualizing, may be one of the greatest contributions in that direction. And I think that by putting myself under pressure at any cost I would be able to contribute."

Like others, District Attorney Dodge was particularly curious about Bob's theft of Lucy Beacco's worthless alarm clock.

"What was there about the clock that attracted you?" he asked.

As before, when Detective Crimmins had posed the same question, Bob grew uncharacteristically flustered.

"Because I looked at the clock and saw the green lights," he said nervously.

"The luminous hands?" said Dodge. "Something about the clock that attracted you and you wanted it?

"It—it wasn't the clock," Bob stammered. "I had a clock. It was the green light . . . not the numbers . . . I don't know."[10]

At 6:35 Monday morning, a little more than an hour after he finally opened up to the officials, Bob was escorted to the basement and placed in Cell No. 1, the same cell once occupied by Joseph Gedeon during his weeklong ordeal. Five minutes later, with a sergeant and two detectives keeping suicide watch, he stretched out on the cot and, despite the bright light burning directly overhead, fell instantly asleep.

He was awakened at 8:00 a.m., given a cup of coffee, and taken to the lineup. Hair mussed, suit rumpled, jaw darkened with a three-day growth of stubble, he went through "the routine questioning with ennui written on his face. He smiled frequently and yawned broadly, covering his mouth with a languid gesture. He slouched so insolently that the officer in charge had to shout through a megaphone, 'Stand up there!'"

With a brawny detective clutching each of his wrists, he was then hustled out the front entrance of headquarters, where a police wagon waited to transport him to his arraignment. Wedged between the two massive lawmen, the slender, five-foot-seven prisoner looked "like a dwarf." Sinking into the back seat, he spotted a copy of that morning's *Daily News* on the cushion beside him. A picture of himself appearing "gay and nonchalant" as he posed for photographers in Chicago occupied the bottom two-thirds of the front page, beneath a headline reading, "IRWIN'S OWN STORY." Snatching up the paper, he immediately began reading and didn't raise his head until the van reached Homicide Court a few blocks away.

A crowd estimated at between 2,500 and 3,000 spectators—the largest such gathering since the mobs that had turned out to gawk at Bruno Richard Hauptmann—surrounded Homicide Court at 301

Mott Street. Though the building had been cleared of everyone who had no official business there, the corridors were jammed with municipal employees and the courtroom itself was packed with reporters, detectives, clerks and attendants. Someone else was present, too: Samuel S. Leibowitz.

The previous day, Bob's one-line telegram had reached the lawyer at his summer home: "WILL YOU PLEASE REPRESENT ME ON MY ARRIVAL IN NEW YORK?" Leibowitz, who frankly admitted how much he thrived on publicity, was immediately intrigued at the thought of defending the nationally known Mad Sculptor. Something else, far less to do with his own love of the limelight, also drew him to the case. His long involvement in the Scottsboro affair had done much to enlarge his social conscience, and he already foresaw that the Irwin trial had a significant societal dimension—the potential to produce, as he put it, "a more logical approach to the problem of dealing with the criminally insane."[11]

Hurrying back to the city, he had arrived at the courtroom not long before Bob was brought in. Having never so much as set eyes on Irwin, Leibowitz made it clear to the presiding magistrate that he was there on a provisional basis. He would represent the prisoner for the moment, but until he had a chance to confer at length with Irwin, he would not commit himself to the case. The arraignment itself lasted only a few minutes. A brief affidavit had been prepared by Detective Crimmins, specifying, in typically stilted legalese, that the defendant had "willfully and feloniously choked and strangled to death" both Mary and Ronnie Gedeon and fatally stabbed Frank Byrnes "with an ice pick held in his hand." After Leibowitz waived the reading of the full complaint, Magistrate Alexander Brough adjourned the proceedings until Wednesday, June 30, then remanded Irwin to the Tombs without bail.

When the proceedings were over, Bob and Leibowitz spoke for ten minutes in the detention pen at one side of the courtroom. Bob was then shackled to two detectives and escorted outside to the police wagon parked at the curb. From the rooftops, windows, and fire escapes of the neighborhood tenements, hundreds of men and women peered down at the celebrity killer, some of them hooting in derision.

A short time later, Leibowitz showed up at the Tombs and conferred with Bob in his cell for an hour and a half. Afterward, a swarm of newsmen surrounded the lawyer, bombarding him with questions. Leibowitz said little, though he confirmed that he had decided to represent Irwin. When one of the reporters asked if he would try for an insanity defense, Leibowitz responded with a legal phrase in Latin: "*Res ipsa loquitur*"—the thing speaks for itself.[12]

That same afternoon, Joseph Gedeon's lawyer, Peter Sabbatino, held a press conference at his East 22nd Street apartment. "We are glad that any suspicion that might have existed against my client has been removed," he read from a prepared statement. "The original arrest of Mr. Gedeon and the impression created by the police department that he was a suspect always left a cloud on his reputation and character, and he felt in the past weeks that people looked upon him as an unproved murderer. His reputation is now cleared."

A strained-looking Ethel, "attired in a black dress and hat that accentuated her pallor," was there with her father. When reporters began peppering her with questions about Bob—"What do you have to say about Irwin? Did you think he was crazy? Was he your lover?"—she burst into tears and fled to a bedroom.

Turning to Gedeon, the reporters then tried asking him about the man who had murdered his wife and younger daughter. To every one of their questions, however, the little upholsterer had the same response.

"Go to hell," he told them.[13]

Gedeon's mistreatment at the hands of the police was the subject of an editorial in the next day's *New York Post*. Headlined "The Irwin Case: Where Were the Cops?," the piece was an attack on the "boob police" practice of relying on "mild or severe third degree methods." The "Gedeon murder case proves the point," asserted the editor:

Robert Irwin is in jail—but only because he wanted to go to jail. Until he made that decision and surrendered he was as safe from police interference as if he had been a United States Senator on a good-will tour.

The cops concentrated their attention on the father of the murdered Veronica Gedeon for almost a week after the Easter Sunday crime. He was "questioned" day after day. The process, so much easier on the gray matter than crime detection, lasted until Irwin was enabled to go to Cleveland and get a job in a hotel.

There this man, who has confessed the murder of Veronica Gedeon, her mother, and a lodger, lived for three months. With his picture in every police station in the country, he was never bothered by a detective. It was a waitress who finally identified him, but even so he gave Cleveland police the slip after she notified them and went on his way to Chicago.

In Chicago, he walked past hundreds of officers to go to a newspaper office, where he finally surrendered.

Clearly, "the usual police policy of dragging the first friendless suspect into custody for 'grilling' and feeding the newspapers with heated suspicions is a life-insurance policy for murderers," the editorial concluded. "We offer humble thanks for waitresses who read mystery magazines."[14]

By the time the editorial appeared, the object of those "humble thanks" was enjoying a head-spinning dose of fifteen-minute celebrity. Two days earlier, Henrietta Koscianski—the "plump and pretty pantry maid," "chubby Cinderella detective," "Public Heroine No. 1," as the tabloids variously dubbed her—had received a telegram from *Inside Detective* editor West Peterson, informing her that she was the winner of the magazine's one-thousand-dollar reward for the capture of Robert Irwin.

"Sure, Irwin surrendered of his own accord," Peterson explained to reporters when the announcement was made. "But we feel that if

Miss Koscianski hadn't recognized his picture in the magazine and reported it through the hotel manager to the Cleveland police, Irwin would never have been forced into flight and surrender. She gets the dough."

On Monday afternoon, June 28, accompanied by her truck-driver father, Henry, she boarded a United Air Liner for her first airplane trip, an experience described in luridly purple prose by a tabloid writer named Dale Harrison: "A scullery girl came out of the kitchen today and followed a bewildering rainbow to a New York pot of gold. Murder painted the rainbow that arched Henrietta Koscianski's journey. The blood of Ronnie Gedeon, her mother and luckless Frank Byrnes dotted it."[15]

At 4:15 p.m., the plane landed at Newark Airport, where West Peterson awaited with a crowd of newspapermen and photographers. Emerging from the cabin, Henrietta posed on the rolling metal stairs, clutching the current issue of *Inside Detective*, its cover prominently displayed. Flanked by her beaming father and Peterson — who kept reminding her to hold up the magazine so the cameramen could see it — she answered a few questions about Bob. Though she had repeatedly turned down his requests for a date, she always found him to be a "perfect gentleman" and hoped he had "no hard feelings" toward her. Since she never read the newspapers — "I get all mixed up when I read them," she explained — she had been completely unaware of the Mad Sculptor case until she had seen the issue of *Inside Detective* the previous Wednesday. "I guess my dad and mother won't kid me so much now about reading all those detective magazines and listening to the crime broadcasts when they want to be hearing music on the radio," she said with a smile. "I don't know why but I've always been interested in reading about detectives and criminals. I like mystery, I guess. But I never picture myself as being a detective. And here I am — a detective in one of the most famous murder cases."

As for what she planned to do with the money, she explained that it would all "go to her family — part of it to pay for her little brother's recent appendectomy, the rest towards buying a family home."

Taxied across the Hudson to Manhattan, Henrietta embarked on a whirlwind of glamorous activities. She made an appearance on the NBC radio show *Vox Pop*, a popular program of short man-on-the-street interviews; had cocktails on the roof garden of the Hotel Astor, where she was introduced to the romantic idol and singing sensation Rudy Vallee; and dined at New York City's hottest cabaret, the Hollywood restaurant, where she was summoned onstage by famed MC Nils T. Granlund and invited to sing. Facing a roomful of Manhattan sophisticates, the nineteen-year-old kitchen girl, whose performing had been limited to her high school glee club, showed no trace of the jitters as she signaled to the bandleader and launched into the hit song "Where Are You?" from the recent movie *Top of the Town*. When she was done, the crowd burst into an ovation.

"I don't ever want to go back to that job in the hotel kitchen," she exulted after returning to her table. "I've always wanted to sing. I've always pictured myself as something like a Kate Smith."[16]

Early the following morning, Tuesday, June 29, she was taken from her suite at the Hotel Astor to the offices of *Inside Detective* and presented with her one-thousand-dollar check. From there, Peterson took her by taxi to the Court of General Sessions, where the grand jury was expected to hand down its indictments. In the corridor outside the grand jury room, Joseph Gedeon, in one of his less pugnacious moods, was talking to some of the same reporters he had cursed at a day earlier. "I wasn't an enemy to Irwin," he said, puffing on a stogie. "He was always a nice boy. What he done he has to suffer for, though. I was always for justice." When one of the newsmen pressed him for more information about Irwin, however, the little upholsterer ignored him, switching to a subject of far greater moment to him. He had been out bowling the night before, Gedeon announced, and had "made a score of 289."[17]

Spotting Henrietta, the photographers on the scene immediately instructed her to stand beside the wizened little man, who brought a flush of dismay to her face by suggesting that they exchange a kiss for the benefit of the cameras. She looked visibly relieved when the photographers explained that a handshake would do, though Gedeon seemed somewhat crestfallen.[18]

The proceedings inside the grand jury room, which began at 11:15 a.m., lasted less than forty-five minutes. Seven witnesses testified: Ethel and Joe Kudner, Dr. Thomas Gonzales, Patrolman Edward (who was present when Joseph Gedeon first identified the bodies of the three murder victims), and Detectives Crimmins, Owens, and Tunney. At a few minutes before noon, Julius Bachrach, acting foreman of the grand jury, handed up the three indictments, each charging Robert Irwin with murder in the first degree. Immediately afterward, Irwin was brought from the Tombs and arraigned before Judge William H. Allen. When clerk Edward Cowing asked the defendant how he pleaded, Leibowitz broke in. "I am not ready to plead for the defendant, Your Honor," he said. "I ask for an adjournment until tomorrow morning. In my opinion, this man is crazy as a bedbug."

District Attorney Dodge begged to differ. "I expect to prove that Irwin was not insane at the time of the murder, and I will prove that he knew the nature and quality of his acts," he told reporters after the prisoner was led back to the Tombs. "I will pit my thirty-one years of experience as a lawyer to prove him guilty of murder."[19]

Among the many who agreed with Dodge was Dr. Russell E. Blaisdell, superintendent of the Rockwell State Hospital. "In picturing Irwin's mental condition at the time of the murders," he told reporters, "it points to his knowledge of the difference between right and wrong. That is the test upon which any decision regarding his legal sanity hinges. While Irwin was suffering from a psychosis, that alone does not establish insanity. We have about two thousand patients suffering from psychoses who are not insane."[20]

Taking issue with Blaisdell was Dr. Louis Berg, former head psychiatrist at New York State Hospital for the Insane, soon to gain nationwide attention for his crusade against daytime radio soap operas, which (so he claimed) caused everything from acute anxiety and increased blood pressure to gastrointestinal disturbances, vertigo, and "nocturnal frights" in their female listeners.[21] Irwin, Berg declared, was both "medically and legally insane." Besides being an incurable paranoid schizophrenic—"a dementia-praecox paranoiac," in the terminology of the time—Irwin also exhibited the "abnormal traits" of extreme exhibitionism and egocentricity. Taken together, Berg declared, "these point to a deep-seated maladjustment" that "so influences the individual that he may not know the difference between right and wrong."[22]

The same conflicting opinions of Bob's mental state were offered by those who had known him. While admitting that he was neither "a doctor nor a lawyer" and thus unqualified to judge "whether or not Bob is insane," Irwin's St. Lawrence friend Anders Lunde stressed that the young sculptor "had never acted in a way that made me think he'd do anything" like commit murder. "He always seemed a fine, brilliant person to me," said Lunde.[23]

Henrietta Koscianski, on the other hand, announced that, should Bob plead insanity, she was prepared to testify on his behalf. After spending an hour closeted with Sam Leibowitz, she emerged from his office to tell reporters that she could truthfully "say Bob was not responsible. He seemed childish. If he broke a glass, he was terribly depressed. If he got a dime tip, he'd sing like mad."[24]

Even the personnel on board the airplane that had conveyed Bob from Chicago to New York City had utterly different impressions of him. To stewardess Bernadette Anderle, "he seemed very nice and courteous. Once I heard him remark about the 'beauty of the cirrus clouds.' He looked like a little boy. If I didn't know about him, I would never dream he was the type of man that could be possibly be guilty of those awful crimes." By contrast, pilot Charles W. Allen was struck by Bob's bizarre indifference to his situation. "He impressed me as looking like a nut."[25]

One person who expressed no doubt at all about Irwin's sanity was Robert Flower. Interviewed at his father's Third Avenue bowling alley, Flower spat out his detestation of the man who had murdered his ex-wife.

"Give me five minutes alone with Robert Irwin and my debt to him will be paid. That scoundrel is accorded more attention than a celebrity and is treated as though he had done something wonderful. Has the public forgotten his crimes? Are they concentrating on his superb acting? Why, he should be sent to the chair so fast there could be no question on the workings of the law. I don't think Irwin is any crazier than I am. I can tell from his confession that he's sane because that's exactly how he talks. I would like to beat every part of him until he could no longer cry out for mercy. He has it coming to him."[26]

Along with a crowd of female "morbid rubberneckers"—"women who seemed to find some form of pleasure at gaping at Irwin"— Flower was present in the Court of General Sessions the next morning. At two minutes before noon, Irwin, badly in need of a shave, his once-crisp linen suit a mass of wrinkles, was led into the room. As he made his way toward the front, Flower leaned over the railing and shouted, "You dog!" Irwin ignored him.

After informing the prisoner that three indictments charging him with murder in the first degree had been returned, Court Clerk Cowing asked how he pleaded.

It was Leibowitz who again spoke up for his client. "He pleads not guilty," said the lawyer, while Irwin looked on in mild indifference, as though he were "a tolerantly interested bystander."

Leibowitz then requested an adjournment to fix a date for the trial. He was scheduled to leave at the end of the week for Decatur, Alabama, to take part once again in the seemingly endless case of the Scottsboro Boys—his fifth trip down South in as many years to defend the falsely accused young black men.[27] Dodge offered no objection and the postponement was granted.

The day before his departure, Leibowitz—who by then had engaged in several jailhouse interviews with his client—met with reporters. "The man is absolutely crazy," he declared. "His brain is like a scrambled egg. He has no conception of the seriousness of the charge against him. The fact that he may go to the electric chair means nothing to him. He laughs when he should cry and cries when he should laugh. He'll answer questions right enough, but if you let him talk, he just raves on and on."

Informed of these remarks, the district attorney countered with his own culinary metaphor. Irwin, he said, was not scrambled but hard-boiled.[28]

To Fredric Wertham—a man generally not given to wisecracks—the opposing statements of Leibowitz and Dodge made it sound as though the fight over Robert Irwin's life would be less of a great legal battle than a cooking contest.[29] As the psychiatrist who had gotten Irwin to open up to the New York City authorities, Wertham found himself much in the news in the days following his former patient's surrender, particularly after reporters learned of the lecture he had delivered the previous March on the "catathymic crisis." Crediting Wertham with identifying a previously unknown mental disease that explained "hitherto baffling crimes of violence," newspapers trumpeted his discovery in dramatic headlines: "IRWIN SLEW IN GRIP OF NEW MANIA," "NEW MENTAL ILLNESS KEY TO CRIME."

Not everyone, of course, was so impressed. To many observers, Wertham's theory was nothing more than psychiatric gobbledygook. The editorial page of the *New York Sun*, for example, conveyed its skepticism in a bit of mocking verse:

> He did not murder anyone
> And such a charge not nice is:
> He's just the charming victim of
> A "catathymic crisis"[30]

Other editorials were every bit as scornful. Under the headline "DUMB — LIKE A FOX," the *New York Post* sneered that, while Irwin might or might not be "crazy as a bedbug," he was certainly sane enough to have hired Sam Leibowitz, "the criminal lawyer who boasts that not one of his clients has ever been sentenced to the electric chair."[31]

Much harsher was an editorial in the June 29 issue of the *Daily News*. Headlined "CRIME AND INSANITY," it freely admitted that Irwin was insane, then argued that there were stronger reasons for "putting the murderously insane quietly and painlessly out of the way than for executing, say, a man who has killed in a moment of passion, or for revenge, or for some other sane though deplorable motive." While such a sane killer might be rehabilitated after "twenty or so years in jail," there "was no such prospect" for the "murderously insane," whose "minds are out of normal gear. In asylums or out, they are continuous threat to the safety of anybody who comes near them. . . . We think the case is clear for the execution of criminally insane killers, on the same grounds that mad dogs are put out of the way."

Should Irwin somehow escape the death penalty, the editorial continued, he should at the very least be subjected to forced sterilization by means of either chemical or surgical castration:

> It is bad enough to think of Irwin's life being spared and Irwin allowed to live on as a menace to his keepers if not society at large. But how would it be to let this man pass on life to another generation? . . . As things go now, the chances are at least fair that Irwin may in time bequeath his twisted mentality and murderous instincts to children of his. Isn't it in society's interest to cut off dangerous strains in the population and encourage only healthy strains, so far as society can do so?[32]

According to one chronicler, this editorial elicited little more than a shrug from Bob. Execution held no terror for him. He had already boasted that he was "not afraid of this thing called death." As for the prospect of castration, it was hardly a threat to a man who had once tried to slice off his penis.[33]

Lunacy

I N A TALK TITLED "Psychiatry in Court," delivered to an audience of mental health professionals in May 1940, Sam Leibowitz spelled out his feelings about the insanity defense.

"Frankly," he said, "I avoid it when I can possibly do so":

> Because jurors abhor the insanity defense. Jurors, frankly speaking, don't like psychiatrists. . . . We may probe into the reasons for that and we won't have to probe very far. The average juror knows nothing about the mind. The mind, to him, is synonymous with the brain. He may walk the street and see a cripple and sympathize with him. He can understand a broken arm or leg. He can understand that a man is suffering from consumption. He can see that from the sallow look. He can understand all these things that mean something to him. But when he walks along the street and sees a nice, rosy-cheeked individual apparently suffering from nothing at all, he cannot understand that that man may be suffering from a mental condition. He has probably never been in an institution. To him, insanity is something abstract. Unless he has had experience with some-

one in his family, the average juror feels that insanity is something cooked-up by the lawyers to save someone, especially for a
fat fee. . . . The public is convinced that psychiatry as practiced
in the courts is a racket.[1]

Leibowitz conceded, however, that there were times when the
insanity defense was a "necessary evil." One of those was the Irwin
case.

Even before he departed for Decatur in the first week of July, Leibowitz began laying the groundwork for his defense of Irwin. One
of his first steps was to invite Fredric Wertham to his office for an
interview that lasted from 5:00 p.m. until midnight. It wasn't long
before Leibowitz—imagining himself as a jury member listening to
"the erudite doctor"—concluded that twelve ordinary men would
be utterly "bewildered by the technical terminology of the psychiatrist" and view the concept of "catathymic crisis" as "nothing but
psychiatric double talk." Indeed, just a few years earlier, Wertham's
testimony as an expert witness had failed to save the life of Albert
Fish, a man so extravagantly deranged that even some jurors who
voted for his conviction believed he was insane. By the time their
lengthy conference was over, Leibowitz, despite his high regard for
"the sincere and capable doctor," had eliminated him as a possible
defense witness.[2]

Leibowitz left for the South on Monday, July 5. Exactly three
weeks later, in the dramatic finale of the Scottsboro case, he made
a triumphant return to New York City with four of the young men,
who had been suddenly freed by the state of Alabama after living
six and a half years in the shadow of the electric chair. Three days
later, at a tumultuous rally at the Hippodrome Theatre, more than
five thousand weeping, cheering, and wildly applauding men and
women greeted the Scottsboro Boys and their attorney with a fifteen-minute standing ovation.[3]

Immediately afterward, Leibowitz threw himself back into the
Irwin case. In his typically exhaustive way, he pored over "every
leading case in which criminal responsibility of the mentally ill was

an issue," interviewed prominent psychiatrists and psychologists, visited Bellevue's mental hygiene ward, and traveled to Rockland State Hospital to inspect Irwin's medical records.[4] Always a master at using the press to his advantage, he also made sure that the public was kept constantly aware of Bob's progressively erratic behavior behind bars.

Consigned to Tier No. 1 of the Tombs, where prisoners regarded as mentally unstable could be kept under close observation, Irwin alternated between periods of seeming normality and frenzied outbursts of emotion. Just a few days after his surrender, he allowed himself to be interviewed in his cell by a female reporter for the *Evening Journal*, Mignon Bushel. Asked about Ethel, Bob's "face contorted" and he screamed, "I love her and I hate her. But I want to see her!" Suddenly catching a glimpse of the prison cat prowling outside his cell, he grew instantly calm and murmured, "Hello, kitty. Hello, kitty." A moment later, in a "voice shrill with hysteria," he cried: "I don't expect to be painted like a lily but I want some consideration for what is in back of all this. This is like an iceberg with nine-tenths underneath water and only one-tenth above." He then "burst into tears uncontrollably, like a child. 'Whatever punishment is coming for me, I'll take it with my chin up,' he sobbed. 'I only ask that people try to understand.'" Bushel was so "bewildered, shocked, and frightened by the changeability of his moods" that she fled in dismay.[5]

Not long afterward—just one day after Warden William A. Adams told reporters that Irwin was "as normal as any man in prison"—Bob erupted in fury at some perceived insult by one of the guards and, grabbing the bars of his cell door, began to shriek, "I've killed before and I'll kill again!" It took the threat of a straitjacket to quiet him down.[6]

He remained quiet and cooperative for another few weeks. At about 2:15 p.m. on Sunday, August 29, however, as the prison physician, Dr. George D'Oronzio, walked past his cell, Bob, without warning, leaped from his cot and threw a cup of water at him.

D'Oronzio immediately informed Deputy Warden John Bockel,

who had a keeper, Edward Cleary, bring Irwin to his office. When Bockel asked him "what the trouble was," Irwin snarled, "I don't want you sending those religious and medical bastards up here to annoy me."

Bockel then informed Bob that he would have to be put in an isolation cell as punishment for hurling the water at D'Oronzio. At that, Bob "drew back his fist and shouted another volley of profanities."

Advising Bob to "calm himself and do nothing rash," Bockel, along with keepers Cleary, Joseph Smith, and Michael O'Connell, escorted the prisoner to the South Annex, where the isolation cells were located. Before Bob was placed in the cell, the deputy warden instructed the guards to search his clothing. "Suddenly," Bockel testified afterward, "Irwin leaped upon McConnell, threw his arms around his neck, and bit him on the back of his neck. It took the combined efforts of the other two keepers and myself to pry him loose. He then started striking with both fists and kicking at anyone of us he thought he could reach." After a ferocious struggle, the four brawny men managed to wrestle the frenzied prisoner into the isolation cell.

When Leibowitz learned of the incident the following day, he hurried to see Irwin, who, by then, had written his own four-page account of the disturbance. "Irwin is very jittery," Leibowitz told reporters after his interview with Bob. "He was beaten unmercifully. He has a five-inch cut going from the right temple to the center of his forehead. There are four welts below his shoulder blades. It looks as if they were inflicted with a rubber pipe. They haven't given that kid a drop of water since yesterday afternoon. He's almost mad with thirst."[7]

At Leibowitz's insistence, Irwin was immediately transferred from the Tombs to the Raymond Street Jail in Brooklyn. There, the ever-canny lawyer saw a prime opportunity for a public relations coup. Knowing that the fracas in the Tombs had left Irwin in a highly unsettled frame of mind, he arranged a meeting between reporters and his client in the anteroom off Warden Harry Schleth's office.

At roughly 12:45 on the last day of August, Bob—haggard, unshaven, dressed in a dirty white shirt and wrinkled gray prison trousers—appeared at the threshold of the interview room. "His eyes were blood-flecked and staring," wrote one observer. "He was trembling."

As he entered the room, he clutched at his throat and screamed: "What is this? What are you doing to me? Who are these people?"

Taking Bob by the arm, Leibowitz, speaking in the soothing tones one might use with a hysterical child, said: "Sit down, Bob. Take it easy, now. They're reporters, they want to help you."

"We're not going to harm you," one of the reporters said. "Please sit down."

With an audible whimper, Bob sank into a chair and began brushing nervously at his hair.

"Have you been mistreated?" someone asked.

"For two weeks," Bob blurted, "they had doctors staring at me. Leering at me with their eyes! I couldn't stand it!"

With that, he burst into sobs, leaped from his chair, and began to mumble incoherently. Straining to hear, the reporters could make out broken sentences: "They beat me from behind . . . beat me with blackjacks . . . six men with blackjacks. . . . I couldn't fight six men with blackjacks."

Falling silent, he stood there trembling for a moment, then began rushing wildly around the room. "I haven't had anything to eat in forty-eight hours," he cried. "Only a bowl of soup and one slice of white bread. I can't stand it!"

As he buried his face in his hands and wept convulsively, Leibowitz signaled to the guards, who pulled Irwin to the door.

Once he was gone, Leibowitz turned to the assembled newsmen and said: "Yesterday, he seemed calm and collected. You saw how he acted today—like a raving maniac. And that's the man the district attorney wants to try for murder!"[8]

Despite his confident pronouncements that he would have no trouble convincing a jury that Irwin was legally sane, District Attorney

Dodge was taking no chances. On August 30—one day after Irwin went berserk in the Tombs—Dodge applied to General Sessions Judge John J. Freschi for the appointment of a lunacy commission to examine Robert Irwin and report on his mental condition. Over the protests of Sam Leibowitz, Judge Freschi granted the DA's request.⁹

Beginning in the late 1800s, New York Criminal Court judges could, at their discretion, appoint a lunacy commission to evaluate the sanity of a defendant charged with homicide. Each commission consisted of three "disinterested men": an attorney, a physician, and a layman, almost always a businessman. After conducting a lengthy investigation, the members would offer an opinion as to whether the defendant was mentally fit to stand trial. In later years, the commissioners were also expected to assess the defendant's state of mind while committing the crime. The role of the commission was strictly advisory—the court was at liberty to approve or dismiss its findings.¹⁰

By the time of the Mad Sculptor murders, the entire lunacy commission system had come under fierce attack by the public, the psychiatric community, and many government officials. An investigating committee established by Mayor Fiorello La Guardia concluded that, between January 1930 and December 1936, "lunacy commissions have cost the City of New York $1,359,949 and that one million dollars of this amount has been sheer waste, since the service performed by lunacy commissions could readily be performed by the psychiatric divisions of the city hospitals with small additional force."

Not only were these commissions a misuse of taxpayers' money, their findings also were generally regarded as "almost valueless by specialists in this field." Until 1936, when the situation was belatedly rectified, none of the three members on a lunacy commission, including the doctor, was "legally required to have any psychiatric knowledge or training." A significant percentage of lunacy commission reports were ultimately "rejected by the court as not reliable." Cases of defendants who managed to escape trial by feigning insanity were rife. In one notorious instance, a career criminal named

Martin Lavin, arrested for killing a man in a bar holdup, convinced a lunacy commission that he was insane by claiming that he "heard voices." Sent to the Matteawan State Hospital for the Criminally Insane, he was discharged as a malingerer shortly after his commitment and, soon afterward, shot and killed a police sergeant while robbing a pawnshop.[11]

In spite of the well-documented deficiencies and abuses associated with the system, lunacy examinations continued to be ordered at a profligate rate. Between 1930 and 1938, one Brooklyn judge alone appointed 1,212 lunacy commissions, doling out the lucrative positions to relatives, friends, and political cronies. Increasingly viewed as nothing more than a flagrant "patronage racket," the system was finally ended by the New York State Legislature in 1939. At the time of its abolition, the case of Robert Irwin, still fresh in the minds of lawmakers, was cited as a glaring example of everything wrong with lunacy commissions.[12]

In later years, Fredric Wertham did nothing to conceal his disdain for Irwin's lunacy commission. Its chairman, attorney Archibald Watson, former corporation counsel for an earlier mayoral administration, had close ties to the city government and would be appointed County Clerk of New York before the commission had finished its work. The second member, Dr. Israel Wechsler, was a physician who specialized in neurology. The third, Dr. Charles Ryan, was a "rich man who had become psychiatrist," in Wertham's dismissive words.[13]

Their first attempt to examine Irwin took place on September 29. In preparation for the interview, Bob had been brought from his cell to the prison counsel room, where inmates were allowed to confer privately with their lawyers. Bob was sitting "alone in the room quietly reading a newspaper before the arrival of the commission," the *New York Times* reported, "but when a keeper started to unlock the door to the room, Irwin pushed a heavy oak table against the door, which opened from inside, and threw his weight against it, barring the commission members." When several keepers managed to force the door open, Bob "attempted to strike one of them with a chair but was overpowered. Because he appeared to be in a state of considerable excitement, the commission ordered Warden Adams to take Irwin back to his cell, where he eventually became quiet."[14]

Two days later, the commissioners were back. When Bob saw them approaching his cell, he began kicking the bars of his cell door and yelling, "Get those fucking bastards out of here! I told you I don't want to see preachers or doctors! Get 'em out of here! Get 'em out!"

Ignoring Bob, the turnkey unlocked the cell door to admit the visitors. No sooner had he done so than "Irwin lunged past him and made for the commissioners. The turnkey grappled with him and shouted for help. Several other guards quickly responded, but it took almost twenty minutes before the kicking, screaming, cursing prisoner was finally brought under control and dragged back into his cell."[15]

The commissioners tried again on February 10, 1938. They found Bob lying on his cot, reading a book on his latest enthusiasm, the esoteric philosophy Rosicrucianism. The moment he became aware that the commissioners were standing outside his cell, "he immediately covered his head with a blanket and retreated to a corner of the cage, huddling there on the floor and occasionally poking his head out from underneath the blanket and yelling, 'Get out of here!' Eventually they left in disgust."[16]

Over the course of their inordinately protracted investigation, the commissioners managed not a single interview with Bob. Their conclusions were based on the testimony of twenty-two witnesses examined over the course of seven months—the equivalent, as Sam Leibowitz observed, of an internist diagnosing a patient's gastrointestinal problems by asking his friends about his eating habits. The transcript of the witness testimony ran to seven hundred and fifty-six typewritten pages. Of that number, more than three hundred were the testimony of Fredric Wertham, who appeared before the commission seven times. Providing lengthy and highly detailed accounts of his interactions with Irwin, Wertham was emphatic in his opinion that "Irwin suffered from a mental disease every time I saw him. That he always suffered from the same mental disease. That if he had not had this mental disease, these murders would not have been committed by him. That the three murders were in my opinion definite symptoms of his mental disease. That he was not in full possession of his mental powers during the night of the murders."[17]

On March 24, 1938—seven months after it was appointed—the commission finally issued its report. It came to a scant seven pages and made no reference at all to Wertham's opinions, giving more prominence to the testimony of Leonora Sheldon, the young socialite who had never met Bob before the afternoon of the murders and whose entire relationship with him consisted of brief visits to the American Museum of Natural History and the Metropolitan Museum of Art, followed by lunch at Schrafft's. While acknowledging that Irwin had been "occasionally treated for mental disorders," it attributed his problems to his "poorly digested reading in philosophy and psychology."[18]

"After careful examination and consideration of the material and relevant testimony and such personal observation of the defendant as there was opportunity to make," the report concluded, "we are of the opinion that the said defendant was not in such a state of idiocy, imbecility, lunacy, or insanity as not to know the nature and quality of the acts for which he has been indicted and not to know that the acts were wrong; that is he not in such a state of idiocy, imbecility, lunacy, or insanity as to be incapable of understanding the proceedings or making his defense."[19]

Printed in *The American Journal of Psychiatry*, the report provoked incredulity and outrage among mental health experts, who assailed it as "patently unsound," "a most injudicial document," "at variance with modern and progressive standards in forensic psychiatry." "The attitude expressed is that of an inquisition," railed one critic. Others complained that it relied on concepts "which are not part of the psychiatric vocabulary," that it "failed to present the attitude of disinterested scientific men," that it could have been written by "any lawyer from newspaper accounts," that it "glossed over any evidence which would indicate mental derangement on the part of the defendant." "If it did not deal with matters of life or death," fumed one eminent psychiatrist, "it might be considered comic."[20]

Newspapers, on the other "hailed the decision with joy," praising the Irwin lunacy commission for its exemplary work in confirming what the press had claimed all along: that the "fiendish sculptor" was nothing but a "classic example of the insanity faker."[21]

One day after the commission submitted its report, Judge Freschi endorsed the findings. "The approved report means that the defendant may now legally be tried," the judge declared. He stressed that the question of Bob's "sanity at the time of the commission of the crime may be raised again and decided at the trial." As far as the commission was concerned, however, "Robert Irwin was then sane."[22]

Plea

I N THE COURSE OF HIS intensive preparations for the Irwin trial, Sam Leibowitz had unearthed a 1915 opinion written by Benjamin Cardozo, future U.S. Supreme Court Justice, then serving as a judge on the New York Court of Appeals. The opinion related to the case of Hans Schmidt, a Roman Catholic priest sent to the electric chair in 1916 for the dismemberment-murder of his pregnant mistress, Anna Aumüller.[1]

In it, Cardozo had argued that "there are times and circumstances in which the word 'wrong' as used in the statutory test of responsibility ought not to be limited to 'legal' wrong. If there is an insane delusion that God has appeared to the defendant and ordained the commission of the crime, we think it cannot be said of an offender that he knows the act to be wrong." Cardozo was quick to add that a defendant could not be excused of responsibility simply because "he has views of right and wrong at variance with those that find expression in the law"—unless, that is, such variation had "its origin in some disease of the mind."

As far as Leibowitz was concerned, Cardozo's criteria applied perfectly to Irwin. That Bob suffered from "some disease of the mind" was a fact uncontested even by the prosecution. Even more to the point, his wild-eyed theory of merging with the "Universal Mind" by perfecting his powers of visualization clearly qualified as an insanely deluded God complex.[2]

To make this case to a jury, Leibowitz knew he needed a particular type of psychiatrist—not the kind who spends so much of his life on the witness stand that he comes across as a medical gun-for-hire but a highly respected practicing physician who appeared only rarely before juries. The men whose services he retained were Dr. Leland E. Hinsie, assistant director of the New York Psychiatric Institute and professor of psychiatry at Columbia University, and Dr. Bernard Glueck, former director of the psychiatric clinic at Sing Sing, who had achieved nationwide prominence as an expert witness at the 1924 trial of Nathan Leopold and Richard Loeb.[3]

In contrast to the members of the lunacy commission—whose contact with Bob consisted entirely of observing him through the bars of his cell while he either ignored or spat curses at them—Hinsie and Glueck spent more than seventy hours interviewing him. Their sessions were held behind the closed doors of the prison counsel room. Bob's wildly, sometimes frighteningly, erratic behavior during these examinations was later described in graphic detail by Dr. Hinsie:

He would begin by excessive talking and would be considerably upset when he was interrupted for explanations on some point he had raised. Upon interruption he would stare at the examiner, grit his teeth, pound the table viciously with his fists and yell that he would not suffer any interruptions. If allowed to talk at free will he would become ecstatic and enthusiastic. Marked emotional instability as revealed by rapid shifts in mood from happiness to sadness and to agitation were quite common. At times, he was in such a vicious frame of mind that the examiner felt some qualms regarding his own safety, more especially since the defendant threatened he would kill the war-

den or the prison physician or guard. He would then pace the
floor and behave like a caged animal.[4]

Irwin worked himself into a pitch of near-frenzied exaltation while
discoursing on his current efforts to transform his body through the
power of electricity. Pulling open his shirt, he displayed several pads
of steel wool stuck to his undershirt, acquired from the men who
cleaned the jail. He wore them, he explained, "as a means to build
up electrical impulses in myself. There is no limit to the extent that
I can build myself mentally and physically through electricity. I can
stop the action of my heartbeat, prevent my lungs from expanding
and contracting, control the passage of food through my body. All
this is done by electricity."

Once he had "developed his electrical powers to the highest extent," he would "be able to become that greatest sculptor in the
world, to make any kind of invention, to learn any language without
studying it, to walk on water, to turn my body into light, to attain
immortality.

"I will have powers over and above all other people in the world,"
he crowed. "I think I can say without bragging that at present I am
further advanced in all my thoughts than any man who has ever
lived. I, therefore, have Godlike qualities absolutely. All I have to do
is wish and I get everything."

To prove his godlike powers, he offered to demonstrate his ability to convert his hair into gold. When Hinsie, after watching Bob's
head for a while, was obliged to inform him that the "experiment
was a failure," Bob became "greatly agitated."

Despite this minor setback, he predicted that "within a period
of three years I'll attain to the translucency of form so that I'll just
evaporate right out of the place. I will walk through matter. I will
walk through a stone wall. Bullets will go through me without af-
fecting me. The electricity will enable me to cure all of my troubles
and to cure other people just like Jesus Christ cured them."

Questioned closely about the murders, he revealed details he had
not previously disclosed. While strangling Ronnie, he said, "there

was sunlight or a beautiful light coming down from above. The light was a living thing, like it was a divinity. It seemed to be a divine message that I was getting nearer to the great white throne, nearer to the crystal sun. My head seemed be surrounded by vibrating electricity."

At the same time, he was aware that he was being watched by "two great evil eyes that grew larger and larger" and seemed to carry a "special significance." Under their influence, he said, he would "have killed forty people if they had been in the room then." Only afterward did he realize that the staring eyes "came from the green dial of the clock."[5]

Their extended examinations of the prisoner led Hinsie and Glueck to the same conclusion. Irwin's "fantastic delusional system" conformed completely to a personality pattern encountered "in patients whose diagnosis is unqualifiedly that of the schizophrenia-hebephrenia form. The murders were committed with the delusion that the accomplishment of this act would bring to the patient control of the universe which he had planned for so many years. Under the stress of these delusions and hallucinations, normal intellectual processes played no essential role. Therefore, Irwin at the time of the murders could not know the nature and quality of his act."

As the two eminent psychiatrists were now prepared to attest on the witness stand, Robert Irwin was "both medically and legally insane."[6]

Owing, among other factors, to the exceedingly slow working of the lunacy commission, Bob's trial was postponed until the fall of 1938. By then the city had a new district attorney: Thomas E. Dewey, the fearless young "gangbuster" whose relentless crusade against racketeers like Dutch Schultz and Lucky Luciano would propel him to the governor's mansion in Albany and two runs for the White House as the Republican presidential candidate in 1944 and 1948.

Though just as eager as his predecessor to see Irwin sent to the chair, Dewey, caught up in his first gubernatorial campaign, turned the prosecution over to his right-hand man, Assistant DA Jacob J. Rosenblum, who, in his short time on the job, had already racked up a record of ten consecutive first-degree murder convictions.[7] As Leibowitz had anticipated, the DA's office announced that Irwin would be tried only for the murder of Frank Byrnes, a seemingly airtight case of coldly premeditated, first-degree homicide, perpetrated, by the defendant's own admission, to eliminate a potential witness. It would be Leibowitz's task to show that the slaying of Byrnes was "merely part of a general pattern of slaughter," the climactic act of an insanity-induced orgy of violence.[8]

"I expect to save this boy's life, for he doesn't belong in the electric chair," Leibowitz told reporters on Sunday, November 6, the day before the trial was scheduled to begin. "He is a dangerous lunatic and should be put away for the rest of his life. Under no circumstance will I attempt to free him. He did not know the nature and quality of his acts, and I can deal with any statement of the prosecutor to show that he did." Referring to Inspector Lyons's widely reported statement shortly after the murders that Irwin, then a fugitive, was "stark mad" and would "never be indicted or go to trial," Leibowitz also announced his intention "to show that the police authorized newspaper announcements that he would be granted immunity if he gave himself up."

Informed of the defense attorney's statement, Rosenblum stressed "that there is no such thing as a jury sending an insane killer away for the rest of his life. He can be released from an institution for the criminally insane any time psychiatrists decide he is sane." As an example, he pointed to the case of Harry K. Thaw, the millionaire playboy found not guilty by reason of insanity for the 1906 murder of famed architect Stanford White in the country's first "Trial of the Century." Sentenced to incarceration for life at Matteawan, Thaw was declared sane eight years later, found not guilty at a second trial, and set free.[9]

On Monday, November 7, 1938, opening day of the Irwin trial, the courtroom was filled to capacity for what newspapers predicted would be the greatest "battle of psychiatrists" since the Thaw case.[10] Among the throng of journalists covering the story were two of the city's celebrity columnists: Damon Runyon—beloved Broadway

chronicler whose 1931 bestseller *Guys and Dolls* had turned the colorful denizens of the "Great White Way" into figures of pop myth
—and Dorothy Kilgallen, best known to a later generation as a tele-
vision personality on the hit 1950s quiz show *What's My Line?* but
at this point in her career a star reporter for the *New York Evening
Journal.*

At precisely 10:30 a.m., the bailiff boomed out the name "Robert Irwin" and a husky guard led Bob into the room. Reporters
who had last seen him a year earlier were startled by the change in
his appearance. Convinced—as he had told Dr. Hinsie—that, with
his newly acquired electrical control over his bodily functions, he
no longer required much food, he had lost more than twenty-five
pounds. "In his double-breasted dark, chalk-striped suit," wrote Damon Runyon, Irwin was "a mere bag o' bones," a "jerky, pallid, little
wraith of a man," his "face so drawn that you could hang your hat
on his cheek bones."[11]

Wearing a smirk and walking with pronounced swagger, Bob
strode to the defense table and dropped into the chair beside Leibowitz's associate counsel, Vincent Impellitteri, former assistant district attorney and future mayor of New York City. Throughout that
long day's proceedings, Bob would alternate between periods of incessant, nervous motion and extended stretches of dozing. Occasionally, he would rise muttering from his chair. His guard, "constantly on the watch for an outburst from the egocentric killer,"
would swiftly move in and forcibly reseat him. "Declared by his attorney 'as crazy as a bedbug,'" remarked Runyon, Irwin "certainly
looked the part."[12]

Jury selection was the first order of business. The previous May,
the female population of New York State had won an important victory in the struggle for equality when, on the last day of its spring
session, the legislature passed a law allowing women to serve on juries.[13] Leibowitz was well pleased, for reasons made clear by Mignon
Bushel, the *Evening Journal* reporter granted an exclusive interview
with Bob just days after his surrender. Bushel had begun her story

by declaring: "I do not know if Robert Irwin is insane in a technical way. But I do know that no jury of women would convict him. For Irwin is a handsome, tragic young man who cannot resist women. And women cannot resist him."[14]

The blue-ribbon panel of 150 potential jurors selected for the Irwin trial, however, consisted entirely of men. When Leibowitz protested, he was informed by Frederick H. Cahoon, Acting Commissioner of Jurors, that, while women now had the option to serve on juries, they were "barred from membership on special panels of talesmen for murder trials." Leibowitz immediately declared that "the procedure was not legal" and that "if Irwin were found guilty of first-degree murder, he would make the exclusion of women talesmen the main contention for a reversal."[15]

In his opening remarks to the panel, Leibowitz, dressed in the outfit he traditionally wore at the start of every trial—blue suit, white shirt, and red tie—suggested that he would rely on what the *Daily News* described as "the highly original defense of 'mental drunkenness.'" "We shall claim," said Leibowitz, "that though Irwin was not intoxicated by reason of liquor, he was intoxicated the night of those murders by reason of mental disease. We say that even if he were not insane under the law, he was still out of his mind that night by reason of his state of mind."[16]

Utterly unawed by his opponent's reputation as a courtroom wizard, Rosenblum promised to call an array of psychiatric experts who would testify that while "Irwin perhaps was abnormal," he was legally sane when he perpetrated the crime he was being tried for. Stressing the premeditated quality of the act, Rosenblum declared that "the People are going to prove that the defendant is guilty of murder in the first degree because he plunged an ice pick into Frank Byrnes's head."[17]

Consistent with his belief that the average person "knows nothing about the mind" and cannot understand that a man who seems superficially normal might be suffering from a mental disease, Leibowitz posed the same question to each potential juror: "Have you any fixed notion of what a crazy man must look like? Do you think he must be in a straitjacket and frothing at the mouth in order to be insane?"

He also addressed the issue that Rosenblum had raised in relation to the Harry Thaw case. "You have heard and read how defendants acquitted in murder cases by reason of insanity have gotten out of the crazy house," said Leibowitz to each venireman. "Tell me, would you feel that if Robert Irwin is put in the crazy house, he might get out one day and take more life—would you vote to put him in the electric chair and be done with him, once and for all?"

When one of the potential jurors answered yes, Leibowitz emitted an incredulous "What?"

"I meant no, actually," the venireman muttered sheepishly. Leibowitz, however, used one of his twenty peremptory challenges to dismiss him.

The most heated exchanges between the two lawyers occurred on the frequent occasions when Leibowitz brought up Thomas Dewey, whose public appeal was such that, after just one year as district attorney, he was already on the ballot as the Republican candidate for governor of New York State. Concerned that some veniremen might be "blinded by Dewey's reputation" as a "Galahad in shining armor," Leibowitz, over Rosenblum's furious protests, asked each of them about his attitude toward the district attorney. "Do you think that because Mr. Dewey's office is prosecuting this case, it has to be absolutely legitimate, otherwise Mr. Dewey wouldn't prosecute?" "Suppose Mr. Dewey comes into court, would you regard anything he said as holy and a symbol of purity and virtue?" "You don't feel that just because the D.A. produces a witness, the witness must be shrouded in purity and truthfulness?" One potential juror, about to be accepted by both sides, was immediately rejected by Leibowitz after admitting that he had attended "a testimonial dinner to Dewey after he convicted Lucky Luciano."[18]

When the trial was adjourned at 6:30 p.m.—eight hours after it began—only three jurors had been seated: Consolidated Edison clerk James H. Day, security analyst Henry Andrews, and Harry

Held Jr., manager of a paint supply firm. Given the pace of the first day's proceedings, the newspapers predicted that the trial would last at least a month.[19]

Tuesday, November 8, was Election Day. In New York, the Democratic incumbent, Herbert Lehman, eked out a victory for his fourth and final term as governor; Dewey would have to wait until 1942 before beginning his own three terms as the state's chief executive. Because of the holiday and Judge James G. Wallace's full schedule on Wednesday, the trial did not resume until noon on Thursday.

It lasted until 4:00 p.m. When the abbreviated session was adjourned, only two more jurors had been seated: hairnet salesman Sidney F. Stern and C. Markham Langham, employee of a shipping firm. In accordance with New York State law requiring a defendant to stand and "look upon" every man chosen to decide his fate, Irwin was made to rise from his chair and stare into the faces of Stern and Langham as clerk Siegfried Steinberg mumbled the swearing-in formula. As he had in the case of the three jurors chosen on Monday, Bob seemed to find the ritual intensely amusing, wearing a "continued grin that was almost a giggle."[20]

Following adjournment, Leibowitz and Rosenblum retreated to Judge Wallace's chambers, where the three remained closeted for an hour. Rumors swirled that a plea bargain was in the offing. According to these unverified reports, the district attorney's office was seriously concerned that Leibowitz, with his formidable powers of persuasion, would have no trouble convincing the jury that his client was a hopeless madman. Should the Great Defender prevail, Irwin could become another Harry K. Thaw, committed to Matteawan only to be released after supposedly regaining his sanity.

For his part, Leibowitz was only concerned that his client, a desperately sick man, escape the electric chair. As he had already made clear, he was no more eager than the prosecution to see Irwin back on the streets. Both sides were said to be amenable to a deal that would spare Irwin from the chair but ensure that he would spend the rest of his days in confinement.[21]

Among the reporters who lingered in court while the lawyers and Judge Wallace conferred was Damon Runyon. When the two attorneys emerged from the judge's chambers, Runyon approached them and asked "if there was any foundation of truth to the report."

Drawing Rosenblum aside, Leibowitz exchanged a few whispered words with his opponent before replying: "We have decided to make no comment."[22]

One day earlier, Germany had been the scene of an appalling outburst of anti-Semitic violence. Following the death of German diplomat Ernst vom Rath, shot in Paris as a radical act of protest by a seventeen-year-old Polish Jew named Herschel Grynszpan, Hitler and his minions seized on the assassination to instigate a nationwide pogrom. On the night of November 9, Nazi storm troopers and rioters throughout Germany burned 267 synagogues, vandalized 7,500 Jewish businesses, killed at least 91 Jews, and rounded up roughly 30,000 Jewish males who were shipped off to concentration camps. The countless shattered storefronts whose shards littered the streets in the aftermath of the rampage gave the episode its infamous name: Kristallnacht, the Night of Broken Glass.

Outraged accounts of the pogrom filled the front pages of the nation's newspapers. Reading about it in his cell in the Tombs, Bob seemed most affected by the plight of the young assassin, Grynszpan. He immediately shared his feelings with Leibowitz, informing his attorney that, to show his sympathy for the boy, he was willing to "take his place and be guillotined."

Leibowitz declined to convey the offer to the French authorities, though he did make sure to share his client's latest bizarre notion with the press.[23]

If the first two days of the Irwin trial were notably lacking in drama, the third made up for that deficiency. "It was the triple-killer himself," the *New York Times* reported, "who transformed the session from a routine circumstance of criminal law into one of the most dramatic denouements that has ever taken place in the Supreme Court Building."[24]

At first, observers assumed it would be another tedious day of jury selection. Forty talesmen were questioned in the morning, with only three more accepted by noon recess, bringing the total to eight. No sooner had court reconvened at 2:20 p.m., however, than Leibowitz requested that all jurors be excused from the room. Once they had filed outside, he approached the bench and—confirming the rumors that Damon Runyon had been the first to report—asked "that a plea of guilty to murder in the second degree be accepted for each indictment."

Though Irwin did not "fit the common conception of insanity," said Leibowitz, it was incontestably the case that he "has been insane since childhood with dementia praecox of the hebephrenic type." In the opinion of the defense experts, his condition was only bound to get worse, "until he is a gibbering idiot, sitting in a corner, smiling to himself."

There was no surer sign of his insanity, said Leibowitz, than his obsession with visualization.

> From seventeen on, he has had a crazy notion that by visualization he could project himself into the past and make such men as Napoleon, Bismarck, or Nietzsche live again. He felt he could do the same thing for the future, so much so that he could change things from one form into another; that he was able to bring about such a cataclysm as would be too terrible to behold; that he would take his place on the throne next to God as a man not only omniscient but omnipotent.

Leibowitz then made a startling disclosure. He had spent much of the noon recess cajoling his client into accepting the guilty plea. Irwin, initially resistant, had finally relented under one condition: that Leibowitz give him five hundred dollars, the total amount (according to Bob's calculations) that he would need over the years to pay a prison guard or fellow inmate twenty-five cents a day to "sit in or near his cell" and help with his visualization experiments.[25]

After Leibowitz took his seat at the defense table, Assistant DA Rosenblum approached the bench. Still in a combative mood, he made it clear that the prosecution still believed that Irwin was sane and "legally responsible" for his acts. As he recapped the facts of the defendant's life, he portrayed Bob as a lifelong criminal, who had first been "adjudged a juvenile delinquent at the age of twelve."

"That's a lie!" Bob snarled. Glaring at the prosecutor, he began to rise from his seat. Three guards quickly moved in and forced him back down.

Rosenblum's tone was so hostile that Judge Wallace finally asked, "Are you opposed to the acceptance of his plea?"

"No," said Rosenblum. "In view of the status of the defendant, we feel the circumstances absolutely warrant our consent to such a plea."

"It requires more than consent," snapped the judge. "It must be a recommendation."

"It is a recommendation," said Rosenblum. "Only we must be absolutely certain that this man will be in an institution for life. Under no circumstances can he ever be allowed to get back into society."

"I am shoulder to shoulder with him on that," interjected Leibowitz.

Turning toward the defense table, Judge Wallace peered over his glasses at Irwin. "Well, what does the defendant have to say? Is he willing to take a plea to murder in the second degree?"

Clearly struggling to control himself, Irwin rose from his chair. Eyes blazing, lips curled in bitterness, he seemed, at first, too overwrought to speak. Once he found his voice, however, his words came pouring out of him in a crazed rush. No one who saw and heard him that day could doubt, as the *Times* reported, "the degree to which he appears demented."[26]

"Do you realize," asked the judge, "that you are admitting by your plea that you committed murder in the second degree?"

"Your Honor, technically, since it seems to me everything is a technicality, I admit that," said Bob. "But actually I do not admit to murder. I have looked up in the dictionary what it says about murder, how it defines murder, and it says, 'The malicious killing of one human being by another.' And there is nothing malicious in what I have done."

"Well, you admit you took an ice pick and killed a man named Byrnes with it?" said Judge Wallace.

Irwin hesitated for a moment, as if thinking hard. Then: "I admit that. Yes, sir."

"You knew at the time that you were killing him?"

"Yes."

"And you admit that you strangled Mrs. Gedeon?"

"Yes," said Bob, growing more excited by the moment. "And I admit I killed Ronnie. But I want to repeat that I take this plea against my better judgment. I have been talked blue in the face—"

Judge Wallace interrupted softly: "No, you don't take any plea against your better judgment."

The judge's soothing tone had its effect. Irwin relaxed somewhat and went on: "I only take it because I have been provided by Mr. Leibowitz, out of his kindness and out of his purse, with a means of continuing the one thing that I put my life into. I don't consider myself a murderer."

"You think you had a right to kill these three people?"

"I think that under the circumstances I had every right. And I want to say this, Your Honor," he continued, casting a baleful glare at the prosecution table. "If I ever talked to that jury, and if this thing had gone to trial, I would have emerged in an entirely different light than those professional liars over there, before the court and the jury—"

Shaking with fury, he shifted his gaze to the press table. "And that goes for a few more people," he shouted. "How abominably you treated me! You dirty dogs! Nobody wants to understand me. Nobody wants to see what I'm driving at. No one!"

Evidently thrown into a quandary by this outburst, Judge Wallace sat silently for a moment. "The important thing for me to make up my mind," he finally murmured, as though debating with himself, "is whether he realizes what he is doing before I accept the plea."

Then, addressing Bob again, he said: "You realize you are going to be sent to prison, probably for the rest of your natural life, on your plea?"

"I realize that, Your Honor," Irwin replied scornfully, "and it makes no difference to me. I prophesy to you that in ten years I will be out."

With that, the plea was accepted, sentencing set for two weeks from that day, and Bob—flashing "a mad toothy grin for the photographers"—was led back to the Tombs.[27]

Thomas Dewey lost no time in releasing a prepared statement from his office:

> It is imperative that the community be permanently protected against Irwin's possible return to society. This man has been previously committed as insane five times. Had the case gone to jury, Irwin might have been held legally insane at the time the murders were committed and he then could have been released on the community again. Now that will never happen. At the time of sentence, Mr. Rosenblum, by my direction, will recommend a sentence of ninety years to life on each of the three murder indictments, to be served consecutively. Such a sentence would ensure Irwin's confinement for the rest of his natural life.[28]

On his way out of the courtroom, Leibowitz, wearing a triumphant look, was surrounded by reporters, all of whom had the same question. What had Bob meant when he predicted that he would be out in ten years?

"Electricity," said Leibowitz, explaining Bob's latest obsession. "He believes that, by 1948, he'll have stored enough energy in his body to melt the prison bars."[29]

Aftermath

E VEN BEFORE BOB WAS SENTENCED, Sam Leibowitz had already found himself involved in another made-for-tabloid murder case.

At around 7:30 p.m. Sunday, November 6, 1938—the eve of the start of Bob's trial—a seventeen-year-old girl named Eva Kopalchak showed up at the Bellevue psychiatric ward, where she had been confined twice before for attempted suicide. Dressed in male drag—her stepfather's trousers, a fedora hat, and a lumberman's jacket—she calmly told the on-duty doctors that she had killed her mother, Mrs. Christina Piatak, earlier that day.

"She didn't like the company I was keeping," said Eva by way of explanation. "She didn't want me to drink and smoke. And she wouldn't give me any money."

After arguing for a while, Eva had taken a .22-caliber rifle from a closet and shot her mother six times in the back, head, and chest, then crushed her skull with an iron shoemaker's last "to put her out of her misery." After donning her stepfather's clothing, she strolled to a bar and grill at 30th Street and First Avenue, smoked a cigar, and had a few shots of whiskey before making her way to Bellevue. Records showed that she had been committed to Rockland State Hospital in February of that year but released at her mother's insistence in July.

Her story of matricide seemed so improbable and Eva's demeanor so patently bizarre that the doctors gave it little credence. It wasn't until Monday morning that policeman August Gillman, sent to Mrs. Piatak's apartment to inform her of her daughter's whereabouts, discovered the middle-aged woman's body lying in a pool of dried blood with six spent rifle cartridges scattered on the floor around her.

Arraigned in the Jefferson Market Court later that day, Eva was asked by Magistrate Abeles if she was sorry for what she did.

"Well after all," Eva said with a shrug, "she *is* my mother."

A week and a half later, on Thursday, November 18, the "female Irwin" (as the tabloids quickly dubbed her) appeared in Homicide Court for a hearing. No longer garbed in her "fantastic attire" but in a prim blue sweater and black skirt, she was accompanied by Sam Leibowitz, who had agreed to represent her after she contacted him by mail. Eva would become yet another killer saved from the chair by the Great Defender. In the end, she was allowed to plead guilty to first-degree manslaughter with a term of ten to twenty years.

"Are you sure of what you are doing in entering this guilty plea?" asked the judge.

"Yes, Your Honor," Eva answered. "My lawyer, Samuel Leibowitz, has told me this is the best thing to do. I think I will be all right when I come out of prison."[1]

Bob arrived for his own sentencing on Monday morning, November 28, looking forward to the chance of delivering one of his grandiosely self-serving speeches. Judge Wallace, however, was in no mood for more of the Mad Sculptor's bombast.

Flanked by four husky bailiffs, the prisoner, wearing a dark suit, gray shirt, and black tie, sauntered into the courtroom shortly after

10:00 a.m. Presented at the bar, he was asked the standard question by the clerk: "Have you anything to say before the sentence is pronounced?"

Clearly determined to take full advantage of his last appearance in the legal spotlight, Irwin placed his hands on the prisoner's rail, leaned forward, and launched into a carefully prepared speech.

"Your Honor," he began in sonorous tones, "ordinarily this business of asking a man if he wants to say anything is a mere formality, for the ordinary prisoner is generally guilty of willful aggression against society or ignorant and unable to speak for himself."

As Bob paused for a moment for rhetorical effect, Sam Leibowitz leaned his head toward the man beside him, Assistant DA Sewell T. Tyng, and muttered, "I just can't keep this fellow from talking."

"I am not guilty of any willful aggression against society," Bob continued in a booming voice. "I am not ignorant. And I certainly can speak for myself. Your Honor, please, will you permit me—"

"Unfortunately, you have pleaded guilty to murder in the second degree," Judge Wallace broke in impatiently. "This is not the time to make an extended oration."

"I'm not!" Bob shouted. "I have some facts—"

"I don't care to hear them," said the judge.

Face contorted in fury, Bob screamed: "This is a farce! I have a definite and real reason why sentence should not be pronounced! You say you represent justice. I say you do not. You represent a rich man's justice!"

Ignoring Irwin's wild taunts, Wallace announced that the guilty pleas had been accepted on the recommendation of the district attorney's office "for the reason there is a question of whether the defendant is of sufficient mentality to be responsible in law for the commission of his acts.

"There is no question the defendant is mentally unsound," he added. "In my opinion, the State has lost nothing in accepting these pleas, except possibly the execution of this defendant, and that would bring no credit to the State."

He then pronounced the sentence: twenty years each for the murders of Veronica and Mary Gedeon and ninety-nine years to life for the murder of Frank Byrnes, the terms to run consecutively for a total of 139 years.

Still tightly gripping the rail, Bob shouted, "Your Honor, you should at least let me present my side of the case!"

At that point, two of the guards stepped forward, locked his arms in theirs, and started leading him way. Crimson with rage, Irwin shrieked at the judge: "You're not as fair to me as I expected you to be! You should have let me talk!"

Just as he reached the door, he managed to yank himself free of the attendants' grasp. Wheeling around to sweep his gaze around the courtroom, he barked out a bitter laugh and cried, "I wonder if Ethel had the courage to show her face here? Is she here?"

In an instant, the guards grabbed him again by the arms. "She hasn't got the courage!" he wailed as they dragged him out the door.[2]

Handcuffed to two detectives, Bob was taken by taxi straight to Grand Central Station. Before boarding the train that would carry him to Sing Sing, he made a final statement to reporters. "I think it's ridiculous," he said calmly, "for the court to ask if a man has anything to say before sentence is pronounced against him and then not let him talk. If the truth of this whole business become known, the people will have a different idea of what justice really is."[3]

Soon after 1:30 p.m., he arrived at the prison and was assigned his new identity: No. 95741. Before relinquishing his civilian clothes, he undid a large safety pin securing the side pocket of his suit jacket, removed five crisp new hundred-dollar bills—the money he had been promised by Sam Leibowitz—and turned it over to an official for safekeeping. It was reportedly the largest sum ever brought to Sing Sing by a prisoner, surpassing even the amount carried by Richard Whitney, former president of the New York Stock Exchange, when he had started his five- to ten-year term in April for embezzlement.[4]

Locked in a padded cell in the solitary confinement unit, Bob was placed under observation by Dr. Amos T. Baker, Sing Sing's chief psychiatrist. Over the course of the next week, Baker spent two to three hours a day with Bob, who was his usual cooperative, often maniacally talkative self. Other prison doctors visited him, too, sometimes bringing him coffee and candy, along with drawing materials. Bob passed much of his time making pencil sketches, including one he sent to Sam Leibowitz as a thank-you gift: a cartoon of a "frock-coated Leibowitz snatching a tiny Irwin from the lethal embrace of the electric chair."[5]

Despite the grim accommodations, Bob immediately felt at home at Sing Sing and was eager to remain there. On December 8, however, Dr. Baker delivered his evaluation to Warden Lewis Lawes. Irwin was "very definitely insane" and "unsuitable for a correctional institution."[6] Hoping to be able to stay at the prison, Bob asked for an interview with Warden Lawes but was refused.

Late on December 9, 1938—ten days after his arrival at Sing Sing—Bob, shackled to two other prisoners, was transported by train and automobile from Ossining to Plattsburgh. At around 8:00 a.m. the following morning, he arrived at his new home, the Dannemora State Hospital. Despite his disappointment at the transfer, Bob—so one hospital official reported to the press—went through his routine admission procedure in "gay spirits."[7]

For a while, he seemed content. Soon after his arrival, he sent a Christmas card to Fredric Wertham. "This institution has more restrictions & it lacks the educational facilities of Sing Sing but the attendants & doctors are friendly to me & they do serve better food than either Sing Sing or Rockland," he wrote. "I suppose that later on things will be much better & I guess it's largely what you make of it & so far I have made only friends & no trouble at all with anybody." He requested two books that Wertham promptly purchased and shipped to him: *Mathematics for the Million* and *Science for the Citizen* by British biologist, statistician, and popularizer Lancelot Hogben.[8]

Like virtually every incarcerated mass killer—even those far less physically attractive than Irwin—he quickly attracted the attention of what a later generation would call a groupie. "A beautiful senorita from Cuba has been writing me in Spanish and I'm in love all over again!" he informed Wertham. To facilitate their communication, he began to teach himself Spanish. Before long, in his characteristically fanatical way, he not only had thrown himself into the study of other foreign tongues—French, German, Latin, Polish, and Italian—but also had invented an international language of his own. "I think I have really got something here," he crowed in a letter to Wertham, "something new in the field of languages—a new principle that neither Esperanto nor any other language ever had; which in addition to many advantages of explicitness, brevity, beauty, uniformity, flexibility, ease of learning, etc., will make the mere speaking of this language tend to improve the health and prolong the life of the speaker."[9]

When he wasn't involved with his new linguistic obsession, he was pursuing other enthusiasms. He continued to be fascinated by the esoteric philosophy of Rosicrucianism and urged Wertham to take a look at Max Heindel's *The Rosicrucian Cosmo-Conception*, "the most wonderful book I ever read in my life, bar none." He became interested in the life of Franz Mesmer and attempted to teach himself hypnotism, which he believed would help him "to learn to visualize." And he developed a hobbyist's passion for ornithology, inspired by his observations of the sparrows that nested right outside his window. He had "become quite a bird lover," he wrote to Wertham's wife, the sculptor Florence Hesketh. One passage from his letter made its way into the newspapers:

> It's cold here; I have a sparrow in a box with his foot frozen off; I'm afraid I'm going to have to kill him as I cannot keep him in that box & he can't possibly live if I turn him loose. This is a tough world for lots of people, including sparrows.[10]

One lifelong passion he felt forced to abandon was art. "I am not permitted to model and I wouldn't want to anyway unless I could cast my statues in plaster & I know that I will never be permitted because of the metal tools I need in that work," he wrote to Wertham. "I was hoping to do some pictures in oil and try to sell them so as to help my two brothers get a little money but the Commissioner of Correction has refused me permission to do so, so I am not interested in doing any art work." Wertham, who believed strongly that his former patient might "reach a certain degree of self-expression and happiness and gain a degree of internal freedom" through his art, appealed to the Department of Corrections on Bob's behalf, but to no avail.[11]

For more than a decade, Wertham and his wife kept up a correspondence with Bob, sending him regular letters and holiday cards, along with chocolates, cigarettes, books, and subscriptions to weekly news magazines. Over the years, the tone of Bob's replies grew increasingly dispirited. At first, he struck a note of confidence, even defiance:

> This prison life is a tough life but there are some indications that things might get better for me here. I hope so & intend to stay out of trouble. Looking back thru the years I remember that my life was always a tough life, but I don't think that it is for nothing & you will see that I will win out in the end and get out of here a free man. I am a long way from being discouraged. An experience like I have been thru will either crush you or make you hard inside. I don't feel crushed.[12]

By the following year, his tone was markedly more subdued: "I think that things might get better for me in time—hope so at any rate—but the mills of the gods grind slow."[13]

After that, his letters grew increasingly despondent. In place of his usual hyperenthusiasm—for philosophy, religion, language—there was a sense of hopelessness and futility. He had even lost interest in visualization: "There is nothing to say about myself." "As for me, there is nothing new I can say." "There is not much I can tell you about myself. This place is always about the same."[14]

Despite his early pledge to "stay out of trouble," he grew increasingly belligerent. Convinced that "the employees were unfriendly to him and that the other patients were talking about him," he eventually assaulted another inmate. When an attendant intervened, Bob ripped the nozzle from a wall-mounted fire extinguisher and threatened to kill the man with it. He was forcibly subdued and thrown into solitary confinement.[15]

He remained in his solitary cell for three years, often refusing to eat, growing emaciated, losing his teeth. In 1951, newspapers reported that he was dying of general paresis brought on by his congenital syphilis.[16]

Occasionally, his name would appear in newspapers and magazines for other reasons. On August 1, 1940, for example, Sydney Pilie, a hotel food checker who ran a sideline in mail-order pornography, was picked up by the police at his fourth-floor apartment at 316 East 50th—"the same apartment," as the *New York Times* reported, "where Robert Irwin, demented sculptor, killed Veronica Gedeon, her mother, and another lodger three years ago." As the cops were about to take Pilie into custody, he went into the kitchen, supposedly to turn off the gas stove, and threw himself out the low-silled window into a courtyard. He died instantly. According to the building superintendent, Fernando Molls, "other tenants had declined to lease the apartment after the Gedeon murders. Pilie, however, took the place without reluctance, declaring he was 'not superstitious.'"[17]

A month later, September 1940—one year after the Nazi invasion of Poland plunged Europe into war—an essay appeared on the newsstands that compared Bob to Adolf Hitler. Published in the pulp magazine *Detective Tales*, the piece described Hitler as a "human monster" who, "in his power-lusting brain, actually believes that the stubborn Poles forced him to bomb Warsaw." Wondering if "a parallel to this egomania can be found in the annals of crime as we know it here in America," the article came up with a ready example: "Robert Irwin, slayer of Ronnie Gedeon, Ronnie's mother, and one other innocent victim":

"Society compelled me to do this," Irwin is reputed to have told the police. And he went on to imply that society, having learned that he was a mental misfit, had failed to cure him; and having failed, had neglected to restrain him from moving with normal men and women. So convinced was he of this opinion, that he was "forced" to make society pay for the errors of its ways. There are many who would agree with Irwin; many who are convinced that society was grossly at fault in his case.[18]

Bob was also invoked in another far more impressive magazine piece, this one by the famous author Theodore Dreiser, whose abiding fascination with sensational murders had resulted in his 1925 masterpiece, *An American Tragedy*. Published in the *North American Review*, the article deals, among other things, with the admixture of good and evil impulses within every person. Addressing his readers directly, Dreiser asks them to consider why they—*we*—derive so much enjoyment from reading about horrific murders. And the example he chooses is the case of Robert Irwin:

Why do so many—not all, but many—run to see a crashed plane, or a train, or two autos with numerous dead about? Why? What is it? Weariness of humdrum and commonplace? Love of change? Horror of the same thing happening to themselves? Or is it something evil in them? In us? Do we like to see other people suffer when we ourselves are safe and don't suffer? Are we really just evil or a mixture of good and evil, whether we want to be or not?

This, too, is something to think of in connection with this Gedeon murder by Robert Irwin. . . . For in connection with this particular murder do you recall the national excitement? Everyone was interested. . . . Do you recall the sales of the newspapers during those four weeks in which the murder was the hourly extra edition feature? Any least little thing in connection with it? When Papa Gedeon was arrested? When the sister was found? When Irwin's name was first mentioned? . . .

If you ran and bought extras, as many of you did, are you evil?
. . . Will you get mad if I suggest that it is because some of you
like murders, terrible ones, particularly where they relieve the
monotony of life?[19]

Dreiser wasn't the only important American novelist fascinated by
the Irwin case. Robert Penn Warren, for example—future U.S. Poet
Laureate and Pulitzer Prize–winning novelist for his 1946 bestseller,
All the King's Men—based the shocking, climactic murder scene of
his second novel, *At Heaven's Gate*, on Bob's strangulation of Ronnie Gedeon.[20]

Far more extensive use of the Irwin case was made by Thomas
Berger, best known for his satiric Western, *Little Big Man*, published
in 1964. Despite a prefatory note advising readers "not to identify
the characters in the narrative which follows—criminals, policemen,
madmen, citizens, or any combination thereof—with real human
beings," his 1967 novel, *Killing Time*, is such a thinly veiled version
of the Irwin case that it amounts to a roman à clef. Only the slightest changes have been made to the real-life facts.

On Christmas Day, an attractive young woman named Betty Bay-
son—along with her husband, Arthur, and her scrawny, hard-drink-
ing father, Andrew Starr—arrives at her mother's apartment to find
a scene of carnage. The naked body of her strangled sister "Billie,"
a promiscuous underwear model, is sprawled on a bed, from beneath which protrude the feet and ankles of their murdered mother.
A male boarder named Appleton lies dead on the floor of the living
room, a screwdriver sticking out his left temple. Old man Starr becomes the immediate suspect and is subjected to a brutal interrogation, though the police quickly realize that he is innocent.

The central figure of the darkly comic novel is the actual killer, a
young sculptor/taxidermist named Joe Detweiler. A likeable fellow
—except for his sporadic outbursts of homicidal rage—Detweiler,
son of a séance-holding mother, has devoted his life to perfecting a
technique called Realization that will allow him to travel through

space "using only his mind." In his effort to concentrate all his energies on developing this technique, he has tried to have his penis amputated. Arrested for the triple murder, he is represented by "the best defense counsel in America," a brilliant courtroom strategist named Henry Webster Melrose who has won eighty-two capital cases and lost none. In the end, Detweiler, after pleading guilty to second-degree murder, is sentenced to life, given an immediate examination by prison psychiatrists who find him insane, and transferred to an "institution for the confinement of felonious lunatics."[21]

Though Berger's book was widely reviewed, there is no indication that Bob was aware of it. By the time of its publication, he had been transferred to the Matteawan State Hospital for the Criminally Insane in Fishkill, New York. Eight years later, after a long, agonizing struggle with cancer, he died there at age sixty-seven.

His former attorney, Sam Leibowitz, outlived him by three years, dying of a stroke in June 1978 at the age of eighty-four. For the last twenty-nine years of his professional life, until his retirement in 1970, Leibowitz had served on the bench, having been elected Justice of the Kings County Court in 1941.

At the time he ran for the judgeship, opponents warned that the man who made his early reputation by representing the likes of Al Capone and Mad Dog Coll would be soft on criminals before the bar. Their predictions proved wildly off the mark. Before long, the Great Defender had acquired a new nickname: "Sentencing Sam." First as a Criminal Court Judge in Brooklyn, later as a State Supreme Court Judge, he referred to accused criminals as "animals" and "rats," spoke harshly in open court to their lawyers, and boasted that he was "tough with hardened criminals because toughness is all they understand." When one felon who had offered to testify suddenly clammed up on the stand, Leibowitz roared: "I'll give you a thousand years, if necessary! You'll be buried in jail so you never see daylight again!"

He was also highly vocal on a charged political issue. Believing that it served as an effective deterrent and helped, as he put it, to "eliminate poisonous snakes from the community," Judge Leibowitz — the former lawyer who had saved more than a hundred clients, including Robert Irwin, from the chair — became a staunch advocate of capital punishment.[22]

Epilogue

The Lonergan Case

I N T H E D E C A D E S before Helen Gurley Brown became its
editor and turned it into a swinging-sixties sex guide for single young women, *Cosmopolitan* magazine was a general interest
monthly, combining fiction and feature articles on myriad subjects.
One of the highlights of its October 1948 issue was a piece titled
"Ten Greatest Crimes of the Century," written by one of the found-
ing fathers of the hard-boiled detective genre, Raymond Chandler,
author of *The Big Sleep*, *The Long Goodbye*, and other noir classics.

No. 1 on Chandler's list is the Lindbergh baby kidnapping. No. 2
is the Ruth Snyder–Henry Judd Gray "Double Indemnity" murder,
the greatest tabloid sensation of the 1920s. The Robert Irwin "Mad
Sculptor" case comes in at No. 3—ahead of the St. Valentine's Day
Massacre (No. 4), the kidnap-murder of Bobby Franks by Leopold
and Loeb (No. 8), and the serial murders committed by William
Heirens, the infamous "Lipstick Killer" (No. 10).

Had the article been written fifty years later—at the end of the
century instead of the middle—it would undoubtedly have included
such sensational crimes as the Manson murders, the Columbine

massacre, and the O. J. Simpson case. Still, Chandler's choices, by and large, have withstood the test of time. Only one has so completely faded from public memory that even most histories of American crime make no mention of it. It appears on Chandler's list as No. 9: the Lonergan case.[1]

Born into a middle-class Catholic family in Toronto, the youngest of three children, Wayne Lonergan grew up possessed of every trait necessary to the career of a professional fortune hunter: dashing good looks, glittering charm, easy sexuality, and a driving desire to enjoy the high life. Celebrity scribe Dominick Dunne aptly compares him to Patricia Highsmith's social-climbing, sociopathic hero, Tom Ripley, described by his creator "suave, agreeable, and utterly amoral."[2]

In the spring of 1939, hungry for the kind of thrills his stodgy hometown couldn't supply, twenty-two-year-old Wayne abandoned Toronto and made his way to New York City, where he promptly found work as a "chair boy" at the newly opened World's Fair. Garbed in a uniform that showed off his physique to best advantage—"khaki shorts, a white shirt rolled up over the elbows, and a pith helmet"—he pushed weary sightseers around the grounds in a rented rattan wheelchair. It was in that capacity that he met Bill Burton.[3]

A roly-poly forty-three-year-old with epicurean tastes, Burton—born William Bernheimer—was heir to a $7 million fortune from his family's flourishing brewery, at one time the world's largest. Married, with a daughter named Patricia, he kept a villa on the French Riviera, dabbled in society portraiture, and played sugar daddy to an endless stream of young male lovers.

Shortly after meeting Burton at the fair, golden-boy Wayne Lonergan—happy to hop into bed with anyone, male or female, who could provide him entrée into Manhattan's fast-living "café-society" set—became the latest of the older man's "protégés."

Bill Burton suffered a fatal heart attack in October 1940. By then, his daughter, Patsy, had become infatuated with her father's former boyfriend. In July 1941, the pair of lovebirds eloped to Las Vegas and were married. "If he was good enough for my father," twenty-one-year-old Patsy explained, "he's good enough for me."[4]

Patsy promptly became pregnant, but neither her delicate condition nor the birth of their son in the spring of 1942 put a damper on their nightlife. When the two weren't out carousing at the Stork Club or El Morocco, they were at each other's throats. "They fought like cats and dogs," one close friend recalled. "There was never any peace between them. Once, when they got into an argument, I heard her say to Wayne, 'I suppose that's to be expected when a girl marries a man who's beneath her.'"

Neighbors complained of the hair-raising screams emanating from the couple's apartment. When questioned about the commotion, Wayne blithely explained, "Oh, we had a row and I beat her up."[5]

To no one's surprise, the couple separated in the summer of 1943, exactly two years after their wedding. Soon afterward, Wayne returned to Toronto, where he joined the Royal Canadian Air Force as a cadet, while Patsy—after cutting him out of her will and naming their infant son, Wayne Jr., as her heir—threw herself into her nightly social whirl with wholehearted abandon.

Her activities on the night of Saturday, October 23, 1943, were typical. At a little after seven o'clock, her date, a forty-three-year-old Italian count named Mario Enzo Gabellini, picked her up and took her to the bar at the Peter Cooper Hotel on East 39th Street, where they rendezvoused with another couple, a magazine publisher named Thomas Farrell and his date. After imbibing a few drinks, the four taxied to a restaurant on East 58th Street, where they consumed several more rounds of liquor with dinner. From there they repaired to the Stork Club for a long evening of dancing and drinking. After closing the place down at 4:00 a.m., they headed for Farrell's apartment for a few more hours of drinking. It was 6:30 a.m. when Gabellini finally took Patsy home. Too exhausted to put on a nightgown or turn down the bed, she stripped off her garments—mink jacket, black dress, girdle, bra, panties and stockings—tossed them onto a cushioned bench and collapsed on top of the covers of her Second Empire–style four-poster.[6]

Wayne had flown to New York City that weekend on a forty-eight-hour pass and was staying at the Upper East Side apartment of a friend, John Harjes. On Saturday, October 23, after lunching with friends, he purchased a stuffed elephant for his eighteen-month-old son at the Fifth Avenue toy emporium FAO Schwarz, then paid a brief visit to the boy, playing with him for about an hour. Sometime around 7:00 p.m., smartly dressed in his RCAF uniform, he headed uptown to pick up his date for the evening, Mrs. Jean Murphy Jaburg, a one-time stage actress and movie bit player, recently separated from her husband. She and Wayne attended the Broadway hit *One Touch of Venus*, followed by a midnight dinner at the '21' Club and drinks at the Blue Angel supper club. At around 3:00 a.m., he dropped her off at her apartment, kissed her good night, and made a lunch date for Sunday at the Plaza Hotel.

When they met the following day around noon, Wayne was no longer dressed in his uniform but in an expensive, if somewhat ill-fitting, suit. He was also wearing Max Factor foundation makeup on his chin, though Mrs. Jaburg appeared not to notice. After lunch, they returned to her apartment for a few hours before Wayne took a cab to LaGuardia Airport for a flight back to Toronto.[7]

Since Patsy frequently needed a full day to recover from her previous night's exploits, no one was immediately worried when she failed to emerge from her bedroom on Sunday. It wasn't until early evening that her naked body was discovered sprawled across her bed, her head beaten in with a pair of fourteen-inch brass candlesticks, the room a shambles. Bits of human flesh were subsequently found under her fingernails, evidently scratched from the face of her killer.

With sixty detectives assigned to the case, Wayne was swiftly tracked to Toronto. The police were quick to note some nasty scratches on his chin. Proclaiming his innocence, Wayne waived extradition and was flown back to New York City, where — so he announced—he intended "to help the authorities" find his wife's killer.

Grilled for twenty-four straight hours, he told a story so unsavory that his interrogators were initially nonplussed. According to Wayne, after bidding Jean Murphy Jaburg good night early Sunday morning following their night on the town, he had picked up an American soldier on Lexington Avenue and brought him back to John Harjes's apartment for sex. Wayne had then fallen asleep, only to awaken sometime later to find the other man rummaging through the pockets of his uniform. He had leaped on the man and, in the bitter fight that ensued, his face had been badly scratched. Finally, the other soldier managed to pull free and escape, making off with Wayne's uniform and all the money in his pockets. Wayne had been forced to borrow one of his friend's suits for his Sunday lunch date at the Plaza with Mrs. Jaburg.

At first, the police were inclined to believe him, since—as one officer put it—"a guilty man would never offer an alibi so degrading."[8] It wasn't until he was confronted with incontrovertible physical evidence—his bloody fingerprints on the candlesticks used to crush the victim's skull—that Wayne broke down and confessed.

At a little before nine o'clock that Sunday morning, he had gone to his wife's apartment and knocked on her bedroom door. Patsy, still completely nude, let him in. Sitting beside each other on the bed, they exchanged increasingly testy words. He accused her of "behaving like a tart." She called him "a couple of names." Finally, she told him to "get the hell out here" and "don't ever come back." As he headed for the door, she shouted, "You'll never see the baby again—ever!"

"I lost my head," Lonergan explained to his interrogators. Grabbing one of the heavy brass candlesticks from the sideboard, he rushed at her and smashed her in the head with such force that the candlestick broke. Blind with rage, he grabbed the second candlestick and struck her again. Still conscious, she clawed at him, raking his chin. He seized her by the throat and choked her. It took her, by his estimate, three minutes to die.

Hurrying back to Harjes's apartment, he scissored his blood-stained uniform to pieces, stuffed them in his duffel bag, weighed the bag down with a dumbbell, and tossed it in the river. He then purchased some makeup at a neighborhood drugstore to conceal the scratches on his face and, borrowing one of his friend's suits, went off to keep his lunch date. "The best-looking degenerate ever to go on trial for murder in the history of the New York court system," he was ultimately convicted of second-degree homicide and sentenced to thirty-five years to life.[9]

With its deliciously scandalous elements—"whispered vices whose details are unprintable and whose character is generally unknown to the average normal person," as the *Journal-American* put it—the Lonergan case was the greatest tabloid sensation in years. Among the lurid rumors that swirled around the crime was a widespread story that Wayne had killed Patsy when she nearly bit off his penis while performing "a final act of fellatio on him."[10]

What made the case so titillating, however, was not just the sex but the setting. The killing took place at 313 East 51st Street, a four-story town house a few blocks from the sites of two other horrors still fresh in the minds of New Yorkers. The brutalized heiress became the third in a trio of lovely young women found naked and slain in the fashionable Manhattan neighborhood. Nancy Titterton. Veronica Gedeon. Now Patsy Burton Lonergan. Once again, as newspapers throughout the country never failed to mention, savage death had visited Beekman Place.[11]

Acknowledgments

I OWE MY GREATEST debt of thanks to my agent, David Patterson, whose guidance and advice were absolutely essential to this project, from conception to realization.

Thanks also to:

Kenneth Cobb, New York City Municipal Archives
Bruce Kirby, Manuscript Reading Room, Library of Congress
Mark McMurray, St. Lawrence University
Thomas Mills, Cornell University Law Library
Richard Pope
Martha Sachs, Penn State University Harrisburg Library
E. Morris Sider, Messiah College
Lewis Titterton

As always, I give thanks to—and for—my dear and loving wife, Kimiko Hahn. As the poet said: "If ever two were one, then surely we."

Notes

Prologue: *268 East 52nd Street, New York City*

1. *New York Journal*, March 29, 1937, p. 8.
2. Box 21, Folder 10, Papers of Fredric Wertham, 1818–1936, Library of Congress Rare Books and Special Collections Division.

Chapter 1. *Dead End*

1. William B. Aitken, *Distinguished Families in America, Descended from Wilhelmus Beekman and Jan Thomasse Van Dyke* (New York: G. P. Putnam's Sons/The Knickerbocker Press, 1912), pp. 3–4, 118–120. Steven Gaines, *The Sky's the Limit: Passion and Property in Manhattan* (New York: Little, Brown, 2005), p. 112.
2. Charles Lockwood, *Manhattan Moves Uptown: An Illustrated History* (New York: Barnes & Noble, 1976), p. 248. Blackwell's Island would undergo several name changes, first to Welfare Island, then to Roosevelt Island. For an excellent description of the neighborhood's transformation, see Robert A. M. Stern, Gregory Gilmartin, and Thomas Mellins, *New York 1930: Architecture and Urbanism Between The Two World Wars* (New York: Rizzoli, 1987), pp. 431–433. Also, see Federal Writers' Project, *New York City Guide: A Comprehensive Guide to the Five Boroughs of the Metropolois—Manhattan, Brooklyn, the Bronx, Queens, and Richmond—Prepared by the Ferderal Writers' Project of the Work Progress Administration in New York City* (New York: Random House, 1939), pp. 226–228.
3. Sidney Kingsley, *Dead End: A Play in Three Acts* (New York: Random House, 1936), pp. 11–13.
4. Jay Maeder, "The Dead End Kids East Side Story," *New York Daily News*, March 4, 1999, p. 31.

Chapter 2. Vera and Fritz

1. *New York Post*, November 14, 1935, p. 1; *New York Daily Mirror*, November 22, 1935, p. 3, and November 20, 1935, p. 1; *New York Daily News*, November 13, 1935, p. 3; *New York Post*, November 16, 1935, p. 1.
2. *New York Daily News*, November 13, 1935, pp. 3 and 5; *New York Times*, November 13, 1935, p. 1; *New York Post*, November 12, 1935, pp. 1 and 4, and March 25, 1936, pp. 1 and 9; Quentin Reynolds, *Courtroom: The Story of Samuel S. Leibowitz* (New York: Farrar, Straus and Company, 1950), pp. 211–214.
3. *New York Daily Mirror*, November 13, 1935, p. 5; Reynolds, *Courtroom*, p. 216.
4. Dorothy Kilgallen, *Murder One* (New York: Random House, 1967), pp. 70–72.
5. *New York Daily News*, November 14, 1935, pp. 3 and 12; *New York Times*, November 14, 1935, p. 4.
6. *New York Daily News*, November 13, 1935, p. 3.
7. Ibid.
8. Fifty years after the Gebhardt murder, the supermarket tabloid *Weekly World News* recalled the case in a piece that perfectly captured the sensationalistic tone of the original coverage. See "Blonde Gets Off Scot-free for Blowing Away Her Nazi Loverboy," *Weekly World News*, July 30, 1985, p. 44.
9. Reynolds, *Courtroom*, pp. 215–216; *New York Times*, November 13, 1935, p 3.
10. *New York Daily Mirror*, November 13, 1935, p. 1; "Blonde Gets Off," p. 44.
11. *New York Daily News*, November 14, 1935, pp. 3 and 18; November 15, 1935, pp. 3 and 6; and November 16, 1935, pp. 3 and 5.
12. *New York Times*, November 15, 1935, p. 13; Reynolds, *Courtroom*, p. 214.
13. The family name was originally Lebeau. According to an oft-repeated anecdote, Samuel's father, Isaac, was advised by a friend that he would fare better in the New World if he Americanized his name, a change he could make by simply spelling it "Leibow" and adding "itz." See Reynolds, *Courtroom*, p. 20, and Robert Leibowitz, *The Defender: The Life and Career of Samuel S. Leibowitz, 1893–1933* (Englewood Cliffs, NJ: Prentice-Hall, 1981), p. 2.
14. Reynolds, *Courtroom*, p. 22; Diana Klebanow and Franklin L. Jonas, *People's Lawyers: Crusaders for Justice in American History* (Armonk, NY: M. E. Sharpe, 2003), p. 161.
15. Klebanow and Jonas, *People's Lawyers*, p. 161; Fred D. Pasley, *Not Guilty: The Story of Samuel S. Leibowitz* (New York: G. P. Putnam's Sons, 1933), p. 68.
16. Klebanow and Jonas, *People's Lawyers*, p. 162.
17. Alva Johnston, "Let Freedom Ring," *The New Yorker*, June 4, 1932, p. 22.
18. Leibowitz, *The Defender*, pp. 105–106.
19. John R. Vile, *Great American Lawyers: An Encyclopedia, Vol. I* (Santa Barbara, CA: ABC-CLIO, 2001), p. 461.
20. Pasley, *Not Guilty*, pp. 134, 141, 145, 151; *The New Yorker*, June 4, 1932, p. 21.
21. Klebanow and Jonas, *People's Lawyers*, p. 183; Reynolds, *Courtroom*, pp. 292–293.
22. Klebanow and Jonas, *People's Lawyers*, p. 185.
23. Ibid., p. 196; Jim Fisher, *The Lindbergh Case* (New Brunswick, NJ: Rutgers University Press, 1994), pp. 403–408.
24. *New York Daily Mirror*, November 30, 1936, p. 3.
25. Ibid. Also, see *New York Times*, November 30, 1935, p. 32.

26. *New York Daily Mirror*, March 28, 1936, p. 3.
27. *New York Post*, March 20, 1936, p. 3, and March 21, 1936, p. 3; *New York Daily Mirror*, March 21, 1936, p. 3. Leibowitz did not conceal his disappointment when, that very night, French's ailing mother died and he was forced to withdraw.
28. *New York Times*, March 24, 1936, p. 3; Reynolds, *Courtroom*, p. 219.
29. Reynolds, *Courtroom*, p. 222.
30. *New York Post*, March 26, 1936, p. 3; Kilgallen, *Murder One*, p. 77.
31. *New York Post*, March 28, 1936, p. 3; *New York Daily Mirror*, March 31, 1936, p. 3.
32. *New York Times*, March 28, 1936, p. 3; Reynolds, *Courtroom*, p. 224; Kilgallen, *Murder One*, p. 78.
33. Kilgallen, *Murder One*, p. 81; *New York Post*, March 26, 1936, p. 3.
34. *New York Daily News*, November 13, 1935, p. 8; *New York Daily Mirror*, March 28, 1936, p. 6.
35. *New York Post*, March 26, 1936, p. 1; Kilgallen, *Murder One*, p. 82.
36. *New York Daily Mirror*, March 28, 1936, p. 3.
37. Reynolds, *Courtroom*, p. 227.
38. *New York Post*, March 28, 1936, p. 3.
39. Quoted by Kilgallen, *Murder One*, pp. 85–86.
40. *New York Daily Mirror*, March 28, 1936, p. 3.
41. *New York Post*, March 26, 1936, p. 1.
42. *New York Post*, March 31, 1936, p. 2; Reynolds, *Courtroom*, p. 238; Kilgallen, *Murder One*, p. 92.
43. *New York Journal-American*, April 2, 1936, p. 11; Kilgallen, *Murder One*, p. 106.
44. *New York Journal-American*, April 2, 1936, pp. 1 and 11.
45. *New York Daily News*, April 4, 1936, pp. 2 and 3; *New York Times*, April 4, 1936, p. 1. The acquittal was not only a personal triumph for Leibowitz but a confirmation of what recent research into cognitive science has shown: that "lawyers whose closing arguments tell a story win jury trials against their legal adversaries who lay out 'the facts of the case.'" See Drew Westen, "What Happened to Obama?," *New York Times Sunday Review*, August 7, 2011, p. 6.
46. *New York Daily News*, April 4, 1936, p. 1.
47. *New York Daily News*, April 5, 1936, pp. 3 and 4; *New York Post*, April 5, 1936, p. 1; *New York Daily Mirror*, April 5, 1936, pp. 3 and 4.
48. *New York Daily Mirror*, April 6, 1936, p. 3.

Chapter 3. *"Beauty Slain in Bathtub"*

1. James Farber, "Murder Victim Won Honors as Student," *New York Daily News*, April 11, 1936, p. 3; "Obituary Notes: Nancy Evans Titterton," *Publishers Weekly*, April 18, 1936, p. 1614.
2. *New York Post*, April 11, 1936, p. 3.
3. "Lewis H. Titterton" in *Current Biography: Who's New and Why 1943*, ed. Maxine Block (New York: H. W. Wilson Company, 1944), pp. 768–770; "Woman Writer Slain in Home," *New York Daily News*, April 11, 1936, p. 3.
4. Eight months after Nancy Titterton's murder, "I Shall Decline My Head" was anthologized—along with stories by such masters of the form as Isak Dinesen, Anton Chekhov, Henry James, Isaac Babel, and Katherine Anne Porter—in *A Book of*

Contemporary Short Stories (New York: Macmillan, 1936), edited by Professor Dorothy Brewster of Columbia University.

5. Joseph Faurot, "The Inside Story of New York's Bathtub Slaying," *Official Detective Stories*, July 1936, p. 7.

6. *New York Post*, April 14, 1936, p. 1; *New York Daily Mirror*, April 13, 1936, pp. 3 and 6; *New York Times*, April 11, 1936, pp. 3.

7. *New York Daily News*, April 22, 1936, pp. 3 and 11; *New York Times*, May 26, 1936, p. 45.

8. *New York Post*, April 21, 1936, p. 4.

9. *New York Daily News*, April 12, 1936, p. 4; *New York Times*, April 11, 1936, p. 1, and April 22, 1936, pp. 1 and 12; Faurot, "New York's Bathtub Slaying," p. 4.

10. Faurot, "New York's Bathtub Slaying," pp. 4–5; Colin Evans, *Blood on the Table: The Greatest Cases of New York City's Office of the Chief Medical Examiner* (New York: Berkley Books, 2008), pp. 69–71.

11. *New York Daily News*, April 22, 1936, p. 6.

12. See *New York Daily News*, April 11, 1936, p. 4, and *New York Times*, April 11, 1936, p. 4.

13. *New York Daily News*, April 11, 1936, p. 3, and April 12, 1936, p. 34.

14. *New York Post*, April 11, 1936, p. 3; *New York Daily Mirror*, April 11, 1936, p. 3; *New York Daily News*, April 15, 1936, p. 3.

15. *New York Daily News*, April 16, 1936, p. 7; *New York Post*, April 16, 1936, p. 9.

16. *New York Daily Mirror*, April 15, 1936, p. 1; April 17, 1936, p. 1; and April 18, 1936, p. 1.

17. Susan Lowndes, ed., *Diaries and Letters of Marie Belloc Lowndes, 1911–1947* (London: Chatto & Windus, 1971), p. 138.

18. Edward Sefton Porter, *Conscience of the Court* (Englewood Cliffs, NJ: Prentice-Hall, 1962), p. 175.

19. *New York Daily Mirror*, April 13, 1936, p. 3; April 14, 1936, p. 12; and April 16, 1936, p. 30. Faurot, "New York's Bathtub Slaying," p. 7. *New York Daily News*, April 13, 1936, p. 6.

20. *New York Daily Mirror*, April 14, 1936, p. 12; *New York Daily News*, April 14, 1936, p. 3. Though Simon turned out to be wrong about the Titterton case, his conjecture perfectly describes a killer who would gain nationwide notoriety several decades later: the Boston Strangler.

21. *New York Daily Mirror*, April 16, 1936, p. 30, and April 18, 1936, pp. 3 and 5.

22. *New York Daily Mirror*, April 12, 1936, p. 6; *New York Daily News*, April 12, 1936, p. 4.

23. *New York Daily News*, April 14, 1936, p. 5.

24. *New York Times*, April 17, 1937, p. 44; *New York Daily Mirror*, April 21, 1936, p. 3.

25. *New York Times*, April 19, 1936, p. E11, and April 26, 1985, p. 35; *New York Post*, April 25, 1936, p. 12; *New York Daily News*, April 14, 1936, p. 5. For a fascinating look at Gettler's career, see Deborah Blum, *The Poisoner's Handbook: Murder and the Birth of Forensic Medicine in Jazz Age New York* (New York: The Penguin Press, 2010).

26. Evans, *Blood on the Table*, p. 85; Faurot, "New York's Bathtub Slaying," p. 43.

27. Porter, *Conscience of the Court*, p. 179.

28. *New York Post*, April 21, 1936, p. 4.
29. Evans, *Blood on the Table*, pp. 79–80; *New York Post*, April 22, 1936, pp. 1 and 14.
30. *New York Daily News*, April 22, 1936, pp. 3 and 20.
31. Porter, *Conscience of the Court*, pp. 179–180.
32. *New York Times*, April 23, 1936, p. 5; Faurot, "New York's Bathtub Slaying," p. 44.
33. *New York Daily Mirror*, April 22, 1936, pp. 3 and 5, and May 22, 1936, pp. 3 and 4; *New York Daily News*, April 22, 1936, pp. 1 and 3; *New York Times*, April 22, 1936, pp. 1 and 12; Evans, *Blood on the Table*, pp. 86–88; Bromberg, *The Mold of Murder: A Psychiatric Study of Homicide.* (New York and London: Grune and Stratton, 1961), p. 152.
34. *New York Daily Mirror*, April 23, 1936, p. 3; *New York Post*, April 23, 1936, pp. 3 and 7; *New York Times*, April 23, 1936, p. 5.
35. *New York Daily Mirror*, April 25, 1936, pp. 2 and 3; April 26, 1936, pp. 3 and 7; April 27, 1936, pp. 3 and 6; April 28, 1936, pp. 3 and 6; April 29, 1936, pp. 4 and 9; and April 30, 1936, pp. 2 and 3.
36. *New York Post*, May 1, 1936, p. 1.
37. *New York Daily News*, April 23, 1936, p. 7.
38. *New York Times*, May 20, 1936, p. 4; May 21, 1936, p. 7; May 26, 1936, p. 48; May 27, 1936, p. 48; May 28, 1936, p. 1; May 29, 1936, p. 44; June 6, 1936, p. 34; and January 22, 1937, p. 42. *New York Daily News*, May 23, 1936, p. 3; May 25, 1936, p. 3; and May 27, 1936, pp. 2 and 3. *New York Post*, May 26, 1936, p. 1 and 13. Evans, *Blood on the Table*, pp. 89–92.

Chapter 4. Sex Fiends

1. See Harold Schechter, *Deranged: The Shocking True Story of America's Fiendish Killer!* (New York: Simon & Schuster/Pocket Books, 1998), and *New York Times*, May 1, 1935, p. 44.
2. See Tamara Rice Lave, "Only Yesterday: The Rise and Fall of Twentieth Century Sexual Psychopath Laws," *Louisiana Law Review*, No. 69 (April 2009), p. 551; "Sex Crime Wave Alarms the U.S.," *Literary Digest*, April 10, 1937, pp. 5–7; and Smith Ely Jelliffe, "Why Do Such Things Happen?," *Cosmopolitan*, July 1937, pp. 56–57, 170–171. In New York City, Hoover's syndicated article appeared in *This Week*, the Sunday magazine section of the *New York Herald Tribune*, September 26, 1937, pp. 2 and 23.
3. Chapters include "The Sex Criminal Emerges," "Is the Sex Deviate Born or Made?," and "What Shall We Do with the Sex Criminal?" See Bertram Pollens, *The Sex Criminal* (New York: Emerson Books, 1938).
4. *New York Times*, March 21, 1937, p. 24; August 9, 1937, p. 1; and August 15, 1937, pp. 1 and 2.
5. Pollens, *The Sex Criminal*, pp. 84–85; Jelliffe, "Why Do Such Things Happen?," p. 56; "Sex Crime Wave Alarms U.S.," p. 5–7; Andrea Friedman, "'The Habitats of Sex-Crazed Perverts': Campaigns Against Burlesque in Depression-Era New York City," *Journal of the History of Sexuality*, Vol. 7, No. 2 (October 1996), pp. 226–227.
6. *New York Daily News*, March 28, 1937, pp. 54–55.
7. "Sex Crime Wave Alarms the U.S.," p. 7.

Chapter 5. The Firebrand

1. Martin H. Schrag, "The Spiritual Pilgrimage of the Reverend Benjamin Hardin Irwin," *Brethren in Christ History and Life*, Vol. 4, No. 1 (June 1981), p. 5.
2. Ibid., p. 6.
3. Ibid., pp. 6–7.
4. Ibid., p. 13.
5. In an interview with probation officer B. G. Dodge, Irwin described his father as "a sort of Elmer Gantry—he set out to reform the world. The only drawback was that he neglected first to reform himself." Dodge's handwritten report is filed in Box 21, Folder 10, Papers of Fredric Wertham. Irwin also calls his father "the Elmer Gantry of his day" in the first part of the serialized autobiography published by the *New York Daily News*, April 12, 1937, p. 8.
6. Schrag, "The Spiritual Pilgrimage," p. 10–11; Vinson Synan, *The Holiness-Pentecostal Tradition: Charismatic Movements in the Twentieth Century.* (Grand Rapids, MI: William B. Eerdmans, 1997), pp. 51–52.
7. Synan, *The Holiness-Pentecostal Tradition*, pp. 52–55.
8. Randall J. Stephens, *The Fire Spreads: Holiness and Pentecostalism in the American South* (Cambridge: Harvard University Press, 2008), pp. 180–181; C. F. Carter, "Fantastic Fanaticisms," *Scrap Book*, Vol. 5, No. 3 (March 1908), p. 406; Schrag, "Benjamin Hardin Irwin and the Brethren in Christ," *Brethren in Christ History and Life*, Vol. 4, No. 2 (December 1981), 109.
9. Synan, *The Holiness-Pentecostal Tradition*, p. 56; Stephens, *The Fire Spreads*, p. 180.
10. Synan, *The Holiness-Pentecostal Tradition*, p. 58.
11. Ibid., p. 58; Schrag, "Benjamin Hardin Irwin," p. 19; R. G. Robins, *A. J. Tomlinson: Plainfolk Modernist* (New York: Oxford University Press, 2004), p. 44.
12. See *New York Daily News*, April 12, 1937, p. 8; Stephens, *The Fire Spreads*, p. 184; and Dr. Harold Hunter, "International Pentecostal Holiness Church," http://www.pctii.org/iphc.html.
13. See Vinson Synan, *The Old-Time Power* (Franklin Springs, GA: Advocate Press, 1973), p. 92; Synan, *The Holiness-Pentecostal Tradition*, p. 89; and Cecil M. Robeck, *The Azusa Street Mission and Revival: The Birth of the Global Pentecostal Movement* (Nashville, TN: Thomas Nelson, 2006), p. 42. The scriptural basis for the belief in glossolalia appears in the second chapter of Acts.
14. Sarah E. Parham, *The Life of Charles F. Parham, Founder of the Apostolic Faith Movement* (Baxter Springs, KS: Apostolic Faith Bible College, 1930), pp. 52–53. Technically speaking, Ozman manifested xenolalia, the spontaneous ability to converse in a real foreign language unknown to the speaker. Glossolalia, the typical Pentecostal "tongue speech," refers to utterances in a completely unrecognizable language.
15. Robeck, *The Azusa Street Mission*, pp. 43–44, 49.
16. Synan, *The Holiness-Pentecostal Tradition*, p. 98.
17. "Weird Babel of Tongues," *Los Angeles Times*, April 18, 1906, p. 1.
18. Edith L. Blumhofer, *Restoring the Faith: The Assemblies of God, Pentecostalism, and American Culture* (Urbana and Chicago: University of Illinois Press, 1993), p. 61.
19. Vinson Synan, *Voices of the Pentecost: Testimonies of Lives Touched by the Holy Spirit*

(Ann Arbor, MI: Servant Publications, 2003), pp. 89–90; Synan, *The Holiness-Pentecostal Tradition*, p. 128.

20. Altogether, Mary bore five children by Benjamin: a twin of Vidalin named Victor, who died at under two weeks, and a girl named Mary Louise who died of "membranous cramp" at three months. (See Edythe K. Bryant, "Family History No. 183, Whittier State School Department of Research," p. 17, in Box 21, Folder 8, Papers of Fredric Wertham.) According to one newspaper account, Mary Louise died "because her father neglected her care when left alone with the baby" (*New York Daily Mirror*, April 17, 1937, p. 6). Grant Wacker writes that it was the "painful experience" of his young daughter's death that "triggered" Irwin's Pentecostal baptism. See *Heaven Below* (Cambridge, MA: Harvard University Press, 2001), p. 60.

21. Fredric Wertham, *The Show of Violence* (Garden City, NY: Doubleday & Company, 1949), p. 111; report of B. G. Dodge, pp. 18–19.

22. See Wertham, *The Show of Violence*, p. 111; report of B. G. Dodge, p. 18; and *New York Daily Mirror*, April 18, 1937, p. 8.

23. Wertham, *The Show of Violence*, p. 111.

Chapter 6. The Brothers

1. Report of B. G. Dodge, p. 16.
2. Ibid., p. 13.
3. Wertham, *The Show of Violence*, p. 111.
4. Fredric Wertham, clinical notes on "James Adamson," January 3, 1933, p. 2, Box 21, Folder 8, Papers of Fredric Wertham, 1818–1936.
5. As religious historian Edith L. Blumhofer writes: "Immersed in a world in which spiritual forces often loomed larger than tangible realities, Pentecostals frequently yielded to inclinations to neglect conventional social obligations to pursue spiritual experiences. Taking literally injunctions to love nothing more than Christ, some virtually abandoned regular family life to 'follow the Lord.' . . . Leaders soon found it advisable to encourage the faithful to acknowledge and fulfill family obligations . . . denouncing as 'false teaching' the idea that God had called married women to do 'mission work and to leave the little children at home to fare the best they can.'" See Blumhofer, *Restoring the Faith*, p. 93.
6. "Robert Irwin's Own Story," *New York Daily News*, April 12, 1937, p. 3.
7. Bryant, "Family History No. 183," p. 11.
8. Ibid., p. 7.
9. Ibid., pp. 4–5, 8.
10. F. C. Nelles, "Purposes of the Whittier State School," *Los Angeles School Journal*, Vol. 6, No. 8 (January 15, 1923), pp. 24–25.
11. Bryant, "Family History No. 183," pp. 2–4, 5.
12. Ibid., pp. 9–10.
13. Ibid., pp. 17–19; William Henry Slingerland, *Child Welfare Work in California: A Study of Agencies and Institutions* (New York: Russell Sage Foundation/Department of Child-Helping, 1915), p. 79.
14. Wertham, *The Show of Violence*, p. 114.
15. Report of B. G. Dodge, p. 12; Wertham, clinical notes on "James Adamson," January 9, 1933, p. 6.

16. Report of B. G. Dodge, p. 12; Wertham, clinical notes on "James Adamson," January 3, 1933, p. 2.

17. Report of B. G. Dodge, p. 13; Wertham, clinical notes on "James Adamson," January 9, 1933, p. 6; Wertham, *The Show of Violence*, pp. 114–115.

18. "Robert Irwin's Own Story," *New York Daily News*, April 12, 1937, p. 3.

19. See Wertham, clinical notes on "James Adamson," January 11, 1933, p. 2 and report of B. G. Dodge, p. 13.

20. Report of B. G. Dodge, pp. 3, 18.

Chapter 7. Epiphany

1. Roberts Liardon, *The Azusa Street Revival: When The Fire Fell* (Shippensburg, PA: Destiny Press, 2006), p. 170.

2. See "A Letter Written from Rose City Camp Ground, Portland, Ore.," www.Apostolicfaith.org, and "Religion: Camp Meeting," *Time*, August 19, 1935, p. 43.

3. Harriet Hammond, "Bob Irwin's Secret Life," *New York Daily Mirror*, April 18, 1937, p. 24.

4. Report of B. G. Dodge, p. 14.

5. Wertham, *The Show of Violence*, p. 111. Pember's official Certificate of Death from the State of California, County of Nevada, Nevada City (File No. 95–038240) lists his last known occupation as "Classical Guitar Teacher."

6. Wertham, clinical notes on "James Adamson," January 6, 1933, p. 8.

7. Ibid.; Hammond, "Bob Irwin's Secret Life," April 22, 1937, p. 14. For a good summary of Simpson's life and career, see Ralph Friedman, *Tracking Down Oregon* (Caldwell, ID: Caxton, 1978), pp. 58–70.

8. Hammond, "Bob Irwin's Secret Life," April 19, 1937, p. 3.

9. Ibid., April 25, 1937, p. 14.

10. Ibid., April 22, 1937, p. 14.

11. L. E. Hinsie, "A Contribution to the Psychopathology of Murder—Study of a Case." *Criminal Psychopathology*, Vol. 2, No. 1 (July 1940), p. 4.

12. Wallace D. Wattles, *The Science of Getting Rich* (Holyoke, MA: Elizabeth Towne, 1910), p. 36. Also, see Catherine L. Albanese, *A Republic of Mind and Spirit: A Cultural History of American Metaphysical Religion* (New Haven, CT: Yale University Press, 2007), and Horatio W. Dresser, *A History of the New Thought Movement* (New York: Thomas Y. Crowell, 1919).

13. Wertham, clinical notes on "James Adamson," January 11, 1933, p. 1; Wertham, *The Show of Violence*, p. 117.

14. Hinsie, "The Psychopathology of Murder," p. 8.

15. Report of B. G. Dodge, p. 15.

16. Ibid., p. 13.

17. Hinsie, "The Psychopathology of Murder," p. 8.

18. For an excellent discussion of Ingersoll in the context of his time, see Susan Jacoby, *Freethinkers: A History of American Secularism* (New York: Henry Holt/Metropolitan Books, 2004).

19. Ingersoll's essays are available online at various sites, including Project Gutenberg (www.gutenberg.org).

20. Wertham, *The Show of Violence*, p. 112.

21. Hammond, "Bob Irwin's Secret Life," April 27, 1937, p. 3.

22. Ibid., April 22, 1937, p. 14.

23. Ibid., April 24, 1927, p. 3.

24. Wertham, clinical notes on "James Adamson," January 4, 1933, p. 4, and January 6, 1933, p. 8.

25. Report of B. G. Dodge, pp. 15–16; Wertham, clinical notes on "James Adamson," January 4, 1933, p. 4; Wertham, *The Show of Violence*, p. 117.

26. 1926 census for Brickstore, Newton County, Georgia, T625, reel 271, ED 109, p. 2A; Hammond, *New York Daily News*, April 18, 1937, p. 24.

27. Wertham, clinical notes on "James Adamson," January 6, 1933, p. 7.

28. Report of B. G. Dodge, p. 18.

Chapter 8. Romanelli and Rady

1. "Irwin Bares His Struggle in Art," *New York Daily News*, April 13, 1937, p. 17.

2. Wertham, clinical notes on "James Adamson," January 10, 1933, p. 5.

3. See Gloria Ricci Lothrop, ed., *Fulfilling the Promise of California: An Anthology of Essays on the Italian American Experience in California* (Spokane, WA: Arthur H. Clark Company, 2000), p. 255.

4. Wertham, clinical notes on "James Adamson," January 7, 1933, p. 1.

5. Ibid., p. 3.

6. Wertham, clinical notes on "James Adamson," January 31, 1933, pp. 3–4; Wertham, *The Show of Violence*, p. 117.

7. Report of B. G. Dodge, p. 18.

8. Wertham, clinical notes on "James Adamson," January 6, 1933, p. 8; *Time*, October 1, 1934, p. 68; report of B. G. Dodge, p. 18.

9. Trygve A. Rovelstad, "Impressions of Lorado Taft," *Papers in Illinois History and Transactions for the Year 1937*, Vol. 44 (1938), pp. 18–33.

10. Allen Weller, "Lorado Taft, the Ferguson Fund, and the Advent of Modernism," in *The Old Guard and the Avant-Garde: Modernism in Chicago, 1910–1940*, ed. Sue Ann Price (Chicago: University of Chicago Press, 1990), p. 40.

11. Henry B. Fuller, "Notes on Lorado Taft," *Century*, Vol. 76 (October 1908), p. 618.

12. Hamlin Garland, "The Art of Lorado Taft," *Mentor*, Vol. 11 (October 1923), p. 19.

13. Timothy J. Garvey, *Public Sculptor: Lorado Taft and the Beautification of Chicago* (Urbana: University of Illinois Press, 1988), p. 60.

14. Rovelstad, "Impressions of Lorado Taft," p. 29.

15. Curtis Gathje, *A Model Crime: A True Fiction* (New York: Donald I. Fine, 1995), p. 114.

16. My description of Irwin's arrival at Taft's atelier draws on Ruth Helming Mose, "Midway Studio," *American Magazine of Art*, August 1928, pp. 413–422. Taft's reaction to the little bust of Charles Lindbergh is recounted by Irwin's Chicago roommate Arthur Halliburton. See the typed transcript, "Mr. Arthur Halliburton, reporter from [Sunday] *Mirror Magazine*, reports about his contact with Robert Irwin," in Box 21, Folder 8, Papers of Fredric Wertham.

17. Weller, "Lorado Taft, the Ferguson Fund," pp. 44–45.

18. "Robert Irwin's Own Life Story," *New York Daily News*, April 14, 1937, p. 3; report of B. G. Dodge, p. 22.

19. Wertham, clinical notes on "James Adamson," January 7, 1933, p. 3, and January 9, 1933, p. 2.

20. Ibid., January 24, 1933, p. 1.

21. Ibid., January 7, 1933, p. 3; January 10, 1933, p. 4; and February 7, 1933, p. 3.

22. Ibid., January 24, 1933, p. 1.

23. From a letter to Alice Ryan, January 1, 1931, transcribed by Wertham, Box 21, Folder 8, Papers of Fredric Wertham.

24. A photograph of the letter, which was typed on White House stationery and hand signed "Lou Henry Hoover," appeared in newspapers around the country on April 10, 1937.

25. Wertham, clinical notes on "James Adamson," November 30, 1932, p. 2.

26. My reconstruction of Bob's speech to Alice Ryan is taken from a letter he wrote to her in late December 1930. The letter—eleven single-spaced pages in its typed form —was transcribed by Wertham in early January and is contained in Box 21, Folder 8, Papers of Fredric Wertham.

27. From a typewritten manuscript dated June 11, 1947, "Mr. Arthur Halliburton, reporter from [Sunday] *Mirror Magazine*, reports about his contact with Robert Irwin," in Box 21, Folder 8, Papers of Fredric Wertham.

28. Wertham, *The Show of Violence*, p. 119; Wertham, clinical notes on "James Adamson," January 6, 1933, p. 7, and January 11, 1933, p. 4.

29. Wertham, clinical notes on "James Adamson," January 6, 1933, p. 7, and January 10, 1933, pp. 3–4.

Chapter 9. Depression

1. John Kenneth Galbraith, *The Great Crash, 1929* (Cambridge, MA: Houghton Mifflin, 1955), pp. 132–133, 146; Frederick Lewis Allen, *Since Yesterday: The 1930s in America, September 3, 1929–September 3, 1939* (New York: Harper & Row/Perennial Library, 1972), p. 27.

2. Wertham, clinical notes on "James Adamson," January 10, 1933, p. 5.

3. James Thurber, "Pets and Trophies," *The New Yorker*, July 27, 1929, p. 8.

4. Will Durant, *The Story of Philosophy: The Lives and Opinions of the Greater Philosophers* (New York: Washington Square Press, 1953), pp. 317–318.

5. Wertham, clinical notes on "James Adamson," January 11, 1933, pp. 3–4.

6. Ibid.; Hinsie, "The Psychopathology of Murder," p. 10.

7. Wertham, *The Show of Violence*, p. 122.

8. Report of B. G. Dodge, p. 22.

9. Report of B. G. Dodge, p. 25; Reynolds, *Courtroom*, p. 114.

10. Wertham, *The Show of Violence*, p. 123.

11. See report of B. G. Dodge, pp. 2, 22, 25.

12. See *New York Times*, December 4, 1909, p. 10, and December 7, 1909, p. 9, as well as Frank K. Sturgis, "The Winifred Masterson Burke Relief Foundation," *Journal of the National Institute of Social Sciences*, Vol. 3 (January 1917), pp. 83–93.

13. "Statement of friend, Charles Smith, 240 E. 53rd Street," in Box 21, Folder 8, Papers of Fredric Wertham.

14. Wertham, clinical notes on "James Adamson," January 6, 1933, p. 8.

Chapter 10. The Gedeons

1. Wertham, clinical notes on "James Adamson," January 26, 1933, p. 2; report of B. G. Dodge, pp. 2, 22.

2. Alan Hynd, *Murder, Mayhem, and Mystery: An Album of American Crime* (New York: A. S. Barnes and Company, 1958), p. 81.
3. Gathje, *A Model Crime*, pp. 22–23, 49.
4. Wertham, clinical notes on "James Adamson," February 7, 1933, p. 5.

Chapter 11. Wertham

1. Wertham, clinical notes on "James Adamson," February 7, 1933, p. 4; Wertham, *The Show of Violence*, pp. 106–107.
2. *New York Times*, November 3, 1941, p. 19, and December 24, 1982, p. B6.
3. James Gilbert, *Cycle of Outrage: America's Reaction to the Juvenile Delinquent in the 1950s* (New York: Oxford University Press, 1986), p. 63.
4. The best book on the anti-comics crusade of the 1950s is David Hajdu's *The Ten-Cent Plague: The Great Comic-Book Scare and How It Changed America* (New York: Farrar, Straus and Giroux, 2008).
5. "Peace Loving Psychiarist," *MD: Medical Newsmagazine*, Vol. 11, No. 7 (July 1997), p. 230.
6. Bart Beaty, *Fredric Wertham and the Critique of Mass Culture* (Jackson: University of Mississippi, 2005), p. 19.
7. My capsule biography of Wertham draws on material from James E. Reibman, "The Life of Dr. Fredric Wertham," in *The Fredric Wertham Collection* (Cambridge, MA: Busch-Reisinger Museum, Harvard University, 1990), pp. 11–22, and Gabriel N. Mendes, "A Deeper Science: Richard Wright, Dr. Fredric Wertham, and the Fight for Mental Health Care in Harlem, NY, 1940–1960" (PhD diss., Brown University, 2010), pp. 59–110.
8. Mendes, "A Deeper Science," p. 100.
9. See Cornelius F. Collins, "N.Y. Court Requests Psychiatric Service Clinic for Criminals Supplemental Memorandum," *Journal of the American Institute for Criminal Law and Criminology*, Vol. 19, No. 3 (November 1928), pp. 337–343, and Emanuel Messinger and Benjamin Apfelberg, "A Quarter Century of Court Psychiatry," *Crime & Delinquency*, Vol. 7, No. 4 (1961), pp. 343–362.
10. Schechter, *Deranged*, pp. 299–300. As it happened, the jurors agreed with Wertham that Fish was insane. They found his crime so appalling, however, that they thought he should be executed anyway.
11. Beaty, *The Critique of Mass Culture*, p. 33.
12. Messinger and Apfelberg, "A Quarter Century of Court Psychiatry," p. 344; Wertham, *The Show of Violence*, p. 107, 110.
13. Among them the Whitney Museum of American Art, the Art Institute of Chicago, the San Francisco Museum of Art, and the Pennsylvania Academy of Fine Arts. See Reibman, "The Life of Dr. Fredric Wertham," p. 13.
14. Wertham, *The Show of Violence*, p. 111.
15. Except where otherwise noted, all quotes from Wertham's psychotherapeutic sessions with Irwin are taken from the transcripts made between December 12, 1932, and March 13, 1933, filed in Box 21, Folder 8, Papers of Fredric Wertham.
16. Wertham, *The Show of Violence*, p. 124.
17. Ibid., p. 126.

Chapter 12. Bug in a Bottle

1. *New York Journal-American*, February 14, 1938, p. 2.
2. See Donna Cornachio, "Changes in Mental Care," *New York Times*, January 3, 1999, p. 7. Bernard's series ran February 14–24, 1938. *The Snake Pit*, published by Random House in 1946, was made into a hugely successful, Oscar-nominated movie two years later.
3. *New York Journal-American*, February 16, 1938, p. 6.
4. Wertham, *The Show of Violence*, p. 129.
5. "Robert Irwin Revealed as Asylum 'Bully,'" *New York Journal-American*, February 26, 1938, p. 4; Gathje, *A Model Crime*, p. 115.
6. *New York Journal-American*, February 14, 1938, p. 2.
7. Fredric Wertham, Letter to Robert Irwin, May 19, 1933, Box 21, Folder 4, Papers of Fredric Wertham.
8. Wertham, *The Show of Violence*, pp. 127–129. As Louis B. Schlesinger explains, "The term *catathymia* is derived from the Greek *kata* ('according to') and *thymos* ('spirits or temper'). Feyerabend's Greek dictionary gives various translations, the most appropriate of which is 'in accordance with emotions.' *Catathymia* (*Katathymie*) was first used by Hans W. Maier [in a paper published in 1912] as a psychodynamic explanation for the development of the content of delusions. The concept later became used, notably by Fredric Wertham, as an explanation for extreme acts of violence and some types of sexual homicide." See Louis B. Schlesinger, *Sexual Murder: Catathymic and Compulsive Homicides* (Boca Raton, FL: CRC Press, 2004), p. 109.
9. Reynolds, *Courtroom*, p. 117.
10. *New York Daily News*, April 6, 1937, p. 8; *New York Journal-American*, April 6, 1937, p. 3.
11. Wertham, *The Show of Violence*, p. 129.
12. T. H. Trent, "Murder of the Model—the Mother—and the Lodger," *Official Detective Stories*, July 1, 1937, p. 13.

Chapter 13. The Snake Woman

1. Gathje, *A Model Crime*, p. 22.
2. *New York Daily Mirror*, April 6, 1937, p 3.
3. Ibid., p. 14.
4. Gathje, *A Model Crime*, p. 44.
5. Ibid., p. 49.
6. *New York Daily Mirror*, July 1, 1937, p. 5.
7. Ibid., July 3, 1937, p. 3.
8. Ibid., July 4, 1937, p. 4.
9. Robert Leibowitz, *The Defender, Casebook II: The Life and Career of Samuel S. Leibowitz, 1933–1941* (Denville, NJ: SBC Enterprises, 2004), p. 334; Wertham, *The Show of Violence*, p. 129.
10. Trent, "Murder of the Model," June 15, 1937, p. 12.
11. *New York Daily Mirror*, June 31, 1937, p. 5; Leibowitz, *The Defender, Casebook II*, p. 334.

12. Wertham, *The Show of Violence*, p. 129; Gathje, *A Model Crime*, p. 116; Reynolds, *Courtroom*, p. 117.
13. Gathje, *A Model Crime*, p. 116.
14. Trent, "Murder of the Model," June 15, 1937, p. 12.
15. Wertham, *The Show of Violence*, p. 130; report of B. G. Dodge, p. 19; Reynolds, *Courtroom*, p. 117.
16. Report of B. G. Dodge, p. 30; *New York Daily News*, April 15, 1937, p. 11.
17. Leibowitz, *The Defender, Casebook II*, p. 335; *New York Daily News*, April 15, 1937, p. 11; report of B. G. Dodge, p. 3.
18. *New York Daily News*, April 16, 1937, p. 6.
19. *New York Evening Journal*, April 6, 1937, p. 1.
20. Report of B. G. Dodge, p. 3; *New York Daily News*, April 16, 1937, p. 6.
21. Report of B. G. Dodge, p. 31.
22. Gathje, *A Model Crime*, p. 134.

Chapter 14. Canton

1. *New York Daily News*, April 16, 1937, p. 6.
2. Reynolds, *Courtroom*, pp. 117–118; Leibowitz, *The Defender, Casebook II*, p. 335; *New York Daily News*, April 12, 1937, p. 8.
3. Reynolds, *Courtroom*, p. 117.
4. Wertham, *The Show of Violence*, p. 130; Gathje, *A Model Crime*, p. 117.
5. Reynolds, *Courtroom*, p. 118; Gathje, *A Model Crime*, p. 117; report of B. G. Dodge, p. 3.
6. *New York Daily News*, April 8, 1937, p. 8; Gathje, *A Model Crime*, p. 117.
7. Kirk Douglas, *The Ragman's Son: An Autobiography* (New York: Simon & Schuster, 1988), p. 52.
8. *New York Evening Journal*, April 8, 1937, p. 1; Trent, "Murder of the Model," June 15, 1937, p. 12.
9. See Leibowitz, *The Defender*, p. 235.
10. Reynolds, *Courtroom*, p. 118.
11. Ibid.; *New York Daily News*, April 12, 1937, pp. 3 and 8.
12. Reynolds, *Courtroom*, p. 118; *Syracuse Herald*, April 6, 1937, p. 2.
13. Report of B. G. Dodge, pp. 4, 46; *Syracuse Herald*, April 6, 1937, p. 2; *New York Daily News*, April 12, 1937, p. 8; Reynolds, *Courtroom*, p. 118.
14. Fredric Wertham, "The Catathymic Crisis: A Clinical Entity," *Archives of Neurology and Psychiatry*, Vol. 37 (April 1937), pp. 974–978; Gathje, p. 117.

Chapter 15. Crisis

1. E. J. Kahn Jr., *The World of Swope* (New York: Simon and Schuster, 1965), p. 37; *New York Mirror*, November 9, 1935, pp. 2 and 6; *New York Daily News*, November 9, 1935, p. 8; *New York Times*, November 9, 1935, p. 18; *New York Journal*, March 29, 1937, p. 3.
2. Lee Horsley, "Dead Dolls and Deadly Dames: The Cover Girls of American True Crime Publishing," in *Crime Culture: Figuring Criminality in Fiction and Film*, eds. Bran Nicol, Patricia Pulham, and Eugene McNulty (London: Continuum, 2011), p. 110; Gathje, *A Model Crime*, pp. 60, 62; West F. Peterson, "Veronica Gedeon, Model for *Inside Detective*, Is Murdered," *Inside Detective*, July 1937, p. 6.

3. Reynolds, *Courtroom*, p. 118. The first giant panda ever shot was killed in April 1928 by Theodore Roosevelt and his son Kermit. For a complete account of Sheldon's experience, see William G. Sheldon, *The Wilderness Home of the Giant Panda* (Amherst: University of Massachusetts Press, 1975).

4. *New York Evening Journal*, April 6, 1937, p. 1; Francis C. Preston, "Unpublished Facts in New York's Artist Model Murders," *True Detective Mysteries*, September 1937, p. 81.

5. *New York Evening Journal*, April 6, 1937, p. 1; Gathje, *A Model Crime*, p. 118.

6. *New York Evening Journal*, April 6, 1937, p. 3; *New York Daily Mirror*, April 6, 1937, pp. 13 and 34; Gathje, *A Model Crime*, pp. 118–119.

7. *New York Daily News*, April 12, 1937, p. 3; *New York Evening Journal*, April 12, 1937, pp. 1 and 3; Gathje, *A Model Crime*, pp. 7–71. For an entertaining biography of Bernard, see Robert Love, *The Great Oom: The Improbable Birth of Yoga in America* (New York: Viking, 2010).

8. Trent, "Murder of the Model," July 1, 1937, p. 46.

9. Ibid., p. 47; Gathje, *A Model Crime*, p. 120.

10. William R. Taylor, ed., *Inventing Times Square: Commerce and Culture at the Crossroads of the World* (Baltimore: The Johns Hopkins University Press, 1996), p. 332. The work that best captures Hubert's ineffably sleazy ambience is Morty Bushmaster, *Hubert's Dime Museum & Flea Circus: An Underground History* (New York: Book Whisperer Press, 2008).

11. After its initial newspaper publication, Bob's confession appeared in many publications. This and other quotes are taken from Lewis J. Valentine, *Night Stick: The Autobiography of Lewis J. Valentine, Former Police Commissioner of New York* (New York: The Dial Press, 1947), p. 175.

12. Gathje, *A Model Crime*, p.119.

13. See *Stage*, March 1935, p. 5.

14. Gathje, *A Model Crime*, p. 120.

15. Hinsie, "The Psychopathology of Murder," pp. 4–7.

16. Wertham, *The Show of Violence*, p. 134; report of B. G. Dodge, p. 8.

Chapter 16. Bloody Sunday

1. *New York Sun*, March 29, 1937, p. 2.

2. See "Murder for Easter," *Time*, April 12, 1937, pp. 67–68.

3. Gathje, *A Model Crime*, p. 11; *New York Evening Journal*, March 30, 1937, p. 3.

4. Gathje, *A Model Crime*, p. 11; *New York Evening Journal*, March 31, 1937, p. 4.

5. *New York Evening Journal*, March 29, 1937, p. 2.

6. Gathje, *A Model Crime*, pp. 11–13; Francis C. Preston, "Unpublished Facts in New York's Artist Model Murders," *True Detective Mysteries*, September 1937, p. 6; *New York Daily Mirror*, April 1, 1937, p. 7.

7. Frederick L. Collins, *Homicide Squad: Adventures of a Headquarters Old Timer* (New York: G. P. Putnam's Sons, 1944), p. 207; Preston, "Unpublished Facts," p. 6; Report of Death on (Mrs.) Mary Gedeon by Thomas A. Gonzales, M.D., Office of the Chief Medical Examiner of the City of New York, Case No. 1898, March 29, 1937, pp. 1–3.

8. Trent, "Murder of the Model," May 15, 1937, pp. 4–5.

9. *New York Daily News*, March 29, 1937, p. 3; Report on Death of Frank Byrnes by

Thomas A. Gonzales, M.D., Office of the Chief Medical Examiner of the City of New York, Case No. 1897, March 29, 1937.

10. Preston, "Unpublished Facts," p. 8.

11. *New York Post*, March 29, 1937, p. 12.

12. Sir Arthur Conan Doyle, *The Memoirs of Sherlock Holmes* (New York: Dover, 2010), p. 17.

13. *New York Post*, March 29, 1937, p. 13; Trent, "Murder of the Model," May 15, 1937, p. 9.

14. Doyle, *The Memoirs of Sherlock Holmes*, p. 20.

15. *New York Sun*, March 29, 1937, p. 2; Trent, "Murder of the Model," May 15, 1937, p. 8.

16. Trent, "Murder of the Model," May 15, 1937, p. 8.

17. Ibid., p. 7.

18. *New York Post*, March 29, 1937, p. 12.

19. Jack Alexander, "Independent Cop—Part I," *The New Yorker*, October 3, 1936, p. 23, and "Independent Cop—Part II," *The New Yorker*, October 10, 1936, p. 30.

20. Gathje, *A Model Crime*, p. 14; Collins, *Homicide Squad*, p. 210.

21. Gathje, *A Model Crime*, pp. 7–8, 14; *New York Post*, March 29, 1937, p. 13.

22. *New York Sun*, March 29, 1937, p. 2; *New York Post*, March 29, 1937, p. 13.

23. *New York Evening Journal*, March 29, 1937, p. 3.

24. *New York Evening Journal*, March 31, 1937, p. 5; Gathje, *A Model Crime*, p. 23.

25. *New York Evening Journal*, March 29, 1937, p. 3.

Chapter 17. The Party Girl

1. Gathje, *A Model Crime*, pp. 1–2. In the same week that *Newsweek* covered the Easter Sunday Massacre, both *Time* and *Life* magazines also ran pieces on the case. See *Time*, April 12, 1937, p. 68, and *Life*, April 12, 1937, p. 31.

2. *New York Evening Journal*, March 29, 1927, pp. 1 and 15; *New York Daily News*, March 29, 1937, p. 3; Preston, "Unpublished Facts," p. 6.

3. *New York Daily News*, March 29, 1937, p. 3.

4. *New York Evening Journal*, March 29, 1937, p. 3; Collins, *Homicide Squad*, pp. 207–208.

5. Gathje, *A Model Crime*, p. 14; Leo E. McGivens, *The News: The First Fifty Years of New York's Picture Newspaper* (New York News Syndicate Co., 1969), p. 215; "Murder for Easter," pp. 67–68.

6. *New York Evening Journal*, March 29, 1937, p. 1; *New York Daily News*, March 31, 1937, p. 33; Gathje, *A Model Crime*, pp. 59–60. One nationally distributed newsstand magazine published several photographs of the fully nude Ronnie. See *Real Detective*, September 1937, pp. 23, 25.

7. Gathje, *A Model Crime*, p. 33; *New York Evening Journal*, March 29, 1937, p. 3; Peterson, "Veronica Gedeon, Model for *Inside Detective*," p. 8.

8. Collins, *Homicide Squad*, p. 213; Peterson, "Veronica Gedeon, Model for *Inside Detective*," p. 8; Gathje, *A Model Crime*, pp. 63–65; Peterson, "Veronica Gedeon, Model for *Inside Detective*," pp. 77–78; Neal Gabler, *Winchell: Gossip, Power and the Culture of Celebrity* (New York: Alfred A. Knopf, 1994), p. 71.

9. Gathje, *A Model Crime*, pp. 29–30; *New York Evening Journal*, March 29, 1937, p. 3.

10. Gathje, *A Model Crime*, p. 30; *New York Post*, March 29, 1937, p. 12.

11. *New York Post*, March 29, 1937, p. 13.
12. *New York Evening Journal*, March 30, 1937, p. 5.
13. *New York Evening Journal*, March 30, 1937, p. 5; Trent, "Murder of the Model," June 1, 1937, p. 12.
14. *New York Post*, March 29, 1937, p. 13.
15. *New York Evening Journal*, March 30, 1937, p. 5; Trent, "Murder of the Model," May 15, 1937, pp. 9, 40.
16. Preston, "Unpublished Facts," p. 76; Collins, *Homicide Squad*, p. 211.
17. *New York Post*, March 30, 1937, p. 3; *New York Evening Journal*, March 29, 1937, p. 1.
18. Benj. Morgan Vance, M.D., Acting Deputy Chief Medical Examiner, City of New York, "Examination of Fingernail Scrapings from Left Hand of Mary Gedeon Taken March 29, 1937," attached to autopsy report; *New York Evening Journal*, March 30, 1937, p. 3; Gathje, *A Model Crime*, p. 50.
19. Preston, "Unpublished Facts," p. 77; Trent, "Murder of the Model," May 15, 1937, p. 41.
20. *New York Post*, March 29, 1937, p. 12.
21. *New York Evening Journal*, March 30, 1937, p. 2, and March 31, 1937, p. 1; Gathje, *A Model Crime*, p. 77.
22. *New York Evening Journal*, March 30, 1937, p. 2; Collins, *Homicide Squad*, p. 214.
23. *New York Post*, March 29, 1937, pp. 1 and 12; Collins, *Homicide Squad*, p. 214; *New York Evening Journal*, March 30, 1937, p. 3.
24. *New York Evening Journal*, March 30, 1937, p. 2; Gathje, *A Model Crime*, pp. 35, 67.
25. *New York Post*, March 29, 1937, p. 1.
26. *New York Post*, March 30, 1937, p. 3; *New York Times*, April 16, 1976, p. 27. The best book-length study of Smith is Glen Jeansonne, *Gerald L. K. Smith: Minister of Hate* (Baton Rouge: Louisiana State University Press, 1997).
27. Preston, "Unpublished Facts," p. 78.

Chapter 18. Murder Sells

1. *New York Daily News*, April 4, 1937, p. 5.
2. *New York Daily News*, March 31, 1937, p. 31. See *Time*, April 12, 1937, p. 68.
3. *New York Daily News*, April 2, 1937, p. 37.
4. *New York Daily Mirror*, April 1, 1937, pp. 3 and 8; April 2, 1937, pp. 20 and 21; and April 4, 1937, p. 20.
5. *New York Post*, March 30, 1937, p. 3.
6. *New York Daily News*, March 31, 1937, p. 3; *New York Times*, March 31, 1937, p. 1.
7. *New York Journal*, March 30, 1937, p. 2; Trent, "Murder of the Model," June 1, 1937, p. 12; Preston, "Unpublished Facts," p. 78; Collins, *Homicide Squad*, p. 215.
8. Gathje, *A Model Crime*, p. 52.
9. Gathje, *A Model Crime*, pp. 67–70; *New York Evening Journal*, March 31, 1937, pp. 3 and 4; *New York Post*, March 31, 1937, p. 3; Preston, "Unpublished Facts," p. 79.
10. *New York Evening Journal*, April 1, 1937, p. 2; Gathje, *A Model Crime*, p. 77.
11. Preston, "Unpublished Facts," p. 79.
12. Gathje, *A Model Crime*, pp. 47–48; Peterson, "Veronica Gedeon, Model for *Inside Detective*," pp. 9, 52; *New York Daily News*, April 1, 1937, p. 10, and April 2, 1937, p. 6.

13. *New York Daily News,* April 2, 1937, p. 6; Preston, "Unpublished Facts," p. 79; Gathje, *A Model Crime,* p. 77.

14. Reynolds, *Courtroom,* p. 109.

15. Peterson, "Veronica Gedeon, Model for *Inside Detective,*" p. 52.

16. *New York Daily News,* April 2, 1937, pp. 3 and 6; Preston, "Unpublished Facts," p. 80.

17. *New York Daily News,* April 1, 1937, pp. 1 and 2; *New York Evening Journal,* April 1, 1937, p. 3; *New York Daily Mirror,* April 1, 1937, pp. 1 and 39. See also Ted Collins, ed., *New York Murders* (New York: Duell, Sloan and Pearce, 1944), pp. 237–238.

18. *New York Daily News,* April 2, 1937, p. 1; *New York Daily Mirror,* April 2, 1937, p. 18.

19. *New York Evening Journal,* April 1, 1937, pp. 1–2; *New York Daily Mirror,* April 2, 1937, p. 5.

20. Gathje, *A Model Crime,* pp. 93–94; *New York Post,* April 1, 1937, p. 1.

21. *New York Post,* April 1, 1937, p. 5.

22. *New York Daily News,* April 1, 1937, p. 6, and April 2, 1937, p. 36.

23. Ibid.; *New York Evening Journal,* April 2, 1937, p. 1; *New York Post,* April 1, 1937, p. 5.

24. *New York Evening Journal,* April 2, 1937, pp. 1 and 3; *New York Post,* April 2, 1927, pp. 1, 2, and 3; *New York Sun,* April 2, 1937, pp. 1 and 21; *New York Mirror,* April 3, 1937, pp. 1 and 3, and April 4, 1937, p. 14.

25. Preston, "Unpublished Facts," p. 80.

26. Gathje, *A Model Crime,* p. 95; *New York Daily Mirror,* April 3, 1937, p. 1; *New York Daily News,* April 3, 1937, p. 1; *New York Journal,* April 3, 1937, p. 1.

27. *New York Daily Mirror,* April 4, 1937, p. 8; *New York Daily News,* April 4, 1937, pp. 6 and 8.

28. *New York Post,* April 3, 1937, p. 1; *New York Sun,* April 3, 1937, p. 1; *New York Evening Journal,* April 3, 1937, pp. 1 and 2; *New York Mirror,* April 4, 1937, p. 3; *New York Times,* April 5, 1937, p. 40; Preston, "Unpublished Facts," p. 80; Gathje, *A Model Crime,* p. 128; Trent, "Murder of the Model," May 15, 1937, p. 8.

29. *New York Herald Tribune,* April 5, 1937, p. 1.

30. *New York Times,* April 5, 1937, p. 40; Preston, "Unpublished Facts," p. 80; Gathje, *A Model Crime,* p. 128; Trent, "Murder of the Model," May 15, 1937, p. 8; Reynolds, *Courtroom,* pp. 112–113.

Chapter 19. Prime Suspect

1. *New York Sun,* April 5, 1937, p. 2.

2. See *New York Post,* April 5, 1937, pp. 1–2; *New York Herald Tribune,* April 5, 1937, pp. 1–2; *New York Sun,* April 5, 1937, pp. 1–2.

3. *New York Post,* April 6, 1937, p. 2; Trent, "Murder of the Model," June 15, 1937, p. 12.

4. *New York Times,* April 6, 1937, p. 1, and April 9, 1937, p. 9; Jennifer Jane Marshall, "Clean Cuts: Procter & Gamble's Depression-Era Soap-Carving Contests," *Winterthur Portfolio,* Vol. 42, No. 1 (Spring 2008), pp. 51–52; Candice Jacobson Fuhrman, *Publicity Stunt!: Great Staged Events that Made the News* (San Francisco: Chronicle Books, 1989), p. 131. Fuhrman's book illustrates how readily truth gets inflated into legend. In her telling, "A New York City soap carver took a turn at practicing his art on a young woman and her mother. Hiding in the home of his

victims while they were out, he gathered a number of cakes of soap from around the house and started carving, and by the time the women returned home he had finished a number of pieces. He then killed them both and fled the scene of the crime, leaving the bodies and the completed soap sculptures. Police brought in Henry Bern, the public relations counsel for the contest, who after many years of judging contests was an expert on carving style. He instantly recognized the work of the previous year's winner."

5. *New York Post,* April 6, 1937, p. 2; *New York Times,* April 6, 1937, p. 6.
6. *New York Daily Mirror,* April 6, 1937, p. 13; *New York Evening Journal,* April 6, 1937, p. 3; *New York Sun,* April 6, 1937, p. 1.
7. *New York Daily Mirror,* April 6, 1937, p. 3.
8. *New York Post,* April 5, 1937, p. 1; *New York Daily Mirror,* April 6, 1937, p. 3; *New York Evening Journal,* April 6, 1937, p. 1; *New York Daily News,* April 6, 1937, p. 3.

Chapter 20. Manhunt

1. *New York Post,* April 5, 1937, p. 15, and April 6, 1937, p. 1; *New York Daily News,* April 7, 1937, pp. 3 and 10; *New York Evening Journal,* April 6, 1937, pp. 1 and 3; Gathje, *A Model Crime,* p. 120; *New York Sun,* April 6, 1937, pp. 1 and 19. On March 22, 1938, Joseph Gedeon would receive a suspended sentence of his possession of an unlicensed pistol. See *New York Times,* March 23, 1938, p. 46.
2. *New York Herald Tribune,* April 5, 1937, p. 2; *New York Post,* April 5, 1937, p. 2; *New York Sun,* April 5, 1937, p. 2.
3. *New York Post,* April 6, 1937, p. 1; *New York Daily News,* April 7, 1937, pp. 6 and 8.
4. *New York Evening Journal,* April 6, 1937, p. 1; *New York Daily Mirror,* April 9, 1937, p. 3.
5. *New York Evening Journal,* April 6, 1937, pp. 1 and 2.
6. *New York Daily News,* April 9, 1937, p. 3.
7. *New York Daily Mirror,* April 7, 1937, p. 4.
8. *New York Daily News,* April 7, 1937, p. 6; *New York Daily Mirror,* April 7, 1937, p. 3; *New York Evening Journal,* April 7, 1937, p. 1.
9. *New York Daily News,* April 9, 1937, pp. 3 and 6; *New York Journal,* April 12, 1937, p. 1.
10. *New York Evening Journal,* April 7, 1937, p. 1; *New York Daily News,* April 7, 1937, p. 3.
11. *New York Evening Journal,* April 7, 1937, p. 3.
12. *New York Daily News,* April 9, 1937, p. 3, and April 10, 1937, p. 1; *New York Times,* April 9, 1937, p. 9.
13. *New York Daily News,* April 9, 1937, p. 3; *New York Times,* April 11, 1937, p. 33; *New York Daily Mirror,* April 13, 1937, p. 3.
14. Gathje, *A Model Crime,* p. 121.
15. *New York Evening Journal,* April 8, 1937, p. 4.
16. *New York Daily News,* April 10, 1937, p. 1; *New York Daily Mirror,* April 11, 1937, p. 3.
17. "Robert Irwin's Own Life Story," *New York Daily News,* April 12, 1937, pp. 3 and 8; April 13, 1937, pp. 2 and 17; April 14, 1937, pp. 3 and 6; April 15, 1937, pp. 3 and 6; and April 16, 1937, p. 6.

18. *New York Evening Journal*, April 13, 1937, pp. 1 and 10; *New York Herald Tribune*, April 14, 1937, p. 4; *New York Sun*, April 13, 1937, p. 1; *New York Daily Mirror*, April 14, 1937, p. 3.

19. *New York Daily Mirror*, April 16, 1937, and April 11, 1937, p. 3; *New York Post*, April 15, 1937, p. 3; *New York Daily News*, April 15, 1937, p. 6; *New York Evening Journal*, April 15, 1937, p. 1.

20. *New York Evening Journal*, April 15, 1937, p. 1.

21. *New York Sun*, June 28, 1937, p. 3

Chapter 21. Murder in Times Square

1. *New York Daily News*, April 19, 1937, pp. 3 and 8; April 20, 1937, pp. 3 and 6; and April 21, 1937, pp. 3 and 6. *New York Times*, April 19, 1937, p. 1; April 20, 1937, p. 1; and April 21, 1937, p. 48. *New York Evening Journal*, April 19, 1937, pp. 1 and 3; April 20, 1937, pp. 1 and 2; and April 21, 1937, p. 4. *New York Post*, April 19, 1937, pp. 1 and 2, and April 20, 1937, p. 3. *New York Sun*, April 19, 1937, pp. 1 and 15.

2. *New York Daily News*, April 22, 1937, pp. 1 and 6; June 8, 1937, p. 2; and June 22, 1937, p. 4. *New York Times*, April 22, 1937, p. 48; June 8, 1937, p. 21; and June 22, 1937, p. 9. *New York Evening Journal*, June 7, 1937, p. 1, and June 21, 1937, p. 1.

Chapter 22. Henrietta

1. Ted Schwarz, *Shocking Stories of the Cleveland Mob* (Charleston, SC: The History Press, 2010), pp. 10, 12, 35, 36.

2. See *Inside Detective*, October 1937, p. 6; *New York Daily News*, June 27, 1937, p. 4.

3. Peterson, "Veronica Gedeon, Model for *Inside Detective*," pp. 8–9.

4. *Inside Detective*, October 1937, p. 9; *New York Sun*, June 26, 1937, p. 24; Gathje, *A Model Crime*, pp. 145–146.

5. *Inside Detective*, October 1937, p. 40.

6. *New York Daily News*, June 27, 1937, p. 4.

Chapter 23. The Front Page

1. All details of Irwin's flight are taken from his confession as reprinted in Valentine, *Night Stick*, pp. 172–182.

2. Gathje, *A Model Crime*, p. 148.

3. Robert Casey, *Such Interesting People* (Indianapolis: Bobbs-Merrill, 1943), p. 273.

4. *New York Post*, June 28, 1937, p. 2.

5. For a lively account of the Wanderer case, see Michael Lesy, *Murder City: The Bloody History of Chicago in the Twenties* (New York: W. W. Norton, 2007), pp. 9–27.

6. See Ben Hecht and Charles MacArthur, *The Front Page: From Theater and Reality*, ed. George W. Hilton (Hanover, NH: Smith and Kraus, 2002).

7. George Johanssen, "What Manner of Man Is This?," *Inside Detective*, October 1937, p. 10; Gathje, *A Model Crime*, pp. 149–150; Reynolds, *Courtroom*, pp. 121–122.

Chapter 24. Confession

1. Report of B. G. Dodge, p. 8.

2. Valentine, *Night Stick*, pp. 172–182; Robert Irwin, "Why I Killed the Beautiful Artist's Model," *Real Detective*, September 1937, pp. 20–25, 67–68.

Chapter 25. Celebrities

1. Gathje, *A Model Crime*, p. 153; Reynolds, *Courtroom*, p. 122.
2. *New York Post*, June 28, 1937, p. 1; Gathje, *A Model Crime*, p. 159.
3. Leibowitz, *The Defender, Casebook II*, p. 324; *Charleston Gazette*, June 28, 1937, p. 1.
4. *New York Daily News*, June 28, 1937, p. 6.
5. Ibid.; Leibowitz, *The Defender, Casebook II*, p. 324.
6. *New York Daily News*, June 28, 1937, p. 3; *New York Herald Tribune*, June 28, 1937, pp. 3 and 7; Gathje, *A Model Crime*, p. 160.
7. *New York Daily Mirror*, June 28, 1937, p.14; *New York Post*, June 28, 1937, p. 3; Reynolds, *Courtroom*, p. 158.
8. *New York Post*, June 28, 1937, p. 2.
9. Valentine, *Night Stick*, p. 183; Reynolds, *Courtroom*, pp. 123–124.
10. Wertham, *The Show of Violence*, pp. 101–106; "Statement of Robert Irwin, at Police Headquarters, June 28, 1937," Box 21, Folder 10, Papers of Fredric Wertham; Reynolds, *Courtroom*, p. 128.
11. *New York Post*, June 30, 1937, p. 6.
12. All citations are from the following newspapers: *New York Sun*, June 28, 1937, pp. 1, 2, and 3; *New York Post*, June 28, 1937, pp. 1, 2, and 3; *New York Daily News*, June 28, 1937, pp. 3, 6, 9, 10, 11, 14, 22, 24, and 25; *New York Herald Tribune*, June 28, 1937, pp. 1 and 3; *New York Daily Mirror*, June 28, 1937, pp. 3, 4, 6, 7, 8, 12, and 14.
13. *New York Times*, June 28, 1937, p. 6.
14. *New York Post*, June 29, 1937, p. 8.
15. The AP story was syndicated in newspapers around the country. This quote is from the *Moberly [MO] Monitor-Index*, June 28, 1937, p. 1.
16. "She Spotted Killer Irwin!," *Inside Detective*, October 1937, p. 49; *New York Daily Mirror*, June 28, 1937, p. 9; *New York Daily News*, June 29, 1937, p. 8; *New York Sun*, June 28, 1937, p. 3, and June 29, 1937, p. 2; *New York Daily Mirror*, June 30, 1937, p. 5; Gathje, *A Model Crime*, pp. 168–170.
17. *New York Daily Mirror*, June 30, 1937, p. 5.
18. *New York Times*, June 30, 1937, p. 46.
19. *New York Post*, June 28, 1937, p. 8.
20. *New York Herald Tribune*, June 30, 1937, p. 4.
21. *New York Daily News*, June 28, 1937, p. 14.
22. See Martha P. Nochimson, *No End to Her: Soap Opera and the Female Subject* (Berkeley: University of California Press, 1993), p. 21.
23. *New York Daily Mirror*, July 2, 1937, p. 6.
24. *New York Daily News*, June 29, 1937, p. 8.
25. *New York Journal-American*, July 4, 1937, p. 1-3.
26. *New York Daily Mirror*, June 28, 1937, p. 14.
27. Ibid., p. 5.
28. *New York Sun*, June 30, 1937, p. 7; *New York Post*, June 30, 1937, p. 6; *New York Daily Mirror*, July 1, 1937, p. 3; Dan T. Carter, *Scottsboro: A Tragedy of the American South* (Baton Rouge: Louisiana State University Press, 2007), p. 367.
29. *New York Daily Mirror*, July 2, 1937, p. 8.

30. Wertham, *The Show of Violence*, p. 139.
31. *New York Daily News*, June 28, 1937, p. 3; *New York American*, June 28, 1937, p. 3.
32. See Leibowitz, *The Defender, Casebook II*, p. 348.
33. *New York Daily News*, July 29, 1937, p. 29.

Chapter 26. Lunacy

1. A typescript of Leibowitz's talk is filed in Box 21, Folder 5, Papers of Fredric Wertham.
2. Reynolds, *Courtroom*, pp. 130–131; Wertham, *The Show of Violence*, pp. 151–156.
3. *New York Times*, July 25, 1937, p. 1; July 26, 1937, p. 1; and July 30, 1937, p. 8.
4. Reynolds, *Courtroom*, p. 133; Leibowitz, *The Defender, Casebook II*, p. 349.
5. *New York Evening Journal*, July 2, 1937, p. 4.
6. Leibowitz, *The Defender, Casebook II*, p. 349.
7. *New York Daily Mirror*, August 31, 1937, pp. 3 and 6; *New York Daily News*, August 31, 1937, pp. 2 and 16.
8. *New York Times*, September 1, 1937, p. 20; Reynolds, *Courtroom*, pp. 141–142; Leibowitz, *The Defender, Casebook II*, pp. 355–356.
9. *New York Times*, August 27, 1937, p. 22, and August 31, 1937, p. 13.
10. Benjamin Apfelberg, "Experiences with a New Criminal Code in New York State," *American Journal of Psychiatry*, Vol. 98 (November 1941), p. 415.
11. *New York Times*, February 4, 1938, p. 22. The only psychiatrist who seems not have been fooled was Fredric Wertham, who insisted that Lavin was "simulating insanity" and was almost "certain to commit another murder."
12. Thomas C. Desmond, "New York Smashes the Lunacy Commission 'Racket,'" *Journal of Criminal Law and Criminology*, Vol. 30, No. 5 (January–February 1940), p. 654; Apfelberg, "Experiences with a New Criminal Code," p. 417.
13. Wertham, *The Show of Violence*, p. 141.
14. *New York Times*, March 25, 1938, p. 4.
15. Leibowitz, *The Defender, Casebook II*, p. 357.
16. Ibid., p. 360.
17. Wertham, *The Show of Violence*, p. 142.
18. Reynolds, *Courtroom*, p. 139.
19. Archibald R. Watson et al., "The People *Versus* Robert Irwin, Charged with the Murder of Three Persons. Report of Commissioners in Lunacy. In the Matter of the Examination into the Mental Condition of the Above Named Robert Irwin, an Alleged Lunatic," *American Journal of Psychiatry*, Vol. 95, No. 1 (July 1938), p. 225.
20. See Wertham, *The Show of Violence*, pp. 144–145.
21. Reynolds, *Courtroom*, p. 140.
22. *New York Times*, March 25, 1938, p. 4.

Chapter 27. Plea

1. For a solid book-length study of the Hans Schmidt case, see Mark Gado, *Killer Priest: The Crimes, Trial, and Execution of Father Hans Schmidt* (Westport, CT: Praeger, 2006).
2. See Reynolds, *Courtroom*, p. 133; Leibowitz, *The Defender, Casebook II*, pp. 364–365.
3. For more on Glueck, see Simon Baatz, *For the Thrill of It: Leopold, Loeb, and the Murder That Shocked Chicago* (New York: HarperCollins, 2008).

4. Hinsie, "The Psychopathology of Murder," p. 18.
5. Ibid, pp. 7, 14–16; Reynolds, *Courtroom*, p. 137.
6. Hinsie, "The Psychopathology of Murder," pp. 17–18, 20.
7. Reynolds, *Courtroom*, p. 142; Leibowitz, *The Defender, Casebook II*, p. 372.
8. Reynolds, *Courtroom*, p. 143.
9. *New York Daily Mirror*, November 7, 1938, p. 3.
10. Ibid.
11. *New York Daily Mirror*, November 8, 1937, p. 2.
12. Ibid.
13. See *New York Times*, May 30, 1937, p. 60; August 29, 1937, p. 35; and December 26, 1937, p. 67.
14. *New York Evening Journal*, July 2, 1937, p. 4.
15. *New York Times*, September 9, 1937, p. 25.
16. Gathje, *A Model Crime*, p. 186; *New York Daily News*, November 8, 1937, pp. 3 and 10.
17. Leibowitz, *The Defender, Casebook II*, p. 374.
18. Reynolds, *Courtroom*, p. 144; Leibowitz, *The Defender, Casebook II*, pp. 375–376.
19. *New York Daily Mirror*, November 7, 1938, p. 3.
20. *New York Daily Mirror*, November 8, 1938, p. 2; *New York Times*, November 11, 1938, p. 52.
21. See Reynolds, *Courtroom*, p. 146.
22. *New York Daily Mirror*, November 11, 1938, p. 3.
23. *New York Daily News*, November 16, 1938, p. 23.
24. *New York Times*, November 15, 1938, p. 1.
25. Ibid., p. 16; Reynolds, *Courtroom*, p. 147.
26. *New York Times*, November 15, 1938, p. 24.
27. Gathje, *A Model Crime*, p. 191.
28. *New York Daily News*, November 18, 1938, p. 16.
29. Leibowitz, *The Defender, Casebook II*, p. 383.

Chapter 28. Aftermath

1. *New York Daily News*, November 8, 1938, p. 3; *New York Daily Mirror*, November 8, 1938, p. 5; *New York Times*, November 10, 1938, p. 22.
2. *New York Post*, November 28, 1938, pp. 1 and 3; *New York Times*, November 29, 1938, p. 48; *New York Daily News*, November 29, 1938, pp. 3 and 8; *New York Herald Tribune*, November 29, 1938, p. 3.
3. *New York Post*, November 28, 1938, p. 1; *New York Daily News*, November 29, 1938, p. 3.
4. *New York Herald Tribune*, November 29, 1938, p. 3; Gathje, *A Model Crime*, p. 193.
5. The description of Bob's cartoon comes from Leibowitz, *The Defender, Casebook II*, p. 385. Bob's feelings about Sing Sing are recorded in a Christmas card he wrote to Fredric Wertham on December 21, 1938. It is filed in Box 21, Folder 4, Papers of Fredric Wertham. All subsequent quotes from Irwin's correspondence are from the cards and letters contained in the same file.
6. Wertham, *The Show of Violence*, p. 165; Gathje, *A Model Crime*, p. 194.
7. *Syracuse Herald*, December 11, 1938, p. 4.
8. Christmas card to Fredric Wertham, December 21, 1938.

9. Letter to Fredric Wertham, January 23, 1941; Reynolds, *Courtroom*, p. 150.
10. Letter to Florence Hesketh, January 25, 1945. The passage was reprinted in Leonard Lyons's *New York Post* column, "The Lyons Den," on February 9, 1945, p. 22, and later quoted by Wertham in *The Show of Violence*, p. 183.
11. See Irwin's letter to Wertham, January 23, 1941; Wertham's letter to Irwin, March 6, 1939; and Wertham, *The Show of Violence*, p. 183.
12. Letter to Fredric Wertham, January 23, 1941.
13. Christmas card to Fredric and Florence Wertham, December 1942.
14. Letters to Fredric Wertham, December 4, 1944, and January 25, 1945; letter to Florence Hesketh, January 1, 1948.
15. Hinsie, "The Psychopathology of Murder," p. 19.
16. *New York Post*, April 16, 1951, p. 28.
17. *New York Times*, August 1, 1940, p. 23.
18. "The Crime of Appeasement," *Detective Tales*, September 1940, p. 4.
19. Theodore Dreiser, "Good and Evil," *North American Review*, Vol. 266, No. 1 (Autumn 1938), pp. 76–77. A condensed version of the essay forms the epilogue of Dreiser's 1947 novel, *The Stoic*.
20. See Randy Hendricks and James A. Perkins, eds., *Selected Letters of Robert Penn Warren, Volume Three: Triumph and Transition, 1943–1952* (Baton Rouge: Louisiana State University Press, 2006), pp. 67–68. The murder scene can be found in Robert Penn Warren, *At Heaven's Gate* (New York: New Directions, 1985), pp. 360–363.
21. Thomas Berger, *Killing Time* (New York: The Dial Press, 1967). According to Brooks Landon, "Berger drew much of his information from . . . Quentin Reynolds's *Courtroom* and Fredric Wertham's *The Show of Violence*." See Landon, *Thomas Berger* (Boston: Twayne Publishers, 1989), p. 67.
22. "Samuel S. Leibowitz, 84, Jurist and Scottsboro Case Lawyer, Dies," *New York Times*, January 12, 1978, p. B2; "Jurist Before the Bar," *Time*, November 15, 1963, pp. 70–71.

Epilogue: The Lonergan Case

1. Raymond Chandler, "Ten Greatest Crimes of the Century," *Cosmopolitan*, October 1948, pp. 50–53.
2. The main works on the Lonergan case are Mel Heimer, *The Girl in Murder Flat* (New York: Fawcett/Gold Medal, 1955) and Hamilton Darby Perry, *A Chair for Wayne Lonergan* (New York: Macmillan, 1971). Dominick Dunne has a lively chapter on the case in his collection *Justice: Crimes, Trials, and Punishments* (New York: Crown, 2001).
3. Dunne, *Justice*, p. 275.
4. Ibid., p. 273.
5. Ibid., p. 277.
6. Heimer, *The Girl in Murder Flat*, p. 12.
7. Perry, *A Chair for Wayne Lonergan*, pp. 42–45.
8. Dunne, *Justice*, pp. 281–282; Perry, *A Chair for Wayne Lonergan*, pp. 40–41, 51.
9. Perry, *A Chair for Wayne Lonergan*, pp. 249–251; Heimer, *The Girl in Murder Flat*, pp. 23–24; Dunne, *Justice*, pp. 285–286. Lonergan was released in 1967, was deported to Canada, and lived quietly in Toronto until his death of cancer at the age

of sixty-seven on January 2, 1986. See Albin Krebbs, "Wayne Lonergan, 67, Killer of Heiress Wife," *New York Times*, January 3, 1986, p. B5.

10. *New York Journal-American*, October 29, 1943, p. 3. Quoted by Dunne, *Justice*, p. 272.

11. See Jack O'Brian, "Murder Murk Hangs Over Fashionable Beekman Hill," *Milwaukee Journal*, November 2, 1943, p. 1. The AP article was syndicated nationwide.

Bibliography

Aitken, William B. *Distinguished Families in America, Descended from Wilhelmus Beek-man and Jan Thomasse Van Dyke*. New York: G. P. Putnam's Sons/The Knicker-bocker Press, 1912.

Albanese, Catherine L. *A Republic of Mind and Spirit: A Cultural History of American Metaphysical Religion*. New Haven, CT: Yale University Press, 2007.

Alexander, Estrelda Y. *Limited Liberty: The Legacy of Four Pentecostal Women Pioneers*. Cleveland: The Pilgrim Press, 2008.

———. *The Women of Azusa Street*. Cleveland: The Pilgrim Press, 2005.

Alexander, Jack. "Independent Cop." *The New Yorker*, October 3, 1936, pp. 21–27; October 10, 1936, pp. 26–30; October 17, 1936, pp. 30–32, 36, 39–40.

Allen, Frederick Lewis. *Since Yesterday: The 1930s in America, September 3, 1929–September 3, 1939*. New York: Harper & Row/Perennial Library, 1972.

Apfelberg, Benjamin. "Experiences with a New Criminal Code in New York State." *American Journal of Psychiatry*, Vol. 98 (November 1941), pp. 415–421.

Baatz, Simon. *For the Thrill of It: Leopold, Loeb, and the Murder that Shocked Chicago*. New York: HarperCollins, 2008.

Balmer, Randall Herbert. *Encyclopedia of Evangelism*. Louisville, KY: John Knox Press, 2002.

Barnes, Harry Elmer, and Negley K. Teeters. *New Horizons in Criminology: The American Crime Problem*. New York: Prentice-Hall, 1943.

Bartleman, Frank. *Azusa Street*. New Kensington, PA: Whitaker House, 1982.

Beaty, Bart. *Fredric Wertham and the Critique of Mass Culture*. Jackson: University of Mississippi, 2005.

Berger, Thomas. *Killing Time*. New York: The Dial Press, 1967.

Bessie, Simon Michael. *Jazz Journalism: The Story of the Tabloid Newspaper.* New York: E. P. Dutton & Co., 1938.

Blum, Deborah. *The Poisoner's Handbook: Murder and the Birth of Forensic Medicine in Jazz Age New York.* New York: The Penguin Press, 2010.

Blumhofer, Edith L. *Restoring the Faith: The Assemblies of God, Pentecostalism, and American Culture.* Urbana and Chicago: University of Illinois Press, 1993.

Boswell, Charles, and Lewis Thompson. *Curriculum of Murder.* New York: Collier Books, 1962.

Brewster, Dorothy, ed. *A Book of Contemporary Short Stories.* New York: Macmillan, 1936.

Bromberg, Walter. *The Mold of Murder: A Psychiatric Study of Homicide.* New York and London: Grune and Stratton, 1961.

———. *Psychiatry Between the Wars, 1918–1945: A Recollection.* Westport, CT: Greenwood Press, 1982.

Bromberg, Walter, and Charles B. Thompson. "The Relation of Psychosis, Mental Defect and Personality Types to Crime." *Journal of Criminal Law and Criminology,* Vol. 28, No. 1 (May–June 1937), pp. 70–89.

Brooks, Landon. *Thomas Berger.* Boston: Twayne Publishers, 1989.

Bryant, John. *Convalescence: Historical and Practical.* White Plains, NY: The Sturgis Fund of the Burke Foundation, 1927.

Bushmaster, Morty. *Hubert's Dime Museum & Flea Circus: An Underground History.* New York: Book Whisperer Press, 2008.

Carey, John. "'He's on Parole.'" *Journal of Criminal Law and Criminology,* Vol. 30, No. 5 (January–February 1940), pp. 741–749.

Carter, C. F. "Fantastic Fanaticisms." *Scrap Book,* Vol. 5, No. 3 (March 1908), p. 406.

Carter, Dan T. *Scottsboro: A Tragedy of the American South.* Baton Rouge: Louisiana State University Press, 2007.

Casey, Robert. *Such Interesting People.* Indianapolis: Bobbs-Merrill, 1943.

Chandler, Raymond. "Ten Greatest Crimes of the Century." *Cosmopolitan,* October 1948, pp. 50–53.

Chávez-García, Miroslava. "Intelligence Testing at Whittier School, 1890–1920." *Pacific Historical Review,* Vol. 76, No. 2 (May 2007), pp. 193–228.

Collins, Cornelius F. "N.Y. Court Requests Psychiatric Service Clinic for Criminals Supplemental Memorandum." *Journal of the American Institute for Criminal Law and Criminology,* Vol. 19, No. 3 (November 1928), pp. 337–343.

———. "Treatment of Criminals in the Court of General Sessions of the County of New York." *Journal of Criminal Law and Criminology,* Vol. 24, No. 4 (November–December 1933), pp. 700–711.

Collins, Frederick L. *Homicide Squad: Adventures of a Headquarters Old Timer.* New York: G. P. Putnam's Sons, 1944.

Collins, Ted, ed. *New York Murders.* New York: Duell Sloan and Pearce, 1944.

Cooper, Page. *The Bellevue Story.* New York: Thomas Y. Crowell, 1948.

Davenport, Frederick Morgan. *Primitive Traits in Religious Revivals.* New York: Macmillan, 1905.

Delaney, Edmund T. *New York's Turtle Bay Old & New.* Barre, MA: Barre Publishers, 1965.

Desmond, Thomas C. "New York Smashes the Lunacy Commission 'Racket.'" *Journal of Criminal Law and Criminology*, Vol. 30, No. 5 (January–February 1940), pp. 653–661.

Douglas, Kirk. *The Ragman's Son: An Autobiography.* New York: Simon & Schuster, 1988.

Doyle, Sir Arthur Conan. *The Memoirs of Sherlock Holmes.* New York: Dover, 2010.

Dreiser, Theodore. "Good and Evil." *North American Review*, Vol. 266, No. 1 (Autumn 1938), pp. 67–86.

Dresser, Horatio W. *A History of the New Thought Movement.* New York: Thomas Y. Crowell, 1919.

Duncombe, Stephen, and Andrew Mattson. *The Bobbed Haired Bandit: A True Story of Crime and Celebrity in 1920s New York.* New York: New York University Press, 2006.

Dunlap, W. C. *Life of S. Miller Willis, The Fire Baptized Evangelist. A Man Who Literally Took God at His Word for Twenty-six Years, and Yet Never Wanted for Any Good Thing.* Atlanta, GA: Constitution Publishing Co., 1892.

Dunne, Dominick. *Justice: Crimes, Trials, and Punishments.* New York: Crown Publishers, 2001.

Durant, Will. *The Story of Philosophy: The Lives and Opinions of the Greater Philosophers.* New York: Washington Square Press, 1953.

Edmiston, Susan, and Linda D. Cirino. *Literary New York: A History and Guide.* New York: Gibbs Smith, 1991.

Evans, Colin. *Blood on the Table: The Greatest Cases of New York City's Office of the Chief Medical Examiner.* New York: Berkley Books, 2008.

Faurot, Joseph A. "The Inside Story of New York's Bathtub Slaying." *Official Detective Stories*, July 1936, pp. 3–7, 43–44.

Federal Writers' Project. *New York City Guide: A Comprehensive Guide to the Five Boroughs of the Metropolis—Manhattan, Brooklyn, the Bronx, Queens, and Richmond—Prepared by the Federal Writers' Project of the Work Progress Administration in New York City.* New York: Random House, 1939.

Fisher, Jim. *The Lindbergh Case.* New Brunswick, NJ: Rutgers University Press, 1994.

Freedman, Estelle B. "'Uncontrolled Desires': The Response to the Sexual Psychopath, 1920–1960." *Journal of American History*, Vol. 74, No. 1 (June 1987), pp. 83–106.

Friedman, Andrea. "'The Habitats of Sex-Crazed Perverts': Campaigns Against Burlesque in Depression-Era New York City." *Journal of the History of Sexuality*, Vol. 7, No. 2 (October 1996), pp. 203–238.

Friedman, Ralph. *Tracking Down Oregon.* Caldwell, ID: Caxton, 1978.

Fuhrman, Candice Jacobson. *Publicity Stunt!: Great Staged Events That Made the News.* San Francisco: Chronicle Books, 1989.

Fuller, Henry B. "Notes on Lorado Taft." *Century*, Vol. 76 (October 1908), pp. 618–621.

Gabler, Neal. *Winchell: Gossip, Power and the Culture of Celebrity.* New York: Alfred A. Knopf, 1994.

Gado, Mark. *Killer Priest: The Crimes, Trial, and Execution of Father Hans Schmidt.* Westport, CT: Paeger, 2006.

Gaines, Steven. *The Sky's the Limit: Passion and Property in Manhattan.* New York: Little, Brown, 2005.

Galbraith, John Kenneth. *The Great Crash, 1929.* Cambridge, MA: Houghton Mifflin, 1955.

Garland, Hamlin. "The Art of Lorado Taft." *Mentor*, Vol. 11 (October 1923), pp. 19–34.

———. *A Daughter of the Middle Border.* New York: Macmillan, 1921.

Garvey, Timothy J. *Public Sculptor: Lorado Taft and the Beautification of Chicago*. Urbana: University of Illinois Press, 1988.

Gathje, Curtis. *A Model Crime: A True Fiction*. New York: Donald I. Fine, 1995.

Gilbert, James. *Cycle of Outrage: America's Reaction to the Juvenile Delinquent in the 1950s*. New York: Oxford University Press, 1986.

Godtland, Eric. *True Crime Detective Magazines, 1924–1969*. Cologne, Germany: Taschen, 2008.

Haines, Max. *Murders Strange But True*. New York: Signet, 1997.

Hajdu, David. *The Ten-Cent Plague: The Great Comic-Book Scare and How It Changed America*. New York: Farrar, Straus and Giroux, 2008.

Hanlon, Pamela. *Manhattan's Turtle Bay: Story of a Midtown Neighborhood*. Charleston, SC: Arcadia Books, 2008.

Hecht, Ben, and Charles MacArthur. *The Front Page: From Theater and Reality*. Edited by George W. Hilton. Hanover, NH: Smith and Kraus, 2002.

Heimer, Mel. *The Girl in Murder Flat*. New York: Fawcett/Gold Medal, 1955.

Hendricks, Randy, and James A. Perkins, eds. *Selected Letters of Robert Penn Warren, Volume Three: Triumph and Transition, 1943–1952*. Baton Rouge: Louisiana State University Press, 2006.

Hinsie, L. E. "A Contribution to the Psychopathology of Murder—Study of a Case." *Criminal Psychopathology*, Vol. 2, No. 1 (July 1940), pp. 1–20.

Holmes, Nickels J., and Lucy Elizabeth Simpson Holmes. *Life Sketches and Sermons*. Royston, GA: Press of the Pentecostal Holiness Church, 1920.

Horsley, Lee. "Dead Dolls and Deadly Dames: The Cover Girls of American True Crime Publishing," in *Crime Culture: Figuring Criminality in Fiction and Film*, edited by Bran Nicol, Patricia Pulham, and Eugene McNulty, pp. 109–121. London: Continuum, 2011.

Hynd, Alan. *Murder, Mayhem, and Mystery: An Album of American Crime*. New York: A. S. Barnes and Company, 1958.

Irwin, B. H. "My Pentecostal Baptism—A Christmas Gift." *Triumphs of Faith* (May 1907), pp. 114–117.

Jakoubek, Robert. *Jack Johnson: Heavyweight Champion*. New York: Chelsea House, 1990.

Jelliffe, Smith Ely. "Why Do Such Things Happen?" *Cosmopolitan*, July 1937, pp. 56–57, 170–171.

Johanssen, George. "What Manner of Man is This?" *Inside Detective*, October 1937, pp. 10–15, 51–52.

Johnston, Alva. "Let Freedom Ring." *The New Yorker*, June 4, 1932, pp. 21–24; June 11, 1932, pp. 18–23.

Kahn, E. J., Jr. *The World of Swope*. New York: Simon and Schuster, 1965.

Kilgallen, Dorothy. *Murder One*. New York: Random House, 1967.

Kingsley, Sidney. *Dead End: A Play in Three Acts*. New York: Random House, 1936.

Klebanow, Diana, and Franklin L. Jonas. *People's Lawyers: Crusaders for Justice in American History*. Armonk, NY: M. E. Sharpe, 2003.

Klein, Maury. *Rainbow's End: The Crash of 1929*. New York: Oxford University Press, 2003.

Knox, Sara L. *Murder: A Tale of Modern American Life*. Durham, NC: Duke University Press, 1998.

Kuhn, Irene. *Assigned to Adventure*. Philadelphia: J. P. Lippincott, 1938.

Landon, Brooks. *Thomas Berger*. Boston: Twayne Publishers, 1989.

Lardner, James, and Thomas Repetto. *NYPD: A City and Its Police*. New York: Henry Holt, 2000.

Lave, Tamara Rice. "Only Yesterday: The Rise and Fall of Twentieth Century Sexual Psychopath Laws." *Louisiana Law Review*, No. 69 (April 2009), pp. 549–591.

Leibowitz, Robert. *The Defender: The Life and Career of Samuel S. Leibowitz, 1893–1933*. Englewood Cliffs, NJ: Prentice-Hall, 1981.

———. *The Defender, Casebook II: The Life and Career of Samuel S. Leibowitz, 1933–1941*. Denville, NJ: SBC Enterprises, 2004.

Lesy, Michael. *Murder City: The Bloody History of Chicago in the Twenties*. New York: W. W. Norton, 2007.

Liardon, Roberts. *The Azusa Street Revival: When The Fire Fell*. Shippensburg, PA: Destiny Press, 2006.

Lockwood, Charles. *Manhattan Moves Uptown: An Illustrated History*. New York: Barnes & Noble, 1976.

Lothrop, Gloria Ricci, ed. *Fulfilling the Promise of California: An Anthology of Essays on the Italian American Experience in California*. Spokane, WA: Arthur H. Clark Company, 2000.

Love, Robert. *The Great Oom: The Improbable Birth of Yoga in America*. New York: Viking, 2010.

Lowndes, Susan, ed. *Diaries and Letters of Marie Belloc Lowndes, 1911–1947*. London: Chatto & Windus, 1971.

Marshall, Jennifer Jane. "Clean Cuts: Procter & Gamble's Depression-Era Soap-Carving Contests." *Winterthur Portfolio*, Vol. 42, No. 1 (Spring 2008), pp. 51–76.

McDowell, John Hugh. *History of the McDowells, Erwins, Irwins and Connections (Being a Compilation from Various Sources)*. Memphis, TN: C. B. Johnson & Co., 1918.

McGivnes, Leo E. *The News: The First Fifty Years of New York's Picture Newspaper*. New York: News Syndicate Co., 1969.

Mendes, Gabriel N. "A Deeper Science: Richard Wright, Dr. Fredric Wertham, and the Fight for Mental Health Care in Harlem, NY, 1940–1960." PhD diss., Brown University, 2010.

Messinger, Emanuel, and Benjamin Apfelberg. "A Quarter Century of Court Psychiatry." *Crime & Delinquency*, Vol. 7, No. 4 (1961), pp. 343–362.

Moler, A. B. *The Manual of Beauty Culture*. n.p., 1911.

Morgan, David. "N. J. Holmes and the Origins of Pentecostalism." *South Carolina Historical Magazine*, Vol. 84, No. 3 (July 1983), pp. 136–151.

Morris, Charles E., III. "Pink Herring & The Fourth Persona: J. Edgar Hoover's Sex Crime Panic." *Quarterly Journal of Speech*, Vol. 88, No. 2 (May 2002), pp. 228–244.

Morris, Lloyd: *Incredible New York: High Life and Low Life of the Last Hundred Years*. New York: Random House, 1951.

Mose, Ruth Helming. "Midway Studio." *American Magazine of Art*, Vol. 19, No. 8 (August 1928), pp. 413–422.

Nast, William. "The Berlin Conference." *Methodist Quarterly Review*, Vol. 40 (July 1858), pp. 432–436.

Nelles, F. C. "Purposes of the Whittier State School." *Los Angeles School Journal*, Vol. 6, No. 8 (January 15, 1923), pp. 24–25.

Nochimson, Martha P. *No End to Her: Soap Opera and the Female Subject*. Berkeley: University of California Press, 1993.

Overholzer, Winfred. "The Place of Psychiatry in the Criminal Law." *Psychiatric Quarterly*, Vol. 10, No. 2 (1936), pp. 197–223.

Parham, Sarah E. *The Life of Charles F. Parham, Founder of the Apostolic Faith Movement*. Baxter Springs, KS: Apostolic Faith Bible College, 1930, pp. 52–53.

Pasley, Fred D. *Not Guilty: The Story of Samuel S. Leibowitz*. New York: G. P. Putnam's Sons, 1933.

Perry, Hamilton Darby. *A Chair for Wayne Lonergan*. New York: Macmillan, 1972.

Peterson, West F. "Veronica Gedeon, Model for *Inside Detective,* Is Murdered." *Inside Detective*, July 1937, pp. 6–12, 52–54.

Pollens, Bertram. *The Sex Criminal*. New York: Macaulay Company, 1938.

Porter, Edward Sefton. *Conscience of the Court*. Englewood Cliffs, NJ: Prentice-Hall, 1962.

Preston, Francis C. "Unpublished Facts in New York's Artist Model Murders." *True Detective Mysteries*, September 1937, pp. 4–10, 76–82.

Price, Sue A., ed. *The Old Guard and the Avant-Garde: Modernism in Chicago, 1910–1940*. Chicago: University of Chicago Press, 1990.

Queen, Ellery. "The Strange Case of the Mad Sculptor." *American Weekly*, March 10, 1957, pp. 15, 28–30.

Radin, Edward D. "The Café Society Murder," in *Murder Cavalcade: An Anthology*, edited by Mystery Writers of America Inc., pp. 377–410. New York: Duell, Sloan and Pearce, 1946.

———. *Crimes of Passion*. New York: G. P. Putnam's Sons, 1953.

Reibman, James E. "The Life of Dr. Fredric Wertham," in *The Fredric Wertham Collection*. Cambridge, MA: Busch-Reisinger Museum, Harvard University, 1990.

Reynolds, Quentin. *Courtroom: The Story of Samuel S. Leibowitz*. New York: Farrar, Straus and Company, 1950.

Robeck, Cecil M. *The Azusa Street Mission and Revival: The Birth of the Global Pentecostal Movement*. Nashville, TN: Thomas Nelson, 2006.

Robins, R. G. *A. J. Tomlinson: Plainfolk Modernist*. New York: Oxford University Press, 2004.

Rovelstad, Trygve A. "Impressions of Lorado Taft." *Papers in Illinois History and Transactions for the Year 1937*, Vol. 44 (1938), pp. 18–33.

Ruben, William. *Grotesque Sex Crimes*. New York: Tower, 1967.

Schechter, Harold. *Deranged: The Shocking True Story of America's Most Fiendish Killer*. New York: Simon & Schuster/Pocket Books, 1990.

Schlesinger, Louis B. *Sexual Murder: Catathymic and Compulsive Homicides*. Boca Raton, FL: CRC Press, 2004.

Schoenberg, Robert J. *Mr. Capone*. New York: William Morrow, 1992.

Schrag, Martin H. "The Spiritual Pilgrimage of the Reverend Benjamin Hardin Irwin." *Brethren in Christ History and Life*, Vol. 4, No. 1 (June 1981), pp. 3–29.

———. "Benjamin Hardin Irwin and the Brethren in Christ." *Brethren in Christ History and Life*, Vol. 4, No. 2 (December 1981), pp. 89–126.

Schultz, Gladys Denny. *How Many More Victims?: Society and the Sex Criminal*. Philadelphia: J. B. Lippincott, 1965.

Schwarz, Ted. *Shocking Stories of the Cleveland Mob*. Charleston, SC: The History Press, 2010.

Sheldon, William G. *The Wilderness Home of the Giant Panda*. Amherst: University of Massachusetts Press, 1975.

Slingerland, William Henry. *Child Welfare Work in California: A Study of Agencies and Institutions*. New York: Russell Sage Foundation/Department of Child-Helping, 1915.

Smith, Alson J. *Chicago's Left Bank*. Chicago: Henry Regnery Company, 1953.

Stephens, Randall J. *The Fire Spreads: Holiness and Pentecostalism in the American South*. Cambridge: Harvard University Press, 2008.

Stevens, John D. *Sensationalism and the New York Press*. New York: Columbia University Press, 1991.

Sturgis, Frank K. "The Winifred Masterson Burke Relief Foundation." *Journal of the National Institute of Social Sciences*, Vol. 3 (January 1917), pp. 83–93.

Swanberg, W. A. *Citizen Hearst*. New York: Scribner, 1961.

Synan, Vinson. *The Holiness-Pentecostal Tradition: Charismatic Movements in the Twentieth Century*. Grand Rapids, MI: William B. Eerdmans, 1997.

———. *The Old-Time Power*. Franklin Springs, GA: Advocate Press, 1973.

———. *Voices of the Pentecost: Testimonies of Lives Touched by the Holy Spirit*. Ann Arbor, MI: Servant Publications, 2003.

Taft, Ada Bartlett. *Lorado Taft: Sculptor and Citizen*. Brattleboro, VT: E. L. Hildreth & Company, 1946.

Taylor, William R., ed. *Inventing Times Square: Commerce and Culture at the Crossroads of the World*. Baltimore: The Johns Hopkins University Press, 1996.

Thurber, James. "Pets and Trophies." *The New Yorker*, July 27, 1929, p. 8.

Trent, T. H. "Murder of the Model—the Mother—and the Lodger." *Official Detective Stories*, May 15, 1937, pp. 3–9, 40–41; June 1, 1937, pp. 10–13, 41–42; June 15, 1937, pp. 10–13, 39–41; July 1, 1937, pp. 10–13, 45–47; July 15, 1937, pp. 12–13, 35–36; and August 1, 1937, pp. 14–17, 35, 38.

Tucher, Andie. *Froth & Scum: Truth, Beauty, Goodness, and the Ax Murder in America's First Mass Medium*. Chapel Hill: University of North Carolina Press, 1994.

Valentine, Lewis J. *Night Stick: The Autobiography of Lewis J. Valentine, Former Police Commissioner of New York*. New York: The Dial Press, 1947.

Vile, John R. *Great American Lawyers: An Encyclopedia, Vol. I*. Santa Barbara, CA: ABC-CLIO, 2001.

Wacker, Grant. *Heaven Below: Early Pentecostals and American Culture*. Cambridge, MA: Harvard University Press, 2001.

Ward, Mary Jane. *The Snake Pit*. New York: Random House, 1946.

Warren, Robert Penn. *At Heaven's Gate*. New York: New Directions, 1985.

Watson, Archibald R., et al. "The People *Versus* Robert Irwin, Charged with the Murder of Three Persons. Report of Commissioners in Lunacy in the Matter of the Examination into the Mental Condition of the Above Named Robert Irwin, an Alleged Lunatic." *American Journal of Psychiatry*, Vol. 95, No. 1 (July 1938), pp. 219–225.

Wattles, Wallace D. *The Science of Getting Rich*. Holyoke, MA: Elizabeth Towne, 1910.

Watts, Steven. *The People's Tycoon: Henry Ford and the American Century*. New York: Alfred A. Knopf, 2005.

Wecter, Dixon. *The Age of the Great Depression, 1929–1941*. New York: Macmillan, 1948.

Wertham, Fredric. "The Catathymic Crisis: A Clinical Entity." *Archives of Neurology and Psychiatry*, Vol. 37 (April 1937), pp. 974–978.

———. *The Circle of Guilt*. London: Denis Dobson, 1955.

———. *The Show of Violence*. Garden City, NY: Doubleday & Company, 1949.

———. *A Sign for Cain: An Exploration of Human Violence*. New York: Macmillan, 1966.

Wolfe, Gerard R. *New York: A Guide to the Metropolis*. New York: McGraw-Hill, 1983.

Wood, Dillard L., and William H. Preskitt Jr. *Baptized with Fire: A History of the Pentecostal Fire-Baptized Holiness Church*. Franklin Springs, GA: Advocate Press, 1982.

Wylie, Max. *Best Broadcasts of 1938–39*. New York: McGraw-Hill, 1939.

———. *Radio Writing*. New York: Rinehart & Company, 1939.

Index